THE WORLD'S 100 GREATEST SPEECHES

THE WORLD'S 100 GREATEST SPEECHES

Selection and Introduction

Terry O'Brien

RUPA

Published by
Rupa Publications India Pvt. Ltd 2016
7/16, Ansari Road, Daryaganj
New Delhi 110 002

Sales centres:
Allahabad Bengaluru Chennai
Hyderabad Jaipur Kathmandu
Kolkata Mumbai

Edition copyright © Rupa Publications India Pvt. Ltd 2016
Introduction copyright © Terry O'Brien 2016

The views and opinions expressed in this book are the author's own
and the facts are as reported by him/her which have been verified to the
extent possible, and the publishers are not in any way liable for the same.

ISBN: 978-81-291-4212-2

Second impression 2017

10 9 8 7 6 5 4 3 2

Printed at HT Media Ltd, Noida

CONTENTS

INTRODUCTION

THE WORLD'S 100 GREATEST SPEECHES is a tribute to those that created a niche for themselves in history by their wisdom and words. In an age where 140 characters are set as a word limit and SMS is the call of the day, I have tried to put in place great speeches over a period of time, that still continue to make an impact across the globe for their oratorical skills. These remain for their outstanding contribution and for bringing about a change in society. If a person wishes to become a great orator, he must first become a student of the great orators who have come before him. He must immerse himself in their texts, listening for the turns of phrases and textual symmetries, the pauses and crescendos, the metaphors and melodies that have enabled the greatest speeches to stand the test of time. Speeches made to an audience, especially a public address needs to be put in print for generations to emulate and be motivated.

Poets are born; orators are made! The brief and terse speech of Abraham Lincoln at Gettysburg is the most quoted definition of DEMOCRACY: 'Government of the people, by the people and for the people.'

Great speech-makers held the power of persuasion and public speaking. These speakers followed the most powerful method of conveying ideas. Their attempt was in gaining the respect of the listeners; it was also a way by which one could appeal to the listeners' emotions, and this included the facts used to convey a message. These great speeches indeed changed the world. Such speeches shook the world!

Practice is a valuable component of great speeches. Within the first few moments of beginning a speech, these great speakers get to the moot point of their talk. They all try to give the audience something that they can take with them. Taking a moment of silence before beginning is a method of gaining the audience's attention. Napoleon Bonaparte was known for doing this with his troops. This strategy adds weight to the words.

Such speeches put on display eloquence or skill in making speeches in public. The extraordinary first inaugural address of Franklin Delano Roosevelt in 1933 ('The only thing we have to fear is fear itself') and 'fireside chats' mesmerized a nation of families huddled about their radio sets. The conviction, confidence, passion, intelligence and wit of FDR pulled the American nation out of the Depression, through the Second World War and into a 'New Deal' between government and the people. Regardless of one's views of FDR's policies, this man was a force of nature and a model of how to use words, voice tone and body language to lead a great nation.

But on 20 January 1961, a very young new president stepped up to that high bar with a speech that has been voted the second-greatest American speech of the 20th century, his 'Ask Not' inaugural address. President John F. Kennedy went on to similarly light up Europe and the world with his 'Ich Bin Ein Berliner' speech to a crowd of a million in Germany, a profound foreign policy address at American University and many others in addition to exhibiting levels of charm, wit and personality at press conferences and elsewhere that redefined the concept of charisma in politics. But added to the spectacular delivery and charisma, it was that very rare quality—vision—that solidifies JFK as America's greatest modern era presidential orator. From the Inaugural addressing a new vision for America and the world, to his challenging Congress and the American people to unite to send a man to the moon by the end of the decade, JFK truly dreamt things that never were and said 'why not'.

Great speakers have worked on every single word. There is no replacement for this and even the greatest delivery skills cannot compensate for words. These speakers are able to use rhythm, body language, pauses and punctuation and nuances in voice tone to set the music of a a speech. Such speeches become their own personal orchestra and that is a level of mastery that few ever reach. They have the ability to excite an audience with energy, ('Visual Language'), give them a compelling story line to follow ('Auditory Language'), rest their anxieties as you show an unshakable grasp of the facts, details and nuances, ('Auditory Digital Language') and, most importantly, to connect with, touch, move and inspire one's audience, ('Kinesthetic Language').

Great speakers don't 'give a speech' when they give their best speeches, they have a conversation. Many speakers 'perform at' their audiences or 'present to' their audiences. The great speaker exemplifies that he/she has a conversation 'with' his/her audiences, a quality that is seen only amongst the greatest political and business speakers.

Nothing is more powerful than the power of words. Especially if the words come from someone we admire and look up to. We meet, watch, hear many leaders every day. Some we agree with and some we don't. But, there are those who leave a great impact on the lives of millions of people around them, they change the fate of the country and they bring a change which once looked like a dream.

Yes, this is the power of words—when spoken, everyone listens.

Happy Reading!

Terry O'Brien

1

I HAVE THE HEART AND
THE STOMACH OF A KING

Queen Elizabeth I

The 'Speech to the Troops' was delivered on 9 August Old Style (19 August New Style) 1588 by Queen Elizabeth of England to the land forces earlier assembled at Tilbury in Essex in preparation for repelling the expected invasion by the Spanish Armada. In her famous speech to rouse the English troops staking out Tilbury at the mouth of the Thames during the Spanish Armada's campaign, Queen Elizabeth is said to have proclaimed, 'I may have the body of a weak, feeble woman; but I have the heart and stomach of a king.' The text was found in a letter from Leonel Sharp sometime after 1624 to the Duke of Buckingham. The speech is a persuasive analysis of how perception of gender roles helped to constitute power in Tudor England.

My loving people:

We have been persuaded by some that are careful of our safety, to take heed how we commit ourselves to armed multitudes for fear of treachery; but I assure you I do not desire to live to distrust my faithful and loving people. Let tyrants fear. I have always so behaved myself that, under God, I have placed my chiefest strength and safeguard in the loyal hearts and goodwill of my subjects; and therefore I am come amongst you, as you see, at this time, not for my recreation and disport, but being resolved, in the midst and heat of the battle, to live and die amongst you all; to lay down for my God, and for my kingdom, and my people, my honour and my blood, even in the dust.

I know I have the body of a weak, feeble woman; but I have the heart and stomach of a king, and of a king of England too, and think foul scorn that Parma or Spain, or any prince of Europe, should dare to invade the borders of my realm; to which rather than any dishonour shall grow by me, I myself will take up arms, I myself will be your general, judge, and rewarder of every one of your virtues in the field.

I know already, for your forwardness you have deserved rewards and crowns; and we do assure you on a word of a prince, they shall be duly paid. In the meantime, my lieutenant general shall be in my stead, than whom never prince commanded a more noble or worthy subject; not doubting but by your obedience to my general, by your concord in the camp, and your valour in the field, we shall shortly have a famous victory over these enemies of my god, of my kingdom and of my people.

2

I GO FROM A CORRUPTIBLE TO AN INCORRUPTIBLE CROWN

King Charles I

This speech was made by King Charles I upon the scaffold at Whitehall Gate, immediately before his execution, on Tuesday, 30 January 1648.

I shall be very little heard of anybody here, I shall therefore speak a word unto you here. Indeed I could hold my peace very well, if I did not think that holding my peace would make some men think that I did submit to the guilt as well as to the punishment. But I think it is my duty to God first and to my country for to clear myself both as an honest man and a good King, and a good Christian. I shall begin first with my innocence. In troth I think it not very needful for me to insist long upon this, for all the world knows that I never did begin a war with the two Houses of Parliament. And I call God to witness, to whom I must shortly make an account, that I never did intend for to encroach upon their privileges. They began upon me, it is the Militia they began upon, they confessed that the Militia was mine, but they thought it fit for to have it from me. And, to be short, if anybody will look to the dates of commissions, of their commissions and mine, and likewise to the declarations, they will see clearly that they began these unhappy troubles, not I. So that as the guilt of these enormous crimes that are laid against me, I hope in God that God will clear me of it, I will not, I am in charity. God forbid that I should lay it upon the two Houses of Parliament; there is no necessity of either, I hope that they are free of this guilt; for I do believe that ill instruments between them and me has been the chief cause of all this bloodshed; so that by way of speaking, as I find myself clear of this, I hope (and pray God) that they may too; yet for all this, God forbid that I should be so ill a Christian as not to say that God's judgments are just upon me. Many times he does pay justice by an unjust sentence, that is ordinary; I will only say this, that an unjust sentence (Strafford) that I suffered for to take effect, is punished now by an unjust sentence upon me; that is, so far as I have said, to show you that I am an innocent man.

Now for to show you that I am a good Christian; I hope there is a good man that will bear me witness that I have forgiven all the world, and even those in particular that have been the chief causes of my death. Who they are, God knows, I do not desire to know, God forgive them. But this is not all, my charity must go further. I wish that they may repent, for indeed they have committed a great sin in that particular. I pray God, with St Stephen, that this be not laid to their charge. Nay, not only so, but that they may take the right way to the peace of the kingdom, for my charity commands me not only to forgive particular men, but my charity commands me to endeavour to the last gasp the peace of the kingdom. So, Sirs, I do wish with all my soul, and I do hope there is some here (turning to some gentlemen that wrote) that will carry it further, that they may endeavour the peace of the Kingdom. Now, (Sirs) I must show you both how you are out of the way and will put you in a way; first, you are out of the way, for certainly all the way you have ever had yet, as I could find by anything, is by way of conquest. Certainly this is an ill way, for conquest, (Sir) in my opinion, is never just, except that there be a good just cause, either for matter of wrong or just title, and then if you go beyond it, the first quarrel that you have to it, that makes it unjust at the end that was just at the first: But if it be only matter of conquest, there is a great robbery; as a pirate said to Alexander, that He was the great robber, he was but a petty robber: and so, Sir, I do think the way that you are in, is much out of the way. Now Sir, for to put you in the way, believe it you will never do right, nor God will never prosper you, until you give God his due, the King his due (that is, my successors) and the people their due; I am as much for them as any of you: You must give God his due by regulating rightly His Church (according to the scripture) which is now out of order. A national synod freely called, freely debating among themselves, must settle this, when that every opinion is freely and clearly heard.

For the King, indeed I will not, (then turning to a gentlemen that touched the ax, said, Hurt not the ax, that may hurt me) [meaning if he did blunt the edge]. For the King: The laws of the land will clearly instruct you for that, therefore, because it concerns my own particular, I only give you a touch of it.

For the people, and truly I desire their liberty and freedom as much as any body whomsoever. But I must tell you that their liberty and freedom, consists in having of government those laws, by which their life and their gods may be most their own. It is not for having share in government (Sir) that is nothing pertaining to them. A subject and a sovereign are clean different things, and therefore until they do that, I mean, that you do put the people in that liberty as I say, certainly they will never enjoy themselves.

Sirs, it was for this that now I am come here. If I would have given way to an arbitrary way, for to have all laws changed according to the power of the sword, I needed not to have come here; and therefore, I tell you (and I pray God it be not laid to your charge) that I am the martyr of the people.

In truth, Sirs, I shall not hold you much longer, for I will only say thus to you. That in truth I could have desired some little time longer, because I would have put then that I have said in a little more order, and a little better digested than I have done. And, therefore, I hope that you will excuse me.

I have delivered my conscience. I pray God, that you do take those courses that are best for the good of the kingdom and your own salvations.

I thank you very heartily (my Lord) for that, I had almost forgotten it. In truth, Sirs, my conscience in religion, I think, is very well known to all the world; and, therefore, I declare before you all that I die a Christian according to the profession of the Church of England, as I found it left me by my father. And this honest man I think will witness it. Sirs, excuse me for this same. I have a good cause, and I have a gracious God; I will say no more. Take care that they do not put me to pain, and Sir this, and it please you. But then a gentleman coming near the ax, the King said, Take heed of the ax. Pray take heed of the ax.

I shall say but very short prayers and, when I thrust out my hands, I have a good cause, and a gracious God on my side. There is but one stage more. This stage is turbulent and troublesome; it is a short one. But you may consider it will soon carry you a very great way; it will carry you from earth to heaven; and there you shall find a great deal of cordial, joy, and comfort.

I go from a corruptible to an incorruptible crown, where no disturbance can be no disturbance in the world.

3

IN THE NAME OF GOD, GO

Oliver Cromwell

Oliver Cromwell (25 April 1599–3 September 1658) was an English statesman, soldier and revolutionary responsible for the overthrow of the monarchy, temporarily turning England into a republican Commonwealth and assuming rule as lord protector of the Commonwealth of England, Scotland and Ireland. 'In the name of God, go!' is an address to the Rump Parliament (20 April 1653). The Rump Parliament was the English Parliament after Colonel Pride purged the Long Parliament on 6 December 1648 of those members hostile to the Grandees' intention to try King Charles I for high treason. 'Rump' normally means the hind end of an animal; its other meaning 'remnant' was first recorded in the above context in English. This short Oliver Cromwell Speech—Dissolution of the Long Parliament—featured is in the form of a transcript, extract, passages or lines and demonstrates the good oratory skills of a great public speaker with the ability to use clear words and text.

It is high time for me to put an end to your sitting in this place, which you have dishonoured by your contempt of all virtue, and defiled by your practice of every vice; ye are a factious crew, and enemies to all good government; ye are a pack of mercenary wretches, and would like Esau sell your country for a mess of pottage, and like Judas betray your god for a few pieces of money.

Is there a single virtue now remaining amongst you? Is there one vice you do not possess? Ye have no more religion than my horse; gold is your god; which of you have not barter'd your conscience for bribes? Is there a man amongst you that has the least care for the good of the Commonwealth?

Ye sordid prostitutes have you not defil'd this sacred place, and turn'd the

Lord's temple into a den of thieves by your immoral principles and wicked practices? Ye are grown intolerably odious to the whole nation; you were deputed here by the people to get grievances redress'd, are yourselves gone! So! Take away that shining bauble there, and lock up the doors.

In the name of God, go!

4

WHAT ENGLAND COULD DO

Keshab Chandra Sen

Keshab Chandra Sen was one of the leading reformers of the nineteenth century. He worked for the values of the Brahmo Samaj. Through his forceful and inspiring lectures, he fought against superstition, idolatory, prejudices, illiteracy and pitiable conditions of women, which was bane of Hindu society. Keshab Chandra was greatly influenced by Western thinkers; he acknowledged this in his lectures. This lecture delivered at the Metropolitan Tabernacle, London, 24 May 1870 was chaired by the ex-governor general of India, Sir John Lawrence who described him as 'an eloquent speaker.'

My lord, ladies, and gentlemen, if you turn your eyes for a moment to yonder east you will see a great country rising from the death-like slumber of ages, and exerting its powers to move onward in the path of true enlightenment and reform. That country is India. You behold a spectacle there which cannot but rivet your interest, which cannot but excite your pity and compassion. In that country, the great work of reform has commenced. In that country, there is an ongoing struggle between old institutions and new ideas, between ancestral notions and prejudices, and modern civilization. The flood of Western education has burst upon India, has made its way into the citadels of idolatry and prejudice, and is sweeping away in its current all the accumulated errors and iniquities of past centuries. The light of truth has dawned over the 180 million people of our country. Every year thousands and tens of thousands are casting away the fetters which have tied them for ages, and confined them in the prison house of ignorance. They are endeavouring, most conscientiously, to vindicate the humanity which dwells within them. That scene is certainly encouraging, but to what is this great work owing? Undoubtedly it is mainly owing to British energy and British enterprise, and the exertions of that paternal government under whose care and providence, in its inscrutable mercy, has placed my great country.

This evening, I stand upon this platform not merely as a learner, but as a representative of my country, as a humble advocate of its interests. I ask you and beseech you to do all that lies within your power to exalt, purify and regenerate the country which has been placed under your protection. I fully agree with the noble lord who sits in the chair, that the British government has been the best that India could possible have; but still there are certain defects in the administration of that country which ought to be rectified. There are certain wants and shortcomings which ought to be redressed. What government on earth is free from errors and shortcomings and it is my desire—certainly it is my humble duty to explain them. I do so with the greatest confidence, for I am about to appeal not to a nation that has no conscience, but to a nation that has a generous heart. A nation that, whatever its shortcomings and imperfections, is anxious to do good to India, if only it can understand full what her wants are. India is now passing through a great crisis, and I trust that my humble words will be received by you in a kindly spirit. I do not, this evening, represent any clique or sect, political or religious; I stand here as a humble representative of the people of India. It is my firm conviction that you Englishmen stand in India merely as trustees. You hold India on trust, and you have no right to say that you will use its property, its riches, its resources, or any or the privileges which God has given you, simply for the purpose of your own selfish aggrandisement and enjoyment. You are accountable to that God who has placed India in your hands, and if there are sins in your administration it is your duty to blot them out as soon as you see them, and believe them to be evil. You are accountable to God for those millions of souls who have been placed under your care. You cannot hold India for the interests of Manchester, nor for the welfare of any other section of the community here, or for the advantage of those merchants who go there and live as birds of passage for a time, and never feel an abiding interest in the country, because they really cannot do so. If you desire to hold India, you can only do so for the good and welfare of India.

The first great duty which the British nation owes to India is to promote education far and wide. It is desirable that you should establish a railway and telegraph network, open up works of irrigation, and try in all possible ways to promote the material prosperity of the country. All these certainly are desirable, but are, after all, only external refinements of civilization, for unless the heart of the nation is reformed and purified, there cannot be anything like true and lasting reformation. If you desire to make the people loyal, you must educate them. A school or college is a better and stronger safeguard of the power and prosperity of the British nation than a citadel of fortress.

If you turn your attention from the schools to the press, you will find that the latter has already commenced to develop itself in a most satisfactory manner. Not only in the larger cities, but also in the smaller towns in the provinces, the press is at work, sending out month by month, new books on literature and science, calculated to improve the mind and heart of the nation; books, not only in the English language, but what is more needed at present, in the vernacular. There are many newspapers which have an extensive circulation, and are being read with great avidity by thousands of educated young men. Everywhere you see, there is a growing taste for English literature. More so, if you educate the people, will you not also encourage them by rewarding them with high appointments, and throwing open posts which are at present enjoyed exclusively by the Europeans? You may talk of pursuing truth for truth's sake, or of acquiring wisdom for wisdom's sake, but the people of the world are not always influenced by these high and transcendental considerations; they must have, something tangible placed before them. You give our people education in schools and colleges; but our people demand a practical training also. If you put them in those higher posts of responsibility and the emolument you give them for that practical training and discipline which is so essential to integrity, honesty, and probity, and a successful discharge of high duty. Let me ask you—are not my countrymen fit for these high posts? Let those who have spent their time in India bear testimony to the fact, if it is established by experience, that the people of India are not unworthy of the high posts which it is possible for the government to confer upon them. There is another thing which distresses me very much and that is the order lately issued (I believe by the Indian Council) abolishing the state scholarships which my countrymen were allowed to enjoy for two years. These scholarships were instituted by the government to enable educated natives to go to England and receive higher training. A more honourable object is impossible to conceive, and when it was carried into execution the entire Indian public welcomed it as an inestimable boon for them and their country. If it is advisable to give the most distinguished of my fellow countrymen a sound education, it is desirable that they should now and then come to England to study English life, literature and science. It is for that reason, I believe, the noble lord in the chair sanctioned this measure after due deliberation and I am glad to say that it is to him India owes this precious boon. But scarcely had my people begun to enjoy the blessing when it was suddenly taken away from them.

As it is the duty of every government to promote general education, it is the special duty of the British government to educate women in India. Unless the women are educated, the education of India will be partial and at best superficial, for it is the women who conserve the traditions that exist in the country. If you don't endeavour to give India good mothers, you will not be able to save the rising generation from those evils which have always acted as a curse in India. If you educate the women, you give my country good mothers, who will train their children in the fear and love of God, and in the appreciation and enjoyment of truth. In this way, our people will not only become intelligent men but will have intelligent and happy homes.

Though the Indian woman is powerful and lively, her position is pathetic and not what it ought to be. Look at the Indian koolin with his fifty wives, who never thinks himself responsible to God or man for the maintenance or education of these fifty women. When he dies, they all become widows, and are doomed to perpetual widowhood. There is none to relieve them— it is altogether impossible for Indian society as it is, to help them in any way. These fifty women, who become widows in a moment, become subject to all those mortifications which a crafty priesthood enjoins upon them. If you wish to rescue her from ignorance and give her all the blessings of true civilization, you must educate her.

Time is running on, and I fear I shall have to conclude: but allow me to advert to one more topic which I have always held dear to my heart as it is one of great importance to India. I refer to the liquor traffic. Allow me to tell you that it has produced demoralizing effects on the people of India, which you may witness with your own eyes. A nation remarkable for abstemiousness, sobriety, and temperance, has, I state, most candidly and emphatically, been demoralized to a certain extent by this traffic, and demoralized not through any innate perversity in their own nature—for I have told you that they are naturally fond of temperance and sobriety. They hate intemperance and drunkenness and drinking has never found any favour amongst them as a custom. They are not going into the paths of intemperance from the inherent depravity of their nature, but because many of the English people there, by the wickedness of their lives, and the English government by bad liquor-traffic rules, have succeeded in placing formidable temptations in the way of the Indian people.

5

SOLDIERS OF MY OLD GUARD,
I BID YOU FAREWELL

Napoleon Bonaparte

On 20 April 1814, a truly dramatic moment in history occurred, as Napoleon Bonaparte, Emperor of France and the would-be ruler of Europe, said goodbye to the Old Guard after his failed invasion of Russia and defeat by the Allies.

Soldiers of my Old Guard:

I bid you farewell. For twenty years I have constantly accompanied you on the road to honour and glory. In these latter times, as in the days of our prosperity, you have invariably been models of courage and fidelity. With men such as you, our cause could not be lost; but the war would have been interminable; it would have been a civil war, and that would have entailed deeper misfortunes on France.

I have sacrificed all of my interests to those of the country.

I go, but you, my friends, will continue to serve France. Her happiness was my only thought. It will still be the object of my wishes. Do not regret my fate; if I have consented to survive, it is to serve your glory. I intend to write the history of the great achievements we have performed together. Adieu, my friends. Would I could press you all to my heart.

6

GOVERNMENT OF THE PEOPLE, BY THE PEOPLE, FOR THE PEOPLE

Abraham Lincoln

On the afternoon of Thursday, 19 November 1863, at the Soldiers' National Cemetery in Gettysburg, Pennsylvania, President Abraham Lincoln made a speech that lasted for just over two minutes, and ended with his hope 'that this nation, under God, shall have a new birth of freedom'. The Gettysburg Address is one of the best-known speeches in American history. Abraham Lincoln's address was one of the greatest and most influential statements of national purpose. Lincoln reiterated the principles of human equality espoused by the Declaration of Independence and proclaimed the Civil War was a struggle for the preservation of the Union sundered by the secession crisis that would bring true equality to all of its citizens. Over time, however, this speech with its ending, 'government of the people, by the people, for the people' has come to symbolize the definition of democracy itself.

Four score and seven years ago our fathers brought forth on this continent, a new nation, conceived in liberty, and dedicated to the proposition that all men are created equal. Now we are engaged in a great civil war, testing whether that nation, or any nation so conceived and so dedicated, can long endure. We are met on a great battlefield of that war. We have come to dedicate a portion of that field, as a final resting place for those who here gave their lives that that nation might live. It is altogether fitting and proper that we should do this.

But in a larger sense, we cannot dedicate—we cannot consecrate—we cannot hallow this ground. The brave men, living and dead, who struggled here, have consecrated it, far above our poor power to add or detract. The world will little note, nor long remember what we say here, but it can never forget what they did here. It is for us the living, rather, to be dedicated here to the unfinished work which they who fought here have thus far so nobly advanced. It is rather for us to be here dedicated to the great task remaining before us—that from these honoured dead we take increased devotion to that cause for which they gave the last full measure of devotion—that we here highly resolve that these dead shall not have died in vain—that this nation, under God, shall have a new birth of freedom—and that government of the people, by the people, for the people, shall not perish from the earth.

7

ARE WOMEN PERSONS?

Susan B. Anthony

In the 1800s, women in the United States had few legal rights and did not have the right to vote. This speech was given by Susan B. Anthony after her arrest for casting an illegal vote in the presidential election of 1872. She was tried and then fined $100, but she refused to pay. The speech was delivered in 1873.

Friends and fellow citizens:

I stand before you tonight under indictment for the alleged crime of having voted at the last presidential election, without having a lawful right to vote. It shall be my work this evening to prove to you that in thus voting, I not only committed no crime, but, instead, simply exercised my citizen's rights, guaranteed to me and all United States citizens by the National Constitution, beyond the power of any state to deny.

The preamble of the Federal Constitution says:

'We, the people of the United States, in order to form a more perfect union, establish justice, insure domestic tranquillity, provide for the common defence, promote the general welfare, and secure the blessings of liberty to ourselves and our posterity, do ordain and establish this Constitution for the United States of America.'

It was we, the people; not we, the white male citizens; nor yet we, the male citizens; but we, the whole people, who formed the Union. And we formed it, not to give the blessings of liberty, but to secure them; not to the half of ourselves and the half of our posterity, but to the whole people—women as well as men. And it is a downright mockery to talk to women of their enjoyment of the blessings of liberty while they are denied the use of the only means of securing them provided by this democratic-republican government—the ballot.

For any state to make sex a qualification that must ever result in the disfranchisement of one entire half of the people, is to pass a bill of attainder, or, an ex post facto law, and is therefore a violation of the supreme law of the land. By it the blessings of liberty are forever withheld from women and their female posterity.

To them this government has no just powers derived from the consent of the governed. To them this government is not a democracy. It is not a republic. It is an odious aristocracy; a hateful oligarchy of sex; the most hateful aristocracy ever established on the face of the globe; an oligarchy of wealth, where the rich govern the poor. An oligarchy of learning, where the educated govern the ignorant, or even an oligarchy of race, where the Saxon rules the African, might be endured; but this oligarchy of sex, which makes father, brothers, husband, sons, the oligarchs over the mother and sisters, the wife and daughters, of every household, which ordains all men sovereigns, all women subjects, carries dissension, discord, and rebellion into every home of the nation.

Webster, Worcester, and Bouvier all define a citizen to be a person in the United States, entitled to vote and hold office.

The only question left to be settled now is: Are women persons? And I hardly believe any of our opponents will have the hardihood to say they are not. Being persons, then, women are citizens; and no state has a right to make any law, or to enforce any old law, that shall abridge their privileges or immunities. Hence, every discrimination against women in the constitutions and laws of the several states is today null and void, precisely as is every one against Negroes.

8

THE ILBERT BILL AND FREEDOM MOVEMENT

Sir Pherozeshah M. Mehta

This speech was delivered in Bombay (now Mumbai) on 28 April, 1883. Sir Courtenay Ilbert, the law member of Viceroy Ripon's council, introduced a bill in the Imperial Legislative Council in 1883. In those days, no white in India could be tried by an Indian judge for his offences in the country. The bill sought to do away with that privilege of the whites. Pherozeshah Mehta ridicules the whites for opposing the bill and at the same time calls it of 'little moment'. The real reason is that 'their fears are aroused as it indicates the shifting of the foundations of the British power in India.'

In the last few days, we have been generously inundated with the advice to preserve the utmost judicial calm and moderation without the slightest admixture of judicial severity, not to allow an angry word or syllable to escape us, while we are also to put forth our case with force and vigor. Now, gentlemen, this advice is more easy to preach than to practice, and though I have resolved to use my best endeavors to achieve this golden mean, I cannot quite escape a feeling of some nervousness as to the success of this rather difficult experiment. Our European friends are disposed to rebuke us for our obstreperousness if we make bold to express our opinion of this bill in this public meeting. They are just as ready to take advantage of us on the score of our indifference if we sit quiet without blowing the feeblest counterblast to the incessant soundings of trumpets and clashing of cymbals which is kept up even now all over the country to frighten away this poor little bill. This attitude may lay claim, I admit, to some amount of rather grim humour, but I trust our European friends will not be very hard upon us if we refuse to be tossed about in this manner on the two horns of such a dilemma as they present to us, and prudently hold fast by the one which does us least injury.

We were told that we have no concern with this bill at all and that it is only a little matter between Lord Ripon and the Europeans in India, in which the parties have got rather hot with each other, and that in fact we have no locus standi at all to take part in the argument. No gentlemen, of all the astonishing things which have been said on the controversy over this bill (and they are not few) it seems to me that this is about the most astonishing, for nothing can be clearer than that the natives have the most immediate and vital concern in the subject matter of this bill. I do not refer here to the handful of native civilians who might get extended jurisdiction under it. I do not speak here of the educated English-speaking natives who may sympathize with native civilians. But I speak of the masses of the native population, and I say that they are as directly and strongly interested in this bill as any European British-born subject. As there are two parties to an offence, the offending party and the suffering party; both are interested in the trial in which they are respectively to appear as complainant and accused.

Has it ever been inquired into, in the course of this controversy, how many offences committed by Europeans have never been brought to the cognizance of the courts of justice in consequence of the difficulties thus created by this 'dear and cherished privilege of being tried by their peers'? A locus standi, gentlemen, we most assuredly have in this controversy; if European British subjects hold that of the accused we have the locus standi of the complainants. They deliberately urge that this bill is in itself a matter of little consequence, but their fears are aroused, as it indicates the shifting of the foundations of the British power in India. Denouncing the wisdom of the declared policy of the crown, or urging that its declarations in that respect were not meant to be practically acted upon, they boldly say that India has been conquered by force and must be governed by force. They ridicule the policy of righteousness as one of weak sentiment and seen almost to adopt, with scarcely disguised approval, the vigorous summary of their position given recently by Mr Bright in his own peculiar manner, that, having won India by breaking all the Ten Commandments, it is too late now to think of maintaining it on the principles of the Sermon on the Mount. For many years the policy of governing India on principles of justice and equality for all the Queen's subjects of whatever caste and creed, has never so openly and so furiously been called in for question as now. The declared policy of the Crown was adopted after a long and careful consideration not on grounds of weak sentiment, or because it was a policy dictated by honour and justice (which we cheerfully and gratefully acknowledge that it is) but also because it was a policy dictated by the true interest of England herself. Also, because in no other way could England hope to preserve her great dependency with the greatest amount of safety and profit to herself.

At present, dire prophesies are proclaimed as to the ill feeling which has been created between the natives and Europeans by the introduction of this bill which is to leave effects for ever so long. In presenting this touching tableau I say, gentlemen, that this bill, which Lord Ripon has introduced in the honest and well considered prosecution of his far-sighted and righteous administration, holds forth hopeful promises of improved relations between the natives and Europeans in this country.

9

I AM HERE AS A SOLDIER

Emmeline Pankhurst

This speech was delivered in Hartford, Connecticut on 13 November 1913. It was significant as a strong statement of the position that women's suffrage advocates. Emmeline Pankhurst addressing an election crowd has become known for her famous 'Freedom or Death' speech at Parson's Theater.

I do not come here as an advocate, because whatever position the suffrage movement may occupy in the United States of America, in England it has passed beyond the realm of advocacy and it has entered into the sphere of practical politics. It has become the subject of revolution and civil war, and so tonight I am not here to advocate woman suffrage. American suffragists can do that very well for themselves.

I am here as a soldier who has temporarily left the field of battle in order to explain—it seems strange it should have to be explained—what civil war is like when civil war is waged by women. I am not only here as a soldier temporarily absent from the field at battle; I am here—and that, I think, is the strangest part of my coming—I am here as a person who, according to the law courts of my country, it has been decided, is of no value to the community at all; and I am adjudged because of my life to be a dangerous person, under sentence of penal servitude in a convict prison.

It is not at all difficult if revolutionaries come to you from Russia, if they come to you from China, or from any other part of the world, if they are men. But since I am a woman it is necessary to explain why women have adopted revolutionary methods in order to win the rights of citizenship. We women, in trying to make our case clear, always have to make as part of our argument, and urge upon men in our audience the fact—a very simple fact—that women are human beings.

Suppose the men of Hartford had a grievance, and they laid that grievance before their legislature, and the legislature obstinately refused to listen to them, or to remove their grievance, what would be the proper and the constitutional and the practical way of getting their grievance removed? Well, it is perfectly obvious at the next general election the men of Hartford would turn out that legislature and elect a new one.

But let the men of Hartford imagine that they were not in the position of being voters at all, that they were governed without their consent being obtained, that the legislature turned an absolutely deaf ear to their demands, what would the men of Hartford do then? They couldn't vote the legislature out. They would have to choose; they would have to make a choice of two evils: they would either have to submit indefinitely to an unjust state of affairs, or they would have to rise up and adopt some of the antiquated means by which men in the past got their grievances remedied.

Your forefathers decided that they must have representation for taxation, many, many years ago. When they felt they couldn't wait any longer, when they laid all the arguments before an obstinate British government that they could think of, and when their arguments were absolutely disregarded, when every other means had failed, they began by the tea party at Boston, and they went on until they had won the independence of the United States of America. It is about eight years since the word militant was first used to describe what we were doing. It was not militant at all, except that it provoked militancy on the part of those who were opposed to it. When women asked questions in political meetings and failed to get answers, they were not doing anything militant. In Great Britain it is a custom, a time-honoured one, to ask questions of candidates for parliament and ask questions of members of the government. No man was ever put out of a public meeting for asking a question. The first people who were put out of a political meeting for asking questions, were women; they were brutally ill-used; they found themselves in jail before 24 hours had expired.

We were called militant, and we were quite willing to accept the name. We were determined to press this question of the enfranchisement of women to the point where we were no longer to be ignored by the politicians.

You have two babies very hungry and wanting to be fed. One baby is a patient baby, and waits indefinitely until its mother is ready to feed it. The other baby is an impatient baby and cries lustily, screams and kicks and makes everybody unpleasant until it is fed. Well, we know perfectly well which baby is attended to first. That is the whole history of politics. You have to make more noise than anybody else, you have to make yourself more obtrusive than anybody else, you have to fill all the papers more than anybody else, in fact you have to be there all the time and see that they do not snow you under.

When you have warfare things happen; people suffer; the noncombatants suffer as well as the combatants. And so it happens in civil war. When your forefathers threw the tea into Boston Harbour, a good many women had to go without their tea. It has always seemed to me an extraordinary thing that you did not follow it up by throwing the whiskey overboard; you sacrificed the women; and there is a good deal of warfare for which men take a great deal of glorification which has involved more practical sacrifice on women than it has on any man. It always has been so. The grievances of those who have got power, the influence of those who have got power commands a great deal of attention; but the wrongs and the grievances of those people who have no power at all are apt to be absolutely ignored. That is the history of humanity right from the beginning. Well, in our civil war people have suffered, but you cannot make omelettes without breaking eggs; you cannot have civil war without damage to something. The great thing is to see that no more damage is done than is absolutely necessary, that you do just as much as will arouse enough feeling to bring about peace, to bring about an honourable peace for the combatants; and that is what we have been doing.

We entirely prevented stockbrokers in London from telegraphing to stockbrokers in Glasgow and vice versa: for one whole day telegraphic communication was entirely stopped. I am not going to tell you how it was done. I am not going to tell you how the women got to the mains and cut the wires; but it was done. It was done, and it was proved to the authorities that weak women, suffrage women, as we are supposed to be, had enough ingenuity to create a situation of that kind. Now, I ask you, if women can do that, is there any limit to what we can do except the limit we put upon ourselves?

If you are dealing with an industrial revolution, if you get the men and women of one class rising up against the men and women of another class, you can locate the difficulty; if there is a great industrial strike, you know exactly where the violence is and how the warfare is going to be waged; but in our war against the government you can't locate it. We wear no mark; we belong to every class; we permeate every class of the community from the highest to the lowest; and so you see in the woman's civil war the dear men of my country are discovering it is absolutely impossible to deal with it: you cannot locate it, and you cannot stop it. 'Put them in prison,' they said, 'that will stop it.' But it didn't stop it at all: instead of the women giving it up, more women did it, and more and more and more women did it until there were 300 women at a time, who had not broken a single law, only 'made a nuisance of themselves' as the politicians say. Then they began to legislate. The British government has passed more stringent laws to deal with this agitation than it ever found necessary during all the history of political agitation in my country. They were able to deal with the revolutionaries of the Chartists' time; they were able to deal with the trades union agitation; they were able to deal with the revolutionaries later on when the Reform Acts were passed: but the ordinary law has not sufficed to curb insurgent women. They had to dip back into the middle ages to find a means of repressing the women in revolt.

They have said to us, government rests upon force, the women haven't force, so they must submit. Well, we are showing them that government does not rest upon force at all: it rests upon consent. As long as women consent to be unjustly governed, they can be, but directly women say: 'We withhold our consent, we will not be governed any longer so long as that government is unjust.' Not by the forces of civil war can you govern the very weakest woman. You can kill that woman, but she escapes you then; you cannot govern her. No power on earth can govern a human being, however feeble, who withholds his or her consent. When they put us in prison at first, simply for taking petitions, we submitted; we allowed them to dress us in prison clothes; we allowed them to put us in solitary confinement; we allowed them to put us amongst the most degraded of criminals; we learned of some of the appalling evils of our so-called civilization that we could not have learned in any other way. It was valuable experience, and we were glad to get it.

I have seen men smile when they heard the words 'hunger strike', and yet I think there are very few men today who would be prepared to adopt a 'hunger strike' for any cause. It is only people who feel an intolerable sense of oppression who would adopt a means of that kind. It means you refuse food until you are at death's door, and then the authorities have to choose between letting you die, and letting you go; and then they let the women go.

Now, that went on so long that the government felt that they were unable to cope. It was [then] that, to the shame of the British government, they set the example to authorities all over the world of feeding sane, resisting human beings by force. There may be doctors in this meeting: if so, they know it is one thing to feed by force an insane person; but it is quite another thing to feed a sane, resisting human being who resists with every nerve and with every fibre of her body the indignity and the outrage of forcible feeding. Now, that was done in England, and the government thought they had crushed us. But they found that it did not quell the agitation, that more and more women came in and even passed that terrible ordeal, and they were obliged to let them go. Then came the legislation—the 'Cat and Mouse Act'. The home secretary said, 'Give me the power to let these women go when they are at death's door, and leave them at liberty under license until they have recovered their health again and then bring them back.' It was passed to repress the agitation, to make the women yield—because that is what it has really come to, ladies and gentlemen. It has come to a battle between the women and the government as to who shall yield first, whether they will yield and give us the vote, or whether we will give up our agitation.

Well, they little know what women are. Women are very slow to rouse, but once they are aroused, once they are determined, nothing on earth and nothing in heaven will make women give way; it is impossible. And so this 'Cat and Mouse Act' which is being used against women today has failed. There are women lying at death's door, recovering enough strength to undergo operations who have not given in and won't give in, and who will be prepared, as soon as they get up from their sick beds, to go on as before. There are women who are being carried from their sick beds on stretchers into meetings. They are too weak to speak, but they go amongst their fellow workers just to show that their spirits are unquenched, and that their spirit is alive, and they mean to go on as long as life lasts.

Now, I want to say to you who think women cannot succeed, we have brought the government of England to this position, that it has to face this alternative: either women are to be killed or women are to have the vote. I ask American men in this meeting, what would you say if in your state you were faced with that alternative, that you must either kill them or give them their citizenship? Well, there is only one answer to that alternative, there is only one way out—you must give those women the vote.

You won your freedom in America when you had the revolution, by bloodshed, by sacrificing human life. You won the civil war by the sacrifice of human life when you decided to emancipate the negro. You have left it to women in your land, the men of all civilized countries have left it to women, to work out their own salvation. That is the way in which we women of England are doing. Human life for us is sacred, but we say if any life is to be sacrificed it shall be ours; we won't do it ourselves, but we will put the enemy in the position where they will have to choose between giving us freedom or giving us death.

So here am I. I come in the intervals of prison appearance. I come after having been four times imprisoned under the 'Cat and Mouse Act', probably going back to be rearrested as soon as I set my foot on British soil. I come to ask you to help to win this fight. If we win it, this hardest of all fights, then, to be sure, in the future it is going to be made easier for women all over the world to win their fight when their time comes.

10

POWER TO THE SOVIETS

Vladimir Ilyich Ulyanov (Lenin)

'All power to the Soviets!' is surely one of the most famous slogans in revolutionary history. This was first published in Pravda No. 99, 18 July 1917. It is here that we get 'Egalité, liberté, fraternité' as a symbol of an entire revolutionary epoch. The Russian word 'sovet' simply means 'advice', and, from that, 'council'. By now, of course, we are very used to the Russian word, because it evokes the specific set of meanings arising out of the revolutionary experience of 1917.

'Drive nature out of the door and she will rush back through the window.' It seems that the Socialist—Revolutionary and Menshevik parties have to 'learn' this simple truth time and again by their own experience. They undertook to be 'revolutionary democrats' and found themselves in the shoes of revolutionary democrats—they are now forced to draw the conclusions which every revolutionary democrat must draw.

Democracy is the rule of the majority. As long as the will of the majority was not clear, as long as it was possible to make it out to be unclear, at least with a grain of plausibility, the people were offered a counter-revolutionary bourgeois government disguised as 'democratic.' But this delay could not last long. During the several months that have passed since 27 February the will of the majority of the workers and peasants, of the overwhelming majority of the country's population, has become clear in more than a general sense. Their will has found expression in mass organizations—the Soviet's of Workers', Soldiers' and Peasants' Deputies.

How, then, can anyone oppose the transfer of all power in the state to the

Soviets? Such opposition means nothing but renouncing democracy! It means no more no less than imposing on the people a government which admittedly can neither come into being nor hold its ground democratically, i.e., as a result of truly free, truly popular elections.

It is a face, strange as it may seem at first sight, that the Socialist—Revolutionaries and Mensheviks have forgotten this perfectly simple, perfectly obvious and palpable truth. Their position is so false, and they are so badly confused and bewildered, that they are unable to 'recover' this truth they have lost. Following the elections in Petrograd and in Moscow, the convocation of the All-Russia Peasant Congress, and the Congress of Soviets, the classes and parties throughout Russia have shown what they stand for so clearly and specifically that people who have not gone mad or deliberately got themselves into a mess and simply cannot have any illusions on this score.

To tolerate the Cadet ministers or the Cadet government or Cadet policies means challenging democrats and democracy. This is the source of the political crises since 27 February, and this also the source of the shakiness and vacillation of our government system. At every turn, daily and even hourly, appeals are being made to the people's revolutionary spirit and to their democracy on behalf of the most authoritative government institutions and congresses. Yet the government's policies in particular, are all departures from revolutionary principles, and breaches in democracy.

This sort of thing will not do.

It is inevitable that a situation like the present should show elements of instability now for one reason, now for another. And it is not exactly a clever policy of jib. Things are moving by fits and starts towards a point where power will be transferred to the Soviets, which is what our Party called for long ago.

11

THE ONLY THING WE HAVE TO FEAR
IS FEAR ITSELF

Franklin D. Roosevelt

In his 1933 inaugural address given on 4 March, Roosevelt stated that he was prepared to recommend measures that he knew could succeed only with strong public pressure in support of extraordinary federal powers to deal with 'extraordinary needs'. This speech is particularly memorable for its attack on the psychology of the Great Depression. Roosevelt planned to expand the power of the federal government to achieve his legislative objectives and thereby ease the effects of the Great Depression. He aimed to declare war on the Great Depression and needed all the executive latitude possible in order to wage that war. In addition to his famous statement, 'The only thing we have to fear is fear itself,' he also said, 'I shall ask the Congress for the one remaining instrument to meet the crisis—broad executive power to wage a war against the emergency, as great as the power that would be given to me if we were in fact invaded by a foreign foe.'

I am certain that my fellow Americans expect that on my induction into the Presidency I will address them with a candour and a decision which the present situation of our nation impels. This is preeminently the time to speak the truth, the whole truth, frankly and boldly. Nor need we shrink from honestly facing conditions in our country today. This great nation will endure as it has endured, will revive and will prosper. So, first of all, let me assert my firm belief that the only thing we have to fear is fear itself—nameless, unreasoning, unjustified terror which paralyses needed efforts to convert retreat into advance. In every dark hour of our national life a leadership of frankness and vigour has met with that understanding and support of the people themselves which is essential to victory. I am convinced that you will again give that support to leadership in these critical days.

In such a spirit on my part and on yours we face our common difficulties. They concern, thank God, only material things. Values have shrunken to fantastic levels; taxes have risen; our ability to pay has fallen; government of all kinds is faced by serious curtailment of income; the means of exchange are frozen in the currents of trade; the withered leaves of industrial enterprise lie on every side; farmers find no markets for their produce; the savings of many years in thousands of families are gone. More important, a host of unemployed citizens face the grim problem of existence, and an equally great number toil with little return. Only a foolish optimist can deny the dark realities of the moment.

Yet our distress comes from no failure of substance. We are stricken by no plague of locusts. Compared with the perils which our forefathers conquered because they believed and were not afraid, we have still much to be thankful for. Nature still offers her bounty and human efforts have multiplied it. Plenty is at our doorstep, but a generous use of it languishes in the very sight of the supply. Primarily this is because the rulers of the exchange of mankind's goods have failed, through their own stubbornness and their own incompetence, have admitted their failure, and abdicated. Practices of the unscrupulous money changers stand indicted in the court of public opinion, rejected by the hearts and minds of men.

True they have tried, but their efforts have been cast in the pattern of an outworn tradition. Faced by failure of credit they have proposed only the lending of more money. Stripped of the lure of profit by which to induce our people to follow their false leadership, they have resorted to exhortations, pleading tearfully for restored confidence. They know only the rules of a generation of self-seekers. They have no vision, and when there is no vision the people perish.

The money changers have fled from their high seats in the temple of our civilization. We may now restore that temple to the ancient truths. The measure of the restoration lies in the extent to which we apply social values more noble than mere monetary profit. Happiness lies not in the mere possession of money; it lies in the joy of achievement, in the thrill of creative effort. The joy and moral stimulation of work no longer must be forgotten in the mad chase of evanescent profits. These dark days will be worth all they cost us if they teach us that our true destiny is not to be ministered unto but to minister to ourselves and to our fellow men.

Recognition of the falsity of material wealth as the standard of success goes hand in hand with the abandonment of the false belief that public office and high political position are to be valued only by the standards of pride of place and personal profit; and there must be an end to a conduct in banking and in business which too often has given to a sacred trust the likeness of callous and selfish wrongdoing. Small wonder that confidence languishes, for it thrives only on honesty, on honour, on the sacredness of obligations, on faithful protection, on unselfish performance; without them it cannot live. Restoration calls, however, not for changes in ethics alone. This nation asks for action, and action now.

Our greatest primary task is to put people to work. This is no unsolvable problem if we face it wisely and courageously. It can be accomplished in part by direct recruiting by the government itself, treating the task as we would treat the emergency of a war, but at the same time, through this employment, accomplishing greatly needed projects to stimulate and reorganize the use of our natural resources.

Hand in hand with this we must frankly recognize the overbalance of population in our industrial centres and, by engaging on a national scale in a redistribution, endeavour to provide a better use of the land for those best fitted for the land. The task can be helped by definite efforts to raise the values of agricultural products and with this the power to purchase the output of our cities. It can be helped by preventing realistically the tragedy of the growing loss through foreclosure of our small homes and our farms. It can be helped by insistence that the federal, state, and local governments act forthwith on the demand that their cost be drastically reduced. It can be helped by the unifying of relief activities which today are often scattered, uneconomical, and unequal. It can be helped by national planning for and supervision of all forms of transportation and of communications and other utilities which have a definitely public character. There are many ways in which it can be helped, but it can never be helped merely by talking about it. We must act and act quickly.

Finally, in our progress toward a resumption of work we require two safeguards against a return of the evils of the old order; there must be a strict supervision of all banking and credits and investments; there must be an end to speculation with other people's money, and there must be provision for an adequate but sound currency.

There are the lines of attack. I shall presently urge upon a new Congress in special session detailed measures for their fulfillment, and I shall seek the immediate assistance of the several states.

Through this program of action we address ourselves to putting our own national house in order and making income balance outgo. Our international trade relations, though vastly important, are in point of time and necessity secondary to the establishment of a sound national economy. I favor as a practical policy the putting of first things first. I shall spare no effort to restore world trade by international economic readjustment, but the emergency at home cannot wait on that accomplishment.

The basic thought that guides these specific means of national recovery is not narrowly nationalistic. It is the insistence, as a first consideration, upon the interdependence of the various elements in all parts of the United States—a recognition of the old and permanently important manifestation of the American spirit of the pioneer. It is the way to recovery. It is the immediate way. It is the strongest assurance that the recovery will endure. In the field of world policy I would dedicate this nation to the policy of the good neighbour—the neighbour who resolutely respects himself and, because he does so, respects the rights of others—the neighbour who respects his obligations and respects the sanctity of his agreements in and with a world of neighbours.

If I read the temper of our people correctly, we now realize as we have never realized before our interdependence on each other; that we can not merely take but we must give as well; that if we are to go forward, we must move as a trained and loyal army willing to sacrifice for the good of a common discipline, because without such discipline no progress is made, no leadership becomes effective. We are, I know, ready and willing to submit our lives and property to such discipline, because it makes possible a leadership which aims at a larger good. This I propose to offer, pledging that the larger purposes will bind upon us all as a sacred obligation with a unity of duty hitherto evoked only in time of armed strife.

With this pledge taken, I assume unhesitatingly the leadership of this great army of our people dedicated to a disciplined attack upon our common problems.

Action in this image and to this end is feasible under the form of government which we have inherited from our ancestors. Our Constitution is so simple and practical that it is possible always to meet extraordinary needs by changes in emphasis and arrangement without loss of essential form. That is why our constitutional system has proved itself the most superbly enduring political mechanism the modern world has produced. It has met every stress of vast expansion of territory, of foreign wars, of bitter internal strife, of world relations.

It is to be hoped that the normal balance of executive and legislative authority may be wholly adequate to meet the unprecedented task before us. But it may be that an unprecedented demand and need for undelayed action may call for temporary departure from that normal balance of public procedure.

I am prepared under my constitutional duty to recommend the measures that a stricken nation in the midst of a stricken world may require. These measures, or such other measures as the Congress may build out of its experience and wisdom, I shall seek, within my constitutional authority, to bring to speedy adoption.

But in the event that the Congress shall fail to take one of these two courses, and in the event that the national emergency is still critical, I shall not evade the clear course of duty that will then confront me. I shall ask the Congress for the one remaining instrument to meet the crisis—broad executive power to wage a war against the emergency, as great as the power that would be given to me if we were in fact invaded by a foreign foe.

For the trust reposed in me I will return the courage and the devotion that befit the time. I can do no less.

We face the arduous days that lie before us in the warm courage of the national unity; with the clear consciousness of seeking old and precious moral values; with the clean satisfaction that comes from the stern performance of duty by old and young alike. We aim at the assurance of a rounded and permanent national life.

We do not distrust the future of essential democracy. The people of the United States have not failed. In their need they have registered a mandate that they want direct, vigorous action. They have asked for discipline and direction under leadership. They have made me the present instrument of their wishes. In the spirit of the gift I take it.

In this dedication of a nation we humbly ask the blessing of God. May He protect each and every one of us. May He guide me in the days to come.

When four years ago we met to inaugurate a President, the Republic, single-minded in anxiety, stood in spirit here. We dedicated ourselves to the fulfillment of a vision—to speed the time when there would be for all the people that security and peace essential to the pursuit of happiness. We of the Republic pledged ourselves to drive from the temple of our ancient faith those who had profaned it; to end by action, tireless and unafraid, the stagnation and despair of that day. We did those first things first.

Our covenant with ourselves did not stop there. Instinctively we recognized a deeper need—the need to find through government the instrument of our united purpose to solve for the individual the ever-rising problems of a complex civilization. Repeated attempts at their solution without the aid of government had left us baffled and bewildered. For, without that aid, we had been unable to create those moral controls over the services of science which are necessary to make science a useful servant instead of a ruthless master of mankind. To do this we knew that we must find practical controls over blind economic forces and blindly selfish men.

We of the Republic sensed the truth that democratic government has innate capacity to protect its people against disasters once considered inevitable, to solve problems once considered unsolvable. We would not admit that we could not find a way to master economic epidemics just as, after centuries of fatalistic suffering, we had found a way to master epidemics of disease. We refused to leave the problems of our common welfare to be solved by the winds of chance and the hurricanes of disaster.

In this we Americans were discovering no wholly new truth; we were writing a new chapter in our book of self-government. This year marks the one hundred and fiftieth anniversary of the Constitutional Convention which made us a nation. At that Convention our forefathers found the way out of the chaos which followed the Revolutionary War; they created a strong government with powers of united action sufficient then and now to solve problems utterly beyond individual or local solution. A century and a half ago they established the Federal government in order to promote the general welfare and secure the blessings of liberty to the American people. Today we invoke those same powers of government to achieve the same objectives.

Four years of new experience have not belied our historic instinct. They hold out the clear hope that government within communities, government within the separate states, and government of the United States can do the things the times require, without yielding its democracy. Our tasks in the last four years did not force democracy to take a holiday.

Nearly all of us recognize that as intricacies of human relationships increase, so power to govern them also must increase—power to stop evil; power to do good. The essential democracy of our nation and the safety of our people depend not upon the absence of power, but upon lodging it with those whom the people can change or continue at stated intervals through an honest and free system of elections. The Constitution of 1787 did not make our democracy impotent.

In fact, in these last four years, we have made the exercise of all power more democratic; for we have begun to bring private autocratic powers into their proper subordination to the public's government. The legend that they were invincible—above and beyond the processes of a democracy—has been shattered. They have been challenged and beaten.

Our progress out of the depression is obvious. But that is not all that you and I mean by the new order of things. Our pledge was not merely to do a patchwork job with secondhand materials. By using the new materials of social justice we have undertaken to erect on the old foundations a more enduring structure for the better use of future generations.

In that purpose we have been helped by achievements of mind and spirit. Old truths have been relearned; untruths have been unlearned. We have always known that heedless self-interest was bad morals; we know now that it is bad economics. Out of the collapse of a prosperity whose builders boasted their practicality has come the conviction that in the long run economic morality pays. We are beginning to wipe out the line that divides the practical from the ideal; and in so doing we are fashioning an instrument of unimagined power for the establishment of a morally better world.

This new understanding undermines the old admiration of worldly success as such. We are beginning to abandon our tolerance of the abuse of power by those who betray for profit the elementary decencies of life.

In this process evil things formerly accepted will not be so easily condoned. Hard-headedness will not so easily excuse hardheartedness. We are moving toward an era of good feeling. But we realize that there can be no era of good feeling save among men of good will.

For these reasons I am justified in believing that the greatest change we have witnessed has been the change in the moral climate of America.

Among men of goodwill, science and democracy together offer an ever-richer life and ever-larger satisfaction to the individual. With this change in our moral climate and our rediscovered ability to improve our economic order, we have set our feet upon the road of enduring progress.

Shall we pause now and turn our back upon the road that lies ahead? Shall we call this the promised land? Or, shall we continue on our way? For 'each age is a dream that is dying, or one that is coming to birth'.

Many voices are heard as we face a great decision. Comfort sa while'. Opportunism says, 'This is a good spot.' Timidity asks, 'How difficult is the road ahead?' True, we have come far from the days of stagnation and despair. Vitality has been preserved. Courage and confidence have been restored. Mental and moral horizons have been extended.

But our present gains were won under the pressure of more than ordinary circumstances. Advance became imperative under the goad of fear and suffering. The times were on the side of progress. To hold to progress today, however, is more difficult. Dulled conscience, irresponsibility, and ruthless self-interest already reappear. Such symptoms of prosperity may become portents of disaster! Prosperity already tests the persistence of our progressive purpose.

Let us ask again: Have we reached the goal of our vision of that fourth day of March 1933? Have we found our happy valley?

I see a great nation, upon a great continent, blessed with a great wealth of natural resources. Its hundred and thirty million people are at peace among themselves; they are making their country a good neighbour among the nations. I see a United States which can demonstrate that, under democratic methods of government, national wealth can be translated into a spreading volume of human comforts hitherto unknown, and the lowest standard of living can be raised far above the level of mere subsistence.

But here is the challenge to our democracy: In this nation I see tens of millions of its citizens—a substantial part of its whole population—who at this very moment are denied the greater part of what the very lowest standards of today call the necessities of life.

I see millions of families trying to live on incomes so meagre that the pall of family disaster hangs over them day by day. I see millions whose daily lives in city and on farm continue under conditions labelled indecent by a so-called polite society half a century ago. I see millions denied education, recreation, and the opportunity to better their lot and the lot of their children. I see millions lacking the means to buy the products of farm and factory and by their poverty denying work and productiveness to many other millions. I see one-third of a nation ill-housed, ill-clad, ill-nourished.

It is not in despair that I paint you that picture. I paint it for you in hope—because the nation, seeing and understanding the injustice in it, proposes to paint it out. We are determined to make every American citizen the subject of his country's interest and concern; and we will never regard any faithful law-abiding group within our borders as superfluous. The test of our progress is not whether we add more to the abundance of those who have much; it is whether we provide enough for those who have too little.

If I know aught of the spirit and purpose of our nation, we will not listen to comfort, opportunism and timidity. We will carry on.

Overwhelmingly, we of the Republic are men and women of goodwill; men and women who have more than warm hearts of dedication; men and women who have cool heads and willing hands of practical purpose as well. They will insist that every agency of popular government use effective instruments to carry out their will. Government is competent when all who compose it work as trustees for the whole people. It can make constant progress when it keeps abreast of all the facts. It can obtain justified support and legitimate criticism when the people receive true information of all that government does.

If I know aught of the will of our people, they will demand that these conditions of effective government shall be created and maintained. They will demand a nation uncorrupted by cancers of injustice and, therefore, strong among the nations in its example of the will to peace.

Today we reconsecrate our country to long-cherished ideals in a suddenly changed civilization. In every land there are always at work forces that drive men apart and forces that draw men together. In our personal ambitions we are individualists. But in our seeking for economic and political progress as a nation, we all go up, or else we all go down, as one people.

To maintain a democracy of effort requires a vast amount of patience in dealing with differing methods, a vast amount of humility. But out of the confusion of many voices rises an understanding of dominant public need. Then political leadership can voice common ideals, and aid in their realization. In taking again the oath of office as President of the United

States, I assume the solemn obligation of leading the American people forward along the road over which they have chosen to advance. While this duty rests upon me I shall do my utmost to speak their purpose and to do their will, seeking divine guidance to help us each and every one to give light to them that sit in darkness and to guide our feet into the way of peace.

12

THE CONGRESS AND THE MUSLIMS

Badruddin Tyabji

This speech was delivered at Madras, 27 December 1887. Badruddin Tyabji was the president of the Third Session of the Congress which met at Madras in 1887 where he delivered the following address. The Congress was taking some shape due to the efforts of its founder Allan Octavian Hume (who had been its general secretary since its inception in 1885) and the number of delegates was increasing every year.

Sir Syed Ahmed Khan through his speeches and writings had been advising the Muslims not to join the Congress or attend its sessions. To counteract that 'fatwa', the Congress had chosen a Muslim to be its president. Tyabji in his speech exhorts the Muslims to join the Congress.

Gentlemen, I did not have the good fortune to be present at the proceedings of the First Session of the Congress, held in Bombay in 1885, nor had I the good fortune to take part in the deliberations of the Second Session, held in Calcutta last year. But, I have read carefully the proceedings of both those Congresses, and I have no hesitation in declaring that they display an amount of talent, wisdom and eloquence of which we have every reason to be proud.

It has been urged in derogation of our character as a representative national gathering, that one great and important community—the Musalman community—has kept aloof from the proceedings of the last two Congresses. In the first place, this is only partially true, and applies only to one particular part of India due to certain special, local, and temporary causes. In the second place, no such reproach can, I think, with

...ow of justice, be urged against this present Congress. I must honestly ...ess to you that one great motive which has induced me, in the present ...ate of my health, to undertake the grave responsibilities of presiding over your deliberations, has been an earnest desire on my part to prove that I at least, not merely in my individual capacity but as representing the Anjuman-i-Islam of Bombay, do not consider that there is anything whatsoever in the position or the relations of the different communities of India—be they Hindus, Musalmans, Parsis, or Christians—which should induce the leaders of any one community to stand aloof from the others in their efforts to obtain those great reforms, those great general rights, which are for the common benefit of us all which, I feel assured, have only to be earnestly and unanimously pressed upon the government to be granted to us.

Gentlemen, it is undoubtedly true that each one of our great Indian communities has its own peculiar social, moral, educational and even political difficulties to surmount. So far as general political questions affecting the whole of India, such as those which alone are discussed by this Congress are concerned, I for one, am utterly at a loss to understand why Musalmans should not work shoulder to shoulder with their fellow-countrymen, of other races and creeds, for the common benefit of all.

Gentlemen, it has been urged as a slur upon our loyalty that this Congress is composed of what are called the educated natives of India. Now; if by this it is intended to convey that we are merely a crowd of people with nothing but our education to commend us, if it is intended to convey that the gentry; the nobility, and the aristocracy of the land have kept aloof from us, I can only meet that assertion by the most direct and the most absolute denial. To any person who made that assertion, I should feel inclined to say: Come with me into this hall and look around you, and tell me where you could wish to see a better representation of the aristocracy; not only by birth and wealth, but by intellect, education and position, than you see gathered within the walls of this hall. But, gentlemen, if no such insinuation is intended to be made, I should only say that I am happy to think that this Congress does consist of the educated natives of India.

I for one, am proud to be called not only educated but a 'native' of this country. And gentlemen, I should like to know, where among all the millions of Her Majesty's subjects in India are to be found more truly loyal, nay, more devoted friends of the British Empire than among these educated natives. To be a true and sincere friend of the British government, it is necessary that one should be in a position to appreciate the great blessings which that government has conferred upon us. I should like to know who is in a better position to appreciate these blessings—the ignorant peasants or the educated natives? Who, for instance, will better appreciate the advantages of good roads, railways, telegraphs and post offices, schools, colleges and universities, hospitals, good laws and impartial courts of justice—the educated natives or the ignorant peasants of this country

No, gentlemen, let our opponents say what they please. We, the educated natives, by the mere force of our education, must be the best appreciators of the blessings of a civilized and enlightened government and therefore in our own interests, the best and staunchest supporters of the British government in India.

Now one word as to the scope of our action and deliberations. It has been urged—solemnly urged—as an objection against our proceedings that this Congress does not discuss the question of social reform. This matter has already been fully dealt with by my friend, Mr Dadabhai Naoroji, who presided over your deliberations last year. I must confess that the objection seems strange to me seeing that this Congress is composed of representatives, not of any one class or community, not of one part of India, but of all the different parts, classes, and communities of India. Whereas any question of social reform must of necessity affect some particular part or some particular community of India only, it seems to me that, although we Musalmans have our own social problems to solve, just as our Hindu and Parsi friends have theirs, yet these questions can be best dealt with by the leaders of the particular corn unities to which they relate. I, therefore think, that the only wise, and indeed the only possible course we can adopt is to confine our discussions to such questions which affect the whole of India at large, and to abstain from the discussion of questions that affect a particular part or a particular community only.

Gentlemen, I do not, at present at least, propose to say anything upon the various problems that will be submitted to you for your consideration. I have no doubt that the questions will be discussed in a manner and in a spirit that will reflect credit upon all of us. I will only say this: be moderate in your demands, be just in your criticism, be accurate in your facts, be logical in your conclusions, and you may rest assured that any propositions you may make to our rulers will be received with that benign consideration which is characteristic of a strong and enlightened government.

13

A DATE WHICH WILL LIVE IN INFAMY

Franklin D. Roosevelt

In this speech, President Roosevelt talks about the impact of 7 December 1941—a date which will live in infamy—the day the United States of America was suddenly and deliberately attacked by the naval and air forces of the Empire of Japan. Pearl Harbor Address to the nation delivered on 8 December 1941, Washington, D.C.

Mr Vice President, Mr Speaker, Members of the Senate, and of the House of Representatives:

Yesterday, 7 December 1941—a date which will live in infamy—the United States of America was suddenly and deliberately attacked by naval and air forces of the Empire of Japan.

The United States was at peace with that nation and, at the solicitation of Japan, was still in conversation with its government and its emperor, looking toward the maintenance of peace in the Pacific.

Indeed, one hour after Japanese air squadrons had commenced bombing in the American island of Oahu, the Japanese ambassador to the United States and his colleague delivered to our Secretary of State a formal reply to a recent American message. And while this reply stated that it seemed useless to continue the existing diplomatic negotiations, it contained no threat or hint of war or of armed attack.

It will be recorded that the distance of Hawaii from Japan makes it obvious that the attack was deliberately planned many days or even weeks ago.

During the intervening time, the Japanese government has deliberately sought to deceive the United States by false statements and expressions of hope for continued peace.

The attack yesterday on the Hawaiian islands has caused severe damage to American naval and military forces. I regret to tell you that very many American lives have been lost. In addition, American ships have been reported torpedoed on the high seas between San Francisco and Honolulu.

Yesterday, the Japanese government also launched an attack against Malaya.

Last night, Japanese forces attacked Hong Kong.

Last night, Japanese forces attacked Guam.

Last night, Japanese forces attacked the Philippine Islands.

Last night, the Japanese attacked Wake Island.

And this morning, the Japanese attacked Midway Island.

Japan has, therefore, undertaken a surprise offensive extending throughout the Pacific area. The facts of yesterday and today speak for themselves. The people of the United States have already formed their opinions and well understand the implications to the very life and safety of our nation.

As Commander-in-Chief of the Army and Navy, I have directed that all measures be taken for our defence. But always will our whole nation remember the character of the onslaught against us.

No matter how long it may take us to overcome this premeditated invasion, the American people in their righteous might will win through to absolute victory.

I believe that I interpret the will of the Congress and of the people when I assert that we will not only defend ourselves to the uttermost, but will make it very certain that this form of treachery shall never again endanger us.

Hostilities exist. There is no blinking at the fact that our people, our territory, and our interests are in grave danger.

With confidence in our armed forces, with the unbounding determination of our people, we will gain the inevitable triumph—so help us God.

I ask that the Congress declare that since the unprovoked and dastardly attack by Japan on Sunday, 7 December 1941, a state of war has existed between the United States and the Japanese empire.

14

I AM FROM NOW ON JUST FIRST SOLDIER OF THE REICH

Adolf Hitler

This is an address by Adolf Hitler, Chancellor of the Reich, before the Reichstag, 1 September 1939.

For months we have been suffering under the torture of a problem which the Versailles Diktat created—a problem which has deteriorated until it becomes intolerable for us. Danzig was and is a German city. The Corridor was and is German. Both these territories owe their cultural development exclusively to the German people. Danzig was separated from us, the Corridor was annexed by Poland. As in other German territories of the East, all German minorities living there have been ill-treated in the most distressing manner. More than 1,000,000 people of German blood had in the years 1919–1920 to leave their homeland.

As always, I attempted to bring about, by the peaceful method of making proposals for revision, an alteration of this intolerable position. It is a lie when the outside world says that we only tried to carry through our revisions by pressure. Fifteen years before the National Socialist Party came to power there was the opportunity of carrying out these revisions by peaceful settlements and understanding. On my own initiative I have, not once but several times, made proposals for the revision of intolerable conditions. All these proposals, as you know, have been rejected—proposals for limitation of armaments and even, if necessary, disarmament, proposals for limitation of war-making, proposals for the elimination of certain methods of modern warfare. You know the proposals that I have made to fulfil the necessity of restoring German sovereignty over German territories. You know the endless attempts I made for a peaceful clarification and understanding of the problem of Austria, and later of the problem of the Sudetenland, Bohemia, and Moravia. It was all in vain.

It is impossible to demand that an impossible position should be cleared up by peaceful revision and at the same time constantly reject peaceful revision. It is also impossible to say that he who undertakes to carry out these revisions for himself transgresses a law, since the Versailles Diktat is not law to us. A signature was forced out of us with pistols at our head and with the threat of hunger for millions of people. And then this document, with our signature, obtained by force, was proclaimed as a solemn law.

In the same way, I have also tried to solve the problem of Danzig, the Corridor, etc., by proposing a peaceful discussion. That the problems had to be solved was clear. It is quite understandable to us that the time when the problem was to be solved had little interest for the Western Powers. But that time is not a matter of indifference to us. Moreover, it was not and could not be a matter of indifference to those who suffer most.

In my talks with Polish statesmen I discussed the ideas which you recognize from my last speech to the Reichstag. No one could say that this was in any way an inadmissible procedure on undue pressure. I then naturally formulated at last the German proposals, and I must once more repeat that there is nothing more modest or loyal than these proposals. I should like to say this to the world. I alone was in the position to make such proposal, for I know very well that in doing so I brought myself into opposition to millions of Germans. These proposals have been refused. Not only were they answered first with mobilization, but with increased terror and pressure against our German compatriots and with a slow strangling of the Free City of Danzig—economically, politically, and in recent weeks by military and transport means.

Poland has directed its attacks against the Free City of Danzig. Moreover, Poland was not prepared to settle the Corridor question in a reasonable way which would be equitable to both parties, and she did not think of keeping her obligations to minorities.

I must here state something definitely; German has kept these obligations; the minorities who live in Germany are not persecuted. No Frenchman can stand up and say that any Frenchman living in the Saar territory is oppressed, tortured, or deprived of his rights. Nobody can say this. For four months I have calmly watched developments, although I never ceased to give warnings. In the last few days I have increased these warnings. I informed the Polish Ambassador three weeks ago that if Poland continued to send to Danzig notes in the form of ultimata, and if on the Polish side an end was not put to Customs measures destined to ruin Danzig's trade, then the Reich could not remain inactive. I left no doubt that people who wanted to compare the Germany of today with the former Germany would be deceiving themselves.

An attempt was made to justify the oppression of the Germans by claiming that they had committed acts of provocation. I do not know in what these provocations on the part of women and children consist, if they themselves are maltreated, in some cases killed. One thing I do know—that no great Power can with honour long stand by passively and watch such events.

I made one more final effort to accept a proposal for mediation on the part of the British government. They proposed, not that they themselves should carry on the negotiations, but rather that Poland and Germany should come into direct contact and once more pursue negotiations.

I must declare that I accepted this proposal, and I worked out a basis for these negotiations which are known to you. For two whole days I sat in my government and waited to see whether it was convenient for the Polish government to send a plenipotentiary or not. Last night they did not send us a plenipotentiary, but instead informed us through their Ambassador that they were still considering whether and to what extent they were in a position to go into the British proposals. The Polish government also said that they would inform Britain of their decision.

Deputies, if the German government and its Leader patiently endured such treatment, Germany would deserve only to disappear from the political stage. But I am wrongly judged if my love of peace and my patience are mistaken for weakness or even cowardice. I, therefore, decided last night and informed the British government that in these circumstances I can no longer find any willingness on the part of the Polish government to conduct serious negotiations with us.

These proposals for mediation have failed because in the meanwhile there, first of all, came as an answer the sudden Polish general mobilization, followed by more Polish atrocities. These were again repeated last night. Recently in one night there were as many as twenty-one frontier incidents: last night there were fourteen, of which three were quite serious. I have, therefore, resolved to speak to Poland in the same language that Poland for months past has used toward us. This attitude on the part of the Reich will not change.

The other European states understand in part our attitude. I should like here above all to thank Italy, which throughout has supported us, but you will understand that for the carrying on of this struggle we do not intend to appeal to foreign help. We will carry out this task ourselves. The neutral states have assured us of their neutrality, just as we had already guaranteed it to them.

When statesmen in the West declare that this affects their interests, I can only regret such a declaration. It cannot for a moment make me hesitate to fulfill my duty. What more is wanted? I have solemnly assured them, and I repeat it, that we ask nothing of those western states and never will ask anything. I have declared that the frontier between France and Germany is a final one. I have repeatedly offered friendship and, if necessary, the closest cooperation to Britain, but this cannot be offered from one side only. It must find response on the other side. Germany has no interests in the West, and our western wall is for all time the frontier of the Reich on the west. Moreover, we have no aims of any kind there for the future. With this assurance we are in solemn earnest, and as long as others do not violate their neutrality we will likewise take every care to respect it.

I am happy particularly to be able to tell you of one event. You know that Russia and Germany are governed by two different doctrines. There was only one question that had to be cleared up. Germany has no intention of

The World's 100 Greatest Speeches

exporting its doctrine. Given the fact that Soviet Russia has no intention of exporting its doctrine to Germany, I no longer see any reason why we should still oppose one another. On both sides we are clear on that. Any struggle between our people would only be of advantage to others. We have, therefore, resolved to conclude a pact which rules out for ever any use of violence between us. It imposes the obligation on us to consult together in certain European questions. It makes possible for us economic co-operation, and above all it assures that the powers of both these powerful states are not wasted against one another. Every attempt of the West to bring about any change in this will fail.

At the same time I should like here to declare that this political decision means a tremendous departure for the future, and that it is a final one. Russia and Germany fought against one another in the World War. That shall and will not happen a second time. In Moscow, too, this pact was greeted exactly as you greet it. I can only endorse word for word the speech of Russian Foreign Commissar, Molotov.

I am determined to solve (1) the Danzig question; (2) the question of the Corridor; and (3) to see to it that a change is made in the relationship between Germany and Poland that shall ensure a peaceful coexistence. In this I am resolved to continue to fight until either the present Polish government is willing to continue to bring about this change or until another Polish government is ready to do so. I am resolved to remove from the German frontiers the element of uncertainty, the everlasting atmosphere of conditions resembling civil war. I will see to it that in the East there is, on the frontier, a peace precisely similar to that on our other frontiers.

In this I will take the necessary measures to see that they do not contradict the proposals I have already made known in the Reichstag itself to the rest of the world, that is to say, I will not war against women and children. I have ordered my air force to restrict itself to attacks on military objectives. If, however, the enemy thinks he can form that draw carte blanche on his side to fight by the other methods, he will receive an answer that will deprive him of hearing and sight.

This night for the first time Polish regular soldiers fired on our territory.

Since 5.45 a.m. we have been returning the fire, and from now on bombs will be met by bombs. Whoever fights with poison gas will be fought with poison gas. Whoever departs from the rules of humane warfare can only expect that we shall do the same. I will continue this struggle, no matter against whom, until the safety of the Reich and its rights are secured.

For six years now I have been working on the building up of the German defences. Over 90 million have in that time been spent on the building up of these defence forces. They are now the best equipped and are above all comparison with what they were in 1914. My trust in them is unshakable. When I called up these forces and when I now ask sacrifices of the German people and if necessary every sacrifice, then I have a right to do so, for I also am today absolutely ready, just as we were formerly, to make every possible sacrifice.

I am asking of no German man more than I myself was ready throughout four years at any time to do. There will be no hardships for Germans to which I myself will not submit. My whole life henceforth belongs more than ever to my people. I am from now on just first soldier of the German Reich. I have once more put on that coat that was the most sacred and dear to me. I will not take it off again until victory is secured, or I will not survive the outcome.

Should anything happen to me in the struggle then my first successor is Party Comrade Göring; should anything happen to Party Comrade Göring my next successor is Party Comrade Hess. You would then be under obligation to give to them as Führer the same blind loyalty and obedience as to myself. Should anything happen to Party Comrade Hess, then by law the Senate will be called, and will choose from its midst the most worthy— that is to say the bravest—successor.

As a National Socialist and as a German soldier I enter upon this struggle with a stout heart. My whole life has been nothing but one long struggle for my people, for its restoration, and for Germany. There was only one watchword for that struggle: faith in this people. One word I have never learned: that is, surrender.

If, however, anyone thinks that we are facing a hard time, I should ask him to remember that once a Prussian King, with a ridiculously small State, opposed a stronger coalition, and in three wars finally came out successful because that state had that stout heart that we need in these times. I would, therefore, like to assure all the world that a November 1918 will never be repeated in German history. Just as I myself am ready at any time to stake my life—anyone can take it for my people and for Germany—so I ask the same of all others.

Whoever, however, thinks he can oppose this national command, whether directly of indirectly, shall fall. We have nothing to do with traitors. We are all faithful to our old principle. It is quite unimportant whether we ourselves live, but it is essential that our people shall live, that Germany shall live. The sacrifice that is demanded of us is not greater than the sacrifice that many generations have made. If we form a community closely bound together by vows, ready for anything, resolved never to surrender, then our will will master every hardship and difficulty. And I would like to close with the declaration that I once made when I began the struggle for power in the Reich. I then said: 'If our will is so strong that no hardship and suffering can subdue it, then our will and our German might shall prevail.'

15

FAREWELL ADDRESS

George Washington

George Washington wrote this farewell address towards the end of his second term to say that he would not run for a third term. It was printed in newspapers and circulated in pamphlet form.

Friends and Citizens:

The period for a new election of a citizen to administer the executive government of the United States being not far distant, and the time actually arrived when your thoughts must be employed in designating the person who is to be clothed with that important trust, it appears to me proper, especially as it may conduce to a more distinct expression of the public voice, that I should now apprise you of the resolution I have formed, to decline being considered among the number of those out of whom a choice is to be made.

I beg you, at the same time, to do me the justice to be assured that this resolution has not been taken without a strict regard to all the considerations appertaining to the relation which binds a dutiful citizen to his country; and that in withdrawing the tender of service, which silence in my situation might imply, I am influenced by no diminution of zeal for your future interest, no deficiency of grateful respect for your past kindness, but am supported by a full conviction that the step is compatible with both.

The acceptance of, and continuance hitherto in, the office to which your suffrages have twice called me have been a uniform sacrifice of inclination to the opinion of duty and to a deference for what appeared to be your desire. I constantly hoped that it would have been much earlier in my power, consistently with motives which I was not at liberty to disregard, to return to that retirement from which I had been reluctantly drawn. The strength of my inclination to do this, previous to the last election, had even led to the preparation of an address to declare it to you; but mature reflection on the then perplexed and critical posture of our affairs with foreign nations, and the unanimous advice of persons entitled to my confidence, impelled me to abandon the idea.

I rejoice that the state of your concerns, external as well as internal, no longer renders the pursuit of inclination incompatible with the sentiment of duty or propriety, and am persuaded, whatever partiality may be retained for my services, that, in the present circumstances of our country, you will not disapprove my determination to retire.

The impressions with which I first undertook the arduous trust were explained on the proper occasion. In the discharge of this trust, I will only say that I have, with good intentions, contributed towards the organization and administration of the government the best exertions of which a very fallible judgment was capable. Not unconscious in the outset of the inferiority of my qualifications, experience in my own eyes, perhaps still more in the eyes of others, has strengthened the motives to diffidence of myself; and every day the increasing weight of years admonishes me more and more that the shade of retirement is as necessary to me as it will be welcome. Satisfied that if any circumstances have given peculiar value to my services, they were temporary, I have the consolation to believe that, while choice and prudence invite me to quit the political scene, patriotism does not forbid it.

In looking forward to the moment which is intended to terminate the career of my public life, my feelings do not permit me to suspend the deep acknowledgment of that debt of gratitude which I owe to my beloved country for the many honours it has conferred upon me; still more for the steadfast confidence with which it has supported me; and for the opportunities I have thence enjoyed of manifesting my inviolable attachment, by services faithful and persevering, though in usefulness unequal to my zeal. If benefits have resulted to our country from these services, let it always be remembered to your praise, and as an instructive example in our annals, that under circumstances in which the passions, agitated in every direction, were liable to mislead, amidst appearances sometimes dubious, vicissitudes of fortune often discouraging, in situations in which not unfrequently want of success has countenanced the spirit of criticism, the constancy of your support was the essential prop of the efforts, and a guarantee of the plans by which they were effected. Profoundly penetrated with this idea, I shall carry it with me to my grave, as a strong incitement to unceasing vows that heaven may continue to you the choicest tokens of its beneficence; that your union and brotherly affection may be perpetual; that the free Constitution, which is the work of your hands, may be sacredly maintained; that its administration in every department may be stamped with wisdom and virtue; that, in fine, the happiness of the people of these States, under the auspices of liberty, may be made complete by so careful a preservation and so prudent a use of this blessing as will acquire to them the glory of recommending it to the applause, the affection, and adoption of every nation which is yet a stranger to it.

Here, perhaps, I ought to stop. But a solicitude for your welfare, which cannot end but with my life, and the apprehension of danger, natural to that solicitude, urge me, on an occasion like the present, to offer to your solemn contemplation, and to recommend to your frequent review, some sentiments which are the result of much reflection, of no inconsiderable observation, and which appear to me all-important to the permanency of your felicity as a people. These will be offered to you with the more freedom, as you can only see in them the disinterested warnings of a parting friend, who can possibly have no personal motive to bias his counsel. Nor can I forget, as an encouragement to it, your indulgent reception of my sentiments on a former and not dissimilar occasion.

Interwoven as is the love of liberty with every ligament of your hearts, no recommendation of mine is necessary to fortify or confirm the attachment.

The unity of government which constitutes you one people is also now dear to you. It is justly so, for it is a main pillar in the edifice of your real independence, the support of your tranquility at home, your peace abroad; of your safety; of your prosperity; of that very liberty which you so highly prize. But as it is easy to foresee that, from different causes and from different quarters, much pains will be taken, many artifices employed to weaken in your minds the conviction of this truth; as this is the point in your political fortress against which the batteries of internal and external enemies will be most constantly and actively (though often covertly and insidiously) directed, it is of infinite moment that you should properly estimate the immense value of your national union to your collective and individual happiness; that you should cherish a cordial, habitual, and immovable attachment to it; accustoming yourselves to think and speak of it as of the palladium of your political safety and prosperity; watching for its preservation with jealous anxiety; discountenancing whatever may suggest even a suspicion that it can in any event be abandoned; and indignantly frowning upon the first dawning of every attempt to alienate any portion of our country from the rest, or to enfeeble the sacred ties which now link together the various parts.

For this you have every inducement of sympathy and interest. Citizens, by birth or choice, of a common country, that country has a right to concentrate your affections. The name of American, which belongs to you in your national capacity, must always exalt the just pride of patriotism more than any appellation derived from local discriminations. With slight shades of difference, you have the same religion, manners, habits, and political principles. You have in a common cause fought and triumphed together; the independence and liberty you possess are the work of joint counsels, and joint efforts of common dangers, sufferings, and successes.

But these considerations, however powerfully they address themselves to your sensibility, are greatly outweighed by those which apply more immediately to your interest. Here every portion of our country finds the most commanding motives for carefully guarding and preserving the union of the whole.

The North, in an unrestrained intercourse with the South, protected by the equal laws of a common government, finds in the productions of the latter great additional resources of maritime and commercial enterprise and precious materials of manufacturing industry. The South, in the same intercourse, benefiting by the agency of the North, sees its agriculture grow and its commerce expand. Turning partly into its own channels the seamen of the North, it finds its particular navigation invigorated; and, while it contributes, in different ways, to nourish and increase the general mass of the national navigation, it looks forward to the protection of a maritime strength, to which itself is unequally adapted. The East, in a like intercourse with the West, already finds, and in the progressive improvement of interior communications by land and water, will more and more find a valuable vent for the commodities which it brings from abroad, or manufactures at home. The West derives from the East supplies requisite to its growth and comfort, and, what is perhaps of still greater consequence, it must of necessity owe the secure enjoyment of indispensable outlets for its own productions to the weight, influence, and the future maritime strength of the Atlantic side of the Union, directed by an indissoluble community of interest as one nation. Any other tenure by which the West can hold this essential advantage, whether derived from its own separate strength, or from an apostate and unnatural connection with any foreign power, must be intrinsically precarious.

While, then, every part of our country thus feels an immediate and particular interest in union, all the parts combined cannot fail to find in the united mass of means and efforts greater strength, greater resource, proportionably greater security from external danger, a less frequent interruption of their peace by foreign nations; and, what is of inestimable value, they must derive from union an exemption from those broils and wars between themselves, which so frequently afflict neighbouring countries not tied together by the same governments, which their own rival ships alone would be sufficient to produce, but which opposite foreign alliances, attachments, and intrigues would stimulate and embitter. Hence, likewise, they will avoid the necessity of those overgrown military establishments which, under any form of government, are inauspicious to liberty, and which are to be regarded as particularly hostile to republican liberty. In this sense, it is that your union ought to be considered as a main prop of your liberty, and that the love of the one ought to endear to you the preservation of the other.

These considerations speak a persuasive language to every reflecting and virtuous mind, and exhibit the continuance of the Union as a primary object of patriotic desire. Is there a doubt whether a common government can embrace so large a sphere? Let experience solve it. To listen to mere speculation in such a case were criminal. We are authorized to hope that a proper organization of the whole with the auxiliary agency of governments for the respective subdivisions, will afford a happy issue to the experiment. It is well worth a fair and full experiment. With such powerful and obvious motives to union, affecting all parts of our country, while experience shall not have demonstrated its impracticability, there will always be reason to distrust the patriotism of those who in any quarter may endeavor to weaken its bands.

In contemplating the causes which may disturb our Union, it occurs as matter of serious concern that any ground should have been furnished for characterizing parties by geographical discriminations, Northern and Southern, Atlantic and Western; whence designing men may endeavor to excite a belief that there is a real difference of local interests and views. One of the expedients of party to acquire influence within particular districts is to misrepresent the opinions and aims of other districts. You cannot shield yourselves too much against the jealousies and heartburnings which spring from these misrepresentations; they tend to render alien to each other those who ought to be bound together by fraternal affection. The inhabitants of our Western country have lately had a useful lesson on this head; they have seen, in the negotiation by the Executive, and in the unanimous ratification by the Senate, of the treaty with Spain, and in the universal satisfaction at that event, throughout the United States, a decisive proof how unfounded were the suspicions propagated among them of a policy in the General Government and in the Atlantic States unfriendly to their interests in regard to the Mississippi; they have been witnesses to the formation of two treaties, that with Great Britain, and that with Spain, which secure to them everything they could desire, in respect to our foreign relations, towards confirming their prosperity. Will it not be their wisdom to rely for the preservation of these advantages on the Union by which they were procured? Will they not henceforth be deaf to those advisers, if such there are, who would sever them from their brethren and connect them with aliens?

To the efficacy and permanency of your Union, a government for the whole is indispensable. No alliance, however strict, between the parts can be an adequate substitute; they must inevitably experience the infractions and interruptions which all alliances in all times have experienced. Sensible of this momentous truth, you have improved upon your first essay, by the adoption of a constitution of government better calculated than your former for an intimate union, and for the efficacious management of your common concerns. This government, the offspring of our own choice, uninfluenced and unawed, adopted upon full investigation and mature deliberation, completely free in its principles, in the distribution of its powers, uniting security with energy, and containing within itself a provision for its own amendment, has a just claim to your confidence and your support. Respect for its authority, compliance with its laws, acquiescence in its measures, are duties enjoined by the fundamental maxims of true liberty. The basis of our political systems is the right of the people to make and to alter their constitutions of government. But the Constitution which at any time exists, till changed by an explicit and authentic act of the whole people, is sacredly obligatory upon all. The very idea of the power and the right of the people to establish government presupposes the duty of every individual to obey the established government.

All obstructions to the execution of the laws, all combinations and associations, under whatever plausible character, with the real design to direct, control, counteract, or awe the regular deliberation and action of the constituted authorities, are destructive of this fundamental principle, and of fatal tendency. They serve to organize faction, to give it an artificial and extraordinary force; to put, in the place of the delegated will of the nation the will of a party, often a small but artful and enterprising minority of the community; and, according to the alternate triumphs of different parties, to make the public administration the mirror of the ill-concerted and incongruous projects of faction, rather than the organ of consistent and wholesome plans digested by common counsels and modified by mutual interests.

However, combinations or associations of the above description may now and then answer popular ends, they are likely, in the course of time and things, to become potent engines, by which cunning, ambitious, and unprincipled men will be enabled to subvert the power of the people and to usurp for themselves the reins of government, destroying afterwards the very engines which have lifted them to unjust dominion.

Towards the preservation of your government, and the permanency of your present happy state, it is requisite, not only that you steadily discountenance irregular oppositions to its acknowledged authority, but also that you resist with care the spirit of innovation upon its principles, however specious the pretexts. One method of assault may be to effect, in the forms of the Constitution, alterations which will impair the energy of the system, and thus to undermine what cannot be directly overthrown. In all the changes to which you may be invited, remember that time and habit are at least as necessary to fix the true character of governments as of other human institutions; that experience is the surest standard by which to test the real tendency of the existing constitution of a country; that facility in changes, upon the credit of mere hypothesis and opinion, exposes to perpetual change, from the endless variety of hypothesis and opinion; and remember, especially, that for the efficient management of your common interests, in a country so extensive as ours, a government of as much vigour as is consistent with the perfect security of liberty is indispensable. Liberty itself will find in such a government, with powers properly distributed and adjusted, its surest guardian. It is, indeed, little else than a name, where the government is too feeble to withstand the enterprises of faction, to confine each member of the society within the limits prescribed by the laws, and to maintain all in the secure and tranquil enjoyment of the rights of person and property.

I have already intimated to you the danger of parties in the State, with particular reference to the founding of them on geographical discriminations. Let me now take a more comprehensive view, and warn you in the most solemn manner against the baneful effects of the spirit of party generally.

This spirit, unfortunately, is inseparable from our nature, having its root in the strongest passions of the human mind. It exists under different shapes in all governments, more or less stifled, controlled, or repressed; but, in those of the popular form, it is seen in its greatest rankness, and is truly their worst enemy.

The alternate domination of one faction over another, sharpened by the spirit of revenge, natural to party dissension, which in different ages and countries has perpetrated the most horrid enormities, is itself a frightful despotism. But this leads at length to a more formal and permanent despotism. The disorders and miseries which result gradually incline the minds of men to seek security and repose in the absolute power of an individual; and sooner or later the chief of some prevailing faction, more able or more fortunate than his competitors, turns this disposition to the purposes of his own elevation, on the ruins of public liberty.

Without looking forward to an extremity of this kind (which nevertheless ought not to be entirely out of sight), the common and continual mischiefs of the spirit of party are sufficient to make it the interest and duty of a wise people to discourage and restrain it. It serves always to distract the public councils and enfeeble the public administration. It agitates the community with ill-founded jealousies and false alarms, kindles the animosity of one part against another, foments occasionally riot and insurrection. It opens the door to foreign influence and corruption, which finds a facilitated access to the government itself through the channels of party passions. Thus the policy and the will of one country are subjected to the policy and will of another.

There is an opinion that parties in free countries are useful checks upon the administration of the government and serve to keep alive the spirit of liberty. This within certain limits is probably true; and in governments of a monarchical cast, patriotism may look with indulgence, if not with favour, upon the spirit of party. But in those of the popular character, in governments purely elective, it is a spirit not to be encouraged. From their natural tendency, it is certain there will always be enough of that spirit for every salutary purpose. And there being constant danger of excess, the effort ought to be by force of public opinion, to mitigate and assuage it. A fire not to be quenched, it demands a uniform vigilance to prevent its bursting into a flame, lest, instead of warming, it should consume.

It is important, likewise, that the habits of thinking in a free country should inspire caution in those entrusted with its administration, to confine themselves within their respective constitutional spheres, avoiding in the exercise of the powers of one department to encroach upon another. The spirit of encroachment tends to consolidate the powers of all the departments in one, and thus to create, whatever the form of government, a real despotism. A just estimate of that love of power, and proneness to abuse it, which predominates in the human heart, is sufficient to satisfy us of the truth of this position. The necessity of reciprocal checks in the exercise of political power, by dividing and distributing it into different depositaries, and constituting each the guardian of the public weal against invasions by the others, has been evinced by experiments ancient and modern; some of them in our country and under our own eyes. To preserve them must be as necessary as to institute them. If, in the opinion of the people, the distribution or modification of the constitutional powers be in any particular wrong, let it be corrected by an amendment in the way which the Constitution designates. But let there be no change by usurpation; for though this, in one instance, may be the instrument of good, it is the customary weapon by which free governments are destroyed. The precedent must always greatly overbalance in permanent evil any partial or transient benefit, which the use can at any time yield.

Of all the dispositions and habits which lead to political prosperity, religion and morality are indispensable supports. In vain would that man claim the tribute of patriotism, who should labour to subvert these great pillars of human happiness, these firmest props of the duties of men and citizens. The mere politician, equally with the pious man, ought to respect and to cherish them. A volume could not trace all their connections with private and public felicity. Let it simply be asked: Where is the security for property, for reputation, for life, if the sense of religious obligation desert the oaths which are the instruments of investigation in courts of justice? And let us with caution indulge the supposition that morality can be maintained without religion. Whatever may be conceded to the influence of refined education on minds of peculiar structure, reason and experience both forbid us to expect that national morality can prevail in exclusion of religious principle.

It is substantially true that virtue or morality is a necessary spring of popular government. The rule, indeed, extends with more or less force to every species of free government. Who that is a sincere friend to it can look with indifference upon attempts to shake the foundation of the fabric?

Promote then, as an object of primary importance, institutions for the general diffusion of knowledge. In proportion as the structure of a government gives force to public opinion, it is essential that public opinion should be enlightened.

As a very important source of strength and security, cherish public credit. One method of preserving it is to use it as sparingly as possible, avoiding occasions of expense by cultivating peace, but remembering also that timely disbursements to prepare for danger frequently prevent much greater disbursements to repel it, avoiding likewise the accumulation of debt, not only by shunning occasions of expense, but by vigorous exertion in time of peace to discharge the debts which unavoidable wars may have occasioned, not ungenerously throwing upon posterity the burden which we ourselves ought to bear. The execution of these maxims belongs to your representatives, but it is necessary that public opinion should cooperate. To facilitate to them the performance of their duty, it is essential that you should practically bear in mind that towards the payment of debts there must be revenue; that to have revenue there must be taxes; that no taxes can be devised which are not more or less inconvenient and unpleasant; that the intrinsic embarrassment, inseparable from the selection of the proper objects (which is always a choice of difficulties), ought to be a decisive motive for a candid construction of the conduct of the government in making it, and for a spirit of acquiescence in the measures for obtaining revenue, which the public exigencies may at any time dictate.

Observe good faith and justice towards all nations; cultivate peace and harmony with all. Religion and morality enjoin this conduct; and can it be, that good policy does not equally enjoin it—it will be worthy of a free, enlightened, and at no distant period, a great nation, to give to mankind the magnanimous and too novel example of a people always guided by an exalted justice and benevolence. Who can doubt that, in the course of time and things, the fruits of such a plan would richly repay any temporary advantages which might be lost by a steady adherence to it? Can it be that Providence has not connected the permanent felicity of a nation with its virtue? The experiment, at least, is recommended by every sentiment which ennobles human nature. Alas! Is it rendered impossible by its vices?

In the execution of such a plan, nothing is more essential than that permanent, inveterate antipathies against particular nations, and passionate attachments for others, should be excluded; and that, in place of them, just and amicable feelings towards all should be cultivated. The nation which indulges towards another a habitual hatred or a habitual fondness is in some degree a slave. It is a slave to its animosity or to its affection, either of which is sufficient to lead it astray from its duty and its interest. Antipathy in one nation against another disposes each more readily to offer insult and injury, to lay hold of slight causes of umbrage, and to be haughty and intractable, when accidental or trifling occasions of dispute occur. Hence, frequent collisions, obstinate, envenomed, and bloody contests. The nation, prompted by ill-will and resentment, sometimes impels to war the government, contrary to the best calculations of policy. The government sometimes participates in the national propensity, and adopts through passion what reason would reject; at other times it makes the animosity of the nation subservient to projects of hostility instigated by pride, ambition, and other sinister and pernicious motives. The peace often, sometimes perhaps the liberty, of nations, has been the victim.

So likewise, a passionate attachment of one nation for another produces a variety of evils. Sympathy for the favorite nation, facilitating the illusion of an imaginary common interest in cases where no real common interest exists, and infusing into one the enmities of the other, betrays the former into a participation in the quarrels and wars of the latter without adequate inducement or justification. It leads also to concessions to the favorite nation of privileges denied to others which is apt doubly to injure the nation making the concessions; by unnecessarily parting with what ought to have been retained, and by exciting jealousy, ill-will, and a disposition to retaliate, in the parties from whom equal privileges are withheld. And it gives to ambitious, corrupted, or deluded citizens (who devote themselves to the favorite nation), facility to betray or sacrifice the interests of their own country, without odium, sometimes even with popularity; gilding, with the appearances of a virtuous sense of obligation, a commendable deference for public opinion, or a laudable zeal for public good, the base or foolish compliances of ambition, corruption, or infatuation.

As avenues to foreign influence in innumerable ways, such attachments are particularly alarming to the truly enlightened and independent patriot. How many opportunities do they afford to tamper with domestic factions, to practice the arts of seduction, to mislead public opinion, to influence or awe the public councils. Such an attachment of a small or weak towards a great and powerful nation dooms the former to be the satellite of the latter.

Against the insidious wiles of foreign influence (I conjure you to believe me, fellow-citizens) the jealousy of a free people ought to be constantly awake, since history and experience prove that foreign influence is one of the most baneful foes of republican government. But that jealousy to be useful must be impartial; else it becomes the instrument of the very influence to be avoided, instead of a defence against it. Excessive partiality for one foreign nation and excessive dislike of another cause those whom they actuate to see danger only on one side, and serve to veil and even second the arts of influence on the other. Real patriots who may resist the intrigues of the favorite are liable to become suspected and odious, while its tools and dupes usurp the applause and confidence of the people, to surrender their interests.

The great rule of conduct for us in regard to foreign nations is in extending our commercial relations, to have with them as little political connection as possible. So far as we have already formed engagements, let them be fulfilled with perfect good faith. Here let us stop. Europe has a set of primary interests which to us have none; or a very remote relation. Hence, she must be engaged in frequent controversies, the causes of which are essentially foreign to our concerns. Hence, therefore, it must be unwise in us to implicate ourselves by artificial ties in the ordinary vicissitudes of her politics, or the ordinary combinations and collisions of her friendships or enmities.

Our detached and distant situation invites and enables us to pursue a different course. If we remain one people under an efficient government. The period is not far off when we may defy material injury from external annoyance; when we may take such an attitude as will cause the neutrality, we may at any time resolve upon to be scrupulously respected; when belligerent nations, under the impossibility of making acquisitions upon us, will not lightly hazard the giving us provocation; when we may choose peace or war, as our interest, guided by justice, shall counsel.

Why forego the advantages of so peculiar a situation? Why quit our own to stand upon foreign ground? Why, by interweaving our destiny with that of any part of Europe, entangle our peace and prosperity in the toils of European ambition, rivalship, interest, humour or caprice?

It is our true policy to steer clear of permanent alliances with any portion of the foreign world; so far, I mean, as we are now at liberty to do it; for let me not be understood as capable of patronizing infidelity to existing engagements. I hold the maxim no less applicable to public than to private affairs, that honesty is always the best policy. I repeat it, therefore, let those engagements be observed in their genuine sense. But, in my opinion, it is unnecessary and would be unwise to extend them.

Taking care always to keep ourselves by suitable establishments on a respectable defensive posture, we may safely trust to temporary alliances for extraordinary emergencies.

Harmony, liberal intercourse with all nations, are recommended by policy, humanity, and interest. But even our commercial policy should hold an equal and impartial hand; neither seeking nor granting exclusive favours or preferences; consulting the natural course of things; diffusing and diversifying by gentle means the streams of commerce, but forcing nothing; establishing (with powers so disposed, in order to give trade a stable course, to define the rights of our merchants, and to enable the government to support them) conventional rules of intercourse, the best that present circumstances and mutual opinion will permit, but temporary, and liable to be from time to time abandoned or varied, as experience and circumstances shall dictate; constantly keeping in view that it is folly in one nation to look for disinterested favours from another; that it must pay with a portion of its independence for whatever it may accept under that character; that, by such acceptance, it may place itself in the condition of having given equivalents for nominal favours, and yet of being reproached with ingratitude for not giving more. There can be no greater error than to expect or calculate upon real favours from nation to nation. It is an illusion, which experience must cure, which a just pride ought to discard.

In offering to you, my countrymen, these counsels of an old and affectionate friend, I dare not hope they will make the strong and lasting impression I could wish; that they will control the usual current of the passions, or prevent our nation from running the course which has hitherto marked the destiny of nations. But, if I may even flatter myself that they may be productive of some partial benefit, some occasional good; that they may now and then recur to moderate the fury of party spirit, to warn against the mischiefs of foreign intrigue, to guard against the impostures of pretended patriotism; this hope will be a full recompense for the solicitude for your welfare, by which they have been dictated.

How far in the discharge of my official duties I have been guided by the principles which have been delineated, the public records and other evidences of my conduct must witness to you and to the world. To myself, the assurance of my own conscience is, that I have at least believed myself to be guided by them.

In relation to the still subsisting war in Europe, my proclamation of the 22 April 1793, is the index of my plan. Sanctioned by your approving voice, and by that of your representatives in both houses of Congress, the spirit of that measure has continually governed me, uninfluenced by any attempts to deter or divert me from it.

After deliberate examination, with the aid of the best lights I could obtain, I was well satisfied that our country, under all the circumstances of the case, had a right to take, and was bound in duty and interest to take, a neutral position. Having taken it, I determined, as far as should depend upon me, to maintain it, with moderation, perseverance, and firmness.

The considerations which respect the right to hold this conduct, it is not necessary on this occasion to detail. I will only observe that, according to my understanding of the matter, that right, so far from being denied by any of the belligerent powers, has been virtually admitted by all.

The duty of holding a neutral conduct may be inferred, without anything more, from the obligation which justice and humanity impose on every nation, in cases in which it is free to act, to maintain inviolate relations of peace and amity towards other nations.

The inducements of interest for observing that conduct will best be referred to your own reflections and experience. With me a predominant motive has been to endeavour to gain time to our country to settle and mature its yet recent institutions, and to progress without interruption to that degree of strength and consistency which is necessary to give it, humanly speaking, the command of its own fortunes.

Though, in reviewing the incidents of my administration, I am unconscious of intentional error, I am nevertheless too sensible of my defects not to think it probable that I may have committed many errors. Whatever they may be, I fervently beseech the Almighty to avert or mitigate the evils to which they may tend. I shall also carry with me the hope that my country will never cease to view them with indulgence; and that, after forty-five years of my life dedicated to its service with an upright zeal, the faults of incompetent abilities will be consigned to oblivion, as myself must soon be to the mansions of rest.

Relying on its kindness in this as in other things, and actuated by that fervent love towards it, which is so natural to a man who views in it the native soil of himself and his progenitors for several generations, I anticipate with pleasing expectation that retreat in which I promise myself to realize, without alloy, the sweet enjoyment of partaking, in the midst of my fellow-citizens, the benign influence of good laws under a free government, the ever-favorite object of my heart, and the happy reward, as I trust, of our mutual cares, labours, and dangers.

16

TONIC FOR THE HINDU MIND

This speech was delivered in Chicago, 11 September 1893. Swami Vivekananda's speech at the Parliament of Religions in Chicago is of immense historical significance. For the first time, a Hindu sanyasi spoke to a Western audience who listened and applauded. He never indulged in politics, but his speeches and later works had a great influence on the political aspirations of Indians. Swami Vivekananda was a powerful speaker. His biographer, the famous French author Romain Rolland wrote, 'Vivekananda's words are great music, phrases in the style of Beethoven, stirring rhythms like the march of Handel choruses.' Indeed, Swami Vivekananda did not belong to a sect; he belonged to India.

Sisters and brothers of America, it fills my heart with unspeakable joy to respond to the warm and cordial welcome which you have given us. I thank you in the name of the most ancient order of monks in the world; I thank you in the name of the mother of religions; and I thank you in the name of the millions and millions of Hindu people of all classes and sects. My thanks, also, to some of the speakers on this platform who, referring to the delegates from the Orient, have told you that these men from far-off nations may well claim the honour of bearing to different lands, the idea of toleration. I am proud to belong to a religion which has taught the world tolerance and universal acceptance. We believe not only in universal toleration but we accept all religions as true. I am proud to belong to a nation which has sheltered the persecuted and the refugees of all religions and nations of the earth. I am proud to tell you that we have gathered in our bosom the purest remnants of the Israelites, who came to southern India and took refuge with us the very year in which their holy temple was shattered to pieces by Roman tyranny. I am proud to belong to the religion which has sheltered and is still fostering the remains of the grand Zoroastrian nation. I will quote to you, brethrens, a few lines from a hymn which I have recited from my earliest boyhood and which is repeated every day by millions of human beings: As the different streams having their sources in different places all mingle their water in the sea, so, O Lord, the different paths which men take through different tendencies, various though they appear, crooked or straight, all lead to Thee.

The present convention, which is one of the most august assemblies ever held, is in itself a vindication, a declaration to the world, of the wonderful doctrine preached in the Bhagvadgita, 'Whosoever comes to Me, through whatsoever form, I reach him; all men are struggling through paths which in the end lead to Me.' Sectarianism, bigotry, and its horrible descendant, fanaticism, have long possessed this beautiful earth. They have filled the earth with violence, drenched it with human blood, destroyed civilizations, and sent whole nations to despair. Had it not been for these horrible demons, human society would be far more advanced than it has now. But now their time has come. I fervently hope that the bell that tolled this morning in honour of this convention may be the death-knell of all fanaticism, of all persecutions with the sword or with the pen, and of all uncharitable feelings between persons wending their way to the same goal.

17

INAUGURAL ADDRESS

Abraham Lincoln

With the Union's victory in the Civil War weeks away and Reconstruction plans already the source of raging debate, Lincoln's second inaugural address looked back at the horror of the conflict but pledged to see it through to the bitter end, even as he hoped for a peaceful reconciliation. This speech was delivered on Saturday, 4 March 1865.

Fellow-Countrymen:

At this second appearing to take the oath of the Presidential office there is less occasion for an extended address than there was at the first. Then a statement somewhat in detail of a course to be pursued seemed fitting and proper. Now, at the expiration of four years, during which public declarations have been constantly called forth on every point and phase of the great contest which still absorbs the attention and engrosses the energies of the nation, little that is new could be presented. The progress of our arms, upon which all else chiefly depends, is as well known to the public as to myself, and it is, I trust, reasonably satisfactory and encouraging to all. With high hope for the future, no prediction in regard to it is ventured.

On the occasion corresponding to this four years ago all thoughts were anxiously directed to an impending civil war. All dreaded it, all sought to avert it. While the inaugural address was being delivered from this place, devoted altogether to saving the Union without war, insurgent agents were in the city seeking to destroy it without war—seeking to dissolve the Union and divide effects by negotiation. Both parties deprecated war, but one of them would make war rather than let the nation survive, and the other would accept war rather than let it perish, and the war came.

One-eighth of the whole population were coloured slaves, not distributed generally over the Union, but localized in the southern part of it. These slaves constituted a peculiar and powerful interest. All knew that this interest was somehow the cause of the war. To strengthen, perpetuate, and extend this interest was the object for which the insurgents would rend the Union even by war, while the Government claimed no right to do more than to restrict the territorial enlargement of it. Neither party expected for the war the magnitude or the duration which it has already attained. Neither anticipated that the cause of the conflict might cease with or even before the conflict itself should cease. Each looked for an easier triumph, and a result less fundamental and astounding. Both read the same Bible and pray to the same God, and each invokes His aid against the other. It may seem strange that any men should dare to ask a just God's assistance in wringing their bread from the sweat of other men's faces, but let us judge not, that we be not judged. The prayers of both could not be answered. That of neither has been answered fully. The Almighty has His own purposes. 'Woe unto the world because of offences; for it must needs be that offences come, but woe to that man by whom the offence cometh.' If we shall suppose that American slavery is one of those offences which, in the providence of God, must needs come, but which, having continued through His appointed time, He now wills to remove, and that He gives to both North and South this terrible war as the woe due to those by whom the offence came, shall we discern therein any departure from those divine attributes which the believers in a living God always ascribe to Him? Fondly do we hope, fervently do we pray, that this mighty scourge of war may speedily pass away. Yet, if God wills that it continue until all the wealth piled by the bondsman's two hundred and fifty years of unrequited toil shall be sunk, and until every drop of blood drawn with the lash shall be paid by another drawn with the sword, as was said three thousand years ago, so still it must be said 'the judgments of the Lord are true and righteous altogether.'

With malice toward none, with charity for all, with firmness in the right as God gives us to see the right, let us strive on to finish the work we are in, to bind up the nation's wounds, to care for him who shall have borne the battle and for his widow and his orphan, to do all which may achieve and cherish a just and lasting peace among ourselves and with all nations.

18

THE FOUR FREEDOMS

Franklin D. Roosevelt

Attempting to secure American support for continued aid to Britain and increased American involvement in WWII, Roosevelt outlined four freedoms America would seek to protect worldwide. This was FDR's State of the Union Address on 6 January 1941.

Mr President, Mr Speaker, Members of the seventy-seventh Congress:

I address you, the Members of this new Congress, at a moment unprecedented in the history of the Union. I use the word 'unprecedented,' because at no previous time has American security been as seriously threatened from without as it is today.

Since the permanent formation of our Government under the Constitution, in 1789, most of the periods of crisis in our history have related to our domestic affairs. And fortunately, only one of these—the four-year War Between the States—ever threatened our national unity. Today, thank God, one hundred and thirty million Americans, in forty-eight States, have forgotten points of the compass in our national unity.

It is true that prior to 1914 the United States often had been disturbed by events in other Continents. We had even engaged in two wars with European nations and in a number of undeclared wars in the West Indies, in the Mediterranean and in the Pacific for the maintenance of American rights and for the principles of peaceful commerce. But in no case had a serious threat been raised against our national safety or our continued independence.

What I seek to convey is the historic truth that the United States as a nation has at all times maintained opposition, clear, definite opposition, to any attempt to lock us in behind an ancient Chinese wall while the procession of civilization went past. Today, thinking of our children and of their children, we oppose enforced isolation for ourselves or for any other part of the Americas.

That determination of ours, extending over all these years, was proved, for example, in the early days during the quarter century of wars following the French Revolution.

While the Napoleonic struggles did threaten interests of the United States because of the French foothold in the West Indies and in Louisiana, and while we engaged in the War of 1812 to vindicate our right to peaceful trade, it is nevertheless clear that neither France nor Great Britain, nor any other nation, was aiming at domination of the whole world.

And in like fashion from 1815 to 1914—ninety-nine years—no single war in Europe or in Asia constituted a real threat against our future or against the future of any other American nation.

Except in the Maximilian interlude in Mexico, no foreign power sought to establish itself in this Hemisphere; and the strength of the British fleet in the Atlantic has been a friendly strength. It is still a friendly strength.

Even when the World War broke out in 1914, it seemed to contain only small threat of danger to our own American future. But, as time went on, as we remember, the American people began to visualize what the downfall of democratic nations might mean to our own democracy.

We need not overemphasize imperfections in the Peace of Versailles. We need not harp on failure of the democracies to deal with problems of world reconstruction. We should remember that the Peace of 1919 was far less unjust than the kind of 'pacification' which began even before Munich, and which is being carried on under the new order of tyranny that seeks to spread over every continent today. The American people have unalterably set their faces against that tyranny.

I suppose that every realist knows that the democratic way of life is at this moment being directly assailed in every part of the world—assailed either by arms, or by secret spreading of poisonous propaganda by those who seek to destroy unity and promote discord in nations that are still at peace.

During sixteen long months this assault has blotted out the whole pattern of democratic life in an appalling number of independent nations, great and small. And the assailants are still on the march, threatening other nations, great and small.

Therefore, as your President, performing my constitutional duty to 'give to the Congress information of the state of the Union,' I find it, unhappily, necessary to report that the future and the safety of our country and of our democracy are overwhelmingly involved in events far beyond our borders.

Armed defence of democratic existence is now being gallantly waged in four continents. If that defence fails, all the population and all the resources of Europe, and Asia, and Africa and Australasia will be dominated by conquerors. And let us remember that the total of those populations in those four continents, the total of those populations and their resources greatly exceeds the sum total of the population and the resources of the whole of the Western Hemisphere—yes, many times over. In times like these it is immature—and incidentally, untrue—for anybody to brag that an unprepared America, single-handed, and with one hand tied behind its back, can hold off the whole world.

No realistic American can expect from a dictator's peace international generosity, or return of true independence, or world disarmament, or freedom of expression, or freedom of religion—or even good business.

Such a peace would bring no security for us or for our neighbours. 'Those, who would give up essential liberty to purchase a little temporary safety, deserve neither liberty nor safety.'

As a nation, we may take pride in the fact that we are soft-hearted; but we cannot afford to be soft-headed.

We must always be wary of those who with sounding brass and a tinkling cymbal preach the 'ism' of appeasement.

We must especially beware of that small group of selfish men who would clip the wings of the American eagle in order to feather their own nests.

I have recently pointed out how quickly the tempo of modern warfare could bring into our very midst the physical attack which we must eventually expect if the dictator nations win this war.

There is much loose talk of our immunity from immediate and direct invasion from across the seas. Obviously, as long as the British Navy retains its power, no such danger exists. Even if there were no British Navy, it is not probable that any enemy would be stupid enough to attack us by landing troops in the United States from across thousands of miles of ocean, until it had acquired strategic bases from which to operate.

But we learn much from the lessons of the past years in Europe-particularly the lesson of Norway, whose essential seaports were captured by treachery and surprise built up over a series of years.

The first phase of the invasion of this Hemisphere would not be the landing of regular troops. The necessary strategic points would be occupied by secret agents and by their dupes—and great numbers of them are already here, and in Latin America.

As long as the aggressor nations maintain the offensive, they not, we will choose the time and the place and the method of their attack.

And that is why the future of all the American Republics is today in serious danger.

That is why this Annual Message to the Congress is unique in our history.

That is why every member of the Executive Branch of the Government and every member of the Congress face great responsibility and great accountability.

The need of the moment is that our actions and our policy should be devoted primarily—almost exclusively—to meeting this foreign peril. For all our domestic problems are now a part of the great emergency.

Just as our national policy in internal affairs has been based upon a decent respect for the rights and the dignity of all of our fellow men within our gates, so our national policy in foreign affairs has been based on a decent respect for the rights and the dignity of all nations, large and small. And the justice of morality must and will win in the end.

Our national policy is this:

First, by an impressive expression of the public will and without regard to partisanship, we are committed to all-inclusive national defence.

Second, by an impressive expression of the public will and without regard to partisanship, we are committed to full support of all those resolute people everywhere who are resisting aggression and are thereby keeping war away from our Hemisphere. By this support, we express our determination that the democratic cause shall prevail; and we strengthen the defence and the security of our own nation.

Third, by an impressive expression of the public will and without regard to partisanship, we are committed to the proposition that principles of morality and considerations for our own security will never permit us to acquiesce in a peace dictated by aggressors and sponsored by appeasers. We know that enduring peace cannot be bought at the cost of other people's freedom.

In the recent national election there was no substantial difference between the two great parties in respect to that national policy. No issue was fought out on this line before the American electorate. And today it is abundantly evident that American citizens everywhere are demanding and supporting speedy and complete action in recognition of obvious danger.

Therefore, the immediate need is a swift and driving increase in our armament production.

Leaders of industry and labour have responded to our summons. Goals of speed have been set. In some cases these goals are being reached ahead of time; in some cases we are on schedule; in other cases there are slight but not serious delays; and in some cases—and I am sorry to say very important cases—we are all concerned by the slowness of the accomplishment of our plans.

The Army and Navy, however, have made substantial progress during the past year. Actual experience is improving and speeding up our methods of production with every passing day. And today's best is not good enough for tomorrow.

I am not satisfied with the progress thus far made. The men in charge of the program represent the best in training, in ability, and in patriotism. They are not satisfied with the progress thus far made. None of us will be satisfied until the job is done.

No matter whether the original goal was set too high or too low, our objective is quicker and better results.

We are behind schedule in turning out finished airplanes; we are working day and night to solve the innumerable problems and to catch up.

We are ahead of schedule in building warships but we are working to get even further ahead of that schedule.

To change a whole nation from a basis of peacetime production of implements of peace to a basis of wartime production of implements of war is no small task. And the greatest difficulty comes at the beginning of the program, when new tools, new plant facilities, new assembly lines, and new ship ways must first be constructed before the actual material begins to flow steadily and speedily from them.

The Congress, of course, must rightly keep itself informed at all times of the progress of the program. However, there is certain information, as the Congress itself will readily recognize, which, in the interests of our own security and those of the nations that we are supporting, must of needs be kept in confidence.

New circumstances are constantly begetting new needs for our safety. I shall ask this Congress for greatly increased new appropriations and authorizations to carry on what we have begun.

I also ask this Congress for authority and for funds sufficient to manufacture additional munitions and war supplies of many kinds, to be turned over to those nations which are now in actual war with aggressor nations.

Our most useful and immediate role is to act as an arsenal for them as well as for ourselves. They do not need manpower, but they do need billions of dollars worth of the weapons of defence.

The time is near when they will not be able to pay for them all in ready cash. We cannot, and we will not, tell them that they must surrender, merely because of present inability to pay for the weapons which we know they must have.

I do not recommend that we make them a loan of dollars with which to pay for these weapons—a loan to be repaid in dollars.

I recommend that we make it possible for those nations to continue to obtain war materials in the United States, fitting their orders into our own program. And nearly all of their material would, if the time ever came, be useful in our own defence.

Taking counsel of expert military and naval authorities, considering what is best for our own security, we are free to decide how much should be kept here and how much should be sent abroad to our friends who by their determined and heroic resistance are giving us time in which to make ready our own defence.

For what we send abroad, we shall be repaid, repaid within a reasonable time following the close of hostilities, repaid in similar materials, or, at our option, in other goods of many kinds, which they can produce and which we need.

Let us say to the democracies: 'We Americans are vitally concerned in your defence of freedom. We are putting forth our energies, our resources and our organizing powers to give you the strength to regain and maintain a free world. We shall send you, in ever-increasing numbers, ships, planes, tanks, guns. This is our purpose and our pledge.'

In fulfillment of this purpose we will not be intimidated by the threats of dictators that they will regard as a breach of international law or as an act of war our aid to the democracies which dare to resist their aggression. Such aid…such aid is not an act of war, even if a dictator should unilaterally proclaim it so to be.

And when the dictators, if the dictators, are ready to make war upon us, they will not wait for an act of war on our part. They did not wait for Norway or Belgium or the Netherlands to commit an act of war.

Their only interest is in a new one-way international law, which lacks mutuality in its observance, and, therefore, becomes an instrument of oppression.

The happiness of future generations of Americans may well depend upon how effective and how immediate we can make our aid felt. No one can tell the exact character of the emergency situations that we may be called upon to meet. The Nation's hands must not be tied when the Nation's life is in danger.

Yes, and we must all prepare—all of us prepare—to make the sacrifices that the emergency—almost as serious as war itself—demands. Whatever stands in the way of speed and efficiency—in defence, preparations of any kind—must give way to the national need.

A free nation has the right to expect full cooperation from all groups. A free nation has the right to look to the leaders of business, of labour, and of agriculture to take the lead in stimulating effort, not among other groups but within their own groups.

The best way of dealing with the few slackers or trouble makers in our midst is; first, to shame them by patriotic example, and, if that fails, to use the sovereignty of government to save government.

As men do not live by bread alone, they do not fight by armaments alone. Those who man our defences, and those behind them who build our defences, must have the stamina and the courage which come from unshakable belief in the manner of life which they are defending. The mighty action that we are calling for cannot be based on a disregard of all the things worth fighting for.

The Nation takes great satisfaction and much strength from the things which have been done to make its people conscious of their individual stake in the preservation of democratic life in America. Those things have toughened the fibre of our people, have renewed their faith and strengthened their devotion to the institutions we make ready to protect.

Certainly this is no time for any of us to stop thinking about the social and economic problems which are the root cause of the social revolution which is today a supreme factor in the world.

For there is nothing mysterious about the foundations of a healthy and strong democracy. The basic things expected by our people of their political and economic systems are simple. They are:

Equality of opportunity for youth and for others.

Jobs for those who can work.

Security for those who need it.

The ending of special privilege for the few.

The preservation of civil liberties for all.

The enjoyment…the enjoyment of the fruits of scientific progress in a wider and constantly rising standard of living.

These are the simple, the basic things that must never be lost sight of in the turmoil and unbelievable complexity of our modern world. The inner and abiding strength of our economic and political systems is dependent upon the degree to which they fulfill these expectations.

Many subjects connected with our social economy call for immediate improvement.

As examples:

We should bring more citizens under the coverage of old-age pensions and unemployment insurance.

We should widen the opportunities for adequate medical care.

We should plan a better system by which persons deserving or needing gainful employment may obtain it.

I have called for personal sacrifice. And I am assured of the willingness of almost all Americans to respond to that call.

A part of the sacrifice means the payment of more money in taxes. In my Budget Message I will recommend that a greater portion of this great defence program be paid for from taxation than we are paying for today. No person should try, or be allowed, to get rich out of the program; and the principle of tax payments in accordance with ability to pay should be constantly before our eyes to guide our legislation.

If the Congress maintains these principles, the voters, putting patriotism ahead of pocketbooks, will give you their applause.

In the future days, which we seek to make secure, we look forward to a world founded upon four essential human freedoms.

The first is freedom of speech and expression—everywhere in the world.

The second is freedom of every person to worship God in his own way—everywhere in the world.

The third is freedom from want—which translated into world terms, means economic understandings which will secure to every nation a healthy peacetime life for its inhabitants everywhere in the world.

The fourth is freedom from fear—which translated into world terms, means a worldwide reduction of armaments to such a point and in such a thorough fashion that no nation will be in a position to commit an act of physical aggression against any neighbour—anywhere in the world.

That is no vision of a distant millennium. It is a definite basis for a kind of world attainable in our own time and generation. That kind of world is the very antithesis of the so-called new order of tyranny which the dictators seek to create with the crash of a bomb.

To that new order we oppose the greater conception—the moral order. A good society is able to face schemes of world domination and foreign revolutions alike without fear.

Since the beginning of our American history, we have been engaged in change—in a perpetual peaceful revolution—a revolution which goes on steadily, quietly adjusting itself to changing conditions—without the concentration camp or the quicklime in the ditch. The world order which we seek is the cooperation of free countries, working together in a friendly, civilized society.

This nation has placed its destiny in the hands and heads and hearts of its millions of free men and women; and its faith in freedom under the guidance of God. Freedom means the supremacy of human rights everywhere. Our support goes to those who struggle to gain those rights and keep them. Our strength is our unity of purpose.

To that high concept there can be no end save victory.

19

THE NAZI INVASION OF RUSSIA

Vyacheslay Molotov

Vyacheslay Molotov (1889–1986) was Foreign Minister of Soviet Russia when the Nazi-Soviet Non-aggression Pact was signed, 23 August 1939. News of the Pact stunned the world and effectively paved the way for the beginning of World War II with Hitler assured the Germans would not face Russian military opposition in response to Nazi aggression in Europe. This speech was delivered on 22 June 1941.

Citizens of the Soviet Union:

The Soviet Government and its head, Comrade Stalin, have authorized me to make the following statement:

Today at 4 o' clock a.m., without any claims having been presented to the Soviet Union, without a declaration of war, German troops attacked our country, attacked our borders at many points and bombed from their airplanes our cities; Zhitomir, Kiev, Sevastopol, Kaunas and some others, killing and wounding over two hundred persons.

There were also enemy air raids and artillery shelling from Rumanian and Finnish territory.

This unheard of attack upon our country is perfidy unparalleled in the history of civilized nations. The attack on our country was perpetrated despite the fact that a treaty of non-aggression had been signed between the U. S. S. R. and Germany and that the Soviet Government most faithfully abided by all provisions of this treaty.

The attack upon our country was perpetrated despite the fact that during the entire period of operation of this treaty, the German Government could not find grounds for a single complaint against the U.S.S.R. as regards observance of this treaty.

Entire responsibility for this predatory attack upon the Soviet Union falls fully and completely upon the German Fascist rulers.

At 5:30 a.m.—that is, after the attack had already been perpetrated, Von der Schulenburg, the German Ambassador in Moscow, on behalf of his government made the statement to me as People's Commissar of Foreign Affairs to the effect that the German Government had decided to launch war against the U.S.S.R. in connection with the concentration of Red Army units near the eastern German frontier.

In reply to this I stated on behalf of the Soviet Government that, until the very last moment, the German Government had not presented any claims to the Soviet Government, that Germany attacked the U.S.S.R. despite the peaceable position of the Soviet Union, and that for this reason Fascist Germany is the aggressor.

On instruction of the government of the Soviet Union I also stated that at no point had our troops or our air force committed a violation of the frontier and therefore the statement made this morning by the Rumanian radio to the effect that Soviet aircraft allegedly had fired on Rumanian airdromes is a sheer lie and provocation.

Likewise a lie and provocation is the whole declaration made today by Hitler, who is trying belatedly to concoct accusations charging the Soviet Union with failure to observe the Soviet-German pact.

Now that the attack on the Soviet Union has already been committed, the Soviet Government has ordered our troops to repulse the predatory assault and to drive German troops from the territory of our country.

This war has been forced upon us, not by the German people, not by German workers, peasants and intellectuals, whose sufferings we well understand, but by the clique of bloodthirsty Fascist rulers of Germany who have enslaved Frenchmen, Czechs, Poles, Serbians, Norway, Belgium, Denmark, Holland, Greece and other nations.

The government of the Soviet Union expresses its unshakable confidence that our valiant army and navy and brave falcons of the Soviet Air Force will acquit themselves with honour in performing their duty to the fatherland and to the Soviet people, and will inflict a crushing blow upon the aggressor.

This is not the first time that our people have had to deal with an attack of an arrogant foe. At the time of Napoleon's invasion of Russia our people's reply was war for the fatherland, and Napoleon suffered defeat and met his doom.

It will be the same with Hitler, who in his arrogance has proclaimed a new crusade against our country. The Red Army and our whole people will again wage victorious war for the fatherland, for our country, for honour, for liberty.

The government of the Soviet Union expresses the firm conviction that the whole population of our country, all workers, peasants and intellectuals, men and women, will conscientiously perform their duties and do their work. Our entire people must now stand solid and united as never before.

Each one of us must demand of himself and of others discipline, organization and self-denial worthy of real Soviet patriots, in order to provide for all the needs of the Red Army, Navy and Air Force, to insure victory over the enemy.

The government calls upon you, citizens of the Soviet Union, to rally still more closely around our glorious Bolshevist party, around our Soviet Government, around our great leader and comrade, Stalin. Ours is a righteous cause. The enemy shall be defeated. Victory will be ours.

Vyacheslav Molotov–22 June 1941

20

MEETING OF SOLDIERS OF
THE IZMAILOVSKY REGIMENT

Vladimir Ilyich Lenin

This speech was delivered on 10 April 1917

Comrade soldiers! The question of the state system is now on the order of the day. The capitalists, in whose hands the state power now rests, desire a parliamentary bourgeois republic, that is, a state system where there is no tsar, but where power remains in the hands of the capitalists who govern the country by means of the old institutions, namely: the police, the bureaucracy, and the standing army.

We desire a different republic, one more in keeping with the interests of the people, more democratic. The revolutionary workers and soldiers of Petrograd have overthrown tsarism, and have cleaned out all the police from the capital. The workers of all the world look with pride and hope to the revolutionary workers and soldiers of Russia as the vanguard of the world's liberating army of the working class. The revolution, once begun, must be strengthened and carried on. We shall not allow the police to be re-established! All power in the state, from the bottom up, from the remotest little village to every street block of Petrograd, must belong to the Soviets of Workers', Soldiers', Agricultural Labourers', Peasants' and other Deputies. The central state power uniting these local Soviets must be the Constituent Assembly, National Assembly, or Council of Soviets—no matter by what name you call it.

Not the police, not the bureaucracy, who are unanswerable to the people and placed above the people, not the standing army, separated from the people, but the people themselves, universally armed and united in the Soviets, must run the state. It is they who will establish the necessary order, it is they whose authority will not only be obeyed, but also respected, by the workers and peasants.

Only this power, only the Soviets of Soldiers' and Peasants' Deputies, can solve the great question of the land in a non-bureaucratic way and not in the interests of the land owners. The land must not belong to the landowners. The peasant committees must take the land away at once from the landowners, while carefully guarding all the property against damage, and seeing to it that grain production is increased in order that the soldiers at the front be better supplied. All the land must belong to the whole nation, and its disposal must be the concern of the local Soviets of Peasants' Deputies. In order that the rich peasants—who are themselves capitalists—may not wrong and deceive the agricultural labourers and the poor peasants, it will be necessary for the latter either to confer, to combine, to unite separately, or to set up Soviets of Agricultural Labourers' Deputies of their own.

Do not allow the police to be re-established, do not let the state power or the administration of the state pass into the hands of the bureaucracy, who are non-elective, undisplaceable, and paid on a bourgeois scale; get together, unite, organize yourselves, trusting no one, depending only on your own intelligence and experience—and Russia will be able to move with a firm, measured, unerring tread toward the liberation of both our own country and of all humanity from the yoke of capital as well as from the horrors of war.

Our government, a government of the capitalists, is continuing the war in the interests of the capitalists. Like the German capitalists, headed by their crowned brigand Wilhelm, the capitalists of all the other countries are carrying on the war only for a division of capitalist profits, for domination over the world. Hundreds of millions of people, almost all the countries in the world, have been dragged into this criminal war. Hundreds of billions of capital have been invested in 'profitable' undertakings, bringing death, hunger, ruin, and barbarism to the peoples and staggering, scandalously high profits to the capitalists. There is only one way to get out of this frightful war and conclude a truly democratic peace not imposed by force, and that is by transferring all the state power to the Soviets of Workers' and Soldiers' Deputies. The workers and poor peasants, who are not interested in preserving the profits of the capitalists and robbing the weaker nations, will be able to do effectively what the capitalists only promise, namely, end the war by concluding a lasting peace that will assure liberty to all peoples without exception.

21

ADDRESS TO THE UNITED NATIONS GENERAL ASSEMBLY

Queen Elizabeth II

This speech was delivered on 21 October 1957.

I thank you, Mr President, for your words of welcome.

I wish first to express to you, to the Secretary-General and to the General Assembly of the United Nations, my great pleasure at being here today.

This Assembly was born of the endeavours of countless men and women from different nations who, over the centuries, have pursued the aims of the preservation of peace between nations, equality of justice for all before the law and the right of the peoples of the world to live their lives in freedom and security.

The Charter of the United Nations was framed with a view to giving expression to these great purposes and so forming a fitting memorial to the men and women whose toil and sacrifices turned those ideas into articles of faith for the nations of today.

Time has in fact made the task of the United Nations more difficult than it seemed when the terms of the charter were agreed at San Francisco twelve years ago. We are still far from the achievement of the ideals which I have mentioned but we must not be discouraged. The peoples of the world expect the United Nations to persevere in its efforts.

Ten Commonwealth countries are represented in this Assembly—countries which form a free association of fully independent states and which have widely different histories, cultures and traditions. Common ideals and hopes, not formal bonds, unite the members of the Commonwealth and promote that association between them which, in my belief, has contributed significantly to the cause of human freedom.

The countries of the Commonwealth regard their continuing association with one another and joint service to their high ideals as still an essential contribution to world peace and justice. They add and will continue to add to a tried element of strength, and of accumulated experience.

The United Nations is an organization, dedicated to peace, where representatives from all over the world meet to examine the problems of the time. In it men and women from all these countries—large or small, powerful or weak—can exercise an influence that might otherwise be denied them. The United Nations also originates and inspires a wide range of social and economic activities for the benefit of the whole human race.

But, Mr President, the future of this Organization will be determined, not only by the degree to which its members observe strictly the provisions of the charter and cooperate in its practical activities, but also by the strength of its people's devotion to the pursuit of those great ideals to which I have referred. When justice and respect for obligations are firmly established, the United Nations will the more confidently achieve the goal of a world at peace, law-abiding and prosperous, for which men and women have striven so long and which is the heart's desire of every nation here represented. I offer you my best wishes in your task and pray that you may be successful.

22

ABDICATION SPEECH

King Edward VIII

Edward VIII (1894-1972) became King of England upon the death of his father, George V, on 20 January 1936. Nearly forty-two years old and a bachelor, Edward then made known his desire to marry an American woman named Wallis Warfield Simpson, whom he had known since 1931. He sought the approval of his family, the Church of England, and the political establishment to marry her, but met with strong opposition. She had been married twice before and her second divorce was still pending. The love affair and possible royal marriage resulted in sensational newspaper headlines around the world and created a storm of controversy, but did not sway Edward. On 10 December 1936, King Edward VIII submitted his abdication and it was endorsed by Parliament the next day. He thus became the only British monarch ever to resign voluntarily. The speech is from 11 December 1936 when Edward publicly announced his decision via radio to a worldwide audience.

At long last I am able to say a few words of my own. I have never wanted to withhold anything, but until now it has not been constitutionally possible for me to speak. A few hours ago I discharged my last duty as King and Emperor, and now that I have been succeeded by my brother, the Duke of York, my first words must be to declare my allegiance to him. This I do with all my heart.

You all know the reasons which have impelled me to renounce the throne. But I want you to understand that in making up my mind I did not forget the country or the empire, which, as Prince of Wales and lately as King, I have for twenty-five years tried to serve. But you must believe me when I tell you that I have found it impossible to carry the heavy burden of responsibility and to discharge my duties as King as I would wish to do without the help and support of the woman I love.

And I want you to know that the decision I have made has been mine and mine alone. This was a thing I had to judge entirely for myself. The other person most nearly concerned has tried up to the last to persuade me to take a different course. I have made this, the most serious decision of my life, only upon the single thought of what would, in the end, be best for all.

This decision has been made less difficult to me by the sure knowledge that my brother, with his long training in the public affairs of this country and with his fine qualities, will be able to take my place forthwith without interruption or injury to the life and progress of the empire. And he has one matchless blessing, enjoyed by so many of you, and not bestowed on me—a happy home with his wife and children. During these hard days I have been comforted by Her Majesty my mother and by my family. The ministers of the crown, and in particular, Mr Baldwin, the Prime Minister, have always treated me with full consideration. There has never been any constitutional difference between me and them, and between me and Parliament. Bred in the constitutional tradition by my father, I should never have allowed any such issue to arise. Ever since I was Prince of Wales, and later on when I occupied the throne, I have been treated with the greatest kindness by all classes of the people wherever I have lived or journeyed throughout the empire. For that I am very grateful.

I now quit altogether public affairs and I lay down my burden. It may be some time before I return to my native land, but I shall always follow the fortunes of the British race and empire with profound interest, and if at any time in the future I can be found of service to His Majesty in a private station, I shall not fail.

And now, we all have a new King. I wish him and you, his people, happiness and prosperity with all my heart. God bless you all! God save the King!

23

GIVE ME LIBERTY OR GIVE ME DEATH

Patrick Henry

Patrick Henry was an American attorney, planter and politician who became known as an orator during the movement for independence in Virginia. This speech was delivered on 23 March 1775.

No man thinks more highly than I do of the patriotism, as well as abilities, of the very worthy gentlemen who have just addressed the House. But different men often see the same subject in different lights; and, therefore, I hope it will not be thought disrespectful to those gentlemen if, entertaining as I do opinions of a character very opposite to theirs, I shall speak forth my sentiments freely and without reserve. This is no time for ceremony. The question before the House is one of awful moment to this country. For my own part, I consider it as nothing less than a question of freedom or slavery; and in proportion to the magnitude of the subject ought to be the freedom of the debate. It is only in this way that we can hope to arrive at truth, and fulfil the great responsibility which we hold to God and our country. Should I keep back my opinions at such a time, through fear of giving offence, I should consider myself as guilty of treason towards my country, and of an act of disloyalty toward the Majesty of Heaven, which I revere above all earthly kings.

Mr President, it is natural to man to indulge in the illusions of hope. We are apt to shut our eyes against a painful truth, and listen to the song of that siren till she transforms us into beasts. Is this the part of wise men, engaged in a great and arduous struggle for liberty? Are we disposed to be of the number of those who, having eyes, see not, and, having ears, hear not, the things which so nearly concern their temporal salvation? For my part, whatever anguish of spirit it may cost, I am willing to know the whole truth; to know the worst, and to provide for it.

I have but one lamp by which my feet are guided, and that is the lamp of experience. I know of no way of judging of the future but by the past. And judging by the past, I wish to know what there has been in the conduct of the British ministry for the last ten years to justify those hopes with which gentlemen have been pleased to solace themselves and the House. Is it that insidious smile with which our petition has been lately received? Trust it not, sir; it will prove a snare to your feet. Suffer not yourselves to be betrayed with a kiss. Ask yourselves how this gracious reception of our petition comports with those warlike preparations which cover our waters and darken our land. Are fleets and armies necessary to a work of love and reconciliation? Have we shown ourselves so unwilling to be reconciled that force must be called in to win back our love? Let us not deceive ourselves, sir. These are the implements of war and subjugation; the last arguments to which kings resort. I ask gentlemen, Sir, what means this martial array, if its purpose be not to force us to submission? Can gentlemen assign any other possible motive for it? Has Great Britain any enemy, in this quarter of the world, to call for all this accumulation of navies and armies? No, Sir, she has none. They are meant for us: they can be meant for no other. They are sent over to bind and rivet upon us those chains which the British ministry have been so long forging. And what have we to oppose to them? Shall we try argument? Sir, we have been trying that for the last ten years. Have we anything new to offer upon the subject? Nothing. We have held the subject up in every light of which it is capable; but it has been all in vain. Shall we resort to entreaty and humble supplication? What terms shall we find which have not been already exhausted? Let us not, I beseech you, Sir, deceive ourselves. Sir, we have done everything that could be done to avert the storm which is now coming on. We have petitioned; we have remonstrated; we have supplicated; we have prostrated ourselves before the throne, and have implored its interposition to arrest the tyrannical hands of the ministry and Parliament. Our petitions have been slighted; our remonstrances have produced additional violence and insult; our supplications have been disregarded; and we have been spurned, with contempt, from the foot of the throne! In vain, after these things, may we indulge the fond hope of peace and reconciliation. There is no longer any room for hope. If we wish to be free—if we mean to preserve inviolate those inestimable privileges for which we have been so long contending—if we mean not basely to abandon the noble struggle in which we have been so long engaged, and which we have pledged ourselves never to abandon until the glorious object of our contest shall be obtained—we must fight! I repeat it, Sir, we must fight! An appeal to arms and to the God of hosts is all that is left us!

They tell us, Sir, that we are weak; unable to cope with so formidable an adversary. But when shall we be stronger? Will it be the next week, or the next year? Will it be when we are totally disarmed, and when a British guard shall be stationed in every house? Shall we gather strength by irresolution and inaction? Shall we acquire the means of effectual resistance by lying supinely on our backs and hugging the delusive phantom of hope, until our enemies shall have bound us hand and foot? Sir, we are not weak if we make a proper use of those means which the God of nature hath placed in our power. The millions of people, armed in the holy cause of liberty, and in such a country as that which we possess, are invincible by any force which our enemy can send against us. Besides, Sir, we shall not fight our battles alone. There is a just God who presides over the destinies of nations, and who will raise up friends to fight our battles for us. The battle, Sir, is not to the strong alone; it is to the vigilant, the active, the brave. Besides, Sir, we have no election. If we were base enough to desire it, it is now too late to retire from the contest. There is no retreat but in submission and slavery! Our chains are forged! Their clanking may be heard on the plains of Boston! The war is inevitable—and let it come! I repeat it, Sir, let it come.

It is in vain, Sir, to extenuate the matter. Gentlemen may cry, Peace, Peace—but there is no peace. The war is actually begun! The next gale that sweeps from the north will bring to our ears the clash of resounding arms! Our brethren are already in the field! Why stand we here idle? What is it that gentlemen wish? What would they have? Is life so dear, or peace so sweet, as to be purchased at the price of chains and slavery? Forbid it, Almighty God! I know not what course others may take; but as for me, give me liberty or give me death!

24

WHY I BECAME A HINDU

Sister Nivedita

Sister Nivedita (1867–1911) born Margaret E. Noble was born in Ireland in an orthodox Christian family. When she grew up she did not find Christian doctrines very convincing to her rational mind. She was influenced by the Vedantic philosophy preached by Swami Vivekananda; she came to Calcutta in 1898 and got 'diksha' (initiation) from Vivekananda and joined the order of the Ramakrishna Mission. She devoted the most part of her life to rouse the national consciousness of Indians through her writings and speeches, which proved a source of great inspiration to young Bengal. The speech was delivered at the Hindu Ladies' Social Club in Bombay (now Mumbai), 2 October 1902.

I am a woman born and bred in England and up to the age of eighteen, I was trained and educated as English girls are. Christian religious doctrines were of course instilled early into me. Even from my childhood I was inclined to venerate all religious teachings. I devotedly worshipped baby Jesus and loved Him with all my heart for the sacrifices, He always willingly underwent. I felt I could not worship Him enough for crucifying Himself to bestow salvation on the human race. But after the age of eighteen, I began to harbour doubts as to the truth of the Christian doctrines. Many of them began to seem false to me and incompatible with truth. These doubts grew stronger and at the same time my faith in Christianity tottered more and more. For seven years I was in this wavering state of mind, very unhappy, and yet, very eager to seek the Truth. I shunned going to the church. Yet, sometimes my longing to bring restfulness to my spirit compelled me to rush there and be absorbed in the service to feel at peace within, as I had hitherto done, and as others around me were doing. But alas, there was no peace, no rest there for my troubled soul all eager to know the Truth.

During the seven years of wavering it occurred to me that in the study of natural science I would surely find the Truth I was seeking. So, ardently I began to study how this world and all things in it were created. I discovered that at least in the laws of nature there was consistency, but it made the doctrines of the Christian religion seem all the more inconsistent. Just then I happened to get to know of Buddha and I found that there was a child who lived many centuries before the child Christ, but whose sacrifices were no less self-abnegating than those of the other. This dear child Gautama made a strong impact on me and for the next three years I plunged myself into the study of the religion of Buddha. I became more and more convinced that the salvation he preached was decidedly more consistent with the Truth than the preachings of Christianity.

Then came the turning point for my faith. A cousin of your great Viceroy Lord Ripon invited me to have tea with him and to meet there a great swami from India who, he said, may perhaps help the search my soul was longing for. The swami I met here was none other than Vivekananda who afterwards became my guru and whose teachings have given relief to my doubting spirit that it had been longing for. Yet it was not during a visit or two that my doubts were dispelled. I had several warm discussions with him and I pondered on his teachings for more than a year. Then he asked me to visit India, to see the yogis and study the subject in the very country of its birth. I found, at last, a faith I could lean upon and obtain my mukti through. The uplifting of the spirit till it is merged into ananda. I have told you how and why I have adopted this religion of yours, and if you care to hear more, I will gladly go on.

I love India as the birthplace of the highest and best of all religions as the country that has the grandest mountains, the Himalayas; as the place where the sublimate of mountains are located. The country where the homes are simple; where domestic happiness is found most; where the woman unselfishly, unobtrusively, ungrudgingly, serves the dear ones from early morn to dewy eve; where the mother and the grandmother study, foresees and contribute to the comfort of their children regardless of their own happiness, and in the unselfishness raises womanhood to its highest status.

You, my sisters, each of whom I dearly love for being the daughter of this lovely land of India, I urge each of you to study the grand literature of the east in preference to that of the west. Your literature will uplift you. Cling to it. Cling to the simplicity and sobriety of your domestic lives. Keep its purity as it was in the ancient times and as it is still existing in your simple homes.

Do not let modern fashions and extravagances of the West and its modern English education spoil your reverential humility, your lovable domestic ties consisting in the loving thoughts the elders display for the beloved ones, depending on them, and the resulting respect accorded by the young to the aged. I make this appeal not to my Hindu sisters only but also to my Mohammedan and other sisters. All are my sisters being the daughters of my land of adoption and where I hope to continue the work of my revered guru, Vivekananda.

25

A PASSIONATE ATTACHMENT OF
ONE NATION FOR ANOTHER PRODUCES
A VARIETY OF EVILS

George Washington

This was George Washington's Farewell Address in 1796. George Washington daringly made his address an open letter of advice and warning to the American people about their long-term safety.

Friends and Citizens:

The period for a new election of a citizen to administer the executive government of the United States being not far distant, and the time actually arrived when your thoughts must be employed in designating the person who is to be clothed with that important trust, it appears to me proper, especially as it may conduce to a more distinct expression of the public voice, that I should now apprise you of the resolution I have formed, to decline being considered among the number of those out of whom a choice is to be made.

I beg you, at the same time, to do me the justice to be assured that this resolution has not been taken without a strict regard to all the considerations appertaining to the relation which binds a dutiful citizen to his country; and that in withdrawing the tender of service, which silence in my situation might imply, I am influenced by no diminution of zeal for your future interest, no deficiency of grateful respect for your past kindness, but am supported by a full conviction that the step is compatible with both.

The acceptance of, and continuance hitherto in, the office to which your suffrages have twice called me have been a uniform sacrifice of inclination to the opinion of duty and to a deference for what appeared to be your desire. I constantly hoped that it would have been much earlier in my power, consistently with motives which I was not at liberty to disregard, to return to that retirement from which I had been reluctantly drawn. The strength of my inclination to do this, previous to the last election, had even led to the preparation of an address to declare it to you; but mature reflection on the then perplexed and critical posture of our affairs with foreign nations, and the unanimous advice of persons entitled to my confidence, impelled me to abandon the idea.

I rejoice that the state of your concerns, external as well as internal, no longer renders the pursuit of inclination incompatible with the sentiment of duty or propriety, and am persuaded, whatever partiality may be retained for my services, that, in the present circumstances of our country, you will not disapprove my determination to retire.

The impressions with which I first undertook the arduous trust were explained on the proper occasion. In the discharge of this trust, I will only say that I have, with good intentions, contributed towards the organization and administration of the government the best exertions of which a very fallible judgment was capable. Not unconscious in the outset of the inferiority of my qualifications, experience in my own eyes, perhaps still more in the eyes of others, has strengthened the motives to diffidence of myself; and every day the increasing weight of years admonishes me more and more that the shade of retirement is as necessary to me as it will be welcome. Satisfied that if any circumstances have given peculiar value to my services, they were temporary, I have the consolation to believe that, while choice and prudence invite me to quit the political scene, patriotism does not forbid it.

In looking forward to the moment which is intended to terminate the career of my public life, my feelings do not permit me to suspend the deep acknowledgment of that debt of gratitude which I owe to my beloved country for the many honours it has conferred upon me; still more for the steadfast confidence with which it has supported me; and for the opportunities I have thence enjoyed of manifesting my inviolable attachment, by services faithful and persevering, though in usefulness unequal to my zeal. If benefits have resulted to our country from these services, let it always be remembered to your praise, and as an instructive example in our annals, that under circumstances in which the passions, agitated in every direction, were liable to mislead, amidst appearances sometimes dubious, vicissitudes of fortune often discouraging, in situations in which not unfrequently want of success has countenanced the spirit of criticism, the constancy of your support was the essential prop of the efforts, and a guarantee of the plans by which they were effected. Profoundly penetrated with this idea, I shall carry it with me to my grave, as a strong incitement to unceasing vows that heaven may continue to you the choicest tokens of its beneficence; that your union and brotherly affection may be perpetual; that the free Constitution, which is the work of your hands, may be sacredly maintained; that its administration in every department may be stamped with wisdom and virtue; that, in fine, the happiness of the people of these states, under the auspices of liberty, may be made complete by so careful a preservation and so prudent a use of this blessing as will acquire to them the glory of recommending it to the applause, the affection, and adoption of every nation which is yet a stranger to it.

Here, perhaps, I ought to stop. But a solicitude for your welfare, which cannot end but with my life, and the apprehension of danger, natural to that solicitude, urge me, on an occasion like the present, to offer to your solemn contemplation, and to recommend to your frequent review, some sentiments which are the result of much reflection, of no inconsiderable observation, and which appear to me all-important to the permanency of your felicity as a people. These will be offered to you with the more freedom, as you can only see in them the disinterested warnings of a parting friend, who can possibly have no personal motive to bias his counsel. Nor can I forget, as an encouragement to it, your indulgent reception of my sentiments on a former and not dissimilar occasion.

Interwoven as is the love of liberty with every ligament of your hearts, no recommendation of mine is necessary to fortify or confirm the attachment.

The unity of government which constitutes you one people is also now dear to you. It is justly so, for it is a main pillar in the edifice of your real independence, the support of your tranquility at home, your peace abroad; of your safety; of your prosperity; of that very liberty which you so highly prize. But as it is easy to foresee that, from different causes and from different quarters, much pains will be taken, many artifices employed to weaken in your minds the conviction of this truth; as this is the point in your political fortress against which the batteries of internal and external enemies will be most constantly and actively (though often covertly and insidiously) directed, it is of infinite moment that you should properly estimate the immense value of your national union to your collective and individual happiness; that you should cherish a cordial, habitual, and immovable attachment to it; accustoming yourselves to think and speak of it as of the palladium of your political safety and prosperity; watching for its preservation with jealous anxiety; discountenancing whatever may suggest even a suspicion that it can in any event be abandoned; and indignantly frowning upon the first dawning of every attempt to alienate any portion of our country from the rest, or to enfeeble the sacred ties which now link together the various parts.

For this you have every inducement of sympathy and interest. Citizens, by birth or choice, of a common country, that country has a right to concentrate your affections. The name of American, which belongs to you in your national capacity, must always exalt the just pride of patriotism more than any appellation derived from local discriminations. With slight shades of difference, you have the same religion, manners, habits, and political principles. You have in a common cause fought and triumphed together; the independence and liberty you possess are the work of joint counsels, and joint efforts of common dangers, sufferings, and successes.

But these considerations, however powerfully they address themselves to your sensibility, are greatly outweighed by those which apply more immediately to your interest. Here every portion of our country finds the most commanding motives for carefully guarding and preserving the union of the whole.

The North, in an unrestrained intercourse with the South, protected by the equal laws of a common government, finds in the productions of the latter great additional resources of maritime and commercial enterprise and precious materials of manufacturing industry. The South, in the same intercourse, benefiting by the agency of the North, sees its agriculture grow and its commerce expand. Turning partly into its own channels the seamen of the North, it finds its particular navigation invigorated; and, while it contributes, in different ways, to nourish and increase the general mass of the national navigation, it looks forward to the protection of a maritime strength, to which itself is unequally adapted. The East, in a like intercourse with the West, already finds, and in the progressive improvement of interior communications by land and water, will more and more find a valuable vent for the commodities which it brings from abroad, or manufactures at home. The West derives from the East supplies requisite to its growth and comfort, and, what is perhaps of still greater consequence, it must of necessity owe the secure enjoyment of indispensable outlets for its own productions to the weight, influence, and the future maritime strength of the Atlantic side of the Union, directed by an indissoluble community of interest as one nation. Any other tenure by which the West can hold this essential advantage, whether derived from its own separate strength, or from an apostate and unnatural connection with any foreign power, must be intrinsically precarious.

While, then, every part of our country thus feels an immediate and particular interest in union, all the parts combined cannot fail to find in the united mass of means and efforts greater strength, greater resource, proportionably greater security from external danger, a less frequent interruption of their peace by foreign nations; and, what is of inestimable value, they must derive from union an exemption from those broils and wars between themselves, which so frequently afflict neighbouring countries not tied together by the same governments, which their own rival ships alone would be sufficient to produce, but which opposite foreign alliances, attachments, and intrigues would stimulate and embitter. Hence, likewise, they will avoid the necessity of those overgrown military establishments which, under any form of government, are inauspicious to liberty, and which are to be regarded as particularly hostile to republican liberty. In this sense it is that your union ought to be considered as a main prop of your liberty, and that the love of the one ought to endear to you the preservation of the other.

These considerations speak a persuasive language to every reflecting and virtuous mind, and exhibit the continuance of the Union as a primary object of patriotic desire. Is there a doubt whether a common government can embrace so large a sphere? Let experience solve it. To listen to mere speculation in such a case were criminal. We are authorized to hope that a proper organization of the whole with the auxiliary agency of governments for the respective subdivisions, will afford a happy issue to the experiment. It is well worth a fair and full experiment. With such powerful and obvious motives to union, affecting all parts of our country, while experience shall not have demonstrated its impracticability, there will always be reason to distrust the patriotism of those who in any quarter may endeavor to weaken its bands.

In contemplating the causes which may disturb our Union, it occurs as matter of serious concern that any ground should have been furnished for characterizing parties by geographical discriminations, Northern and Southern, Atlantic and Western; whence designing men may endeavor to excite a belief that there is a real difference of local interests and views. One of the expedients of party to acquire influence within particular districts is to misrepresent the opinions and aims of other districts. You cannot shield yourselves too much against the jealousies and heartburnings which spring from these misrepresentations; they tend to render alien to each other those who ought to be bound together by fraternal affection. The inhabitants of our Western country have lately had a useful lesson on this head; they have seen, in the negotiation by the Executive, and in the unanimous ratification by the Senate, of the treaty with Spain, and in the universal satisfaction at that event, throughout the United States, a decisive proof how unfounded were the suspicions propagated among them of a policy in the general government and in the Atlantic states unfriendly to their interests in regard to the Mississippi; they have been witnesses to the formation of two treaties, that with Great Britain, and that with Spain, which secure to them everything they could desire, in respect to our foreign relations, towards confirming their prosperity. Will it not be their wisdom to rely for the preservation of these advantages on the Union by which they were procured ? Will they not henceforth be deaf to those advisers, if such there are, who would sever them from their brethren and connect them with aliens?

To the efficacy and permanency of your Union, a government for the whole is indispensable. No alliance, however strict, between the parts can be an adequate substitute; they must inevitably experience the infractions and interruptions which all alliances in all times have experienced. Sensible of this momentous truth, you have improved upon your first essay, by the adoption of a Constitution of government better calculated than your former for an intimate union, and for the efficacious management of your common concerns. This government, the offspring of our own choice, uninfluenced and unawed, adopted upon full investigation and mature deliberation, completely free in its principles, in the distribution of its powers, uniting security with energy, and containing within itself a provision for its own amendment, has a just claim to your confidence and your support. Respect for its authority, compliance with its laws, acquiescence in its measures, are duties enjoined by the fundamental maxims of true liberty. The basis of our political systems is the right of the people to make and to alter their constitutions of government. But the Constitution which at any time exists, till changed by an explicit and authentic act of the whole people, is sacredly obligatory upon all. The very idea of the power and the right of the people to establish government presupposes the duty of every individual to obey the established government.

All obstructions to the execution of the laws, all combinations and associations, under whatever plausible character, with the real design to direct, control, counteract, or awe the regular deliberation and action of the constituted authorities, are destructive of this fundamental principle, and of fatal tendency. They serve to organize faction, to give it an artificial and extraordinary force; to put, in the place of the delegated will of the nation the will of a party, often a small but artful and enterprising minority of the community; and, according to the alternate triumphs of different parties, to make the public administration the mirror of the ill-concerted and incongruous projects of faction, rather than the organ of consistent and wholesome plans digested by common counsels and modified by mutual interests.

However combinations or associations of the above description may now and then answer popular ends, they are likely, in the course of time and things, to become potent engines, by which cunning, ambitious, and unprincipled men will be enabled to subvert the power of the people and to usurp for themselves the reins of government, destroying afterwards the very engines which have lifted them to unjust dominion.

Towards the preservation of your government, and the permanency of your present happy state, it is requisite, not only that you steadily discountenance irregular oppositions to its acknowledged authority, but also that you resist with care the spirit of innovation upon its principles, however specious the pretexts. One method of assault may be to effect, in the forms of the Constitution, alterations which will impair the energy of the system, and thus to undermine what cannot be directly overthrown. In all the changes to which you may be invited, remember that time and habit are at least as necessary to fix the true character of governments as of other human institutions; that experience is the surest standard by which to test the real tendency of the existing Constitution of a country; that facility in changes, upon the credit of mere hypothesis and opinion, exposes to perpetual change, from the endless variety of hypothesis and opinion; and remember, especially, that for the efficient management of your common interests, in a country so extensive as ours, a government of as much vigor as is consistent with the perfect security of liberty is indispensable. Liberty itself will find in such a government, with powers properly distributed and adjusted, its surest guardian. It is, indeed, little else than a name, where the government is too feeble to withstand the enterprises of faction, to confine each member of the society within the limits prescribed by the laws, and to maintain all in the secure and tranquil enjoyment of the rights of person and property.

I have already intimated to you the danger of parties in the state, with particular reference to the founding of them on geographical discriminations. Let me now take a more comprehensive view, and warn you in the most solemn manner against the baneful effects of the spirit of party generally.

This spirit, unfortunately, is inseparable from our nature, having its root in the strongest passions of the human mind. It exists under different shapes in all governments, more or less stifled, controlled, or repressed; but, in those of the popular form, it is seen in its greatest rankness, and is truly their worst enemy.

The alternate domination of one faction over another, sharpened by the spirit of revenge, natural to party dissension, which in different ages and countries has perpetrated the most horrid enormities, is itself a frightful despotism. But this leads at length to a more formal and permanent despotism. The disorders and miseries which result gradually incline the minds of men to seek security and repose in the absolute power of an individual; and sooner or later the chief of some prevailing faction, more able or more fortunate than his competitors, turns this disposition to the purposes of his own elevation, on the ruins of public liberty.

Without looking forward to an extremity of this kind (which nevertheless ought not to be entirely out of sight), the common and continual mischiefs of the spirit of party are sufficient to make it the interest and duty of a wise people to discourage and restrain it.

It serves always to distract the public councils and enfeeble the public administration. It agitates the community with ill-founded jealousies and false alarms, kindles the animosity of one part against another, foments occasionally riot and insurrection. It opens the door to foreign influence and corruption, which finds a facilitated access to the government itself through the channels of party passions. Thus the policy and the will of one country are subjected to the policy and will of another.

There is an opinion that parties in free countries are useful checks upon the administration of the government and serve to keep alive the spirit of liberty. This within certain limits is probably true; and in governments of a monarchical cast, patriotism may look with indulgence, if not with favor, upon the spirit of party. But in those of the popular character, in governments purely elective, it is a spirit not to be encouraged. From their natural tendency, it is certain there will always be enough of that spirit for every salutary purpose. And there being constant danger of excess, the effort ought to be by force of public opinion, to mitigate and assuage it. A fire not to be quenched, it demands a uniform vigilance to prevent its bursting into a flame, lest, instead of warming, it should consume.

It is important, likewise, that the habits of thinking in a free country should inspire caution in those entrusted with its administration, to confine

The World's 100 Greatest Speeches

themselves within their respective constitutional spheres, avoiding in the exercise of the powers of one department to encroach upon another. The spirit of encroachment tends to consolidate the powers of all the departments in one, and thus to create, whatever the form of government, a real despotism. A just estimate of that love of power, and proneness to abuse it, which predominates in the human heart, is sufficient to satisfy us of the truth of this position. The necessity of reciprocal checks in the exercise of political power, by dividing and distributing it into different depositories, and constituting each the guardian of the public weal against invasions by the others, has been evinced by experiments ancient and modern; some of them in our country and under our own eyes. To preserve them must be as necessary as to institute them. If, in the opinion of the people, the distribution or modification of the constitutional powers be in any particular wrong, let it be corrected by an amendment in the way which the Constitution designates. But let there be no change by usurpation; for though this, in one instance, may be the instrument of good, it is the customary weapon by which free governments are destroyed. The precedent must always greatly overbalance in permanent evil any partial or transient benefit, which the use can at any time yield.

Of all the dispositions and habits which lead to political prosperity, religion and morality are indispensable supports. In vain would that man claim the tribute of patriotism, who should labour to subvert these great pillars of human happiness, these firmest props of the duties of men and citizens. The mere politician, equally with the pious man, ought to respect and to cherish them. A volume could not trace all their connections with private and public felicity. Let it simply be asked: Where is the security for property, for reputation, for life, if the sense of religious obligation desert the oaths which are the instruments of investigation in courts of justice? And let us with caution indulge the supposition that morality can be maintained without religion. Whatever may be conceded to the influence of refined education on minds of peculiar structure, reason and experience both forbid us to expect that national morality can prevail in exclusion of religious principle.

It is substantially true that virtue or morality is a necessary spring of popular government. The rule, indeed, extends with more or less force to every species of free government. Who that is a sincere friend to it can look with indifference upon attempts to shake the foundation of the fabric?

Promote then, as an object of primary importance, institutions for the general diffusion of knowledge. In proportion as the structure of a government gives force to public opinion, it is essential that public opinion should be enlightened.

As a very important source of strength and security, cherish public credit. One method of preserving it is to use it as sparingly as possible, avoiding occasions of expense by cultivating peace, but remembering also that timely disbursements to prepare for danger frequently prevent much greater disbursements to repel it, avoiding likewise the accumulation of debt, not only by shunning occasions of expense, but by vigorous exertion in time of peace to discharge the debts which unavoidable wars may have occasioned, not ungenerously throwing upon posterity the burden which we ourselves ought to bear. The execution of these maxims belongs to your representatives, but it is necessary that public opinion should cooperate. To facilitate to them the performance of their duty, it is essential that you should practically bear in mind that towards the payment of debts there must be revenue; that to have revenue there must be taxes; that no taxes can be devised which are not more or less inconvenient and unpleasant; that the intrinsic embarrassment, inseparable from the selection of the proper objects (which is always a choice of difficulties), ought to be a decisive motive for a candid construction of the conduct of the government in making it, and for a spirit of acquiescence in the measures for obtaining revenue, which the public exigencies may at any time dictate.

Observe good faith and justice towards all nations; cultivate peace and harmony with all. Religion and morality enjoin this conduct; and can it be, that good policy does not equally enjoin it—it will be worthy of a free, enlightened, and at no distant period, a great nation, to give to mankind the magnanimous and too novel example of a people always guided by an exalted justice and benevolence. Who can doubt that, in the course of time and things, the fruits of such a plan would richly repay any temporary advantages which might be lost by a steady adherence to it? Can it be that providence has not connected the permanent felicity of a nation with its virtue? The experiment, at least, is recommended by every sentiment which ennobles human nature. Alas! Is it rendered impossible by its vices?

In the execution of such a plan, nothing is more essential than that permanent, inveterate antipathies against particular nations, and passionate attachments for others, should be excluded; and that, in place of them, just and amicable feelings towards all should be cultivated. The nation which indulges towards another a habitual hatred or a habitual fondness is in some degree a slave. It is a slave to its animosity or to its affection, either of which is sufficient to lead it astray from its duty and its interest. Antipathy in one nation against another disposes each more readily to offer insult and injury, to lay hold of slight causes of umbrage, and to be haughty and intractable, when accidental or trifling occasions of dispute occur. Hence, frequent collisions, obstinate, envenomed, and bloody contests. The nation, prompted by ill-will and resentment, sometimes impels to war the government, contrary to the best calculations of policy. The government sometimes participates in the national propensity, and adopts through passion what reason would reject; at other times it makes the animosity of the nation subservient to projects of hostility instigated by pride, ambition, and other sinister and pernicious motives. The peace often, sometimes perhaps the liberty, of nations, has been the victim.

So likewise, a passionate attachment of one nation for another produces a variety of evils. Sympathy for the favorite nation, facilitating the illusion of an imaginary common interest in cases where no real common interest exists, and infusing into one the enmities of the other, betrays the former into a participation in the quarrels and wars of the latter without adequate inducement or justification. It leads also to concessions to the favorite nation of privileges denied to others which is apt doubly to injure the nation making the concessions; by unnecessarily parting with what ought to have been retained, and by exciting jealousy, ill-will, and a disposition to retaliate, in the parties from whom equal privileges are withheld. And it gives to ambitious, corrupted, or deluded citizens (who devote themselves to the favorite nation), facility to betray or sacrifice the interests of their own country, without odium, sometimes even with popularity; gilding, with the appearances of a virtuous sense of obligation, a commendable deference for public opinion, or a laudable zeal for public good, the base or foolish compliances of ambition, corruption, or infatuation.

As avenues to foreign influence in innumerable ways, such attachments are particularly alarming to the truly enlightened and independent patriot. How many opportunities do they afford to tamper with domestic factions, to practice the arts of seduction, to mislead public opinion, to influence or awe the public councils. Such an attachment of a small or weak towards a great and powerful nation dooms the former to be the satellite of the latter.

Against the insidious wiles of foreign influence (I conjure you to believe me, fellow-citizens) the jealousy of a free people ought to be constantly awake, since history and experience prove that foreign influence is one of the most baneful foes of republican government. But that jealousy to be useful must be impartial; else it becomes the instrument of the very influence to be avoided, instead of a defence against it. Excessive partiality for one foreign nation and excessive dislike of another cause those whom they actuate to see danger only on one side, and serve to veil and even second the arts of influence on the other. Real patriots who may resist the intrigues of the favorite are liable to become suspected and odious, while its tools and dupes usurp the applause and confidence of the people, to surrender their interests.

The great rule of conduct for us in regard to foreign nations is in extending our commercial relations, to have with them as little political connection as possible. So far as we have already formed engagements, let them be fulfilled with perfect good faith. Here let us stop. Europe has a set of primary interests which to us have none; or a very remote relation. Hence she must be engaged in frequent controversies, the causes of which are essentially foreign to our concerns. Hence, therefore, it must be unwise in us to implicate ourselves by artificial ties in the ordinary vicissitudes of her politics, or the ordinary combinations and collisions of her friendships or enmities.

Our detached and distant situation invites and enables us to pursue a different course. If we remain one people under an efficient government. the period is not far off when we may defy material injury from external annoyance; when we may take such an attitude as will cause the neutrality we may at any time resolve upon to be scrupulously respected; when belligerent nations, under the impossibility of making acquisitions upon us, will not lightly hazard the giving us provocation; when we may choose peace or war, as our interest, guided by justice, shall counsel.

Why forego the advantages of so peculiar a situation? Why quit our own to stand upon foreign ground? Why, by interweaving our destiny with that of any part of Europe, entangle our peace and prosperity in the toils of European ambition, rivalship, interest, humour or caprice?

It is our true policy to steer clear of permanent alliances with any portion of the foreign world; so far, I mean, as we are now at liberty to do it; for let me not be understood as capable of patronizing infidelity to existing engagements. I hold the maxim no less applicable to public than to private affairs, that honesty is always the best policy. I repeat it, therefore, let those engagements be observed in their genuine sense. But, in my opinion, it is unnecessary and would be unwise to extend them. Taking care always to keep ourselves by suitable establishments on a respectable defensive posture, we may safely trust to temporary alliances for extraordinary emergencies. Harmony, liberal intercourse with all nations, are recommended by policy, humanity, and interest. But even our commercial policy should hold an equal and impartial hand; neither seeking nor granting exclusive favours or preferences; consulting the natural course of things; diffusing and diversifying by gentle means the streams of commerce, but forcing nothing; establishing (with powers so disposed, in order to give trade a stable course, to define the rights of our merchants, and to enable the government to support them) conventional rules of intercourse, the best that present circumstances and mutual opinion will permit, but temporary, and liable to be from time to time abandoned or varied, as experience and circumstances shall dictate; constantly keeping in view that it is folly in one nation to look for disinterested favours from another; that it must pay with a portion of its independence for whatever it may accept under that character; that, by such acceptance, it may place itself in the condition of having given equivalents for nominal favours, and yet of being reproached with ingratitude for not giving more. There can be no greater error than to expect or calculate upon real favours from nation to nation. It is an illusion, which experience must cure, which a just pride ought to discard.

In offering to you, my countrymen, these counsels of an old and affectionate friend, I dare not hope they will make the strong and lasting impression I could wish; that they will control the usual current of the passions, or prevent our nation from running the course which has hitherto marked the destiny of nations. But, if I may even flatter myself that they may be productive of some partial benefit, some occasional good; that they may now and then recur to moderate the fury of party spirit, to warn against the mischiefs of foreign intrigue, to guard against the impostures of pretended patriotism; this hope will be a full recompense for the solicitude for your welfare, by which they have been dictated. How far in the discharge of my official duties I have been guided by the principles which have been delineated, the public records and other evidences of my conduct must witness to you and to the world. To myself, the assurance of my own conscience is, that I have at least believed myself to be guided by them.

In relation to the still subsisting war in Europe, my proclamation of the 22 April 1793, is the index of my plan. Sanctioned by your approving voice, and by that of your representatives in both houses of Congress, the spirit of that measure has continually governed me, uninfluenced by any attempts to deter or divert me from it. After deliberate examination, with the aid of the best lights I could obtain, I was well satisfied that our country, under all the circumstances of the case, had a right to take, and was bound in duty and interest to take, a neutral position. Having taken it, I determined, as far as should depend upon me, to maintain it, with moderation, perseverance, and firmness.

The considerations which respect the right to hold this conduct, it is not necessary on this occasion to detail. I will only observe that, according to my understanding of the matter, that right, so far from being denied by any of the belligerent powers, has been virtually admitted by all. The duty of holding a neutral conduct may be inferred, without anything more, from the obligation which justice and humanity impose on every nation, in cases in which it is free to act, to maintain inviolate the relations of peace and amity towards other nations.

The inducements of interest for observing that conduct will best be referred to your own reflections and experience. With me a predominant motive has been to endeavour to gain time to our country to settle and mature its yet recent institutions, and to progress without interruption to that degree of strength and consistency which is necessary to give it, humanly speaking, the command of its own fortunes. Though, in reviewing the incidents of my administration, I am unconscious of intentional error, I am nevertheless too sensible of my defects not to think it probable that I may have committed many errors. Whatever they may be, I fervently beseech the Almighty to avert or mitigate the evils to which they may tend. I shall also carry with me the hope that my country will never cease to view them with indulgence; and that, after forty-five years of my life dedicated to its service with an upright zeal, the faults of incompetent abilities will be consigned to oblivion, as myself must soon be to the mansions of rest.

Relying on its kindness in this as in other things, and actuated by that fervent love towards it, which is so natural to a man who views in it the native soil of himself and his progenitors for several generations, I anticipate with pleasing expectation that retreat in which I promise myself to realize, without alloy, the sweet enjoyment of partaking, in the midst of my fellow-citizens, the benign influence of good laws under a free government, the ever-favorite object of my heart, and the happy reward, as I trust, of our mutual cares, labours, and dangers.

26

IT IS IMPERATIVE THAT WE AGREE TO CONCLUDE THE PACT

Joseph Stalin

Joseph Stalin's speech to the Soviet Politburo on 19 August 1939 reveals his deliberations prior to signing a pact with Nazi Germany on 22 August, in which the two countries agreed to divide Poland and not fight each other. This was a duplicitous agreement between two dictators who mistrusted each other and hated each other's ideology. At that point, however, the pact was expedient to both.

The question of war and peace has entered a critical phase for us. Its solution depends entirely on the position which will be taken by the Soviet Union. We are absolutely convinced that if we conclude a mutual assistance pact with France and Great Britain, Germany will back off from Poland and seek a modus vivendi with the Western powers. War would be avoided, but further events could prove dangerous for the USSR.

On the other hand, if we accept Germany's proposal, that you know, and conclude a non-aggression pact with her, she will certainly invade Poland, and the intervention of France and England is then unavoidable. Western Europe would be subjected to serious upheavals and disorder. In this case we will have a great opportunity to stay out of the conflict, and we could plan the opportune time for us to enter the war.

The experience of the last twenty years has shown that in peacetime the Communist movement is never strong enough for the Bolshevik Party to seize power. The dictatorship of such a party will only become possible as the result of a major war.

Our choice is clear. We must accept the German proposal and, with a refusal, politely send the Anglo-French mission home.

It is not difficult to envisage the importance which we would obtain in this way of proceeding. It is obvious, for us, that Poland will be destroyed even before England and France are able to come to her assistance. In this case Germany will cede to us a part of Poland... Our immediate advantage will be to take Poland all the way to the gates of Warsaw, as well as Ukrainian Galicia.

This is in the case that Germany would emerge victorious from the war. We must, however, envisage the possibilities that will result from the defeat as well as from the victory of Germany. In case of her defeat, a Sovietization of Germany will unavoidably occur and a communist government will be created.

We should not forget that a Sovietized Germany would bring about great danger, if this Sovietization is the result of German defeat in a transient war. England and France will still be strong enough to seize Berlin and to destroy a Soviet Germany. We would be unable to come effectually to the aid of our Bolshevik comrades in Germany.

'Our goal is that Germany should carry out the war as long as possible so that England and France grow weary and become exhausted.'

Therefore, our goal is that Germany should carry out the war as long as possible so that England and France grow weary and become exhausted to such a degree that they are no longer in a position to put down a Sovietized Germany.

Our position is this. Maintaining neutrality and waiting for the right time, the USSR will presently assist Germany economically and supply her with raw materials and provisions. It goes without saying that our assistance should not exceed a certain limit; we must not send so much as to weaken our economy or the power of our army.

At the same time we must carry on active Communist propaganda in the Anglo-French bloc, and predominantly in France. We must expect that in that country in times of war, the party should quit the legal means of warfare and turn underground. We know that their work will demand great sacrifices, but our French comrades will not hesitate. Their first task will be to decompose and demoralize the army and the police. If this preparatory work is fulfilled properly, the safety of Soviet Germany will be assured, and this will contribute to the Sovietization of France.

For the realization of these plans it is essential that the war continue for as long as possible, and all forces, which we have available in Western Europe and the Balkans, should be directed toward this goal.

Now let us consider the second possibility, a German victory. Some think that this would confront us with a serious danger. There is some truth in this, but it would be a mistake to regard the danger as so close at hand or as great as has been proposed.

If Germany should prove to be victorious, she will leave the war too weakened to start a war with the USSR within a decade at least. She will have to supervise the occupation of France and England and restore herself.

In addition, a victorious Germany will have vast colonies, the exploitation of those and their adaptation to German methods will also absorb Germany during several decades.

We must strengthen our propaganda work in the belligerent countries, in order to be prepared when the war ends.

Obviously, this Germany will be too busy elsewhere to turn against us. There is one additional thing that will strengthen our safety. In a conquered France, the French Communist Party will always be very strong. A Communist revolution will unavoidably break out, and we will be able to exploit the situation and to come to the aid of France and make her our ally. In addition, all the nations that fall under the 'protection' of a victorious Germany will become our allies. This presents for us a broad field of action for the initiation of world revolution.

Comrades, I have presented my considerations to you. I repeat that it is in the interest of the USSR, the workers' homeland, that a war breaks out between the Reich and the capitalist Anglo-French bloc. Everything should be done so that it drags out as long as possible with the goal of weakening both sides. For this reason, it is imperative that we agree to conclude the pact proposed by Germany, and then work in such a way that this war, once it is declared, will be prolonged maximally. We must strengthen our propaganda work in the belligerent countries, in order to be prepared when the war ends.

27

ASK NOT WHAT YOUR COUNTRY
CAN DO FOR YOU

John F. Kennedy

The inauguration of John F. Kennedy as the 35th President of the United States was held on Friday, 20 January 1961 at the eastern portico of the United States Capitol in Washington, D.C. This 44th presidential inauguration marked the commencement of the term of John F. Kennedy as President and Lyndon B. Johnson as Vice President. In 1960, Kennedy gained the Democratic Party's nomination for President, and millions watched his televised debates with Richard M. Nixon, the Republican candidate. Kennedy won by a narrow margin in the November 1960 election, and became the youngest man and the first Roman Catholic elected and inaugurated as President of the United States.

His inaugural address encompassed the major themes of his campaign and would define his eventual presidency during a time of economic prosperity, emerging social changes, and diplomatic challenges.

We observe today not a victory of party, but a celebration of freedom—symbolizing an end, as well as a beginning—signifying renewal, as well as change. For I have sworn before you and Almighty God the same solemn oath our forebears prescribed nearly a century and three quarters ago.

The world is very different now. For man holds in his mortal hands the power to abolish all forms of human poverty and all forms of human life. And yet the same revolutionary beliefs for which our forebears fought are still at issue around the globe—the belief that the rights of man come not from the generosity of the state, but from the hand of God.

We dare not forget today that we are the heirs of that first revolution. Let the word go forth from this time and place, to friend and foe alike, that the torch has been passed to a new generation of Americans—born in this century, tempered by war, disciplined by a hard and bitter peace, proud of our ancient heritage—and unwilling to witness or permit the slow undoing of those human rights to which this nation has always been committed, and to which we are committed today at home and around the world.

Let every nation know, whether it wishes us well or ill, that we shall pay any price, bear any burden, meet any hardship, support any friend, oppose any foe, in order to assure the survival and the success of liberty.

This much we pledge—and more.

To those old allies whose cultural and spiritual origins we share, we pledge the loyalty of faithful friends. United, there is little we cannot do in a host of cooperative ventures. Divided, there is little we can do—for we dare not meet a powerful challenge at odds and split asunder.

To those new states whom we welcome to the ranks of the free, we pledge our word that one form of colonial control shall not have passed away merely to be replaced by a far more iron tyranny. We shall not always expect to find them supporting our view. But we shall always hope to find them strongly supporting their own freedom—and to remember that, in the past, those who foolishly sought power by riding the back of the tiger ended up inside.

To those peoples in the huts and villages across the globe struggling to break the bonds of mass misery, we pledge our best efforts to help them help themselves, for whatever period is required—not because the Communists may be doing it, not because we seek their votes, but because it is right. If a free society cannot help the many who are poor, it cannot save the few who are rich.

To our sister republics south of our border, we offer a special pledge—to convert our good words into good deeds—in a new alliance for progress—to assist free men and free governments in casting off the chains of poverty.

But this peaceful revolution of hope cannot become the prey of hostile powers. Let all our neighbours know that we shall join with them to oppose aggression or subversion anywhere in the Americas. And let every other power know that this hemisphere intends to remain the master of its own house.

To that world assembly of sovereign states, the United Nations, our last best hope in an age where the instruments of war have far outpaced the instruments of peace, we renew our pledge of support—to prevent it from becoming merely a forum for invective—to strengthen its shield of the new and the weak—and to enlarge the area in which its writ may run.

Finally, to those nations who would make themselves our adversary, we offer not a pledge but a request: that both sides begin anew the quest for peace, before the dark powers of destruction unleashed by science engulf all humanity in planned or accidental self-destruction.

We dare not tempt them with weakness. For only when our arms are sufficient beyond doubt can we be certain beyond doubt that they will never be employed.

But neither can two great and powerful groups of nations take comfort from our present course—both sides overburdened by the cost of modern weapons, both rightly alarmed by the steady spread of the deadly atom, yet both racing to alter that uncertain balance of terror that stays the hand of mankind's final war.

So let us begin anew—remembering on both sides that civility is not a sign of weakness, and sincerity is always subject to proof. Let us never negotiate out of fear. But let us never fear to negotiate.

Let both sides explore what problems unite us instead of belabouring those problems which divide us.

Let both sides, for the first time, formulate serious and precise proposals for the inspection and control of arms—and bring the absolute power to destroy other nations under the absolute control of all nations.

Let both sides seek to invoke the wonders of science instead of its terrors.

Together let us explore the stars, conquer the deserts, eradicate disease, tap the ocean depths, and encourage the arts and commerce.

Let both sides unite to heed in all corners of the earth the command of Isaiah—to 'undo the heavy burdens, and to let the oppressed go free.'

And if a beachhead of cooperation may push back the jungle of suspicion, let both sides join in creating a new endeavour, not a new balance of power, but a new world of law, where the strong are just and the weak secure and the peace preserved.

All this will not be finished in the first 100 days. Nor will it be finished in the first 1,000 days, nor in the life of this administration, nor even perhaps in our lifetime on this planet. But let us begin.

In your hands, my fellow citizens, more than in mine, will rest the final success or failure of our course. Since this country was founded, each generation of Americans has been summoned to give testimony to its national loyalty. The graves of young Americans who answered the call to service surround the globe.

Now the trumpet summons us again—not as a call to bear arms, though arms we need; not as a call to battle, though embattled we are—but a call to bear the burden of a long twilight struggle, year in and year out, 'rejoicing in hope, patient in tribulation'—a struggle against the common enemies of man: tyranny, poverty, disease, and war itself.

Can we forge against these enemies a grand and global alliance, North and South, East and West, that can assure a more fruitful life for all mankind? Will you join in that historic effort?

In the long history of the world, only a few generations have been granted the role of defending freedom in its hour of maximum danger. I do not shrink from this responsibility—I welcome it. I do not believe that any of us would exchange places with any other people or any other generation. The energy, the faith, the devotion which we bring to this endeavour will light our country and all who serve it—and the glow from that fire can truly light the world.

And so, my fellow Americans: ask not what your country can do for you—ask what you can do for your country.

My fellow citizens of the world: ask not what America will do for you, but what together we can do for the freedom of man.

Finally, whether you are citizens of America or citizens of the world, ask of us the same high standards of strength and sacrifice which we ask of you. With a good conscience our only sure reward, with history the final judge of our deeds, let us go forth to lead the land we love, asking His blessing and His help, but knowing that here on earth God's work must truly be our own.

28

THE SWADESHI MOVEMENT

Gopal Krishan Gokhale

The Swadeshi movement, part of the Indian independence movement and the developing Indian nationalism, was an economic strategy aimed at removing the British Empire from power and improving economic conditions in India by following the principles of swadeshi (self-sufficiency), which had some success. Strategies of the Swadeshi movement involved boycotting British products and the revival of domestic products and production processes. This significant speech on the ramifications of the swadeshi movement was delivered at Lucknow, 9 February 1907.

One of the most gratifying signs of the present times is the rapid growth of the swadeshi sentiment all over the country during the last two years. I have said it more than once here, but I think the idea bears repetition, that swadeshism at its highest is not merely an industrial movement, but that it affects the whole life of the nation—that swadeshism at its highest is a deep, passionate, fervent, all-embracing love of the motherland, and that this love seeks to show itself, not in one sphere of activity but all spheres of life, it invades the entire being of man, and it will not rest until it has raised all of mankind. The first thing I want to say about this movement is that it has now come to stay.

Our Principal Needs

Our resources are small, and our difficulties are huge. It behoves us, therefore, not to disregard any cooperatior, from whatever quarter it may be forthcoming. Remember that, though there is certain scope for small village industries, our main reliance now—exposed as we are to world competition—must be on production with the aid of steam and machinery. From this standpoint, what are our principal needs today? In the first place, there is geneal ignorance throughout the country about the industrial condition of the world. Very few of us understand where we are, as compared with others, and why we are where we are and why others are where they are. Secondly, our available capital is small, and moreover, it is timid. Confidence in one another in the spirit of cooperation for industrial purposes is weak, and joint stock enterprise is therefore, feeble. Thirdly, there is a lack of facilities for higher scientific and technical instructions in the country Lastly, the new articles we succeed in manufacturing find themselves exposed at once to world competition, and in the beginning at any rate, as they are bound to be somewhat inferior in quality and probably higher in price, it is difficult for them to make their place in the Indian market.

Forms of Swadeshi

Now as our needs are various, the swadeshi cause requires to be served in a variety of ways. We should be careful not to quarrel with others, simply because they serve the cause in a different way from our own. Thus, whoever tries to spread in the country a correct knowledge of the industrial conditions of the world and points out how we may ourselves advance, is a promoter of the swadeshi cause. Whosoever, again, contributes capital to be applied to the industrial development of the country must be regarded as a benefactor of the country and a valued supporter of the Swadeshi Movement. Those who organize funds for sending Indian students to foreign countries for acquiring industrial or scientific education—and in our present state we must, for some time to come, depend upon foreign countries for such education—are friends of the Swadeshi Movement. Those who proceed to foreign countries for such education and try to start new industries on their return, or those who promote technical, industrial and scientific education in the country itself, are all noble workers in the swadeshi field. These three ways of serving the swadeshi cause are, however, open to a limited number of persons only. But there is a fourth way open to all of us, and in the case of most, it is perhaps the only way in which they can help forward the Swadeshi Movement. The way is for us to use, as far as possible, only swadeshi articles and to preach to others that they should do the same. By this we shall 'ensure the consumption of indigenous articles and also stimulate the production of new articles by creating a demand for them. The masses cannot contribute much capital to the industrial development of the country; nor can they render much assistance in the matter of promoting higher scientific, technical or industrial knowledge among us. They can render a most important and most necessary service to the swadeshi cause by undergoing a little sacrifice to extend a kind of voluntary protection to swadeshi industries in their early days of stress and struggle. In course of time, the quality of swadeshi articles is bound to improve and lead to a reduction in the cost of production. It is no merit if you buy them when they can hold their own against foreign articles in quality or price. It is by ensuring the consumption of indigenous articles in their early stage, when their quality is inferior or their price is higher, or when they labour under both these disadvantages, that we can do for our industries what protectionist governments have done for theirs by means of state protection. Those who preach to the people that they should use swadeshi articles only as far as possible, are engaged in sacred work and I say to them: go forward boldly and preach your gospel enthusiastically, Swadeshi and Boycott. In this connection I think I ought to say a word about an expression which has of late, found considerable favour with a section of my countrymen: 'the boycott of foreign goods'. I am sure most of those who speak of this 'boycott' mean by it only the use, as far as possible, of swadeshi articles in preference to foreign articles. Now such use is really included in true swadeshi but unfortunately the word 'boycott' has a sinister meaning; it implies a vindictive desire to injure another, no matter what harm you may thereby cause to yourself I think we would do well to use only the word swadeshi to describe our present movement, leaving alone the word 'boycott' which creates an unnecessary ill will against ourselves. Moreover, remember that a strict 'boycott' of foreign goods is not at all practicable in our present industrial condition. For when you 'boycott' foreign goods you must not touch even a particle of imported articles. We only make ourselves ridiculous by talking of a resolution which we cannot enforce.

29

DECLARATION OF SENTIMENTS

Elizabeth Cady Stanton

Elizabeth Cady Stanton: The Declaration of Sentiments from the Seneca Falls Women's Convention, 1848. She was a prominent 19th century suffragist and civil rights activist Elizabeth Cady Stanton (1815-1902) became involved in the abolitionist movement after a progressive upbringing. She helped organize the world's first women's rights convention in 1848, and formed the National Women's Loyal League with Susan B. Anthony in 1863. Declaration of Sentiments, document, outlining the rights that American women should be entitled to as citizens, that emerged from the Seneca Falls Convention in New York in July 1848.

When, in the course of human events, it becomes necessary for one portion of the family of man to assume among the people of the earth a position different from that which they have hitherto occupied, but one to which the laws of nature and of nature's god entitle them, a decent respect to the opinions of mankind requires that they should declare the causes that impel them to such a course.

We hold these truths to be self-evident: that all men and women are created equal; that they are endowed by their creator with certain inalienable rights; that among these are life, liberty, and the pursuit of happiness; that to secure these rights governments are instituted, deriving their just powers from the consent of the governed. Whenever any form of government becomes destructive of these ends, it is the right of those who suffer from it to refuse allegiance to it, and to insist upon the institution of a new government, laying its foundation on such principles, and organizing its powers in such form, as to them shall seem most likely to effect their safety and happiness. Prudence, indeed, will dictate that governments long established should not be changed for light and transient causes; and accordingly all experience hath shown that mankind are more disposed to suffer, while evils are sufferable, than to right themselves by abolishing the forms to which they are accustomed. But when a long train of abuses and usurpations, pursuing invariably the same object, evinces a design to reduce them under absolute despotism, it is their duty to throw off such government, and to provide new guards for their future security. Such has been the patient sufferance of the women under this government, and such is now the necessity which constrains them to demand the equal station to which they are entitled.

The history of mankind is a history of repeated injuries and usurpations on the part of man toward woman, having in direct object the establishment of an absolute tyranny over her. To prove this, let facts be submitted to a candid world. He has never permitted her to exercise her inalienable right to the elective franchise.

He has compelled her to submit to laws, in the formation of which she had no voice. He has withheld from her rights which are given to the most ignorant and degraded men—both natives and foreigners.

Having deprived her of this first right of a citizen, the elective franchise, thereby leaving her without representation in the halls of legislation, he has oppressed her on all sides.

He has made her, if married, in the eye of the law, civilly dead. He has taken from her all right in property, even to the wages she earns. He has made her, morally, an irresponsible being, as she can commit many crimes with impunity, provided they be done in the presence of her husband. In the covenant of marriage, she is compelled to promise obedience to her husband, he becoming, to all intents and purposes, her master—the law giving him power to deprive her of her liberty, and to administer chastisement. He has so framed the laws of divorce, as to what shall be the proper causes, and in case of separation, to whom the guardianship of the children shall be given, as to be wholly regardless of the happiness of women—the law, in all cases, going upon a flase supposition of the supremacy of man, and giving all power into his hands.

After depriving her of all rights as a married woman, if single, and the owner of property, he has taxed her to support a government which recognizes her only when her property can be made profitable to it.

He has monopolized nearly all the profitable employments, and from those she is permitted to follow, she receives but a scanty remuneration. He closes against her all the avenues to wealth and distinction which he considers most honourable to himself. As a teacher of theoloy, medicine, or law, she is not known. He has denied her the facilities for obtaining a thorough education, all colleges being closed against her.

He allows her in church, as well as state, but a subordinate position, claiming apostolic authority for her exclusion from the ministry, and, with some exceptions, from any public participation in the affairs of the church.

He has created a false public sentiment by giving to the world a different code of morals for men and women, by which moral delinquencies which exclude women from society, are not only tolerated, but deemed of little account in man.

He has usurped the prerogative of Jehovah himself, claiming it as his right to assign for her a sphere of action, when that belongs to her conscience and to her god. He has endeavoured, in every way that he could, to destroy her confidence in her own powers, to lessen her self-respect, and to make her willing to lead a dependent and abject life.

Now, in view of this entire disfranchisement of one-half the people of this country, their social and religious degradation—in view of the unjust laws above mentioned, and because women do feel themselves aggrieved, oppressed, and fraudulently deprived of their most sacred rights, we insist that they have immediate admission to all the rights and privileges which belong to them as citizens of the United States.

30

THE HYPOCRISY OF
AMERICAN SLAVERY, 1852

Frederick Douglass

Born a slave in Maryland, Douglas escaped in 1838 and earned widespread acclaim for his 1845 autobiography. Invited to speak as part of July 4 festivities in his adopted hometown of Rochester, N.Y., the abolitionist took the opportunity to rage at the injustice of slavery. This speech was delivered on 4 July 1852.

Fellow citizens, pardon me, and allow me to ask, why am I called upon to speak here today? What have I or those I represent to do with your national independence? Are the great principles of political freedom and of natural justice, embodied in that Declaration of Independence, extended to us? And am I, therefore, called upon to bring our humble offering to the national altar, and to confess the benefits, and express devout gratitude for the blessings resulting from your independence to us?

Would to God, both for your sakes and ours, that an affirmative answer could be truthfully returned to these questions. Then would my task be light, and my burden easy and delightful. For who is there so cold that a nation's sympathy could not warm him? Who so obdurate and dead to the claims of gratitude, that would not thankfully acknowledge such priceless benefits? Who so stolid and selfish that would not give his voice to swell the hallelujahs of a nation's jubilee, when the chains of servitude had been torn from his limbs? I am not that man. In a case like that, the dumb might eloquently speak, and the 'lame man leap as an hart.'

But such is not the state of the case. I say it with a sad sense of disparity between us. I am not included within the pale of this glorious anniversary! Your high independence only reveals the immeasurable distance between us. The blessings in which you this day rejoice are not enjoyed in common. The rich inheritance of justice, liberty, prosperity, and independence bequeathed by your fathers is shared by you, not by me. The sunlight that brought life and healing to you has brought stripes and death to me. This Fourth of July is yours, not mine. You may rejoice, I must mourn. To drag a man in fetters into the grand illuminated temple of liberty, and call upon him to join you in joyous anthems, were inhuman mockery and sacrilegious irony. Do you mean, citizens, to mock me, by asking me to speak today? If so, there is a parallel to your conduct. And let me warn you, that it is dangerous to copy the example of a nation (Babylon) whose crimes, towering up to heaven, were thrown down by the breath of the Almighty, burying that nation in irrecoverable ruin.

Fellow citizens, above your national, tumultuous joy, I hear the mournful wail of millions, whose chains, heavy and grievous yesterday, are today rendered more intolerable by the jubilant shouts that reach them. If I do forget, if I do not remember those bleeding children of sorrow this day, 'may my right hand forget her cunning, and may my tongue cleave to the roof of my mouth!'

To forget them, to pass lightly over their wrongs and to chime in with the popular theme would be treason most scandalous and shocking, and would make me a reproach before God and the world.

My subject, then, fellow citizens, is 'American Slavery.' I shall see this day and its popular characteristics from the slave's point of view. Standing here, identified with the American bondman, making his wrongs mine, I do not hesitate to declare, with all my soul, that the character and conduct of this nation never looked blacker to me than on this Fourth of July.

Whether we turn to the declarations of the past, or to the professions of the present, the conduct of the nation seems equally hideous and revolting. America is false to the past, false to the present, and solemnly binds herself to be false to the future. Standing with God and the crushed and bleeding slave on this occasion, I will, in the name of humanity, which is outraged, in the name of liberty, which is fettered, in the name of the Constitution and the Bible, which are disregarded and trampled upon, dare to call in question and to denounce, with all the emphasis I can command, everything that serves to perpetuate slavery—the great sin and shame of America! 'I will not equivocate—I will not excuse.' I will use the severest language I can command, and yet not one word shall escape me that any man, whose judgment is not blinded by prejudice, or who is not at heart a slave-holder, shall not confess to be right and just.

But I fancy I hear some of my audience say it is just in this circumstance that you and your brother Abolitionists fail to make a favorable impression on the public mind. Would you argue more and denounce less, would you persuade more and rebuke less, your cause would be much more likely to succeed. But, I submit, where all is plain there is nothing to be argued. What point in the anti-slavery creed would you have me argue? On what branch of the subject do the people of this country need light? Must I undertake to prove that the slave is a man? That point is conceded already. Nobody doubts it. The slave-holders themselves acknowledge it in the enactment of laws for their government. They acknowledge it when they punish disobedience on the part of the slave. There are seventy-two crimes in the State of Virginia, which, if committed by a black man (no matter how ignorant he be), subject him to the punishment of death; while only two of these same crimes will subject a white man to like punishment.

What is this but the acknowledgment that the slave is a moral, intellectual, and responsible being? The manhood of the slave is conceded. It is admitted in the fact that Southern statute books are covered with enactments, forbidding, under severe fines and penalties, the teaching of the slave to read and write. When you can point to any such laws in reference to the beasts of the field, then I may consent to argue the manhood of the slave. When the dogs in your streets, when the fowls of the air, when the cattle on your hills, when the fish of the sea, and the reptiles that crawl, shall be unable to distinguish the slave from a brute, then I will argue with you that the slave is a man!

For the present it is enough to affirm the equal manhood of the Negro race. Is it not astonishing that, while we are plowing, planting, and reaping, using all kinds of mechanical tools, erecting houses, constructing bridges, building ships, working in metals of brass, iron, copper, silver, and gold; that while we are reading, writing, and ciphering, acting as clerks, merchants, and secretaries, having among us lawyers, doctors, ministers, poets, authors, editors, orators, and teachers; that we are engaged in all the enterprises common to other men—digging gold in California, capturing the whale in the Pacific, feeding sheep and cattle on the hillside, living, moving, acting, thinking, planning, living in families as husbands, wives, and children, and above all, confessing and worshipping the Christian God, and looking hopefully for life and immortality beyond the grave—we are called upon to prove that we are men?

Would you have me argue that man is entitled to liberty? That he is the rightful owner of his own body? You have already declared it. Must I argue the wrongfulness of slavery? Is that a question for republicans? Is it to be settled by the rules of logic and argumentation, as a matter beset with great difficulty, involving a doubtful application of the principle of justice, hard to understand? How should I look today in the presence of Americans, dividing and subdividing a discourse, to show that men have a natural right to freedom, speaking of it relatively and positively, negatively and affirmatively? To do so would be to make myself ridiculous, and to offer an insult to your understanding. There is not a man beneath the canopy of heaven who does not know that slavery is wrong for him.

What! Am I to argue that it is wrong to make men brutes, to rob them of their liberty, to work them without wages, to keep them ignorant of their relations to their fellow men, to beat them with sticks, to flay their flesh with the lash, to load their limbs with irons, to hunt them with dogs, to sell them at auction, to sunder their families, to knock out their teeth, to burn their flesh, to starve them into obedience and submission to their masters? Must I argue that a system thus marked with blood and stained with pollution is wrong? No—I will not. I have better employment for my time and strength than such arguments would imply.

What, then, remains to be argued? Is it that slavery is not divine; that God did not establish it; that our doctors of divinity are mistaken? There is blasphemy in the thought. That which is inhuman cannot be divine. Who can reason on such a proposition? They that can, may—I cannot. The time for such argument is past.

At a time like this, scorching irony, not convincing argument, is needed. Oh! Had I the ability, and could I reach the nation's ear, I would today pour out a fiery stream of biting ridicule, blasting reproach, withering sarcasm, and stern rebuke. For it is not light that is needed, but fire; it is not the gentle shower, but thunder. We need the storm, the whirlwind, and the earthquake. The feeling of the nation must be quickened; the conscience of the nation must be roused; the propriety of the nation must be startled; the hypocrisy of the nation must be exposed; and its crimes against God and man must be denounced.

What to the American slave is your Fourth of July? I answer, a day that reveals to him more than all other days of the year, the gross injustice and cruelty to which he is the constant victim. To him your celebration is a sham; your boasted liberty an unholy licence; your national greatness, swelling vanity; your sounds of rejoicing are empty and heartless; your shouts of liberty and equality, hollow mock; your prayers and hymns, your sermons and thanks givings, with all your religious parade and solemnity, are to him mere bombast, fraud, deception, impiety, and hypocrisy—a thin veil to cover up crimes which would disgrace a nation of savages. There is not a nation of the earth guilty of practices more shocking and bloody than are the people of these United States at this very hour.

Go search where you will, roam through all the monarchies and despotisms of the Old World, travel through South America, search out every abuse and when you have found the last, lay your facts by the side of the everyday practices of this nation, and you will say with me that, for revolting barbarity and shameless hypocrisy, America reigns without a rival.

31

NATIONALISM IN INDIA

Rabindranath Tagore

Rabindranath Tagore delivered this speech at Ohio, 30 December 1916. Tagore had become an internationally known man, and at the same time an 'embodiment, in the world's eyes, of Indian culture and of national identity.' In this lecture, Tagore compares the problems faced by India with those faced by the West.

Our real problem in India is not political. It is social. This is a condition prevailing not only in India, but among all nations. I do not believe in an exclusive political interest. Politics in the West have dominated Western ideals, and we in India are trying to imitate you. We have to remember that in Europe, where people had racial unity from the very beginning, and where natural resources were insufficient for the inhabitants, civilization has naturally taken on the character of political and commercial aggressiveness. For, on the one hand they had no internal complications, while on the other they had to deal with neighbours who were strong and rapacious. To have a perfect combination among themselves and a watchful attitude of animosity against others was taken as the solution to their problem. In former days, they organized and plundered; in the present age the same spirit continued—they organize and exploit the entire world.

From the earliest beginnings of history India has had her own problem constantly before her—it is the problem concerning race. Each nation must be conscious of its mission, and we in India must realize that we cut a sorry figure when we try to be political, simply because we have not yet been finally able to accomplish what was set before us.

This problem of uniting the races which we have been trying to solve for so many years has likewise to be faced by you here in America. Many people in this country ask me what is happening to the caste distinctions in India. But when this question is asked of me, it is usually done with an air of superiority I feel tempted to put the same question to our American critics with a slight modification: 'What have you done with the Red Indian and the Negro?' You have not got over your attitude of caste towards them. You have used violent methods to keep aloof from other races, but until you have solved the issues here in America, you have no right to question India.

In spite of our great difficulty India has done something. She has tried to make an adjustment of races, to acknowledge the real differences between them, where these exist, and yet seek some basis for unity This basis has come through our saints, like Nanak, Kabir, Chaitanya and others, preaching one God to all races of India.

In finding the solution to our problem we shall have helped solve the world problem as well. What India has been, the entire world is now becoming one through scientific facility. The moment is arriving when you must also find a basis of unity which is not political. If India can offer to the world her solution, it will be a contribution to humanity There is only one history— the history of man. All national histories are merely chapters in the larger one. And we are content in India to suffer for such a great cause.

Each individual has his self-love. Therefore his brute instinct leads him to fight with others in the sole pursuit of his self-interest. But man has also his higher instincts of sympathy and mutual help. People who lack this higher moral power and who cannot conjoin with one another must perish or live in a state of degradation. Only those peoples who have this spirit of cooperation strong in them have survived. We find, therefore, that from the earliest times men had to choose between fighting with one another and combining, between serving their own interest or the common interests of all. In our early history, when the geographical limits of each country and also the facilities of communication were small, this problem was comparatively small in dimension. It was sufficient for men to develop their sense of unity within their area of segregation. They combined among themselves and fought against others. But it was this moral spirit which was the true basis of their greatness, and this fostered their art, science and religion. At that early time the most important fact that man had to take count of was members of one particular race coming in close contact with one another. Those who truly grasped this fact through their higher nature made their mark in history. The most important fact today is that all the different races of men have come closer together. We are again confronted with two alternatives. The problem is whether the different groups of peoples shall go on fighting with one another or find some true basis of reconciliation and mutual help; whether it will be interminable competition or cooperation. I have no hesitation in saying that those who are gifted with the moral power of love and vision of spiritual unity, who have the least feeling of enmity against aliens, and the sympathetic insight to place themselves in somebody else's position, will be the fittest to take their permanent place in times to come. Those who are constantly developing their instincts for a battle will be eliminated. For, this is the problem before us, and we have to prove our humanity by solving it through the help of our higher nature. The gigantic organizations for hurting others and warding off their blows, for making money by dragging others will not help us. On the contrary, by their crushing weight, their enormous cost and their deadening effect on living humanity, they will seriously impede our freedom in the larger life of a higher civilization. It is given at all to the West to struggle out of these tangles and rise to the spiritual summit of humanity then I cannot but think that it is America's special mission to fulfill this hope of both God and man. You are the country of expectation, desiring something else than what is. Europe has her subtle habits of mind and her conventions. But America, as yet, has come to no conclusions. I realize how much America is untrammelled by the traditions of the past, and I can appreciate that experimentalism is a sign of America's youth. The foundation of her glory is in the future, rather than in the past, and if one is gifted with the power of clairvoyance, one will be able to love the America that is to be. America is destined to justify Western civilization to the east. Europe has lost faith in humanity. It has become distrustful and sickly.

Not merely freedom from your habits, but also freedom of your history from all unclean entanglements, befits you in holding the banner of future civilization. All the great nations of Europe have their victims in other parts of the world. This not only deadens their moral sympathy but also their intellectual sympathy, which is so necessary for the understanding of races which are different from one's own. Englishmen can never truly understand India, because their minds are not interested in that country. If you compare England with Germany or France you will find she has produced the smallest number of scholars who have studied Indian literature and philosophy with any sympathetic insight or with assiduity. This attitude of apathy and contempt is natural where the relationship is abnormal and founded upon national selfishness and pride. But your history has been disinterested, and that is why you have been able to help Japan in her lessons in Western civilization, and that is why China can look upon you with the best confidence in this, her darkest period of danger. In fact you are carrying the entire responsibility of a great future because you are untrammelled by the grasping miserliness of a past. Therefore, of all countries on earth, America has to be fully conscious of this future; her vision must not be obscured and her faith in humanity must be strong with the strength of youth. A parallelism exists between America and India— the parallelism of welding together into one body, various races.

In my country we have been seeking to find out something common to all races, which will prove their real unity. No nation looking for a mere political or commercial basis of unity will find such a solution sufficient. Men of thought and power will discover the spiritual unity, will realize it, and preach it. India has never had a real sense of nationalism. Even though from my childhood I had been taught that idolatry of the nation is almost better than reverence for God and humanity, I believe I have outgrown that teaching, and it is my conviction that my countrymen will truly gain their India by fighting against the education which teaches them that a country is greater than the ideals of humanity. Europe has her past. Europe's strength, therefore, lies in her history. We, in India, must makeup our minds that we cannot borrow other people's history and that if we stifle our own we are committing suicide. When you borrow things that do not belong to your life, they only serve to crush your life. Therefore, I believe that it does India no good to compare with Western civilization on its own field. But we shall be more than compensated if, in spite of the insult heaped upon us, we follow our own destiny.

32

ADDRESS AT KINGSLEY HALL

Mohandas Karamchand Gandhi

In October 1931, Mahatma Gandhi visited London where he addressed a large gathering. The Mahatma's address took place at the Kingsley Hall. He called this address as his spiritual message.

There is an indefinable mysterious power that pervades everything. I feel it, though I do not see it. It is this unseen power which makes itself felt and yet defies all proof because it is so unlike all that I perceive through my senses. It transcends the senses.

But it is possible to reason out the existence of God to an (unintelligible) exchange. Even in ordinary affairs we know that people do not know who rules, or why, and how he rules. And yet they know that there is a power that certainly rules.

In my tour last year in Mysore I met many poor villagers and I found upon inquiry that they did not know who ruled Mysore. They simple said some God ruled it. If the knowledge of these poor people was so limited about their ruler, I, who am infinitely lesser in respect to God than they to their ruler need not be surprised if I do not realize the presence of God, the king of kings.

Nevertheless I do feel as the poor villagers felt about Mysore, that there is orderliness in the universe. There is an unalterable law governing everything and every being that exists or lives. It is not a blind law, for no blind law can govern the conduct of living beings. And thanks to the marvellous researches of Sir J.C. Bose, it can now be proved that even matter is life.

That law then which governs all life is God. Law and the lawgiver are one. I may not deny the law or the lawgiver because I know so little about it or him, just as my denial or ignorance of the existence of an earthly power will avail me nothing. Even so, my denial of God and his law will not liberate me from its operation. Whereas, humble and mute acceptance of divine authority makes life's journey easier even as the acceptance of earthly rule makes life under it easier.

I do dimly perceive that whilst everything around me is ever dying, ever guiding, there is underlying all that change a living power that is changeless, that holds all together; that creates, dissolves, and recreates. That informing power of spirit is God. And since nothing else that I see merely through the senses can or will persist, he alone is.

And if this power is benevolent or malevolent, I see it as purely benevolent. For, I can see that in the midst of death, life persists. In the midst of untruth, truth persists. In the midst of darkness, light persists. Hence I gather that God is life, truth, light. He is love. He is the supreme good. But, he is no God who merely satisfies.the intellect, if he ever does. God to be God must rule the heart and transform it. He must express himself in ever smallest act of his (goodery?). This can only be done through a definite realization more real than the fives senses can ever prove use.

Sense perceptions can be and often are false and deceptive however real they may appear to us. Where there is realization outside the senses it is (imperial?), it is proved not by extreme extraneous evidence, but in the transformed conduct and character of those who have felt the real presence of God within. Such testimony is to be found in the experiences of an unbroken line of prophets and sages in all countries and climes. To reject this evidence is to deny oneself. This realization is preceded by an immovable faith. He who would in his own person, test the fact of God's presence can do so by a living faith.

And since faith itself cannot be proved by extraneous evidence, the safest course is to believe in the moral government of the world and therefore in the supremacy of the moral law, the law of truth and love. Exercise of faiths will be the safest where there is the clear determination summarily to reject all that is contrary to truth and love.

I confess that I have no argument to convince through reason. Faith transcends reason. All that I can advise is not to attempt the impossible.

33

WAR MESSAGE

Thomas Woodrow Wilson

Woodrow Wilson, War Message to Congress, 1917. Wilson's re-election in 1916 owed a great deal to the campaign slogan, 'He kept us out of war.' But the resumption of unrestricted submarine warfare by Germany in 1917 significantly changed the international situation. Several US merchant ships were sunk in March by German U-boats. That April, Wilson called Congress into extraordinary session to ask for a declaration of war against Germany. Within four days both the Senate and the House voted overwhelmingly to support the President.

On the third of February last I officially laid before you the extraordinary announcement of the Imperial German government that on and after the first day of February it was its purpose to put aside all restraints of law or of humanity and use its submarines to sink every vessel that sought to approach either the ports of Great Britain and Ireland or the western coasts of Europe or any of the ports controlled by the enemies of Germany within the Mediterranean. That had seemed to be the object of the German submarine warfare earlier in the war, but since April of last year the imperial government had somewhat restrained the commanders of its undersea craft in conformity with its promise then given to us that passenger boats should not be sunk and that due warning would be given to all other vessels which its submarines might seek to destroy, when no resistance was offered or escape attempted, and care taken that their crews were given at least a fair chance to save their lives in their open boats. The precautions taken were meager and haphazard enough, as was proved in distressing instance after instance in the progress of the cruel and unmanly business, but a certain degree of restraint was observed. The new policy has swept every restriction aside. Vessels of every kind, whatever their flag, their character, their cargo, their destination, their errand, have been ruthlessly sent to the bottom without warning and without thought of help or mercy for those on board, the vessels of friendly neutrals along with those of belligerents. Even hospital ships and ships carrying relief to the sorely bereaved and stricken people of Belgium, though the latter were provided with safe conduct through the proscribed areas by the German government itself and were distinguished by unmistakable marks of identity, have been sunk with the same reckless lack of compassion or of principle.

I was for a little while unable to believe that such things would in fact be done by any government that had hitherto subscribed to the humane practices of civilized nations. International law had its origin in the attempt to set up some law which would be respected and observed upon the seas, where no nation had right of dominion and where lay the free highways of the world…This minimum of right the German government has swept aside under the plea of retaliation and necessity and because it had no weapons which it could use at sea except these which it is impossible to employ as it is employing them without throwing to the winds an scruples of humanity or of respect for the understandings that were supposed to underlie the intercourse of the world. I am not now thinking of the loss of property involved, immense and serious as that is, but only of the wanton and wholesale destruction of the lives of non-combatants, men, women, and children, engaged in pursuits which have always, even in the darkest periods of modern history, been deemed innocent and legitimate. Property can be paid for, the lives of peaceful and innocent people cannot be. The present German submarine warfare against commerce is a warfare against mankind.

It is a war against all nations. American ships have been sunk, American lives taken, in ways which it has stirred us very deeply to learn of, but the ships and people of other neutral and friendly nations have been sunk and overwhelmed in the waters in the same way. There has been no-discrimination. The challenge is to all mankind. Each nation must decide for itself how it will meet it. The choice we make for ourselves must be made with a moderation of counsel and a temperateness of judgment befitting our character and our motives as a nation. We must put excited feeling away. Our motive will not be revenge or the victorious assertion of the physical might of the nation, but only the vindication of right, of human right, of which we are only a single champion. With a profound sense of the solemn and even tragical character of the step I am taking and of the grave responsibilities which it involves, but in unhesitating obedience to what I deem my constitutional duty, I advise that the Congress declare the recent course of the imperial German government to be in fact nothing less war against the government and people of the United States; that it formally accept the status of belligerent which has thus been thrust upon it; and that it take immediate steps not only to put the country in a more thorough state of defence but also to exert all its power and employ all its resources to bring the government of the German empire to terms and end the war.

While we do these things, these deeply momentous things, let us be very clear, and make very clear to all the world what our motives and our objects are. My own thought has not been driven from its habitual and normal course by the unhappy events of the last two months, and I do not believe that the thought of the nation has been altered or clouded by them. I have exactly the same things in mind now that I had in mind when I addressed the Senate on 22 January last; the same that I had in mind when I addressed the Congress on 3 February and on 26 February. Our object now, as then, is to vindicate the principles of peace and justice in the life of the world as against selfish and autocratic power and to set up amongst the really free and self-governed peoples of the world such a concert of purpose and of action as will henceforth insure the observance of those principles. Neutrality is no longer feasible or desirable where the peace of the world is involved and the freedom of its peoples, and the menace to that peace and freedom lies in the existence of autocratic governments backed by organized force which is controlled wholly by their will, not by the will of their people. We have seen the last of neutrality in such circumstances. We are at the beginning of an age in which it will be insisted that the same standards of conduct and of responsibility for wrong done shall be observed among nations and their governments that are observed among the individual citizens of civilized states.

We have no quarrel with the German people. We have no feeling towards them but one of sympathy and friendship. It was not upon their impulse that their government acted in entering this war. It was not with their previous knowledge or approval. It was a war determined upon as wars used to be determined upon in the old, unhappy days when peoples were nowhere consulted by their rulers and wars were provoked and waged in the interest of dynasties or of little groups of ambitious men who were accustomed to use their fellow men as pawns and tools.

We are accepting this challenge of hostile purpose because we know that in such a government, following such methods, we can never have a friend; and that in the presence of its organized power, always lying in wait to accomplish we know not what purpose, there can be no assured security for the democratic governments of the world. We are now about to accept gauge of battle with this natural foe to liberty and shall, if necessary, spend the whole force of the nation to check and nullify its pretensions and its power. We are glad, now that we see the facts with no veil of false pretense about them, to fight thus for the ultimate peace of the world and for the liberation of its peoples, the German peoples included: for the rights of nations great and small and the privilege of men everywhere to choose their way of life and of obedience. The world must be made safe for democracy. Its peace must be planted upon the tested foundations of political liberty. We have no selfish ends to serve. We desire no conquest, no dominion. We seek no indemnities for ourselves, no material compensation for the sacrifices we shall freely make. We are but one of the champions of the rights of mankind. We shall be satisfied when those rights have been made as secure as the faith and the freedom of nations can make them.

It is a distressing and oppressive duty, gentlemen of the Congress, which I have performed in thus addressing you. There are, it may be, many months of fiery trial and sacrifice ahead of us. It is a fearful thing to lead this great peaceful people into war, into the most terrible and disastrous of all wars, civilization itself seeming to be in the balance. But the right is more precious than peace, and we shall fight for the things which we have always carried nearest our hearts—for democracy, for the right of those who submit to authority to have a voice in their own governments, for the fights and liberties of small nations, for a universal dominion of right by such a concert of free peoples as shall bring peace and safety to all nations and make the world itself at last free. To such a task we can dedicate our lives and our fortunes, everything that we are and everything that we have, with the pride of those who know that the day has come when America is privileged to spend her blood and her might for the principles that gave her birth and happiness and the peace which she has treasured. God helping her, she can do no other.

34

FREEDOM IS MY BIRTHRIGHT

Bal Gangadhar Tilak

The speech reproduced below was given by Bal Gangadhar Tilak at Nasik on 17 May 1917, at the first anniversary of the forming of the Home Rule League.

I am young in spirit though old in body. I do not wish to lose this privilege of youth. Whatever I am going to speak today is eternally young. The body might grow old, decrepit and it might perish, but the seal is immortal. Similarly, if there might be an apparent lull in our home rule activities, the freedom of the spirit behind it is eternal and indestructible, and it will secure liberty for us. Freedom is my birthright. So long as it is awake within me, I am not old. No weapon can cut this spirit, no fire can burn it, no water can wet it, no wind can dry it. We ask for home rule and we must get it. The science which ends in home rule is the science of politics and not the one which ends in slavery. The science of politics is the 'veda' of the country. You have a soul and I only, want to awaken it up. I want to tear off the blind that has been let down by ignorant, conniving and selfish people. The science of politics consists of two parts. The first is divine and the second is demonic. The slavery of a nation constitutes the latter. There cannot be a moral justification for the demonic part of the science of politics. A nation which might justify this, is guilty of sin in the sight of God. Some people do and some do not have the courage to declare what is harmful for them. Political and religious teaching consists in giving the knowledge of this principle. Religious and political teachings are not separate, though they appear to be so on account of foreign rule. All philosophies are included in the science of politics.

Who does not know the meaning of home rule? Who does not want it? Would you like it if I enter your house and take a possession of your kitchen? I must have the right to manage the affairs in my own house. We are told we are not fit for home rule. A century has passed and the British Rule has not made us fit for home rule; now we will make our own efforts and make ourselves fit for it. To offer irrelevant excuses, to hold out any temptations and to make other offers will be putting a stigma on English policy. England is trying to protect the small state of Belgium with India's help; how can it then say that we should not have home rule? Those who find fault with us are avaricious people. But there are people who find fault even with the all-merciful God. We must work hard to save the soul of our nation without caring for anything. The good of our country consists in guarding this birthright. The Congress has passed this home rule resolution.

In practical politics some futile objections are raised to oppose our desire for swaraj. Illiteracy of the bulk of our people is one of such objections; but to my mind it ought not to be allowed to stand in our way. It would be sufficient for us even if the illiterate in our country have only a vague conception of swaraj, just as it all goes well with them if they simply have a hazy idea about God. Those who can efficiently manage their own affairs may be illiterate; but they are not idiots. They are as intelligent as any other educated man and if they could understand their immediate concerns they would not find any difficulty in grasping the principle of swaraj. If illiteracy is not a disqualification in civil law there is no reason why it should not be so in nature's law also. Even the illiterate are our brethren; they have the same rights and are actuated by the same aspirations. It is, therefore, our bounded duty to awaken the masses. Circumstances have changed, and are favourable. The voice has gone forth 'Now or Never'. Rectitude and constitutional agitation is alone what is expected of you. Turn not back, and confidently leave the ultimate issue to the benevolence of the Almighty.

35

GIVE ME BLOOD, AND I SHALL GIVE YOU FREEDOM

Subhas Chandra Bose

Subhas Chandra Bose was an extremely loved leader, known for his motivational speeches. And of all the speeches he made, none was more popular than the 'Give me blood, and I shall give you freedom' speech that he made in Burma in 1944 to the members of the Indian National Army.

Friends! Twelve months ago a new programme of total mobilization or maximum sacrifice was placed before Indians in East Asia. Today I shall give you an account of our achievements during the past year and shall place before you are demands for the coming year. But, before I do so, I want you to realize once again what a golden opportunity you have for winning freedom. The British are engaged in a worldwide struggle and in the course of struggle they have suffered defeat after defeat on so many fronts. The enemy having being thus considerably weakened, our fight for liberty has become very much easier than it was five years ago. Such a rare and God-given opportunity comes once in a century for liberating our motherland from the British yoke.

I am so very hopeful and optimistic about the outcome of our struggle, because I do not rely merely on the efforts on three million Indians in East Asia. There is a gigantic movement going on inside India and millions of our countrymen are prepared for maximum suffering and sacrifice in order to achieve liberty. Unfortunately, ever since the great fight of 1857, our countrymen are disarmed, whereas the enemy is armed to the teeth. Without arms and without a modern army it is impossible for a disarmed people to win freedom in this modern age. Through the grace of Providence and through the help of generous Nippon, it has become possible for Indians in East Asia are united to a man in the endeavour to win freedom and all the religious and other differences that the British tried to engineer inside India, simply do not exist in East Asia. Consequently, we have now an ideal combination of circumstances favouring the success of our struggle—and all that is wanted is that Indians should themselves come forward to pay the price of liberty. According to the programme of 'total mobilization', I demanded of you men, money, and materials. Regarding men, I am glad to tell you that I have obtained sufficient recruits already. Recruits have come to us from every corner of East Asia—China, Japan, Indo-China, Philippines, Java, Borneo, Celebes, Sumatra, Malaya, Thailand, and Burma...

You must continue the mobilization of men, money and materials with greater vigour and energy, in particular, the problem of supplies and transport has to be solved satisfactorily.

We require more men and women of all categories for administration and reconstruction in liberated areas. We must be prepared for a situation in which the enemy will ruthlessly apply the scorched earth policy, before withdrawing from a particular area and will also force the civilian population to evacuate as was attempted in Burma.

The most important of all is the problem of sending reinforcements in men and in supplies to the fighting fronts. If we do not do so, we cannot hope to maintain our success at the fronts. Nor can we hope to penetrate deeper into India.

Those of you who will continue to work on the Home Front should never forget that East Asia—and particularly Burma—form our base for the war of liberation. If this base is not strong, our fighting forces can never be victorious. Remember that this is a 'total war' and not merely a war between two armies. That is why for a full one year I have been laying so much stress on 'total mobilization' in the East.

There is another reason why I want you to look after the Home Front properly. During the coming months I and my colleagues on the war committee of the cabinet desire to devote our whole attention to the fighting front—and also to the task of working up the revolution in side India. Consequently, we want to be fully assured that the work at the base will go on smoothly and uninterruptedly even in our absence.

Friends, one year ago, when I made certain demands of you, I told you that if you give me 'total mobilization', I would give you a 'second front'. I have redeemed that pledge. The first phase of our campaign is over. Our victorious troops, fighting side by side with Nipponese troops, have pushed back the enemy and are not fighting bravely on the sacred soil of our dear motherland.

Grid up your loins for the task that now lies ahead. I had asked you for men, money and materials. I have got them in generous measure. Now I demand more of you. Men, money and materials have the motive power that will inspire us to brave deeds and heroic exploits.

It will be a fatal mistake for you to wish to live and see India free simply because victory is now within reach. No one here should have the desire to live to enjoy freedom. A long fight is till in front of us. We should have but one desire today—the desire to die so that India may live, the desire to face a martyr's death so that the path to freedom may be paved with the martyr's blood.

Friends! My comrades in the War of Liberation! Today I demand of you one thing, above all. I demand of you blood. It is blood alone that can avenge the blood that the enemy has spilt. It is blood alone that can pay the price of freedom. Give me blood and I promise you freedom!

36

QUIT INDIA SPEECH

Mohandas Karamchand Gandhi

The speech delivered by Gandhi on 8 August 1942, addressed the A.I.C.C. at Mumbai (then Bombay) on the eve of Quit India Movement is considered one of his best speeches. He called for determined, but passive resistance that signified the certitude that Gandhi foresaw for the movement is best described by his call to Do or Die. His speech was issued at the Gowalia Tank Maidan in Bombay (now Mumbai), since renamed August Kranti Maidan (August Revolution Ground).

Before you discuss the resolution, let me place before you one or two things, I want you to understand two things very clearly and to consider them from the same point of view from which I am placing them before you. I ask you to consider it from my point of view, because if you approve of it, you will be enjoined to carry out all I say. It will be a great responsibility. There are people who ask me whether I am the same man that I was in 1920, or whether there has been any change in me. You are right in asking that question.

Let me, however, hasten to assure that I am the same Gandhi as I was in 1920. I have not changed in any fundamental respect. I attach the same importance to non-violence that I did then. If at all, my emphasis on it has grown stronger. There is no real contradiction between the present resolution and my previous writings and utterances.

Occasions like the present do not occur in everybody's and but rarely in anybody's life. I want you to know and feel that there is nothing but purest Ahimsa in all that I am saying and doing today. The draft resolution of the Working Committee is based on Ahimsa, the contemplated struggle similarly has its roots in Ahimsa. If, therefore, there is any among you who has lost faith in Ahimsa or is wearied of it, let him not vote for this resolution. Let me explain my position clearly. God has vouchsafed to me a priceless gift in the weapon of Ahimsa. I and my Ahimsa are on our trail today. If in the present crisis, when the earth is being scorched by the flames of Himsa and crying for deliverance, I failed to make use of the God given talent, God will not forgive me and I shall be judged unworthy of the great gift. I must act now. I may not hesitate and merely look on, when Russia and China are threatened.

Ours is not a drive for power, but purely a non-violent fight for India's independence. In a violent struggle, a successful general has been often known to effect a military coup and to set up a dictatorship. But under the Congress scheme of things, essentially non-violent as it is, there can be no room for dictatorship. A non-violent soldier of freedom will covet nothing for himself, he fights only for the freedom of his country. The Congress is unconcerned as to who will rule, when freedom is attained. The power, when it comes, will belong to the people of India, and it will be for them to decide to whom it placed in the entrusted. May be that the reins will be placed in the hands of the Parsis, for instance—as I would love to see happen—or they may be handed to some others whose names are not heard in the Congress today. It will not be for you then to object saying, 'This community is microscopic. That party did not play its due part in the freedom's struggle; why should it have all the power?' Ever since its inception the Congress has kept itself meticulously free of the communal taint. It has thought always in terms of the whole nation and has acted accordingly…I know how imperfect our Ahimsa is and how far away we are still from the ideal, but in Ahimsa there is no final failure or defeat. I have faith, therefore, that if, in spite of our shortcomings, the big thing does happen, it will be because God wanted to help us by crowning with success our silent, unremitting Sadhana for the last twenty-two years.

I believe that in the history of the world, there has not been a more genuinely democratic struggle for freedom than ours. I read Carlyle's French Revolution while I was in prison, and Pandit Jawaharlal has told me something about the Russian revolution. But it is my conviction that inasmuch as these struggles were fought with the weapon of violence they failed to realize the democratic ideal. In the democracy which I have envisaged, a democracy established by non-violence, there will be equal freedom for all. Everybody will be his own master. It is to join a struggle for such democracy that I invite you today. Once you realize this you will forget the differences between the Hindus and Muslims, and think of yourselves as Indians only, engaged in the common struggle for independence.

Then, there is the question of your attitude towards the British. I have noticed that there is hatred towards the British among the people. The people say they are disgusted with their behavior. The people make no distinction between British imperialism and the British people. To them, the two are one. This hatred would even make them welcome the Japanese. It is most dangerous. It means that they will exchange one slavery for another. We must get rid of this feeling. Our quarrel is not with the British people, we fight their imperialism. The proposal for the withdrawal of British power did not come out of anger. It came to enable India to play its due part at the present critical juncture. It is not a happy position for a big country like India to be merely helping with money and material obtained willy-nilly from her, while the United Nations are conducting the war. We cannot evoke the true spirit of sacrifice and velour, so long as we are not free. I know the British Government will not be able to withhold freedom from us, when we have made enough self-sacrifice. We must, therefore, purge ourselves of hatred. Speaking for myself, I can say that I have never felt any hatred. As a matter of fact, I feel myself to be a greater friend of the British now than ever before. One reason is that they are today in distress. My very friendship, therefore, demands that I should try to save them from their mistakes. As I view the situation, they are on the brink of an abyss. It, therefore, becomes my duty to warn them of their danger even though it may, for the time being, anger them to the point of cutting off the friendly hand that is stretched out to help them. People may laugh, nevertheless that is my claim. At a time when I may have to launch the biggest struggle of my life, I may not harbour hatred against anybody.

37

WHY I LEFT THE SWARAJ PARTY

Lala Lajpat Rai

The following election speech was delivered by Lala Lajpat Rai at Lucknow on 25 September 1926, after resigning from the Swaraj Party and forming a new party, the Nationalist Party, in collaboration with Madan Mohan Malaviya. Lajpat Rai realized that several acts of the Swarajist leaders were not in the interest of the country nor were they doing justice to the Hindus. He was the only Swarajist to win Assembly seat in that state.

It gave me no pleasure to sever my connection with the Swaraj Party, specially after all that I had done to strengthen, aid, and solidify the party in spite of my non-agreement with its leaders on more than one important point. I was released from jail in August 1923. The Swaraj Party had already been formed at Gaya in December 1922. In September, we held a special session of the Congress at Delhi to consider the question of council entry. From my sick bed at Solan I did all I could to support the cause of Deshbandhu and Pandit Motilal viz., to get the permission of the congress to contest the elections. Shortly after that came the elections and although I did not agree with the election slogan of the Swaraj Part i.e. uniform, continuous and consistent obstruction, I did all I could to help them in the election. Practically single handed, I ran the election for them in Punjab and obtained notable victories. After the elections when the Assembly met in Delhi, I stayed for days and days together to help them in their efforts to establish united Nationalist Party and actually canvassed votes for them there. Later on when I went to England I conducted negotiations on their behalf with the Labour Government and throughout that trip espoused their cause and explained their position, although I was not a member of the party and had not accepted the programme of obstruction. My first difference with the Swaraj Party came in relation to the Hindu-Muslim Pact of Bengal propounded by the late Mr Das. I do not propose to revive that controversy, but it would be well to remind that Pact was an act of gross indiscipline on the part of the Bengal Swarajist leaders. The special Congress in Calcutta had appointed a sub-committee consisting of Dr Ansari and myself to draw a national pact. We had drawn a pact with the advice and consent of Maulana Abul Kalam Azad and the leaders of the Swaraj Party knew of that pact. Yet the Bengal Pact was propounded before the other proposed Pact drafted by us was published. After my return from Europe my differences assumed a rather acute shape, but still I entertained hope that I might be able to cooperate with Pandit Motilal Nehru at least, if not with Deshbandhu Das. After the much lamented death of Deshbandhu Das, I appealed to the country once more to forget the differences and to rally round the banner of the Swaraj Party. I could not do so myself, as there were some points of principles on which I could not see eye to eye with the leaders of the Swaraj Party. After all, I joined the Swaraj Party in January 1926, after having made my position clear in the letter I addressed at the time to Pandit Motilal Nehru. That letter has been made public and I need only remind you that I distinctly said in that letter that I believed in the Council work and was opposed to wholesale obstruction and to boycott the Councils. I joined the Swaraj Party in the hope that 1 would be able to pull on with them, but soon after I found that I was mistaken. On my return from England this year, I found the situation so hopeless that considered I could no longer remain in the party. I would have gladly withdrawn from any kind of contest with the Swaraj Party had my sense of duty to the country allowed me to do so. I owe it to myself and the country to vindicate the principles for what I stand. What are those principles? 1 will try to restate them as briefly as possible. Non-cooperation or wholesale obstruction has for the present been frustrated on account of the Muslim community It could only be practicable if the country supported it united. The Muslims never supported the movement wholeheartedly, and whatever support these principles received from the section of the Muslim community has for the present vanished. In the circumstances, the policy of non-cooperation or obstruction by one community only has no chance of success. The leaders of the Muslim community claim certain rights for their community, the acceptance of which will reduce the Hindu community to a position of subordination, if not immediately but, at least in the future. In my judgment it is not in the interests of the country at large that the Hindus should accept those claims. In the circumstances, the Muslims have allied themselves with the government. In their love for their religion and their community they are unable to see the injustice or the incongruity of their claims. They are determined to have the whole loaf either by agreement with the Hindus or by alliance with the Government They find that cooperation with the Government gives them better chance of success than cooperation with the Hindus. Consequently, they have thrown their lot with the Government and the Government is trying its level best to satisfy them in every possible way. The joint strategy of the Government and the Muslims only lead to the isolation of the Hindus. What then should the Hindus do? Should they throw themselves into the arms of the bureaucracy and enter into a counter-alliance with the Government? I would be the last person to suggest or to advocate such a step. The first thing that the Hindus should do, is to abandon, at least for the time being the mentality that led to non-cooperation or wholesale obstruction in the legislatures. Going into the legislatures with the mentality of non-cooperation is not only futile but harmful. One may not fully cooperate with the Government, in fact no Indian patriot can do so, but if one allows himself to be the mentality of boycott he is sure to fall into ways and methods that may spell disaster to the country in general, and the Hindus in particular. What would be the position of the Hindus after ten or twenty years hereafter if the present alliance of the Government and the Muslims continues and the Hindus continue to allow themselves to be influenced by the mentality of non-cooperation and boycott? In my judgment there will be only one result of this, viz, that the Hindus will come to occupy a position of inferiority and subordination. The Swaraj leaders are not troubled by that contingency, but I and men of my thinking cannot but be disturbed by a prospect of that kind. I want freedom for my country, but I must be sure that I get that freedom without losing my status as a Hindu. I do not want to change masters.

38

THE FUNDAMENTAL PRINCIPLE
OF A REPUBLIC

Anna Howard Shaw

Fundamental Principles of a Republic, Albany NY, 21 June 1915 by Anna Howard Shaw. In her speech called 'The Fundamental Principle of a Republic,' she made arguments regarding the value of both genders, reinforcing the fact that there would be no society without men nor would there be one without women.

When I came into your hall tonight, I thought of the last time I was in your city.

Twenty-one years ago I came here with Susan B. Anthony, and we came for exactly the same purpose as that for which we are here tonight. Boys have been born since that time and have become voters, and the women are still trying to persuade American men to believe in the fundamental principles of democracy.

I never quite feel as if it was a fair field to argue this question with men, because in doing it you have to assume that a man who professes to believe in a republican form of government does not believe in a republican form of government, for the only thing that women's enfranchisement means at all is that a government which claims to be a republic should be a republic, and not an aristocracy.

Now one of two things is true: either a republic is a desirable form of government, or else it is not. If it is, then we should have it, if it is not, then we ought not to pretend that we have it. We ought, at least, to be true to our ideals, and the men of New York have, for the first time in their lives, the rare opportunity, on the second day of next November, of making this state truly a part of a republic.

If women's suffrage is wrong, it is a great wrong; if it is right, it is a profound and fundamental principle, and we all know—if we know what a republic is—that it is the fundamental principle upon which a republic must rise. Let us see where we are as a people; how we act here and what we think we are.

The difficulty with the men of this country is that they are so consistent in their inconsistency that they are not aware of having been inconsistent; because their consistency has been so continuous, and their inconsistency so consecutive, that it has never been broken, from the beginning of our nation's life to the present time.

If we trace our history back, we will find that from the very dawn of our existence as a people, men have been imbued with a spirit and a vision more lofty than they have been able to live. They have been led by visions of the sublimest truth, both in regard to religion and in regard to government that ever inspired the souls of men from the time the Puritans left the Old World to come to this country, led by the Divine ideal which is the sublimest and supremest ideal in religious freedom which men have ever known: the theory that a man has a right to worship God according to the dictates of his own conscience, without the intervention of any other man or any other group of men. And it was this theory, this vision of the right of the human soul, which led men first to the shores of this country.

Now, nobody can deny that [these were] sincere, honest and earnest men. No one can deny that the Puritans were men of profound conviction, and yet these men, who gave up everything in behalf of an ideal, hardly established their communities in this new country before they began to practice exactly the same sort of persecutions on other men which had been practiced upon them. They settled in their communities on the New England shores, and when they formed their compacts by which they governed their local societies, they permitted no man to have a voice in their affairs unless he was a member of the church, and not a member of any church, but a member of the particular church which dominated the particular community in which he happened to be. In Massachusetts they drove the Baptists down to Rhode Island; in Connecticut they drove the Presbyterians over to New Jersey; they burned the Quakers in Massachusetts and ducked the witches, and no colony, either Catholic or Protestant, allowed a Jew to have a voice. And so a man must worship God according to the conscience of the particular community in which he was located.

[Even though] they called that religious freedom, they were not able to live the ideal of religious liberty, and from that time to this, the men of this government have been following along the same line of inconsistency, while they, too, have been following a vision of equal grandeur and power.

Never in the history of the world did it dawn upon the human mind as it dawned upon your ancestors, what it would mean for men to be free. They got the vision of a government in which the people would be the supreme power, and so inspired by this vision, men wrote such documents as were sent from Massachusetts legislature, from the New York legislature and from the Pennsylvania group over to the Parliament of Great Britain, which rang with the profoundest measures of freedom and justice. They did not equivocate in a single word when they wrote the Declaration of Independence; no one can dream that these men had not got the sublimest ideal of democracy which had ever dawned upon the souls of men.

But as soon as the war was over and our government was formed, instead of asking the question, who shall be the governing force in this great new republic, when they brought those thirteen little territories together, they began to eliminate instead of include the men who should be the great governing forces. And they said, who shall have the voice in this great new republic, and you would have supposed that such men as fought the Revolutionary War would have been able to answer that every man who has fought, every one who has given up all he has and all he has been able to accumulate, shall be free, yet it never entered their minds. These excellent ancestors of yours had not been away from the Old World long enough to realize that a man is of more value than his purse, so they said every man who has an estate in the government shall have a voice. They [asked] what shall that estate be? And they answered that a man who had property valued at two hundred and fifty dollars will be able to cast a vote, and so they sang about 'the land of the free and the home of the brave.' And they wrote into their Constitution, 'All males who pay taxes on $250 shall cast a vote,' and they called themselves a republic, and we call ourselves a republic [too].

We might call ourselves angels, but that wouldn't make us angels. You have got to be an angel before you are an angel, and you have got to be a republic before you are a republic.

Now what did we do? Before the word 'male' in the local compacts they wrote the word 'church member;' after that they rubbed out 'church member' and they wrote in the word 'tax-payer.'

Then there arose a great Democrat, Thomas Jefferson, who looked down into the day when you and I are living and saw that the rapidly accumulated wealth in the hands of a few men would endanger the liberties of the people, and he knew what you and I know, that no power under heaven or among men is known in a republic by which men can defend their liberties except by the power of the ballot, and so the Democratic party took another step in the evolution of a republic out of a monarchy, and they rubbed out the word 'tax-payer' and wrote in the word 'white,' and then the Democrats thought the millennium had come, and they sang 'the land of the free and the home of the brave' as lustily as the Republicans had sung it before them, and they spoke of the divine right of motherhood with the same thrill in their voices and at the same time they were selling mother's babies by the pound on the auction block and forcing mothers apart from their babies.

Another arose who said a man is not a good citizen because he is white, he is a good citizen because he is a man, and the Republican party took out that progressive evolutionary eraser and rubbed out the word 'white' from before the word 'male' and could not think of another word to put in there—they were all in, black and white, rich and poor, wise and otherwise, drunk and sober; not a man left out to be put in, and so the Republicans could not write anything before the word 'male,' and they had to let that little word 'male' stay alone by itself.

And God said in the beginning 'It is not good for man to stand alone,' Genesis 2:18. That is why we are here tonight, and that is all that women's suffrage means; just to repeat again and again that first declaration of the Divine, 'It is not good for man to stand alone,' and so the women of this state are asking that the word 'male' shall be stricken out of the Constitution altogether, and that the Constitution stand as it ought to have stood in the beginning, and as it must before this state is any part of a republic.

Now what is a republic? Take your dictionary, encyclopedia, lexicon, or anything else you like, and look up the definition and you will find that a republic is a form of government in which the laws are enacted by representatives elected by the people. Now when did the people of New York ever elect their representatives? Never in the world. The men of New York have, and I grant you that men are people—admirable people, as far as they go—but they only go half-way. There is still another half of the people who have not elected representatives, and you never read a definition of a republic in which half of the people elect representatives to govern the whole of the people. That is an aristocracy and that is just what we are. We have been many kinds of aristocracies. We have been a hierarchy of church members, then an aristocracy of wealth, then an oligarchy of sex.

There are two old theories which are dying today. Dying hard, but dying. One of them is dying on the plains of Flanders and the Mountains of Galicia and Austria and that is the theory of the divine right of kings. The other is dying here in the states of New York and Massachusetts and New Jersey and Pennsylvania and that is the divine right of sex. Neither of them has a foundation in reason, or justice or common sense.

The difficulty with the men of this country is that they are so consistent in their inconsistency that they are not aware of having been inconsistent.

Whenever a republic prescribes the qualifications as apply equally to all the citizens of the republic, so that when the republic says in order to vote, a citizen must be twenty-one years of age, it applies to all alike, there is no discrimination against any race or sex. When the government says that a citizen must be a native-born citizen or a naturalized citizen, that applies to all; we are either born or naturalized, somehow or other we are here. Whenever the government says that a citizen, in order to vote, must be a resident of a community a certain length of time, and of the state a certain length of time, and of the nation a certain length of time, that applies to all equally. There is no discrimination.

But when the government says not only that you must be twenty-one years of age, a resident of the community and a native born or naturalized, those are qualifications, but when it says that an elector must be a male, that is not a qualification for citizenship; that is an insurmountable barrier between half of the people and the other half, and no government which erects an insurmountable barrier between one half of the citizens and their rights as citizens can call itself a republic!

Men know the inconsistencies themselves; they realize it in one way while they do not realize it in another, because you never heard a man make a political speech when he did not speak of this country as a whole as though the thing existed which does not exist and that is that the people were equally free, because you hear them declare over and over again on the Fourth of July, 'under God, the people rule.' They know it is not true but they say it with a great hurrah, and then they repeat over and over again that clause from the Declaration of Independence, 'governments derive their just powers from the consent of the governed,' and then they see how they can prevent half of us from giving our consent to anything, and then they give it to us on the Fourth of July in two languages, so if [it] is not true in one, it will be in the other, 'vox populi, vox Dei.' 'The voice of the people is the voice of God,' and the orator forgets that in the people's voice there is a soprano as well as a bass. If the voice of the people is the voice of God, how are we ever going to know what God's voice is when we are content to listen to a bass solo? Now if it is true that the voice of the people is the voice of God, we will never know what the Deity's voice in government is until the bass and soprano are mingled together, the result of which will be the divine harmony!

Men are so sentimental. We used to believe that women were the sentimental sex, but they cannot hold a tallow candle compared with the arc light of

The World's 100 Greatest Speeches

the men...I think the average man recognizes that he has no more right to anything at the hands of the government than has every other man. He has no right at all to anything to which every other man has not an equal right with himself. He says why have I a right to certain things in the government; why have I a right to life and liberty; why have I a right to this or this? Does he say because I am a man? Not at all, because I am human, and being human, I have a right to everything which belongs to humanity, and every right which any other human being has, I have. And then he says of his neighbour and my neighbour, he also is human, therefore every right which belongs to me as a human being, belongs to him as a human being, and I have no right to anything under the government to which he is not equally entitled.

And then up comes a woman, and then they say, now she's a woman; she is not quite human, but she is my wife, or my sister, or my daughter, or an aunt, or my cousin. She is not quite human, she is only related to a human, and being related to a human, a human will take care of her. So we have had that care-taking human being to look after us, and they have not recognized that women too are equally human with men.

What are the arguments which our good 'Anti-' friends give us? We know that lately they have stopped to argue and call suffragists all sorts of creatures....[They say] suffragists are feminists, and when I ask what that is, no one is able to tell me...Then they cry that we are Socialists, and anarchists. Just how a human can be both at the same time, I really do not know. If I know what socialism means it means absolute government, and anarchism means no government at all. So we are feminists, Socialists, anarchists and Mormons or spinsters! Now that is about the list, [although] I have not heard the last speech.

Now, as a matter of fact, as a unit we are nothing, as individuals we are like all other individuals. We have our theories, our beliefs, but as suffragists we have but one belief, but one principle, but one theory and that is the right of a human being to have a voice in the government under which he or she lives. On that we agree, if on nothing else. Whether we agree or not on religion or politics, we are not concerned.

A clergyman asked me the other day, 'By the way, what church does your official board belong to?' I said, 'I don't know.'

He said, 'Don't you know what religion your official board believes?' I said, 'Really it never occurred to me, but I will hunt them up and see, they are not elected to my board because they believe in any particular church. We had no concern either as to what we believe as religionists or as to what we believe as women in regard to theories of government, except that one fundamental theory in the right of democracy. We do not believe in this fad or the other, but whenever any question is to be settled in any community, then the people of that community shall settle that question, the women-people equally with the men-people.' That is all there is to it.

[When] it comes to arguing our case, [anti-suffragists] bring up all sorts of arguments, and the beauty of it is, they always answer all their own arguments! I was followed up last year by a young married woman from New Jersey. She left her husband and home for three months to tell the women that their place was at home, and that they could not leave home long enough to go to the ballot box, and she brought all her arguments out in pairs and backed them up by statistics.

She started by proving that it was no use to give the women the ballot because if they did have it they would not use it, and she had statistics to prove it. If we would not use it, then I really cannot see the harm of giving it to us, we would not hurt anybody with it and what an easy way for you men to get rid of us. No more suffrage meetings, never any nagging you again, no one could blame you for anything that went wrong with the town; if it did not run right, all you would have to say is, you have the power, why don't you go ahead and clean up. Then the young lady, unfortunately for her first argument, proved, by statistics, of which she had many, the awful results which happened where women did have the ballot[—]how deeply women get interested in politics, because women are hysterical, and we cannot think of anything else, we just forget our families, cease to care for our children, cease to love our husbands, and just go to the polls and vote and keep on voting for ten hours a day, 365 days in the year, and never let up! If we ever get to the polls once, you will never get us home So that the women will not vote at all, and they will not do anything but vote

Now these are two very strong anti-suffrage arguments, and they can prove them, by figures.

Then they will tell you that if women are permitted to vote, it will be a great expense and no use because wives will vote just as their husbands do; even if we have no husbands, that would not affect the result because we would vote just as our husbands would vote if we had one. How I wish the anti-suffragists could make the men believe that; if they could make men believe that the women would vote just as they wanted them to, do you think we would ever have to make another speech or hold another meeting? We would have to vote whether we wanted to or not.

And then the very one who will tell you that women will vote just as their husbands do will tell you in five minutes that they will not vote as their husbands will, and then warn you of the discord in the homes, and the divorce. Why, they have discovered that in Colorado, there are more divorces now than there were before women began to vote, but they have forgotten to tell you that there are four times as many people in Colorado today as there were when women began to vote, and that may have some effect.

Then they will tell you all the trouble that happens in the home. A gentleman told me that in California—and when he was talking I had a wonderful thing pass through my mind, because he said he and his wife had lived together for twenty years and never had a difference in opinion in the whole twenty years, and he was afraid if women began to vote that his wife would vote differently from him and then that beautiful harmony which they had had for twenty years would be broken, and all the time he was talking I could not help wondering which was the idiot—because I knew that no intelligent human beings could live together for twenty years and not have differences of opinion. All the time he was talking, I looked at that splendid type of manhood and thought, how would a man feel being tagged up by a little woman for twenty years saying, 'me too, me too.' I would not want to live in a house with a human being for twenty hours who agreed with everything I said. The stagnation of a frog pond would be hilarious compared to that What a reflection is that on men…great big overgrown babies! Cannot be disputed without having a row!…In fact my theory of the whole matter is exactly opposite, because instead of believing that men and women will quarrel, I think just the opposite thing will happen. I think just about six weeks before election, a sort of honeymoon will start and it will continue until they will think they are again hanging over the gate, all in order to get each other's votes. When men want each other's votes they do not go up and knock them down; they are very solicitous of each other, [especially] if they are thirsty or need a smoke!

The husband and wife who are quarreling after the vote are quarreling now.

…I remember hearing Rev. Dr Abbott speak before the anti-suffrage meeting in Brooklyn, and he stated that if women were permitted to vote we could not have so much time for charity and philanthropy, and I would like to say: 'Thank God, there will not be so much need of charity and philanthropy!' The end and aim of the suffrage movement is not to furnish an opportunity for excellent old ladies to be charitable. There are two words that we ought to be able to get along without, and they are 'charity' and 'philanthropy.' They are not needed in a republic. If we put in the word 'opportunity' instead, that is what republics stand for. Our doctrine is not to extend the length of our bread lines or the size of our soup kitchens; what we need is the opportunity for people to buy their own bread and eat their own soup! We will either vote as our husbands vote, or we will not vote as our husbands vote. We either have time to vote, or we don't have time to vote. We will either not vote at all, or we will vote all the time. It reminds me of the story of the old Irish woman who had twin boys, and they were so much alike that the neighbours could not tell them apart, and the mother always seemed to be able to tell them apart, so one of the neighbours said, 'Now Mrs Mahoney, you have two of the finest twin boys I ever saw in all my life, but how do you know them apart.' 'Oh,' she says, 'That's easy enough, anyone could tell them apart. When I want to know which is which I just put my finger in Patsey's mouth, and, if he bites, it is Mikey!' Now what does it matter whether the women will vote as their husbands do or will not vote; whether they have time or have not, or [even] whether they will vote for prohibition or not? What has that to do with the fundamental question of democracy, no one has yet discovered. But they cannot argue on that; they cannot argue on the fundamental basis of our existence so that they have to get off on all these side tracks to get anything approaching an argument.

And so our good friends go on with one thing after another, and they say if women should vote they will have to sit on the jury, and they ask whether we will like to see a woman sitting on a jury. I have seen some juries that ought to be sat on, and I have seen some women that would be glad to sit on anything! When a woman stands up all day behind a counter, or when she stands all day doing a washing, she is glad enough to sit; and when she stands for seventy-five cents, she would like to sit for two dollars a day. But don't you think we need some women on juries in this country? You read your paper, and you read that one day last week, or the week before, or the week before a little girl went out to school and never came back; another little girl was sent on an errand and never came back; another little girl was left in charge of a little sister, and her mother went out to work, and when she returned the little girl was not there, and you read it over and over again, and the horror of it strikes you. You read that in these United States, five thousand young girls go out and never come back, don't you think that the men and women, the vampires of our country who fatten and grow rich on the ignorance and innocence of children, would rather face Satan himself than a jury of mothers?

When I was speaking in North Dakota from an automobile in front of a great crowd,…a man who had been sitting in front of a store whittling a stick called out: 'If women get the vote, will they go over to Germany and fight the Germans?' I said, 'Why no? Why should we women fight men? But if Germany should send an army of women over here, then we would show you what we would do. We would go down and meet them and say, 'Come on, let's go up to the opera house and talk this matter over!'

It might grow wearisome, but it would not be death. Would it not be better if the heads of the governments in Europe had talked things over? What might have happened to the world if a dozen men had gotten together in Europe and settled the awful controversy which is today decimating the nations of Europe? When I turned away from that place up in North Dakota, that man in the crowd called out again, just as we were leaving and said, 'Well, what does a woman know about war anyway?'

I had read my paper that morning, and I knew what the awful headline was. I saw a gentleman standing in the crowd with a paper in his pocket, and I said, will that gentleman hold the paper up, and he held it up, and the headline read, '250,000 Men Killed Since the War Began.'

I said you ask me what a woman knows about war? No woman can read that line and comprehend the awful horror; no woman knows the significance of 250,000 dead men, but you tell me that one man lay dead, and I might be able to tell you something of its awful meaning to one woman. I would know that years before, a woman whose heart beat in unison with her love and her desire for motherhood walked day by day with her face to an open grave, with courage, which no man has ever surpassed, and if she did not fill that grave, if she lived, and if there was laid in her arms a tiny little bit of helpless humanity, I would know that there went out from her soul such a cry of thankfulness as none save a mother could know. And then I would know, what men have not yet learned, that women are human; that they have human hopes and human passions, aspirations and desires as men have, and I would know that that mother who had laid aside all those hopes and aspirations of herself, but never for one moment did she lay them aside for her boy, and if, after years had passed by, she forgot her nights of sleeplessness and her days of fatiguing toil in her care of her growing boy, and when, at last, he became a man, and she stood looking up into his eyes and beheld him, bone of her bone and flesh of her flesh, for out of her woman's life she had carved twenty beautiful years that went into the making of a man, and there he stands, the most wonderful thing in all the world, for in all the universe of God, there is nothing more sublimely wonderful than a strong limbed, clean hearted, keen brained, aggressive young man, standing as he does on the border line of life, ready to reach out and grapple with its problems. Oh, how wonderful he is, and he is hers. She gave her life for him, and, in an hour, this country calls him out, and, in an hour, he lies dead; that wonderful, wonderful thing lies dead, and sitting by his side, that mother looking into the dark years to come knows that when her son died her life's hope died with him, and in the face of that wretched motherhood, what man dare ask what a woman knows of war?

And that is not all. Read your papers, you cannot read it because it is not printable; you cannot tell it because it is not speakable, you cannot even think it because it is not thinkable, the horrible crimes perpetrated against women by the blood-drunken men of the war. You read your paper again and the second headline reads, 'It Costs Twenty Millions of Dollars a Day.' For what? To buy the material to slaughter the splendid results of civilization of the centuries. Men whom it has taken centuries to build up and make into great scientific forces of brain, the flower of the manhood of the great nations of Europe, and we spend twenty millions of dollars a day to blot out all the results of civilization of hundreds and hundreds of years. And what do we do? We lay a mortgage on every unborn child for a hundred and more years to come. Mortgage his brain, his brawn, every pulse of his heart in order to pay the debt, to buy the material to slaughter the men of our country. Read what they are doing. They are calling out every man, every young man, every virile man from seventeen to forty-five or fifty years-old…to be food for the cannon…The crime of crimes of the war is the crime against the unborn children that we take from them what every child has a right to, that is a virile father, and we rob women of fit mates to become the fathers of their children. In the face of these crimes against women and against children, and in the face of the fact that women are driven out of the home, shall men ask if women shall fight, if they are permitted to vote?

No, we women do not want the ballot in order that we may fight, but we do want the ballot in order that we may help men to keep from fighting, whether it is in war or in peace; whether it is in the home or in the state, just as the home is not without the man, so the state is not without the woman, and you can no more build up homes without men than you can build up the state without women. We are needed everywhere where human life is. We are needed everywhere where human problems are [needed] to be solved.

Men and women must go through this world together from the cradle to the grave; it is God's way, and it is the fundamental principle of a republican form of government.

39

THE ARSENAL OF DEMOCRACY

Franklin D. Roosevelt

The 'Arsenal of Democracy' in World War II was a slogan used by US President Franklin D. Roosevelt, in a radio broadcast delivered on 29 December 1940. Roosevelt promised to help the United Kingdom fight Nazi Germany by giving them military supplies while the United States stayed out of the actual fighting. The announcement was made a year before the Attack on Pearl Harbor, at a time when Germany had occupied much of Europe and threatened Britain.

My friends:

This is not a fireside chat on war. It is a talk on national security; because the nub of the whole purpose of your President is to keep you now, and your children later, and your grandchildren much later, out of a last-ditch war for the preservation of American Independence, and all of the things that American Independence means to you and to me and to ours.

Tonight, in the presence of a world crisis, my mind goes back eight years to a night in the midst of a domestic crisis. It was a time when the wheels of American industry were grinding to a full stop, when the whole banking system of our country had ceased to function. I well remember that while I sat in my study in the White House, preparing to talk with the people of the United States, I had before my eyes the picture of all those Americans with whom I was talking. I saw the workmen in the mills, the mines, the factories, the girl behind the counter, the small shopkeeper, the farmer doing his spring plowing, the widows and the old men wondering about their life's savings. I tried to convey to the great mass of American people what the banking crisis meant to them in their daily lives.

Tonight, I want to do the same thing, with the same people, in this new crisis which faces America. We met the issue of 1933 with courage and realism. We face this new crisis, this new threat to the security of our nation, with the same courage and realism. Never before since Jamestown and Plymouth Rock has our American civilization been in such danger as now. For on 27 September 1940—this year—by an agreement signed in Berlin, three powerful nations, two in Europe and one in Asia, joined themselves together in the threat that if the United States of America interfered with or blocked the expansion program of these three nations—a program aimed at world control—they would unite in ultimate action against the United States.

The Nazi masters of Germany have made it clear that they intend not only to dominate all life and thought in their own country, but also to enslave the whole of Europe, and then to use the resources of Europe to dominate the rest of the world. It was only three weeks ago that their leader stated this: 'There are two worlds that stand opposed to each other.' And then in defiant reply to his opponents he said this: 'Others are correct when they say: "With this world we cannot ever reconcile ourselves." I can beat any other power in the world.' So said the leader of the Nazis.

In other words, the Axis not merely admits but the Axis proclaims that there can be no ultimate peace between their philosophy—their philosophy of government—and our philosophy of government. In view of the nature of this undeniable threat, it can be asserted, properly and categorically, that the United States has no right or reason to encourage talk of peace until the day shall come when there is a clear intention on the part of the aggressor nations to abandon all thought of dominating or conquering the world.

At this moment the forces of the States that are leagued against all peoples who live in freedom are being held away from our shores. The Germans and the Italians are being blocked on the other side of the Atlantic by the British and by the Greeks, and by thousands of soldiers and sailors who were able to escape from subjugated countries. In Asia the Japanese are being engaged by the Chinese nation in another great defence. In the

Pacific Ocean is our fleet.

Some of our people like to believe that wars in Europe and in Asia are of no concern to us. But it is a matter of most vital concern to us that European and Asiatic war-makers should not gain control of the oceans which lead to this hemisphere. One hundred and seventeen years ago the Monroe Doctrine was conceived by our government as a measure of defence in the face of a threat against this hemisphere by an alliance in Continental Europe. Thereafter, we stood guard in the Atlantic, with the British as neighbours. There was no treaty. There was no 'unwritten agreement.' And yet there was the feeling, proven correct by history, that we as neighbours could settle any disputes in peaceful fashion. And the fact is that during the whole of this time the Western Hemisphere has remained free from aggression from Europe or from Asia.

Does anyone seriously believe that we need to fear attack anywhere in the Americas while a free Britain remains our most powerful naval neighbour in the Atlantic? And does anyone seriously believe, on the other hand, that we could rest easy if the Axis powers were our neighbours there? If Great Britain goes down, the Axis powers will control the continents of Europe, Asia, Africa, Austral-Asia, and the high seas. And they will be in a position to bring enormous military and naval resources against this hemisphere. It is no exaggeration to say that all of us in all the Americas would be living at the point of a gun—a gun loaded with explosive bullets, economic as well as military. We should enter upon a new and terrible era in which the whole world, our hemisphere included, would be run by threats of brute force. And to survive in such a world, we would have to convert ourselves permanently into a militaristic power on the basis of war economy.

Some of us like to believe that even if Britain falls, we are still safe, because of the broad expanse of the Atlantic and of the Pacific. But the width of those oceans is not what it was in the days of clipper ships. At one point between Africa and Brazil the distance is less than it is from Washington to Denver, Colorado, five hours for the latest type of bomber. And at the north end of the Pacific Ocean, America and Asia almost touch each other. Why, even today we have planes that could fly from the British Isles to New England and back again without refueling. And remember that the range of the modern bomber is ever being increased.

During the past week many people in all parts of the nation have told me what they wanted me to say tonight. Almost all of them expressed a courageous desire to hear the plain truth about the gravity of the situation. One telegram, however, expressed the attitude of the small minority who want to see no evil and hear no evil, even though they know in their hearts that evil exists. That telegram begged me not to tell again of the ease with which our American cities could be bombed by any hostile power which had gained bases in this Western Hemisphere. The gist of that telegram was: 'Please, Mr President, don't frighten us by telling us the facts.' Frankly and definitely there is danger ahead—danger against which we must prepare. But we well know that we cannot escape danger, or the fear of danger, by crawling into bed and pulling the covers over our heads.

Some nations of Europe were bound by solemn non-intervention pacts with Germany. Other nations were assured by Germany that they need never fear invasion. Non-intervention pact or not, the fact remains that they were attacked, overrun, thrown into modern slavery at an hour's notice—or even without any notice at all. As an exiled leader of one of these nations said to me the other day, 'The notice was a minus quantity. It was given to my government two hours after German troops had poured into my country in a hundred places.' The fate of these nations tells us what it means to live at the point of a Nazi gun.

The Nazis have justified such actions by various pious frauds. One of these frauds is the claim that they are occupying a nation for the purpose of 'restoring order.' Another is that they are occupying or controlling a nation on the excuse that they are 'protecting it' against the aggression of somebody else. For example, Germany has said that she was occupying Belgium to save the Belgians from the British. Would she then hesitate to say to any South American country: 'We are occupying you to protect you from aggression by the United States'? Belgium today is being used as an invasion base against Britain, now fighting for its life. And any South American country, in Nazi hands, would always constitute a jumping off place for German attack on any one of the other republics of this hemisphere.

Analyze for yourselves the future of two other places even nearer to Germany if the Nazis won. Could Ireland hold out? Would Irish freedom be permitted as an amazing pet exception in an unfree world? Or the islands of the Azores, which still fly the flag of Portugal after five centuries? You and I think of Hawaii as an outpost of defence in the Pacific. And yet the Azores are closer to our shores in the Atlantic than Hawaii is on the other side.

There are those who say that the Axis powers would never have any desire to attack the Western Hemisphere. That is the same dangerous form of wishful thinking which has destroyed the powers of resistance of so many conquered peoples. The plain facts are that the Nazis have proclaimed, time and again, that all other races are their inferiors and therefore subject to their orders. And most important of all, the vast resources and wealth of this American hemisphere constitute the most tempting loot in all of the round world.

Let us no longer blind ourselves to the undeniable fact that the evil forces which have crushed and undermined and corrupted so many others are already within our own gates. Your government knows much about them and every day is ferreting them out. Their secret emissaries are active in our own and in neighbouring countries. They seek to stir up suspicion and dissension, to cause internal strife. They try to turn capital against labour, and vice versa. They try to reawaken long slumbering racial and religious enmities which should have no place in this country. They are active in every group that promotes intolerance. They exploit for their own ends our own natural abhorrence of war. These trouble-breeders have but one purpose. It is to divide our people, to divide them into hostile groups and to destroy our unity and shatter our will to defend ourselves.

There are also American citizens, many of them in high places, who, unwittingly in most cases, are aiding and abetting the work of these agents. I do not charge these American citizens with being foreign agents. But I do charge them with doing exactly the kind of work that the dictators want done in the United States. These people not only believe that we can save our own skins by shutting our eyes to the fate of other nations. Some of them go much further than that. They say that we can and should become the friends and even the partners of the Axis powers. Some of them even suggest that we should imitate the methods of the dictatorships. But Americans never can and never will do that.

The experience of the past two years has proven beyond doubt that no nation can appease the Nazis. No man can tame a tiger into a kitten by stroking it. There can be no appeasement with ruthlessness. There can be no reasoning with an incendiary bomb. We know now that a nation can have peace with the Nazis only at the price of total surrender. Even the people of Italy have been forced to become accomplices of the Nazis; but at this moment they do not know how soon they will be embraced to death by their allies.

The American appeasers ignore the warning to be found in the fate of Austria, Czechoslovakia, Poland, Norway, Belgium, the Netherlands, Denmark, and France. They tell you that the Axis powers are going to win anyway; that all of this bloodshed in the world could be saved, that the United States might just as well throw its influence into the scale of a dictated peace and get the best out of it that we can. They call it a 'negotiated peace.' Nonsense! Is it a negotiated peace if a gang of outlaws surrounds your community and on threat of extermination makes you pay tribute to save your own skins? For such a dictated peace would be no peace at all. It would be only another armistice, leading to the most gigantic armament race and the most devastating trade wars in all history. And in these contests the Americas would offer the only real resistance to the Axis power. With all their vaunted efficiency, with all their parade of pious purpose in this war, there are still in their background the concentration camp and the servants of God in chains.

The history of recent years proves that the shootings and the chains and the concentration camps are not simply the transient tools but the very altars of modern dictatorships. They may talk of a 'new order' in the world, but what they have in mind is only a revival of the oldest and the worst tyranny. In that there is no liberty, no religion, no hope. The proposed 'new order' is the very opposite of a United States of Europe or a United States of Asia. It is not a government based upon the consent of the governed. It is not a union of ordinary, self-respecting men and women to protect themselves and their freedom and their dignity from oppression. It is an unholy alliance of power and pelf to dominate and to enslave the human race.

The British people and their allies today are conducting an active war against this unholy alliance. Our own future security is greatly dependent on the outcome of that fight. Our ability to 'keep out of war' is going to be affected by that outcome. Thinking in terms of today and tomorrow, I make the direct statement to the American people that there is far less chance of the United States getting into war if we do all we can now to support the nations defending themselves against attack by the Axis than if we acquiesce in their defeat, submit tamely to an Axis victory, and wait our turn to be the object of attack in another war later on.

If we are to be completely honest with ourselves, we must admit that there is risk in any course we may take. But I deeply believe that the great majority of our people agree that the course that I advocate involves the least risk now and the greatest hope for world peace in the future.

The people of Europe who are defending themselves do not ask us to do their fighting. They ask us for the implements of war, the planes, the tanks, the guns, the freighters which will enable them to fight for their liberty and for our security. Emphatically, we must get these weapons to them, get them to them in sufficient volume and quickly enough so that we and our children will be saved the agony and suffering of war which others have had to endure.

Let not the defeatists tell us that it is too late. It will never be earlier. Tomorrow will be later than today.

Certain facts are self-evident. In a military sense Great Britain and the British Empire are today the spearhead of resistance to world conquest. And they are putting up a fight which will live forever in the story of human gallantry. There is no demand for sending an American expeditionary force outside our own borders. There is no intention by any member of your government to send such a force. You can therefore, nail, nail any talk about sending armies to Europe as deliberate untruth. Our national policy is not directed toward war. Its sole purpose is to keep war away from our country and away from our people.

Democracy's fight against world conquest is being greatly aided, and must be more greatly aided, by the rearmament of the United States and by sending every ounce and every ton of munitions and supplies that we can possibly spare to help the defenders who are in the front lines. And it is no more un-neutral for us to do that than it is for Sweden, Russia, and other nations near Germany to send steel and ore and oil and other war materials into Germany every day in the week.

We are planning our own defence with the utmost urgency, and in its vast scale we must integrate the war needs of Britain and the other free nations which are resisting aggression. This is not a matter of sentiment or of controversial personal opinion. It is a matter of realistic, practical military policy, based on the advice of our military experts who are in close touch with existing warfare. These military and naval experts and the members of the Congress and the Administration have a single-minded purpose: the defence of the United States.

This nation is making a great effort to produce everything that is necessary in this emergency, and with all possible speed. And this great effort requires great sacrifice. I would ask no one to defend a democracy which in turn would not defend everyone in the nation against want and privation. The strength of this nation shall not be diluted by the failure of the government to protect the economic well-being of its citizens. If our capacity to produce is limited by machines, it must ever be remembered that these machines are operated by the skill and the stamina of the workers.

As the government is determined to protect the rights of the workers, so the nation has a right to expect that the men who man the machines will discharge their full responsibilities to the urgent needs of defence. The worker possesses the same human dignity and is entitled to the same security of position as the engineer or the manager or the owner. For the workers provide the human power that turns out the destroyers, and the planes, and the tanks. The nation expects our defence industries to continue operation without interruption by strikes or lockouts. It expects and insists that management and workers will reconcile their differences by voluntary or legal means, to continue to produce the supplies that are so sorely needed. And on the economic side of our great defence program, we are, as you know, bending every effort to maintain stability of prices and with that the stability of the cost of living.

Nine days ago I announced the setting up of a more effective organization to direct our gigantic efforts to increase the production of munitions. The appropriation of vast sums of money and a well-coordinated executive direction of our defence efforts are not in themselves enough. Guns, planes, ships and many other things have to be built in the factories and the arsenals of America. They have to be produced by workers and managers and engineers with the aid of machines which in turn have to be built by hundreds of thousands of workers throughout the land. In this great work there has been splendid cooperation between the government and industry and labour. And I am very thankful.

American industrial genius, unmatched throughout all the world in the solution of production problems, has been called upon to bring its resources and its talents into action. Manufacturers of watches, of farm implements, of Linotypes and cash registers and automobiles, and sewing machines and lawn mowers and locomotives, are now making fuses and bomb packing crates and telescope mounts and shells and pistols and tanks.

But all of our present efforts are not enough. We must have more ships, more guns, more planes—more of everything. And this can be accomplished only if we discard the notion of 'business as usual.' This job cannot be done merely by superimposing on the existing productive facilities the added requirements of the nation for defence. Our defence efforts must not be blocked by those who fear the future consequences of surplus plant capacity. The possible consequences of failure of our defence efforts now are much more to be feared. And after the present needs of our defence are past, a proper handling of the country's peacetime needs will require all of the new productive capacity, if not still more. No pessimistic policy about the future of America shall delay the immediate expansion of those industries essential to defence. We need them.

I want to make it clear that it is the purpose of the nation to build now with all possible speed every machine, every arsenal, every factory that we need to manufacture our defence material. We have the men, the skill, the wealth, and above all, the will. I am confident that if and when production of consumer or luxury goods in certain industries requires the use of machines and raw materials that are essential for defence purposes, then such production must yield, and will gladly yield, to our primary and compelling purpose.

So I appeal to the owners of plants, to the managers, to the workers, to our own government employees to put every ounce of effort into producing these munitions swiftly and without stint. With this appeal I give you the pledge that all of us who are officers of your government will devote ourselves to the same wholehearted extent to the great task that lies ahead.

As planes and ships and guns and shells are produced, your government, with its defence experts, can then determine how best to use them to defend this hemisphere. The decision as to how much shall be sent abroad and how much shall remain at home must be made on the basis of our overall military necessities.

We must be the great arsenal of democracy.

For us this is an emergency as serious as war itself. We must apply ourselves to our task with the same resolution, the same sense of urgency, the same spirit of patriotism and sacrifice as we would show were we at war.

We have furnished the British great material support and we will furnish far more in the future. There will be no 'bottlenecks' in our determination to aid Great Britain. No dictator, no combination of dictators, will weaken that determination by threats of how they will construe that determination. The British have received invaluable military support from the heroic Greek Army and from the forces of all the governments in exile. Their strength is growing. It is the strength of men and women who value their freedom more highly than they value their lives.

I believe that the Axis powers are not going to win this war. I base that belief on the latest and best of information.

We have no excuse for defeatism. We have every good reason for hope— hope for peace, yes, and hope for the defence of our civilization and for the building of a better civilization in the future. I have the profound conviction that the American people are now determined to put forth a mightier effort than they have ever yet made to increase our production of all the implements of defence, to meet the threat to our democratic faith.

As President of the United States, I call for that national effort. I call for it in the name of this nation which we love and honour and which we are privileged and proud to serve. I call upon our people with absolute confidence that our common cause will greatly succeed.

40

FIRST INAUGURAL SPEECH

George Washington

17 April 1789. On this day, George Washington was sworn in as the first American president and delivered the first inaugural speech at Federal Hall in New York City. Elements of the ceremony set tradition; presidential inaugurations have deviated little in the two centuries since Washington's inauguration. In front of 10,000 spectators, Washington appeared in a plain brown broadcloth suit holding a ceremonial army sword. At 6' 3, Washington presented an impressive and solemn figure as he took the oath of office standing on the second balcony of Federal Hall. With Vice President John Adams standing beside him, Washington repeated the words prompted by Chancellor Robert R. Livingston, kissed the Bible and then went to the Senate chamber to deliver his inaugural address.

Fellow-Citizens of the Senate and of the House of Representatives:

Among the vicissitudes incident to life no event could have filled me with greater anxieties than that of which the notification was transmitted by your order, and received on the 14th day of the present month. On the one hand, I was summoned by my Country, whose voice I can never hear but with veneration and love, from a retreat which I had chosen with the fondest predilection, and, in my flattering hopes, with an immutable decision, as the asylum of my declining years—a retreat which was rendered every day more necessary as well as more dear to me by the addition of habit to inclination, and of frequent interruptions in my health to the gradual waste committed on it by time. On the other hand, the magnitude and difficulty of the trust to which the voice of my country called me, being sufficient to awaken in the wisest and most experienced of her citizens a distrustful scrutiny into his qualifications, could not but overwhelm with despondence one who (inheriting inferior endowments from nature and unpracticed in the duties of civil administration) ought to be peculiarly conscious of his own deficiencies. In this conflict of emotions, all I dare aver is that it has been my faithful study to collect my duty from a just appreciation of every circumstance by which it might be affected. All I dare hope is that if, in executing this task, I have been too much swayed by a grateful remembrance of former instances, or by an affectionate sensibility to this transcendent proof of the confidence of my fellow-citizens, and have thence too little consulted my incapacity as well as disinclination for the weighty and untried cares before me, my error will be palliated by the motives which mislead me, and its consequences be judged by my country with some share of the partiality in which they originated.

Such being the impressions under which I have, in obedience to the public summons, repaired to the present station, it would be peculiarly improper to omit in this first official act my fervent supplications to that Almighty Being who rules over the universe, who presides in the councils of nations, and whose providential aids can supply every human defect, that His benediction may consecrate to the liberties and happiness of the people of the United States a Government instituted by themselves for these essential purposes, and may enable every instrument employed in its administration to execute with success the functions allotted to his charge. In tendering this homage to the Great Author of every public and private good, I assure myself that it expresses your sentiments not less than my own, nor those of my fellow-citizens at large less than either. No people can be bound to acknowledge and adore the Invisible Hand which conducts the affairs of men more than those of the United States. Every step by which they have advanced to the character of an independent nation seems to have been distinguished by some token of providential agency; and in the important revolution just accomplished in the system of their united government the tranquil deliberations and voluntary consent of so many distinct communities from which the event has resulted can not be compared with the means by which most governments have been established without some return of pious gratitude, along with a humble anticipation of the future blessings which the past seem to presage. These reflections, arising out of the present crisis, have forced themselves too strongly on my mind to be suppressed. You will join with me, I trust, in thinking that there are none under the influence of which the proceedings of a new and free government can more auspiciously commence.

By the article establishing the executive department it is made the duty of the President 'to recommend to your consideration such measures as he shall judge necessary and expedient.' The circumstances under which I now meet you will acquit me from entering into that subject further than to refer to the great constitutional charter under which you are assembled, and which, in defining your powers, designates the objects to which your attention is to be given. It will be more consistent with those circumstances, and far more congenial with the feelings which actuate me, to substitute, in place of a recommendation of particular measures, the tribute that is due to the talents, the rectitude, and the patriotism which adorn the characters selected to devise and adopt them. In these honourable qualifications I behold the surest pledges that as on one side no local prejudices or attachments, no separate views nor party animosities, will misdirect the comprehensive and equal eye which ought to watch over this great assemblage of communities and interests, so, on another, that the foundation of our national policy will be laid in the pure and immutable principles of private morality, and the pre-eminence of free government be exemplified by all the attributes which can win the affections of its citizens and command the respect of the world. I dwell on this prospect with every satisfaction which an ardent love for my country can inspire, since there is no truth more thoroughly established than that there exists in the economy and course of nature an indissoluble union between virtue and happiness; between duty and advantage; between the genuine maxims of an honest and magnanimous policy and the solid rewards of public prosperity and felicity; since we ought to be no less persuaded that the propitious smiles of heaven can never be expected on a nation that disregards the eternal rules of order and right which heaven itself has ordained; and since the preservation of the sacred fire of liberty and the destiny of the republican model of government are justly considered, perhaps, as deeply, as finally, staked on the experiment entrusted to the hands of the American people.

Besides the ordinary objects submitted to your care, it will remain with your judgment to decide how far an exercise of the occasional power delegated by the fifth article of the Constitution is rendered expedient at the present juncture by the nature of objections which have been urged against the system, or by the degree of inquietude which has given birth to them. Instead of undertaking particular recommendations on this subject, in which I could be guided by no lights derived from official opportunities, I shall again give way to my entire confidence in your discernment and pursuit of the public good; for I assure myself that whilst you carefully avoid every alteration which might endanger the benefits of an united and effective government, or which ought to await the future lessons of experience, a reverence for the characteristic rights of freemen and a regard for the public harmony will sufficiently influence your deliberations on the question how far the former can be impregnably fortified or the latter be safely and advantageously promoted. To the foregoing observations I have one to add, which will be most properly addressed to the House of Representatives. It concerns myself, and will therefore be as brief as possible. When I was first honoured with a call into the service of my country, then on the eve of an arduous struggle for its liberties, the light in which I contemplated my duty required that I should renounce every pecuniary compensation. From this resolution I have in no instance departed; and being still under the impressions which produced it, I must decline as inapplicable to myself any share in the personal emoluments which may be indispensably included in a permanent provision for the executive department, and must accordingly pray that the pecuniary estimates for the station in which I am placed may during my continuance in it be limited to such actual expenditures as the public good may be thought to require.

Having thus imparted to you my sentiments as they have been awakened by the occasion which brings us together, I shall take my present leave; but not without resorting once more to the benign Parent of the Human Race in humble supplication that, since He has been pleased to favour the American people with opportunities for deliberating in perfect tranquillity, and dispositions for deciding with unparalleled unanimity on a form of government for the security of their union and the advancement of their happiness, so His divine blessing may be equally conspicuous in the enlarged views, the temperate consultations, and the wise measures on which the success of this Government must depend.

41

GANDHI, HIS GURU

Sardar Vallabhbhai Patel

Sardar Vallabhbhai Patel's speeches were always brief and to the point. He was a man of action and seldom indulged in verbosity. This speech was delivered at Ahmedabad on 9 July 1928 after being presented with an address by the citizens, is typical of his style. He accepts Gandhi as his 'guru' unreservedly. He is full of humility unlike some of the other followers of Gandhi. He does not even take credit for the success of the Bardoli Satyagraha which had made him 'Sardar'. Patel remained a follower of Gandhi and was a source of great strength to him during their long association.

The citizens of Ahmedabad in giving me this address have described me as the chief disciple of Gandhiji. I only wish that I deserved this description; I know, however, that I am not worthy of it. I do not know how often I shall have to be reborn in order to achieve that distinction. Truly, you have been so carried away by your affection for me, and have used such exaggerated expressions about me that I can scarcely accept them. You have all heard of the Bhil disciple of Dronacharya in the Mahabharta. He never had the good fortune of learning directly under Dronacharya, but he used to worship an earthen figure of his guru. It was through his devotion that he acquired all that Dronacharya had to teach. Indeed, he learnt more than what Dronacharya's other disciples ever learnt. How is that to be explained? It is quite simple. He worshipped his guru with a pure heart, devotedly and with complete faith. He had thus the basic qualities which are necessary. In my case, I have access to the guru whose disciple you say I am. So far from being his chief disciple, I doubt if I am fit even to rank among one of his many disciples. If I had that fitness, I would have accomplished today what you hope I shall accomplish in the future. I am confident that there exist today in India many disciples of his who have never seen him but who have completely mastered his teachings. People often say, what will happen when Gandhiji has gone? I have no fear on that account. He would have accomplished by then whatever he sought to accomplish. What remains will be for you and for me to achieve. Only if we do so, he will have no regrets. He has given us whatever he had to give, and it is now up to us to do our duty.

I do not deserve the honour which you are bestowing on me because of Bardoli. The condition of the peasants in India is akin to that of a bed-ridden patient suffering from an incurable disease, waiting only, as it were, to depart from this world and then suddenly getting restored to life by taking some miracle medicine given to him by a sanyasi. I am merely the instrument through whose hands the sanyasi administered the medicine to the patient. If anyone deserves honour, it is the giver of that medicine. Some honour is also due to the patient who carried out the strict injunctions of the sanyasi, for without the self-control that he exercised, the medicine could not have achieved its effect. If anyone else deserves to be honoured, it is my colleagues who showed astonishing discipline, and who had complete confidence in me. It was not I who trained such colleagues. If we have such men of whom the whole of Gujarat is so justly proud, the credit again goes only to Gandhiji.

42

1918 STATEMENT TO THE COURT

Eugene Victor Debs

Eugene Victor 'Gene' Debs (5 November 1855–20 October 1926) was an American union leader, one of the founding members of the Industrial Workers of the World (IWW or the Wobblies), and the candidate of the Socialist Party of America for President of the United States five times. Through his presidential candidacies, as well as his work with labour movements, Debs eventually became one of the best-known Socialists living in the United States. Debs was noted for his oratory skills, and his speech denouncing American participation in World War I led to his second arrest in 1918. He was convicted under the Sedition Act of 1918 and sentenced to a term of ten years. President Warren G. Harding commuted his sentence in December 1921. Debs died in 1926, not long after being admitted to a sanatorium, due to cardiovascular problems that developed during his time in prison. He has since been cited as the inspiration for numerous politicians.

Your Honour:

Years ago I recognized my kinship with all living beings, and I made up my mind that I was not one bit better than the meanest on earth. I said then, and I say now, that while there is a lower class, I am in it; and while there is a criminal element, I am of it; and while there is a soul in prison, I am not free.

If the law under which I have been convicted is a good law, then there is no reason why sentence should not be pronounced upon me. I listened to all that was said in this court in support and justification of this prosecution, but my mind remains unchanged. I look upon the Espionage Law as a despotic enactment in flagrant conflict with democratic principles and with the spirit of free institutions.

Your Honour, I have stated in this court that I am opposed to form of our present government; that I am opposed to the social system in which we live; that I believed in the change of both—but by perfectly peaceable and orderly means.

Let me call your attention to the fact this morning that in this system 5 per cent of our people own and control two-thirds of our wealth; 65 per cent of the people, embracing the working class who produce all wealth, have but 5 per cent to show for it.

Standing here this morning, I recall my boyhood. At fourteen I went to work in a railroad shop; at sixteen I was firing a freight engine on a railroad. I remember all the hardships and privations of that earlier day, and from that time until now my heart has been with the working class. I could have been in congress long ago. I have preferred to go to prison. The choice has been deliberately made. I could not have done otherwise. I have no regret.

In the struggle, the unceasing struggle, between the toilers and producers and their exploiters, I have tried, as best I might, to serve those among whom I was born, with whom I expect to share my lot until the end of my days.

I am thinking this morning of the men in the mills and factories; I am thinking of the men in the mines and on the railroads; I am thinking of the women who, for a paltry wage, are compelled to work out their lives; of the little children, who in this system, are robbed of their childhood, and in their early, tender years are seized in the remorseless grasp of Mammon, and forced into the industrial dungeons, there to feed the machines while they themselves are being starved body and soul. I see them dwarfed, diseased, stunted, their little lives broken, and their hopes blasted, because in this high noon of our twentieth-century civilization money is still so much more important than human life. Gold is God and rules in the affairs of men.

The little girls, and there are a million of them in this country, this, the most favoured land beneath the bending skies, a land in which we have vast areas of rich and fertile soil, material resources in inexhaustible abundance, the most marvellous productive machinery on earth, millions of eager workers ready to apply their labour to that machinery to produce in abundance for every man, woman, and child—and if there are still vast numbers of our people who are the victims of poverty and whose lives are an unceasing struggle all the way from youth to old age, until at last death comes to their rescue and stills the aching heart, it is not the fault of the Almighty, it cannot be charged to nature, but it is due entirely to the outgrown social system that ought to be abolished, not only in the interest of the working class, but in a higher interest of all humanity.

I think of these little children, the girls that are in the textile mills of all description in the east and in the cotton factories of the south, I think of them at work in a vitiated atmosphere; I think of them at work when they ought to be at play or at school; I think that when they do grow up, if they live long enough to approach the marriage state, they are unfit for it. Their nerves are worn out, their tissue is exhausted, their vitality is spent. They have been fed to industry. Their lives have been coined into gold. Their offspring are born tired. That is why there are so many failures in our modern life.

Your Honour, the 5 per cent of the people that I have made reference to constitute that element that absolutely rules our country. They privately own all our public necessities. They wear no crowns; they wield no sceptres, they sit upon no thrones; and yet they are our economic masters and our political rulers. They control this government and all of its institutions. They control the courts.

And Your Honour, if you will permit me, I wish to make just one correction. It was stated here that I had charged that all federal judges are crooks. The charge is absolutely untrue. I did say that all federal judges are appointed through the influence and power of the capitalist class and not the working class. If that statement is not true, I am more than willing to retract it.

The 5 per cent of our people who own and control all of the sources of wealth, all of the nation's industries, all of the means of our common life, it is they who declare war. It is they who make peace. It is they who control our destiny. And so long as this is true, we can make no just claim to being a democratic government, a self-governing people.

I believe, Your Honour, in common with all Socialists, that this nation ought to own and control its own industries. I believe, as all Socialists do, that all things that are jointly needed and used ought to be jointly owned— that industry, the basis of life, instead of being the private property of the few and operated for their enrichment, ought to be the common property of all, democratically administered in the interest of all.

John D. Rockefeller has today an income of 60 million dollars a year, five million dollars a month, two hundred thousand dollars a day. He does not produce a penny of it. I make no attack upon Mr Rockefeller personally. I do not in the least dislike him. If he were in need, and it were in my power to serve him, I should serve him as gladly as I would any other human being. I have no quarrel with Mr Rockefeller personally, nor with any other capitalist. I am simply opposing a social order in which it is possible for one man who does absolutely nothing that is useful to amass a fortune of hundreds of millions of dollars, while millions of men and women who work all of the days of their lives secure barely enough for existence.

This order of things cannot always endure. I have registered my protest against it. I recognize the feebleness of my effort, but, fortunately, I am not alone. There are multiplied thousands of others who, like myself, have come to realize that before we may truly enjoy the blessings of civilized life, we must reorganize society upon a mutual and cooperative basis; and to this end we have organized a great economic and political movement that spreads over the face of all the earth.

There are today upwards of sixty millions of Socialists, loyal, devoted adherents to this cause, regardless of nationality, race, creed, colour or sex. They are all making common cause. They are spreading the propaganda of the new social order. They are waiting, watching, and working through all the hours of the day and night. They are still in the minority. But they have learned how to be patient and to bide their time. They feel—they know, indeed—that the time is coming, in spite of all opposition, all persecution, when this emancipating gospel will spread among all the peoples, and when this minority will become the triumphant majority and, sweeping into power, inaugurate the greatest social and economic change in history.

In that day we shall have the universal commonwealth—not the destruction of the nation, but, on the contrary, the harmonious cooperation of every nation with every other nation on earth. In that day, war will curse this earth no more.

I have been accused, Your Honour, of being an enemy of the soldier. I hope I am laying no flattering unction to my soul when I say that I don't believe the soldier has a more sympathetic friend than I am. If I had my way, there would be no soldiers. But I realize the sacrifice they are making, Your Honour. I can think of them. I can feel for them. I can sympathize with them. That is one of the reasons why I have been doing what little has been in my power to bring about a condition of affairs in this country worthy of the sacrifices they have made and that they are now making in its behalf.

Your Honour, in a local paper yesterday there was some editorial exultation about my prospective imprisonment. I do not resent it in the least. I can understand it perfectly. In the same paper there appears an editorial this morning that has in it a hint of the wrong to which I have been trying to call attention. [He reads:]

'A Senator of the United States receives a salary of $7,500 to $45,000 for the six years for which he is elected. One of the candidates for Senator from a state adjoining Ohio is reported to have spent through his committee $150,000 to secure the nomination. For advertising he spent $35,000; for printing $30,000; for traveling expenses $10,000, and the rest in ways known to political managers.'

The theory is that public office is as open to a poor man as to a rich man. One may easily imagine, however, how slight a chance one of ordinary resources would have in a contest against this man who was willing to spend more than three times his six years' salary merely to secure a nomination. Were these conditions to hold in every state, the Senate would soon become again what it was once held to be, a rich men's club.

Campaign expenditures have been the subject of much restrictive legislation in recent years, but it has not always reached the mark. The authors of primary reform have accomplished some of the things they set out to do, but they have not yet taken the bankroll out of politics.

They never will take it out of politics, they never can take it out of politics, in this system.

Your Honour, I wish to make acknowledgment of my thanks to the counsel for the defence. They have not only defended me with exceptional legal ability, but with a personal attachment and devotion of which I am deeply sensible, and which I can never forget.

Your Honour, I ask no mercy. I plead for no immunity. I realize that finally the right must prevail. I never so clearly comprehended as now the great struggle between the powers of greed on the one hand and upon the other the rising hosts of freedom.

I can see the dawn of a better day for humanity. The people are awakening. In due course, they will come to their own.

When the mariner, sailing over tropic seas, looks for relief from his weary watch, he turns his eyes toward the southern cross, burning luridly above the tempest-vexed ocean. As the midnight approaches, the southern cross begins to bend, and the whirling worlds change their places, and with starry finger-points the Almighty marks the passage of time upon the dial of the universe, and though no bell may beat the glad tidings, the lookout knows that the midnight is passing and that relief and rest are close at hand.

Let the people everywhere take heart and hope everywhere, for the cross is bending, the midnight is passing, and joy cometh with the morning.

Your Honour, I thank you, and I thank all of this Court for their courtesy, for their kindness, which I shall remember always. I am prepared to receive your sentence.

43

FIRST FIRESIDE CHAT

Franklin D. Roosevelt

Franklin D. Roosevelt's First Fireside Chat was given on Sunday, 12 March 1933

I want to talk for a few minutes with the people of the United States about banking—with the comparatively few who understand the mechanics of banking but more particularly with the overwhelming majority who use banks for the making of deposits and the drawing of checks. I want to tell you what has been done in the last few days, why it was done, and what the next steps are going to be. I recognize that the many proclamations from State capitols and from Washington, the legislation, the Treasury regulations, etc., couched for the most part in banking and legal terms, should be explained for the benefit of the average citizen. I owe this in particular because of the fortitude and good temper with which everybody has accepted the inconvenience and hardships of the banking holiday. I know that when you understand what we in Washington have been about I shall continue to have your cooperation as fully as I have had your sympathy and help during the past week.

First of all, let me state the simple fact that when you deposit money in a bank, the bank does not put the money into a safe deposit vault. It invests your money in many different forms of credit—bonds, commercial paper, mortgages and many other kinds of loans. In other words, the bank puts your money to work to keep the wheels of industry and of agriculture turning around. A comparatively small part of the money you put into the bank is kept in currency—an amount which in normal times is wholly sufficient to cover the cash needs of the average citizen. In other words, the total amount of all the currency in the country is only a small fraction of the total deposits in all of the banks.

What, then, happened during the last few days of February and the first few days of March? Because of undermined confidence on the part of the public, there was a general rush by a large portion of our population to turn bank deposits into currency or gold—a rush so great that the soundest banks could not get enough currency to meet the demand. The reason for this was that on the spur of the moment it was, of course, impossible to sell perfectly sound assets of a bank and convert them into cash except at panic prices far below their real value.

By the afternoon of March 3rd scarcely a bank in the country was open to do business. Proclamations temporarily closing them in whole or in part had been issued by the Governors in almost all the States.

It was then that I issued the proclamation providing for the nationwide bank holiday, and this was the first step in the Government's reconstruction of our financial and economic fabric.

The second step was the legislation promptly and patriotically passed by the Congress confirming my proclamation and broadening my powers so that it became possible in view of the requirement of time to extend the holiday and lift the ban of that holiday gradually. This law also gave authority to develop a program of rehabilitation of our banking facilities. I want to tell our citizens in every part of the Nation that the national Congress—Republicans and Democrats alike—showed by this action a devotion to public welfare and a realization of the emergency and the necessity for speed that is difficult to match in our history.

The third stage has been the series of regulations permitting the banks to continue their functions to take care of the distribution of food and household necessities and the payment of payrolls.

This bank holiday, while resulting in many cases in great inconvenience, is affording us the opportunity to supply the currency necessary to meet the situation. No sound bank is a dollar worse off than it was when it closed its doors last Monday. Neither is any bank which may turn out not to be in a position for immediate opening. The new law allows the twelve Federal Reserve Banks to issue additional currency on good assets and thus the banks which reopen will be able to meet every legitimate call. The new currency is being sent out by the Bureau of Engraving and Printing in large volume to every part of the country. It is sound currency because it is backed by actual, good assets.

A question you will ask is this: why are all the banks not to be reopened at the same time? The answer is simple. Your Government does not intend that the history of the past few years shall be repeated. We do not want and will not have another epidemic of bank failures.

As a result, we start tomorrow, Monday, with the opening of banks in the twelve Federal Reserve Bank cities—those banks which on first examination by the Treasury have already been found to be all right. This will be followed on Tuesday by the resumption of all their functions by banks already found to be sound in cities where there are recognized clearing houses. That means about 250 cities of the United States.

On Wednesday and succeeding days banks in smaller places all through the country will resume business, subject, of course, to the Government's physical ability to complete its survey. It is necessary that the reopening of banks be extended over a period in order to permit the banks to make applications for necessary loans, to obtain currency needed to meet their requirements and to enable the Government to make common sense checkups.

Let me make it clear to you that if your bank does not open the first day you are by no means justified in believing that it will not open. A bank that opens on one of the subsequent days is in exactly the same status as the bank that opens tomorrow. I know that many people are worrying about State banks not members of the Federal Reserve System. These banks can and will receive assistance from member banks and from the Reconstruction Finance Corporation. These State banks are following the same course as the National banks except that they get their licenses to resume business from the State authorities, and these authorities have been asked by the

Secretary of the Treasury to permit their good banks to open up on the same schedule as the national banks. I am confident that the State Banking Departments will be as careful as the national Government in the policy relating to the opening of banks and will follow the same broad policy.

It is possible that when the banks resume a very few people who have not recovered from their fear may again begin withdrawals. Let me make it clear that the banks will take care of all needs—and it is my belief that hoarding during the past week has become an exceedingly unfashionable pastime. It needs no prophet to tell you that when the people find that they can get their money—that they can get it when they want it for all legitimate purposes—the phantom of fear will soon be laid. People will again be glad to have their money where it will be safely taken care of and where they can use it conveniently at any time. I can assure you that it is safer to keep your money in a reopened bank than under the mattress.

The success of our whole great national program depends, of course, upon the cooperation of the public—on its intelligent support and use of a reliable system.

Remember that the essential accomplishment of the new legislation is that it makes it possible for banks more readily to convert their assets into cash than was the case before. More liberal provision has been made for banks to borrow on these assets at the Reserve Banks and more liberal provision has also been made for issuing currency on the security of these good assets. This currency is not fiat currency. It is issued only on adequate security, and every good bank has an abundance of such security.

One more point before I close. There will be, of course, some banks unable to reopen without being reorganized. The new law allows the Government to assist in making these reorganizations quickly and effectively and even allows the Government to subscribe to at least a part of new capital which may be required. I hope you can see from this elemental recital of what your Government is doing that there is nothing complex, or radical, in the process.

We had a bad banking situation. Some of our bankers had shown themselves either incompetent or dishonest in their handling of the peoples' funds. They had used the money entrusted to them in speculations and unwise loans. This was, of course, not true in the vast majority of our banks, but it was true in enough of them to shock the people for a time into a sense of insecurity and to put them into a frame of mind where they did not differentiate, but seemed to assume that the acts of a comparative few had tainted them all. It was the Government's job to straighten out this situation and do it as quickly as possible. And the job is being performed.

I do not promise you that every bank will be reopened or that individual losses will not be suffered, but there will be no losses that possibly could be avoided; and there would have been more and greater losses had we continued to drift. I can even promise you salvation for some at least of the sorely pressed banks. We shall be engaged not merely in reopening sound banks but in the creation of sound banks through reorganization.

It has been wonderful to me to catch the note of confidence from all over the country. I can never be sufficiently grateful to the people for the loyal support they have given me in their acceptance of the judgment that has dictated our course, even though all our processes may not have seemed clear to them.

After all, there is an element in the readjustment of our financial system more important than currency, more important than gold, and that is the confidence of the people. Confidence and courage are the essentials of success in carrying out our plan. You people must have faith; you must not be stampeded by rumours or guesses. Let us unite in banishing fear. We have provided the machinery to restore our financial system; it is up to you to support and make it work. It is your problem no less than it is mine. Together we cannot fail.

44

DANDI MARCH

Mohandas Karamchand Gandhi

On the 11 March 1930, the crowd swelled to 10,000 at the evening prayer held on the Sabarmati sands at Ahmedabad. At the end, Gandhi delivered a memorable speech on the eve of his historic march. In the speech, Gandhi advises his followers what to do if he and his companions were arrested.

In all probability this will be my last speech to you. Even if the Government allow me to march tomorrow morning, this will be my last speech on the sacred bank of the Sabarmati. Possibly these may be the last words of my life here.

I have already told you yesterday what I had to say. Today I shall confine myself to what you should do after I and my companions are arrested. The programme of the march to Jalalpur must be fulfilled as originally settled. The enlistment of volunteers for this purpose should be confined to Gujarat. From what I have seen and heard during the last fortnight I am inclined to believe that the stream of civil resisters will flow unbroken.

But let there be not a semblance of breach of peace even after all of us have been arrested. We have resolved to utilize all our resources in the pursuit of an exclusively non-violent struggle. Let riot one commit a wrong in anger. This is my hope and prayer. I wish these words of mine reached every nook and corner of the land. My task shall be done if I perish and so do my comrades. It will then be for the Working Committee of the Congress to show you the way and it will be up to you to follow its leads. That is the only meaning of the Working Committee's resolution. The reins of the movement will still remain in the hands of those of my associates who believe in non-violence as an article of faith. Of course, the Congress will be free to chalk out what course of action commands itself to it. So long as I have not reached Jalalpur, let nothing be done in contravention to the authority vested in me by the Congress. But once I am arrested, the whole general responsibility shifts to the Congress. No one who believes in non-violence, as a creed, need therefore sit still. My compact with the Congress ends as soon as I am arrested. In that case, there should be no slackness in the enrolment of volunteers. Wherever possible, civil disobedience of salt laws should be started. These laws can be violated in three ways. It is an offence to manufacture salt wherever there are facilities for doing so. The possession and sale of contraband salt (which includes natural salt or earth salt) is also an offence. The purchasers of such salt will be equally guilty. To carry away the natural salt depots on the seashore is likewise a violation of law. So is the hawking of such salt. In short, you may choose anyone or all of these devices to break the salt monopoly.

We are however, not to be content with this alone. Wherever there are Congress Committees there is no ban by the Congress and wherever the local workers have self-confidence, other suitable means may be adopted. I prescribe only one condition, viz let our pledge of truth and non-violence as the only means for the attainment of swaraj be faithfully kept. For the rest, everyone has a free hand. But that does not give a licence to all and sundry to carry on their individual responsibility. Where there are no leaders and only a handful of men, have faith in the program, they may do what they can, if they have enough self-confidence. They have a right, nay it is their duty to do so. The history of the world is full of instances of men who rose to leadership by sheer force of self-confidence, bravery and tenacity. We too, if we aspire to swaraj and are impatient to attain it, should have similar self-confidence. Our ranks will swell and our hearts strengthen as the number of our arrests by Government increases.

Let nobody assume that after I am arrested there will be no one left to guide them. It is not I but Pandit Jawaharlal who is your guide. He has the capacity to lead. Though the fact is that those who have learnt the lesson of fearlessness and self-effacement need no leader, but if we lack these virtues, not even Jawaharlal will be able to produce them in us.

Much can be done in other ways besides these. Liquor and foreign cloth shops can be picketed. We can refuse to pay taxes if we have the requisite strength. The lawyers can give up practice. The public can boycott the courts by refraining from litigation. Government servants can resign their posts. This is the easiest solution of the problem of freedom. Let all who are cooperating with the Government in one way or another, be it by paying taxes, keeping titles, or sending children to official schools, etc., withdraw their cooperation in all or as many ways as possible. One can devise other methods, too, of non-cooperation with the Government. And then there are women who can stand shoulder to shoulder with men in this struggle.

You may take it as my will. It was the only message that I desired to impart to you before starting on the march or for the jail. I wish there to be no suspension or abandonment of the war that commences tomorrow morning or earlier if I am arrested before that time. I shall eagerly await the news that ten batches are ready as soon as my batch is arrested. I believe there are men in India to complete the work begun by me today. I have faith in the righteousness of our cause and the purity of our weapons. And where the means are clean, there God is undoubtedly present with His blessings. And where these three combine, there defeat is an impossibility. A satyagrahi, whether free or incarcerated, is ever victorious. He is vanquished only when he forsakes truth and non-violence and turns a deaf ear to the inner voice. If, therefore, there is such a thing as defeat for even a satyagrahi, he alone is the cause of it. God bless you all and keep off all obstacles from the path in the struggle that begins tomorrow. Let this be our prayer.

45

AMERICAN UNIVERSITY
COMMENCEMENT ADDRESS

John F. Kennedy

The American University speech, titled 'A Strategy of Peace' was a commencement address delivered by President John F. Kennedy at the American University in Washington, D.C., on Monday, 10 June 1963. Delivered at the height of his rhetorical powers and widely considered one of his most powerful speeches, Kennedy not only outlined a plan to curb nuclear arms, but also 'laid out a hopeful, yet realistic route for world peace at a time when the US and Soviet Union faced the potential for an escalating nuclear arms race.' In the speech, Kennedy announced his agreement to negotiations 'toward early agreement on a comprehensive test ban treaty' (which resulted in the Nuclear Test-Ban Treaty) and also announced, for the purpose of showing 'good faith and solemn convictions', his decision to unilaterally suspend all US atmospheric testing of nuclear weapons as long as all other nations would do the same.

President Anderson, members of the faculty, Board of Trustees, distinguished guests, my old colleague, Senator Bob Byrd, who has earned his degree through many years of attending night law school, while I am earning mine in the next thirty minutes, ladies and gentlemen:

It is with great pride that I participate in this ceremony of the American University, sponsored by the Methodist Church, founded by Bishop John Fletcher Hurst, and first opened by President Woodrow Wilson in 1914. This is a young and growing university, but it has already fulfilled Bishop Hurst's enlightened hope for the study of history and public affairs in a city devoted to the making of history and to the conduct of the public's business. By sponsoring this institution of higher learning for all who wish to learn whatever their colour or their creed, the Methodists of this area and the nation deserve the nation's thanks, and I commend all those who are today graduating.

Professor Woodrow Wilson once said that every man sent out from a university should be a man of his nation as well as a man of his time, and I am confident that the men and women who carry the honour of graduating from this institution will continue to give from their lives, from their talents, a high measure of public service and public support.

'There are few earthly things more beautiful than a University,' wrote John Masefield, in his tribute to the English Universities—and his words are equally true here. He did not refer to spires and towers, to campus greens and ivied walls. He admired the splendid beauty of the University, he said, because it was 'a place where those who hate ignorance may strive to know, where those who perceive truth may strive to make others see.'

I have, therefore, chose this time and this place to discuss a topic on which ignorance too often abounds and the truth is to rarely perceived—yet it is the most important topic on earth: world peace.

What kind of peace do I mean? What kind of peace do we seek? Not a Pax Americana enforced on the world by American weapons of war. Not the peace of the grave or the security of the slave. I am talking about genuine peace—the kind of peace that makes life on earth worth living—the kind that enables man and nations to grow and to hope and to build a better life for their children—not merely peace for Americans but peace for all men and women—not merely peace in our time but peace for all time.

I speak of peace because of the new face of war. Total war makes no sense in an age when great powers can maintain large and relatively invulnerable nuclear forces and refuse to surrender without resort to those forces. It makes no sense in an age when a single nuclear weapon contains almost ten times the explosive force delivered by all of the Allied air forces in the Second World War. It makes no sense in an age when the deadly poisons produced by a nuclear exchange would be carried by the wind and water and soil and seed to the far corners of the globe and to generations unborn.

Today the expenditure of billions of dollars every year on weapons acquired for the purpose of making sure we never need to use them is essential to keeping the peace. But surely the acquisition of such idle stockpiles—which can only destroy and never create—is not the only, much less the most efficient, means of assuring peace.

I speak of peace, therefore, as the necessary rational end of rational men. I realize that the pursuit of peace is not as dramatic as the pursuit of war—and frequently the words of the pursuer fall on deaf ears. But we have no more urgent task.

Some say that it is useless to speak of world peace or world law or world disarmament—and that it will be useless until the leaders of the Soviet Union adopt a more enlightened attitude. I hope they do. I believe we can help them do it. But I also believe that we must re-examine our own attitude—as individuals and as a nation—for our attitude is as essential as theirs. And every graduate of this school, every thoughtful citizen who despairs of war and wishes to bring peace, should begin by looking inward—by examining his own attitude toward the possibilities of peace, toward the Soviet Union, toward the course of the Cold War and toward freedom and peace here at home.

First: Let us examine our attitude toward peace itself. Too many of us think it is impossible. Too many of us think it is unreal. But that is dangerous, defeatist belief. It leads to the conclusion that war is inevitable—that mankind is doomed—that we are gripped by forces we cannot control.

We need not accept that view. Our problems are man-made—therefore, they can be solved by man. And man can be as big as he wants. No problem of human destiny is beyond human beings. Man's reason and spirit have often solved the seemingly unsolvable—and we believe they can do it again.

I am not referring to the absolute, infinite concept of universal peace and goodwill of which some fantasies and fanatics dream. I do not deny the values of hopes and dreams but we merely invite discouragement and incredulity by making that our only and immediate goal.

Let us focus instead on a more practical, more attainable peace—based not on a sudden revolution in human nature but on a gradual evolution in human institutions—on a series of concrete actions and effective agreements which are in the interest of all concerned. There is no single, simple key to this peace—no grand or magic formula to be adopted by one or two powers. Genuine peace must be the product of many nations, the sum of many acts. It must be dynamic, not static, changing to meet the challenge of each new generation. For peace is a process—a way of solving problems.

With such a peace, there will still be quarrels and conflicting interests, as there are within families and nations. World peace, like community peace, does not require that each man love his neighbour—it requires only that they live together in mutual tolerance, submitting their disputes to a just and peaceful settlement. And history teaches us that enmities between nations, as between individuals, do not last forever. However fixed our likes and dislikes may seem the tide of time and events will often bring surprising changes in the relations between nations and neighbours.

So let us persevere. Peace need not be impracticable—and war need not be inevitable. By defining our goal more clearly—by making it seem more manageable and less remote—we can help all peoples to see it, to draw hope from it, and to move irresistibly toward it.

Second: Let us re-examine our attitude toward the Soviet Union. It is discouraging to think that their leaders may actually believe what their propagandists write. It is discouraging to read a recent authoritative Soviet text on Military Strategy and find, on page after page, wholly baseless and incredible claims—such as the allegation that 'American imperialist circles are preparing to unleash different types of wars…that there is a very real threat of a preventive war being unleashed by American imperialists against the Soviet Union…(and that) the political aims of the American imperialists are to enslave economically and politically the European and other capitalist countries…(and) to achieve world domination.'

Truly, as it was written long ago: 'The wicked flee when no man pursueth.' Yet it is sad to read these Soviet statements—to realize the extent of the gulf between us. But it is also a warning—a warning to the American people not to fall into the same trap as the Soviets, not to see only a distorted and desperate view of the other side, not to see conflict as inevitable, accommodations as impossible and communication as nothing more than an exchange of threats.

No government or social system is so evil that its people must be considered as lacking in virtue. As Americans, we find communism profoundly repugnant as a negation of personal freedom and dignity. But we can still hail the Russian people for their many achievements—in science and space, in economic and industrial growth, in culture and in acts of courage.

Among the many traits the peoples of our two countries have in common, none is stronger than our mutual abhorrence of war. Almost unique, among the major world powers, we have never been at war with each other. And no nation in the history of battle ever suffered more than the Soviet Union suffered in the course of the Second World War. At least 20 million lost their lives. Countless millions of homes and farms were burned or sacked. A third of the nation's territory, including nearly two-thirds of its industrial base, was turned into a wasteland—a loss equivalent to the devastation of this country east of Chicago.

Today, should total war ever break out again—no matter how—our two countries would become the primary targets. It is an ironical but accurate fact that the two strongest powers are the two in the most danger of devastation. All we have built, all we have worked for, would be destroyed in the first twenty-four hours. And even in the Cold War, which brings burdens and dangers to so many countries, including this nation's closest allies—our two countries bear the heaviest burdens. For we are both devoting massive sums of money to weapons that could be better devoted to combating ignorance, poverty and disease. We are both caught up in a vicious and dangerous cycle in which suspicion on one side breeds suspicion on the other, and new weapons beget counter-weapons.

In short, both the United States and its allies, and the Soviet Union and its allies, have a mutually deep interest in a just and genuine peace and in halting the arms race. Agreements to this end are in the interests of the Soviet Union as well as ours—and even the most hostile nations can be relied upon to accept and keep those treaty obligations, and only those treaty obligations, which are in their own interest.

So, let us not be blind to our differences—but let us also direct attention to our common interests and to means by which those differences can be resolved. And if we cannot end now our differences, at least we can help make the world safe for diversity. For, in the final analysis, our most basic common link is that we all inhabit this planet. We all breathe the same air. We all cherish our children's future. And we are all mortal.

Third: Let us re-examine our attitude toward the Cold War, remembering that we are not engaged in a debate, seeking to pile up debating points. We are not here distributing blame or pointing the finger of judgment. We must deal with the world as it is, and not as it might have been had history of the last eighteen years been different.

We must, therefore, preserve in the search for peace in the hope that constructive changes within the Communist bloc might bring within reach solutions which now seem beyond us. We must conduct our affairs in such a way that it becomes in the Communists' interest to agree on a genuine peace. Above all, while defending our vital interest, nuclear powers must avert those confrontations which bring an adversary to a choice of either a humiliating retreat or a nuclear war. To adopt that kind of course in the nuclear age would be evidence only of the bankruptcy of our policy—or of a collective death wish for the world.

To secure these ends, America's weapons are non-provocative, carefully controlled, designed to deter and capable of selective use. Our military forces are committed to peace and disciplines in self-restraint. Our diplomats are instructed to avoid unnecessary irritants and purely rhetorical hostility.

For we can seek a relaxation of tensions without relaxing our guard. And, for our part, we do not need to use threats to prove that we are resolute. We do not need to jam foreign broadcasts out of fear our faith will be eroded. We are unwilling to impose our system on any unwilling people—but we are willing and able to engage in peaceful competition with any people on earth.

Meanwhile, we seek to strengthen the United Nations, to help solve its financial problems, to make it a more effective instrument of peace, to develop it into a genuine world security system—a system capable of resolving disputes on the basis of law, of insuring the security of the large and the small, and of creating conditions under which arms can finally be abolished.

At the same time we seek to keep peace inside the non-communist world, where many nations, all of them our friends, are divided over issues which weaken western unity, which invite communist intervention or which threaten to erupt into war. Our efforts in West New Guinea, in the Congo, in the Middle East and in the Indian subcontinent, have been persistent and patient despite criticism from both sides. We have also tried to set an example for others—by seeking to adjust small but significant differences with our own closest neighbours in Mexico and in Canada.

Speaking of other nations, I wish to make one point clear. We are bound to many nations by alliances. These alliances exist because our concern and theirs substantially overlap. Our commitment to defend Western Europe and West Berlin for example, stands undiminished because of the identity of our vital interests. The United States will make no deal with the Soviet Union at the expense of other nations and other peoples, not merely because they are our partners, but also because their interests and ours converge.

Our interests converge, however not only in defending the frontiers of freedom, but in pursuing the paths of peace. It is our hope—and the purpose of Allied policies—to convince the Soviet Union that she, too, should let each nation choose its own future, so long as that choice does not interfere with the choices of others. The communist drive to impose their political and economic system on others is the primary cause of world tension today. For there can be no doubt that if all nations could refrain from interfering in the self-determination of others, then peace would be much more assured.

This will require a new effort to achieve world law—a new context for world discussions. It will require increased understanding between the

Soviets and ourselves. And increased understanding will require increased contact and communications. One step in this direction is the proposed arrangement for a direct line between Moscow and Washington, to avoid on each side the dangerous delays, misunderstandings, and misreadings of the other's actions which might occur at a time of crisis.

We have also been talking in Geneva about other first-step measures of arms control, designed to limit the intensity of the arms race and to reduce the risks of accidental war. Our primary long-range interest in Geneva, however, is general and complete disarmament—designed to take place by stages, permitting parallel political developments to build the new institutions of peace which would take the place of arms. The pursuit of disarmament has been an effort of this government since the 1920s. It has been urgently sought by the past three Administrations. And however dim the prospects may be today, we intend to continue this effort—to continue it in order that all countries, including our own, can better grasp what the problems and possibilities of disarmament are.

The one major area of these negotiations where the end is in sight—yet where a fresh start is badly needed—is in a treaty to outlaw nuclear tests. The conclusion of such a treaty—so near and yet so far—would check the spiralling arms race in one of its most dangerous areas. It would place the nuclear powers in a position to deal more effectively with one of the greatest hazards which man faces in 1963, the further spread of nuclear arms. It would increase our security—it would decrease the prospects of war. Surely this goal is sufficiently important to require our steady pursuit, yielding neither to the temptation to give up the whole effort nor the temptation to give up our insistence on vital and responsible safeguards.

I am taking this opportunity, therefore, to announce two important decisions in this regard.

First: Chairman Khrushchev, Prime Minister Macmillan and I have agreed that high-level discussions will shortly begin in Moscow looking toward early agreement on a comprehensive test ban treaty. Our hopes must be tempered with the caution of history—but with our hopes go the hopes of all mankind.

Second: To make clear our good faith and solemn convictions on the matter, I now declare that the United States does not propose to conduct nuclear tests in the atmosphere so long as other states do not do so. We will not be the first to resume. Such a declaration is no substitute for a formal binding treaty—but I hope it will help us achieve one. Nor would such a treaty be a substitute for disarmament—but I hope it will help us achieve it.

Finally, my fellow Americans, let us examine our attitude toward peace and freedom here at home. The quality and spirit of our won society must justify and support our efforts abroad. We must show it in the dedication of our own lives—as many of you who are graduating today will have a unique opportunity to do, by serving without pay in the Peace Corps abroad or in the proposed National Service Corps here at home.

But wherever we are, we must all, in our daily lives, live up to the age-old faith that peace and freedom walk together. In too many of our duties today, the peace is not secure because freedom is incomplete.

It is the responsibility of the Executive Branch at all levels of government—local, state and national—to provide and protect that freedom for all of our citizens by all means within their authority. It is the responsibility of the Legislative Branch at all levels, wherever that authority is not now adequate, to make it adequate. And it is the responsibility of all citizens in all sections of this country to respect the rights of all others and to respect the law of the land.

All this is not unrelated to world peace. 'When a man's ways please the Lord,' the Scriptures tell us, 'he maketh even his enemies to be at peace with him.' And is not peace, in the last analysis, basically a matter of human rights—the right to live out our lives without fear of devastation—the right to breathe air as nature provided it—the right of future generations to a healthy existence?

While we proceed to safeguard our national interests, let us also safeguard human interests. And the elimination of war and arms is clearly in the interest of both. No treaty, however much it may be to the advantage of all, however tightly it may be worded, can provide absolute security against the risks of deception and evasion. But it can—if it is sufficiently effective in its enforcement and if it is sufficiently in the interests of its signers—offer far more security and far fewer risks than an unabated, uncontrolled, unpredictable arms race.

The United States, as the world knows, will never start a war. We do not want a war. We do not now expect a war. This generation of Americans has already had enough—more than enough—of war and hate and oppression. We shall be prepared if others wish it. We shall be alert to try to stop it. But we shall also do our part to build a world of peace where the weak are safe and the strong are just. We are not helpless before that task or hopeless of its success. Confident and unafraid, we labour on—not toward a strategy of annihilation but toward a strategy of peace.

46

THE FOURTEEN POINTS

Thomas Woodrow Wilson

In this 8 January 1918 address to Congress, President Woodrow Wilson proposed a 14-point program for world peace. These points were later taken as the basis for peace negotiations at the end of the First World War.

It will be our wish and purpose that the processes of peace, when they are begun, shall be absolutely open and that they shall involve and permit henceforth no secret understandings of any kind. The day of conquest and aggrandizement is gone by; so is also the day of secret covenants entered into in the interest of particular governments and likely at some unlooked-for moment to upset the peace of the world. It is this happy fact, now clear to the view of every public man whose thoughts do not still linger in an age that is dead and gone, which makes it possible for every nation whose purposes are consistent with justice and the peace of the world to avow nor or at any other time the objects it has in view.

We entered this war because violations of right had occurred which touched us to the quick and made the life of our own people impossible unless they were corrected and the world secure once for all against their recurrence. What we demand in this war, therefore, is nothing peculiar to ourselves. It is that the world be made fit and safe to live in; and particularly that it be made safe for every peace-loving nation which, like our own, wishes to live its own life, determine its own institutions, be assured of justice and fair dealing by the other peoples of the world as against force and selfish aggression. All the peoples of the world are in effect partners in this interest, and for our own part we see very clearly that unless justice be done to others it will not be done to us. The program of the world's peace, therefore, is our program; and that program, the only possible program, as we see it, is this:

I. Open covenants of peace, openly arrived at, after which there shall be no private international understandings of any kind but diplomacy shall proceed always frankly and in the public view.

II. Absolute freedom of navigation upon the seas, outside territorial waters, alike in peace and in war, except as the seas may be closed in whole or in part by international action for the enforcement of international covenants.

III. The removal, so far as possible, of all economic barriers and the establishment of an equality of trade conditions among all the nations consenting to the peace and associating themselves for its maintenance.

IV. Adequate guarantees given and taken that national armaments will be reduced to the lowest point consistent with domestic safety.

V. A free, open-minded, and absolutely impartial adjustment of all colonial claims, based upon a strict observance of the principle that in determining all such questions of sovereignty the interests of the populations concerned must have equal weight with the equitable claims of the government whose title is to be determined.

VI. The evacuation of all Russian territory and such a settlement of all questions affecting Russia as will secure the best and freest cooperation of the other nations of the world in obtaining for her an unhampered and unembarrassed opportunity for the independent determination of her own political development and national policy and assure her of a sincere welcome into the society of free nations under institutions of her own choosing; and, more than a welcome, assistance also of every kind that she may need and may herself desire. The treatment accorded Russia by her sister nations in the months to come will be the acid test of their goodwill, of their comprehension of her needs as distinguished from their own interests, and of their intelligent and unselfish sympathy.

VII. Belgium, the whole world will agree, must be evacuated and restored, without any attempt to limit the sovereignty which she enjoys in common with all other free nations. No other single act will serve as this will serve to restore confidence among the nations in the laws which they have themselves set and determined for the government of their relations with one another. Without this healing act the whole structure and validity of international law is forever impaired.

VIII. All French territory should be freed and the invaded portions restored, and the wrong done to France by Prussia in 1871 in the matter of Alsace-Lorraine, which has unsettled the peace of the world for nearly fifty years, should be righted, in order that peace may once more be made secure in the interest of all.

IX. A readjustment of the frontiers of Italy should be effected along clearly recognizable lines of nationality.

X. The peoples of Austria-Hungary, whose place among the nations we wish to see safeguarded and assured, should be accorded the freest opportunity to autonomous development.

XI. Rumania, Serbia, and Montenegro should be evacuated; occupied territories restored; Serbia accorded free and secure access to the sea; and the relations of the several Balkan states to one another determined by friendly counsel along historically established lines of allegiance and nationality; and international guarantees of the political and economic independence and territorial integrity of the several Balkan states should be entered into.

XII. The Turkish portion of the present Ottoman Empire should be assured a secure sovereignty, but the other nationalities which are now under Turkish rule should be assured an undoubted security of life and an absolutely unmolested opportunity of autonomous development, and the Dardanelles should be permanently opened as a free passage to the ships and commerce of all nations under international guarantees.

XIII. An independent Polish state should be erected which should include the territories inhabited indisputably by Polish populations, which should be assured a free and secure access to the sea, and whose political and economic independence and territorial integrity should be guaranteed by international covenant.

XIV. A general association of nations must be formed under specific covenants for the purpose of affording mutual guarantees of political independence and territorial integrity to great and small states alike.

In regard to these essential rectifications of wrong and assertions of right we feel ourselves to be intimate partners of all the governments and peoples associated together against the Imperialists. We cannot be separated in interest or divided in purpose. We stand together until the end.

For such arrangements and covenants we are willing to fight and to continue to fight until they are achieved; but only because we wish the right to prevail and desire a just and stable peace such as can be secured only by removing the chief provocations to war, which this program does remove. We have no jealousy of German greatness, and there is nothing in this program that impairs it. We grudge her no achievement or distinction of learning or of pacific enterprise such as have made her record very bright and very enviable. We do not wish to injure her or to block in any way her legitimate influence or power. We do not wish to fight her either with arms or with hostile arrangements of trade if she is willing to associate herself with us and the other peace-loving nations of the world in covenants of justice and law and fair dealing. We wish her only to accept a place of equality among the peoples of the world—the new world in which we now live—instead of a place of mastery.

47

I AM STILL ALIVE

Subhas Chandra Bose

This speech of Subhas Bose aired in Germany, 25 March 1942 on radio is very compelling and revealing. It shows how much the British government was afraid of Bose and his activities in Europe. They wanted to see him dead. The canard which the British propaganda spread about the death of Bose in an air crash on way to Tokyo, while he was still in Germany, was refuted by Bose himself through this broadcast which was heard by millions in India and throughout the world. There are millions of people in India who still do not believe that Bose died in an air crash over Formosa on 18 August 1945.

This is Subhas Chandra Bose, who is still alive, speaking to you over the Azad Hind radio. British news agencies have spread all over the world the report that I died in an aeroplane crash on my way to Tokyo to attend an important conference there. Ever since I left India, last year, British propaganda agencies have, from time to time, given contradictory reports of my whereabouts, while newspapers in England have not hesitated to use uncomplimentary language about me. The latest report about my death is perhaps an instance of wishful thinking. I can imagine that the British government would, at this critical hour in India's history; like to see me dead since they are now trying their level best to win India over to their side for the purpose of their imperialistic war. I do not have before me the full particulars of the aeroplane disaster referred to above. I cannot, therefore, say if it was the result of sabotage on the part of our enemy. In any case, I beg to offer my respectful homage to the memory of those who lost their lives in that tragic event. Their names will be written in letters of gold in the history of our struggle for independence.

I have considered very carefully the offer of the British government to India and the radio speech of Sir Stafford Cripps in that connection. I feel perfectly convinced that it is now quite clear that Sir Stafford has gone to India to try the age-long policy of British imperialism—'divide and rule'. Many people in India did not expect Sir Stafford Cripps to play a role which might very well have been reserved for a conservative politician like Mr Amery. Sir Stafford has himself assured us that the terms offered to India are, in his opinion, the soundest and the best, and that the members of the British Cabinet were all unanimous over these proposals. This affords one further proof that, in Britain, all party differences disappear when the question of India comes up. Sir Stafford has told us that India is a subcontinent inhabited by many races and peoples. I would like to remind him that India was unified under the empire of Ashoka the Great, several centuries before the Christian era—more than a thousand years before England was unified. Britain has, in other parts of her Empire, for instance in Ireland and Palestine, used the religious issue in order to divide the people. She has been utilizing in India for that same purpose not only this issue but other imperial weapons like the Indian princes, depressed classes, etc. Now Sir Stafford is in India to use the same instruments for imperialistic ends. It is no less striking that he is applying the old imperialist policy for working out a compromise with one section of the people while simultaneously suppressing the other. This is why on one side Sir Stafford is conferring with one set of politicians, while on the other the fearless and uncompromising fighters for independence are safely lodged behind prison. The Indian people are fully aware of this nefarious policy of British politicians.

I have no doubt that the spirit of our freedom fighters will hurl down the prison walls and inspire the people of India to know that this is an insult to India's self-respect and honour.

As the London paper, *The Daily Telegraph*, has remarked, Sir Stafford's proposals contain nothing that is fundamentally new. The essence is dominion status within the Empire, which will be realized only when the war is over. But according to the terms of the offer, the speech of Sir Stafford Cripps, and the comments of English papers like The Manchester Guardian, it is quite clear that the real intention of the British government is to split India into a number of states, just as Ireland was split up at the end of the last war. I am doubtful whether India will even look at such an offer. Indians by nature are hospitable, and Sir Stafford will be committing a grievous mistake if he interpreted such hospitality to mean the acceptance of his offer.

Sir Stafford reached the height of imperialist hypocrisy when, at a press conference at Delhi, he remarked that the Indians have not been able to produce an agreed constitution. But the Indian people know from their bitter experience that only the British government is responsible for the corruption and bribery in India. The Indian people are, therefore, convinced that they can no longer hope to win their freedom by discussion or argument, propaganda and passive resistance, but must now resort to other methods which are more effective and powerful.

Sir Stafford also mentioned that while the war is going on, a new constitution cannot be framed for India, and hence the inauguration of dominion status will begin on the termination of the war. I may remind Sir Stafford Cripps that, as early as October 1939, I replied to the British government by suggesting that a provisional national government, commanding the confidence of the majority of the people, should be set up at once. This provisional national government could be made responsible to the present Indian Legislative Assembly. This suggestion was first of all put forward by me on behalf of the Forward Bloc of the Congress, and being practicable and reasonable, the official Congress Committee also adopted it as their own demand. The fact, however, is that the British government is not ready to part with power at the present moment. By raising the issue of the minorities, princes or of the so-called depressed classes, they can at any time find a plea that the Indians are not united. Sir Stafford must be living in a fool's paradise if he thinks that by making such hopeless offers, he can satisfy India's hunger for freedom. In the last World War, with the help of India, the war was won by England, but India's reward was further suppression and massacre. India has not forgotten those episodes, and she will see that the present golden opportunity is not lost.

Since the beginning of this century, the British government has been using another organization as a counter-blast to the Congress in order to reject its demands. It has been using the Muslim League for this purpose, because that party is regarded as pro-British in its outlook. In fact, British propaganda has tried to create the impression that the Muslim League is almost as influential a body as the Congress, and that it represents the majority of India's Muslims. This, however, is far from the truth. In reality, there are several influential and important Muslim organizations which are thoroughly nationalist. Moreover, of the eleven provinces in British India, out of which only four have a majority of Muslims, only one, the Punjab, has a cabinet which may be regarded as a Muslim League Cabinet. But even the Punjab premier is strongly opposed to the main program of the Muslim League, namely the division of India. But even then it is said that the majority of the Muslims will not stand for Indian independence.

As far as the defence of India is concerned, it is stated in the British proposals that, so long as the war lasts, the full military control of India will be directly in the hands of Britain, not even in the hands of the viceroy or the commander-in-chief in India. By this policy, Britain wants to achieve a twofold purpose. She desires, on the one hand, to utilize to the fullest extent India's resources for the whole Empire, and on the other, to force thereby, the enemies of Britain to attack Britain's military base in India, so that the Indian people may be provoked into voluntarily entering the war as Britain's ally. I would like to affirm, with all the emphasis at my command, that all the pro-British Indians who are participating in Britain's war will alone be responsible if the war comes ultimately to India. Further, I would like to warn my countrymen that Britain's sole object flow is to drag the Indian people into the war. It has been a successful game of the British people to get other nations involved in the war. Up to the present time, they have been carrying out glorious retreats and successful evacuations. Recently they have adopted a novel policy of burning and destroying everything before taking to their heels. If the British government apply these scorched earth tactics to their own county—that is no concern of ours. But I have every reason to believe that they have decided to apply these scorched earth tactics in Ceylon and India, should the war come there. Therefore, participation in Britain's war will not only hinder Britain's defeat and overthrow but will also delay the attainment of independence for Indians.

48

LEAGUE OF NATIONS: FINAL ADDRESS

Thomas Woodrow Wilson

The Pueblo speech was an address in favour of the League of Nations, given by US President Woodrow Wilson on 25 September 1919. This was the last such address he gave due to ill health. It was held in Pueblo, Colorado, hence its name. In the wake of the settlements agreed at the Paris Peace Conference President Wilson set about the task of convincing the United States Congress to ratify both the treaty and to approve American participation in Wilson's own invention, the League of Nations. This task was then considered impossible due to a majority of the Congress being Wilson's political enemies. Wilson embarked on a tour of the country to canvass support in favour of both the treaty and League, until illness forced him to return home after the Pueblo speech. The United States never joined the League of Nations.

Mr Chairman and fellow countrymen:

It is with a great deal of genuine pleasure that I find myself in Pueblo, and I feel it a compliment in this beautiful hall. One of the advantages of this hall, as I look about, is that you are not too far away from me, because there is nothing so reassuring to men who are trying to express the public sentiment as getting into real personal contact with their fellow citizens. I have gained a renewed impression as I have crossed the continent this time of the homogeneity of this great people to whom we belong. They come from many stocks, but they are all of one kind. They come from many origins, but they are all shot through with the same principles and desire, the same righteous and honest things. I have received a more inspiring impression this time of the public opinion of the United States than it was ever my privilege to receive before.

The chief pleasure of my trip has been that it has nothing to do with my personal fortunes, that it has nothing to do with my personal reputation, that it has nothing to do with anything except great principles uttered by Americans of all sorts and of all parties which we are now trying to realize at this crisis of the affairs of the world. But there have been unpleasant impressions as well as pleasant impressions, my fellow citizens, as I have crossed the continent. I have perceived more and more that men have been busy creating an absolutely false impression of what the treaty of peace and the Covenant of the League of Nations contain and mean. I find, moreover, that there is an organized propaganda against the League of Nations and against the treaty proceeding from exactly the same sources that the organized propaganda proceeded from which threatened this country here and there with disloyalty, and I want to say—I cannot say too often—any man who carries a hyphen about with him carries a dagger that he is ready to plunge into the vitals of this Republic whenever he gets ready.

If I can catch any man with a hyphen in this great contest I will know that I have got an enemy of the Republic. My fellow citizens, it is only certain bodies of foreign sympathies, certain bodies of sympathy with foreign nations that are organized against this great document which the American representatives have brought back from Paris. Therefore, in order to clear away the mists, in order to remove the impressions, in order to check the falsehoods that have clustered around this great subject, I want to tell you a few very simple things about the treaty and the covenant.

Do not think of this treaty of peace as merely a settlement with Germany. It is that. It is a very severe settlement with Germany, but there is not anything in it that she did not earn. Indeed, she earned more than she can ever be able to pay for, and the punishment exacted of her is not a punishment greater than she can bear, and it is absolutely necessary in order that no other nation may ever plot such a thing against humanity and civilization. But the treaty is so much more than that. It is not merely a settlement with Germany; it is a readjustment of those great injustices which underlie the whole structure of European and Asiatic society. This is only the first of several treaties. They are all constructed upon the same plan. The Austrian treaty follows the same lines. The treaty with Hungary follows the same lines. The treaty with Bulgaria follows the same lines. The treaty with Turkey, when it is formulated, will follow the same lines.

What are those lines? They are based upon the purpose to see that every government dealt with in this great settlement is put in the hands of the people and taken out of the hands of coteries and of sovereigns, who had no right to rule over the people. It is a people's treaty, that accomplishes by a great sweep of practical justice the liberation of men who never could have liberated themselves, and the power of the most powerful nations has been devoted not to their aggrandizement but to the liberation of people whom they could have put under their control if they had chosen to do so. Not one foot of territory is demanded by submission to their authority is demanded by them. The men who sat around the table in Paris knew that the time had come when the people were no longer going to consent to live under masters, but were going to live the lives that they chose themselves, to live under such governments as they chose themselves to erect. That is the fundamental principle of this great settlement.

And we did not stop with that. We added a great international charter for the rights of labour. Reject this treaty, impair it, and this is the consequence of the labouring men of the world, that there is no international tribunal which can bring the moral judgments of the world to bear upon the great labour questions of the day. What we need to do with regard to the labour questions of the day, my fellow countrymen, is to lift them into the light, is to lift them out of the haze and distraction of passion, of hostility, out into the calm spaces where men look at things without passion.

The more men you get into a great discussion the more you exclude passion. Just as soon as the calm judgment of the worlds is directed upon the question of justice to labour, labour is going to have to forum such as it never was supplied with before, and men everywhere are going to see that the problem of labour is nothing more not less than the problem of the elevation of humanity. We must see that all the questions which have disturbed the world, all the questions which have disturbed the processes of industry, shall be brought out where men of all points of view, men of all attitudes of mind, men of all kinds of experience, may contribute their part of the settlement of the great questions which we must settle and cannot ignore.

At the front of this great treaty is put the Covenant of the League of Nations. It will also be at the front of the Austrian treaty and the Hungarian treaty and the Bulgarian treaty and the treaty with Turkey. Every one of them will contain the Covenant of the League of Nations, because you cannot work any of them without the Covenant of the League of Nations. Unless you get the united, concerted purpose and power of the great governments of the world behind this settlement, it will fall down like a house of cards. There is only one power to put behind the liberation of mankind, and that is the power of mankind. It is the power of the united moral forces of the world, and in the Covenant of the League of Nations the moral forces of the world are mobilized.

For what purpose? Reflect, my fellow citizens, that the membership of this great League is going to include all the great fighting nations of the world, as well as the weak ones. It is not for the present going to include Germany, but for the time being Germany is not a great fighting country. All the nations that have power that can be mobilized are going to be members of this League, including the United States.

And what do they unite for? They enter into a solemn promise to one another they will never use their power against one another for aggression; that they never will impair the territorial integrity of a neighbour; that they never will interfere with the political independence of a neighbour; that they will abide by the principle that great populations are entitled to determine their own destiny and that they will not interfere with that destiny; and that no matter what differences arise amongst them they will never resort to war without first having done one or other of two things—either submitted the matter of controversy to arbitration, in which case they agree to abide by the result without question, or submitted it to the consideration of the council of the League of Nations, laying before that council all the documents, all the facts, agreeing that the council can publish the documents, all the facts, agreeing that the council can publish the documents and the facts to the whole world, agreeing that there shall be six months allowed for the mature consideration of those facts by the council, and agreeing that at the expiration of the six months, even if they are not then ready to accept the advice of the council with regard to the settlement of the dispute, they will still not go to war for another three months.

In other words, they consent, no matter what happens, to submit every matter of difference between them to the judgment of mankind, and just so certainly as they do that, my fellow citizens, war will be in the far background, war will be pushed out of that foreground of terror in which it has kept the world for generation after generation, and men will know that there will be a calm time of deliberate counsel. The most dangerous thing for a bad cause is to expose it to the opinion of the world. The most certain way that you can prove that a man is mistaken is by letting all his neighbours know what he thinks, by letting all his neighbours discuss what he thinks, and if he is in the wrong you will notice that he will stay at home, he will not walk on the street. He will be afraid of the eyes of his neighbours. He will be afraid of their judgment of his character. He will know that his cause is lost unless he can sustain it by the arguments of right and of justice. The same law that applies to individuals applies to nations.

But, you say, 'We have heard that we might be at a disadvantage in the League of Nations.' Well, whoever told you that either was deliberately falsifying or he had not read the Covenant of the League of Nations. I leave him the choice. I want to give you a very simple account of the organization of the League of Nations and let you judge for yourselves. It is a very simple organization. The power of the League, or rather the activities of the league, lie in two bodies. There is the council, which consists of one representative from each of the principal allied and associated powers—that is to say, the United States, Great Britain, France, Italy, and Japan, along with four other representatives of smaller powers chosen out of the general body of the membership of the League.

The council is the source of very active policy of the League, and no active policy of the League can be adopted without a unanimous vote of the council. That is explicitly stated in the Covenant itself. Does it not evidently follow that the League of Nations can adopt no policy whatever without the consent of the United States? The affirmative vote of the representative of the United States is necessary in every case. Now, you have heard of six votes belonging to the British Empire. Those six votes are not in the council. They are in the assembly, and the interesting thing is that the assembly does not vote. I must qualify that statement a little, but essentially it is absolutely true. In every matter in which the assembly is given a voice, and there are only four or five, its vote does not count unless concurred in by the representatives of all the nations represented on the council, so there is no validity to any vote of the assembly unless in that vote the representative of the United States concurs. That one vote of the United States is as big as the six votes of the British Empire. I am not jealous for advantage, my fellow citizens, but I think that is a perfectly safe situation. There is no validity in a vote, either by the council or the assembly, in which we do not concur. So much for the statements about the six votes for the British Empire.

Look at it in another aspect. The assembly is the talking body. The assembly was created in order that anybody that purposed anything wrong should be subjected to the awkward circumstance that everybody could talk about it. This is the great assembly in which all the things that are likely to disturb the peace of the world or the good understanding between nations are to be exposed to the general view, and I want to ask you if you think it was unjust, unjust to the United States, that speaking parts should be assigned to the several portions of the British Empire? Do you think it unjust that there should be some spokesman in debate for that fine little stout Republic down in the Pacific, New Zealand? Do you think it was unjust that Australia should be allowed to stand up and take part in the debate—Australia, from which we have learned some of the most useful progressive policies of modern time, a little nation only five million in a great continent, but counting for several times five in its activities and in its interest in liberal reform? Do you think it unjust that that little Republic down in South Africa, whose gallant resistance to being subjected to any outside authority at all we admired for so many months and whose fortunes we followed with such interest, should have a speaking part? Great Britain obliged South Africa to submit to her sovereignty, but she immediately after that felt that it was convenient and right to hand the whole self-government of that colony over to the very men whom she had beaten.

The representatives of South Africa in Paris were two of the most distinguished generals of the Boer Army, two of the realest men I ever met, two men that could talk sober counsel and wise advice, along with the best statesmen in Europe. To exclude Gen. Botha and Gen. Smuts from the right to stand up in the parliament of the world and say something concerning the affairs of mankind would be absurd. And what about

Canada? Is not Canada a good neighbour? I ask you, is not Canada more likely to agree with the United States than with Great Britain? Canada has a speaking part. And then, for the first time in the history of the world, that great voiceless multitude, that throng hundreds of millions strong in India, has a voice, and I want to testify that some of the wisest and most dignified figures in the peace conference at Paris came from India, men who seemed to carry in their minds an older wisdom than the rest of us had, whose traditions ran back into so many of the unhappy fortunes of mankind that they seemed very useful counselors as to how some ray of hope and some prospect of happiness could be opened to its people. I for my part have no jealousy whatever of those five speaking parts in the assembly. Those speaking parts cannot translate themselves into five votes that can in any matter override the voice and purpose of the United States.

Let us sweep aside all this language of jealousy. Let us be big enough to know the facts and to welcome the facts, because the facts are based upon the principle that America has always fought for, namely, the equality of self-governing peoples, whether they were big or little—not counting men, but counting rights, not counting representation, but counting the purpose of that representation. When you hear an opinion quoted you do not count the number of persons who hold it; you ask, 'Who said that?' You weigh opinions, you do not count them, and the beauty of all democracies is that every voice can be heard, every voice can have its effect, every voice can contribute to the general judgment that is finally arrived at. That is the object of democracy. Let us accept what America has always fought for, and accept it with pride that America showed the way and made the proposal. I do not mean that America made the proposal in this particular instance; I mean that the principle was an American principle, proposed by America.

When you come to the heart of the Covenant, my fellow citizens, you will find it in article ten, and I am very much interested to know that the other things have been blown away like bubbles. There is nothing in the other contentions with regard to the League of Nations, but there is something in article ten that you ought to realize and ought to accept or reject. Article ten is the heart of the whole matter. What is article ten? I never am certain that I can from memory give a literal repetition of its language, but I am sure that I can give an exact interpretation of its meaning. Article ten provides that every member of the League covenants to respect and preserve the territorial integrity and existing political independence of every other member of the league as against external aggression. Not against internal disturbance. There was not a man at that table who did not admit the sacredness of the right of self-determination, the sacredness of the right of any body of people to say that they would not continue to live under the government they were then living under, and under article eleven of the Covenant they are given a place to say whether they will live under it or not. For following article ten is article eleven, which makes it the right of any member of the League at any time to call attention to anything, anywhere, that is likely to disturb the peace of the world or the good understanding between nations upon which the peace of the world depends. I want to give you an illustration of what that would mean.

You have heard a great deal—something that was true and a great deal that was false—about the provision of the treaty which hands over to Japan the rights which Germany enjoyed in the Province of Shantung in China. In the first place, Germany did not enjoy any rights there that other nations had not already claimed. For my part, my judgment, my moral judgment, is against the whole set of concessions. They were all of them unjust to China, they ought never to have been exacted, they were all exacted by duress, from a great body of thoughtful and ancient and helpless people. There never was any right in any of them. Thank God, America never asked for any, never dreamed of asking for any.

But when Germany got this concession in 1898, the government of the United States made no protest whatever. That was not because the government of the United States was not in the hands of high-minded and conscientious men. It was. William McKinley was President and John Hay was Secretary of State—as safe hands to leave the honour of the United States in as any that you can cite. They made no protest because the state of international law at that time was that it was none of their business unless they could show that the interests of the United States were affected, and the only thing that they could show with regard to the interests of the United States was that Germany might close the doors of Shantung Province against the trade of the United States.

The World's 100 Greatest Speeches

They, therefore, demanded and obtained promises that we could continue to sell merchandise in Shantung. Immediately following that concession to Germany there was a concession to Russia of the same sort, of Port Arthur, and Port Arthur was handed over subsequently to Japan on the very territory of the United States. Don't you remember that when Russia and Japan got into war with one another the war was brought to a confusion by a treaty written at Portsmouth, NH, and in that treaty without the slightest intimation from any authoritative sources in America that the government of the United States had any objection, Port Arthur, Chinese territory, was turned over to Japan? I want you distinctly to understand that there is no thought of criticism in my mind. I am expounding to you a state of international law.

Now, read articles ten and eleven. You will see that international law is revolutionized by putting morals into it. Article ten says that no member of the League, and that includes all these nations that have demanded these things unjustly of China, shall impair the territorial integrity or the political independence of any other member of the League. China is going to be a member of the League. Article eleven says that any member of the League can call attention to anything that is likely to disturb the peace of the world or the good understanding between nations, and China is for the first time in the history of mankind afforded a standing before the jury of the world. I, for my part, have a profound sympathy for China, and I am proud to have taken part in an arrangement which promises the protection of the world to the rights of China. The whole atmosphere of the world is changed by a thing like that, my fellow citizens. The whole international practice of the world is revolutionized.

But, you will say, 'What is the second sentence of article ten? That is what gives very disturbing thoughts.' The second sentence is that the council of the League shall advise what steps, if any, are necessary to carry out the guaranty of the first sentence, namely, that the members will respect and preserve the territorial integrity and political independence of the other members. I do not know any other meaning for the word 'advise' except 'advise.' The council advises, and it cannot advise without the vote of the United States. Why gentlemen should fear that the Congress of the United States would be advised to do something that it did not want to do I frankly cannot imagine, because they cannot even be advised to do anything unless their own representative has participated in the advice.

It may be that that will impair somewhat the vigour of the League, but, nevertheless, the fact is so, that we are not obliged to take any advice except our own, which to any man who wants to go his own course is a very satisfactory state of affairs. Every man regards his own advice as best, and I dare say every man mixes his own advice with some thought of his own interest. Whether we use it wisely or unwisely, we can use the vote of the United States to make impossible drawing the United States into any enterprise that she does not care to be drawn into.

Yet article ten strikes at the taproot of war. Article ten is a statement that the very things that have always been sought in imperialistic wars are henceforth foregone by every ambitious nation in the world. I would have felt very much disturbed if, sitting at the peace table in Paris, I had supposed that I was expounding my own ideas. Whether you believe it or not, I know the relative size of my own ideas; I know how they stand related in bulk and proportion to the moral judgments of my fellow countrymen, and I proposed nothing whatever at the peace table at Paris that I had not sufficiently certain knowledge embodied the moral judgment of the citizens of the United States. I had gone over there with, so to say, explicit instruction. Don't you remember that we laid down fourteen points which should contain the principles of the settlement? They were not my points. In every one of them I was conscientiously trying to read the thought of the people of the United States, and after I uttered those points I had every assurance given me that could be given me that they did speak the moral judgment of the United States and not my single judgment.

Then when it came to that critical period just a little less than a year ago, when it was evident that the war was coming to its critical end, all the nations engaged in the war accepted those fourteen principles explicitly as the basis of the armistice and the basis of the peace. In those circumstances I crossed the ocean under bond to my own people and to the other governments with which I was dealing. The whole specification of the method of settlement was written down and accepted before hand, and we were architects building on those specifications. It reassures me and fortifies my position to find how, before I went over men whose judgment the United States has often trusted were of exactly the same opinion that I went abroad to express. Here is something I want to read from Theodore Roosevelt:

'The one effective move for obtaining peace is by an agreement among all the great powers in which each should pledge itself not only to abide by the decisions of a common tribunal but to back its decisions by force. The great civilized nations should combine by solemn agreement in a great world league for the peace of righteousness; a court should be established. A changed and amplified Hague court would meet the requirements, composed of representatives from each nation, whose representatives are sworn to act as judges in each case and not in a representative capacity.' Now there is article ten. He goes on and says this: 'The nations should agree on certain rights that should not be questioned, such as territorial integrity, their right to deal with their domestic affairs, and with such matters as whom they should admit to citizenship. All such guarantee each of their number in possession of these rights.'

Now, the other specification is the Covenant. The Covenant in another portion guarantees to the members independent control of their domestic questions. There is not a leg for these gentlemen to stand on when they say that the interests of the United States are not safeguarded in the very points where we are most sensitive. You do not need to be told again that the Covenant expressly says that nothing in this covenant shall be construed as affecting the validity of the Monroe doctrine, for example. You could not be more explicit than that. And every point of interest is covered, partly for one very interesting reason. This is not the first time that the Foreign Relations Committee of the Senate of the United States has read and considered this covenant. I brought it to this country in March last in a tentative, provisional form, in practically the form that it now has, with the exception of certain additions which I shall mention immediately. I asked the Foreign Relations Committees of both Houses to come to the White House and we spent a long evening in the frankest discussion of every portion that they wished to discuss. They made certain specific suggestions as to what should be contained in this document when it was to be revised. I carried those suggestions to Paris, and every one of them was adopted.

What more could I have done? What more could have been obtained? The very matters upon which these gentlemen were most concerned were, the right of withdrawal, which is now expressly stated; the safeguarding of the Monroe doctrine, which is now accomplished; the exclusion from action by the League of domestic questions, which is now accomplished. All along the line, every suggestion of the United States was adopted after the Covenant had been drawn up in its first form and had been published for the criticism of the world. There is a very true sense in which I can say this is a tested American document.

I am dwelling upon these points, my fellow citizens, in spite of the fact that I dare say to most of you they are perfectly well know, because in order to meet the present situation we have got to know what we are dealing with. We are not dealing with the kind of document which this is represented by some gentlemen to be; and inasmuch as we are dealing with a document simon-pure in respect of the very principles we have professed and lived up to, we have got to do one or other of two things—we have got to adopt it or reject it. There is no middle course. You cannot go in on a special-privilege basis of your own.

I take it that you are too proud to ask to be exempted from responsibilities which the other members of the League will carry. We go in upon equal terms or we do not go in at all; and if we do not go in, my fellow citizens, think of the tragedy of that result—the only sufficient guaranty to the peace of the world withheld! Ourselves drawn apart with that dangerous pride which means that we shall be ready to take care of ourselves, and that means that we shall maintain great standing armies and an irresistible envy; that means we shall have the organization of a military nation; that means we shall have a general staff, with the kind of power that the general staff of Germany had; to mobilize this great manhood of the nation when it pleases, all the energy of our young men drawn into the thought and preparation for war. What of our pledges to the men that lie dead in France? We said that they went over there not to prove the prowess of America or her readiness for another war but to see to that there never was such a war again. It always seems to make it difficult for me to say anything my fellow citizens, when I think of my clients in this case. My clients are the children; my clients are the next generation. They do not know what promises and bonds I undertook when I ordered the armies of the United States to the soil of France, but I know, and I intend to redeem my pledges to the children; they shall not be sent upon a similar errand.

Again and again, my fellow citizens, mothers who lost their sons in France have come to me and, taking my hand, have shed tears upon it not only, but they added, 'God bless you, Mr President!' Why, my fellow citizens, should they pray God to bless me? I advised the Congress of the United States to create the situation that led to the death of their sons. I ordered their sons overseas. I consented to their sons being put in the most difficult parts of the battle line, where death was certain, as in the impenetrable difficulties of the forest of Argonne. Why should they weep upon my hand and call down the blessings of God upon me? Because they believe that their boys died for something that vastly transcends any of the immediate and palpable objects of the war. They believe, and they rightly believe, that their sons saved the liberty of the world. They believe that wrapped up with the liberty of the world is the continuous protection of that liberty by the concerted powers of all civilized people. They believe that this sacrifice was made in order that other sons should not be called upon for a similar gift—the gift of life, the gift of all that died—and if we did not see this thing through, if we fulfilled the dearest present wish of Germany and now dissociated ourselves from those alongside whom we fought in the world, would not something of the halo go away from the gun over the mantelpiece, or the sword? Would not the old uniform lose something of its significance? These men were crusaders. They were not going forth to prove the might of the United States. They were going forth to prove the might of justice and right, and all the world accepted them as crusaders, and their transcendent achievement has made all the world believe in America as it believes in no other nation organized in the modern world. There seem to me to stand between us and the rejection or qualification of this treaty the serried ranks of those boys in khaki, not only these boys who came home, but those dear ghosts that still deploy upon the fields of France.

My friends, on last Decoration day, I went on a beautiful hillside near Paris, where was located the cemetery of Suresnes, a cemetery given over to the burial of the American dead. Behind me on the slopes was rank upon rank of living American soldiers, and lying before me upon the levels of the plain was rank upon rank of departed American soldiers. Right by the side of the stand where I spoke there was a little group of French women who had adopted those graves, had made themselves mothers of those dear ghosts by putting flowers every day upon those graves, taking them as their own sons, their own beloved, because they had died in the same cause—France was free and the world was free because America had come! I wish some men in public life who are now opposing the settlement for which these men died could visit such a spot as that. I wish that the thought that comes out of those graves could penetrate their consciousness. I wish that they could feel the moral obligation that rests upon us not to go back on those boys, but to see the thing through, to see it through to the end and make good their redemption of the world. For nothing less depends upon this decision, nothing less than liberation and salvation of the world.

You will say, 'Is the League an absolute guaranty against war?' No; I do not know any absolute guaranty against the errors of human judgment or the violence of human passion, but I tell you this: With a cooling space of nine months for human passion, not much of it will keep hot. I had a couple of friends who were in the habit of losing their tempers, and when they lost their tempers they were in the habit of using very unparlimentary language. Some of their friends induced them to make a promise that they never would swear inside the town limits. When the impulse next came upon them, they took a streetcar to go out of town to swear, and by the time they got out of town they did not want to swear. They came back convinced that they were just what they were, a couple of unspeakable fools, and the habit of getting angry and of swearing suffered great inroads upon it by that experience. Now, illustrating the great by the small, that is true of the passions of nations. It is true of the passions of men however you combine them. Give them space to cool off. I ask you this: If it is not an absolute insurance against war, do you want no insurance at all? Do you want nothing? Do you want not only no probability that war will not recur, but the probability that it will recur? The arrangements of justice do not stand of themselves, my fellow citizens. The arrangements of this treat are just, but they need the support of the combined power of the great nations of the world. And they will have that support. Now that the mists of this great question have cleared away, I believe that men will see the truth, eye to eye and face to face.

There is one thing that the American people always rise to and extend their hand to, and that is the truth of justice and of liberty and of peace. We have accepted the truth and we are going to be led by it, and it is going to lead us, and through us the world, out into pastures of quietness and peace such as the world never dreamed of before.

49

THE MAN WITH THE MUCK RAKE

Theodore Roosevelt

This speech was given on Sunday, 15 April 1906, at the laying of the corner stone of the Cannon Office Building in Washington, DC. In political science and communication studies, Theodore Roosevelt is said to have ushered in a 'rhetorical presidency.' More than leaders before him, he spoke directly to the people and press to push his agenda. This speech exhibits several key concepts that come to the fore during 9th and 10th grade students' explorations of American history: The relationship of the president to the press; the growing strength of the national government during the Progressive Era; the importance of character to early 20th century reformers; and the increasing role of investigative journalism in pursuing a progressive agenda.

Over a century ago, Washington laid the corner stone of the Capitol in what was then little more than a tract of wooded wilderness here beside the Potomac. We now find it necessary to provide by great additional buildings for the business of the government.

This growth in the need for the housing of the government is but a proof and example of the way in which the nation has grown and the sphere of action of the national government has grown. We now administer the affairs of a nation in which the extraordinary growth of population has been outstripped by the growth of wealth in complex interests. The material problems that face us today are not such as they were in Washington's time, but the underlying facts of human nature are the same now as they were then. Under altered external form we war with the same tendencies toward evil that were evident in Washington's time, and are helped by the same tendencies for good. It is about some of these that I wish to say a word today.

In Bunyan's 'Pilgrim's Progress' you may recall the description of the Man with the Muck Rake, the man who could look no way but downward, with the muck rake in his hand; who was offered a celestial crown for his muck rake, but who would neither look up nor regard the crown he was offered, but continued to rake to himself the filth of the floor.

In 'Pilgrim's Progress' the Man with the Muck Rake is set forth as the example of him whose vision is fixed on carnal instead of spiritual things. Yet he also typifies the man who in this life consistently refuses to see aught that is lofty, and fixes his eyes with solemn intentness only on that which is vile and debasing.

Now, it is very necessary that we should not flinch from seeing what is vile and debasing. There is filth on the floor, and it must be scraped up with the muck rake; and there are times and places where this service is the most needed of all the services that can be performed. But the man who never does anything else, who never thinks or speaks or writes, save of his feats with the muck rake, speedily becomes, not a help but one of the most potent forces for evil.

There are in the body politic, economic and social, many and grave evils, and there is urgent necessity for the sternest war upon them. There should be relentless exposure of and attack upon every evil man, whether politician or business man, every evil practice, whether in politics, business, or social life. I hail as a benefactor every writer or speaker, every man who, on the platform or in a book, magazine, or newspaper, with merciless severity makes such attack, provided always that he in his turn remembers that the attack is of use only if it is absolutely truthful.

The liar is no whit better than the thief, and if his mendacity takes the form of slander he may be worse than most thieves. It puts a premium upon knavery untruthfully to attack an honest man, or even with hysterical exaggeration to assail a bad man with untruth.

An epidemic of indiscriminate assault upon character does no good, but very great harm. The soul of every scoundrel is gladdened whenever an honest man is assailed, or even when a scoundrel is untruthfully assailed.

Now, it is easy to twist out of shape what I have just said, easy to affect to misunderstand it, and if it is slurred over in repetition not difficult really to misunderstand it. Some persons are sincerely incapable of understanding that to denounce mud slinging does not mean the endorsement of whitewashing; and both the interested individuals who need whitewashing and those others who practice mud slinging like to encourage such confusion of ideas.

One of the chief counts against those who make indiscriminate assault upon men in business or men in public life is that they invite a reaction which is sure to tell powerfully in favour of the unscrupulous scoundrel who really ought to be attacked, who ought to be exposed, who ought, if possible, to be put in the penitentiary. If Aristides is praised overmuch as just, people get tired of hearing it; and overcensure of the unjust finally and from similar reasons results in their favor.

Any excess is almost sure to invite a reaction; and, unfortunately, the reactions instead of taking the form of punishment of those guilty of the excess, is apt to take the form either of punishment of the unoffending or of giving immunity, and even strength, to offenders. The effort to make financial or political profit out of the destruction of character can only result in public calamity. Gross and reckless assaults on character, whether on the stump or in newspaper, magazine, or book, create a morbid and vicious public sentiment, and at the same time act as a profound deterrent to able men of normal sensitiveness and tend to prevent them from entering the public service at any price.

As an instance in point, I may mention that one serious difficulty encountered in getting the right type of men to dig the Panama canal is the certainty that they will be exposed, both without, and, I am sorry to say, sometimes within, Congress, to utterly reckless assaults on their character and capacity.

At the risk of repetition let me say again that my plea is not for immunity to, but for the most unsparing exposure of, the politician who betrays his trust, of the big business man who makes or spends his fortune in illegitimate or corrupt ways. There should be a resolute effort to hunt every such man out of the position he has disgraced. Expose the crime, and hunt down the criminal; but remember that even in the case of crime, if it is attacked in sensational, lurid, and untruthful fashion, the attack may do more damage to the public mind than the crime itself.

It is because I feel that there should be no rest in the endless war against the forces of evil that I ask the war be conducted with sanity as well as with resolution. The men with the muck rakes are often indispensable to the well being of society; but only if they know when to stop raking the muck, and to look upward to the celestial crown above them, to the crown of worthy endeavor. There are beautiful things above and round about them; and if they gradually grow to feel that the whole world is nothing but muck, their power of usefulness is gone.

If the whole picture is painted black there remains no hue whereby to single out the rascals for distinction from their fellows. Such painting finally induces a kind of moral colour blindness; and people affected by it come to the conclusion that no man is really black, and no man really white, but they are all gray.

In other words, they neither believe in the truth of the attack, nor in the honesty of the man who is attacked; they grow as suspicious of the accusation as of the offence; it becomes well nigh hopeless to stir them either to wrath against wrongdoing or to enthusiasm for what is right; and such a mental attitude in the public gives hope to every knave, and is the despair of honest men. To assail the great and admitted evils of our political and industrial life with such crude and sweeping generalizations as to include decent men in the general condemnation means the searing of the public conscience. There results a general attitude either of cynical belief in and indifference to public corruption or else of a distrustful inability to discriminate between the good and the bad. Either attitude is fraught with untold damage to the country as a whole.

The fool who has not sense to discriminate between what is good and what is bad is well nigh as dangerous as the man who does discriminate and yet chooses the bad. There is nothing more distressing to every good patriot, to every good American, than the hard, scoffing spirit which treats the allegation of dishonesty in a public man as a cause for laughter. Such laughter is worse than the crackling of thorns under a pot, for it denotes not merely the vacant mind, but the heart in which high emotions have been choked before they could grow to fruition. There is any amount of good in the world, and there never was a time when loftier and more disinterested work for the betterment of mankind was being done than now. The forces that tend for evil are great and terrible, but the forces of truth and love and courage and honesty and generosity and sympathy are also stronger than ever before. It is a foolish and timid, no less than a wicked thing, to blink the fact that the forces of evil are strong, but it is even worse to fail to take into account the strength of the forces that tell for good.

Hysterical sensationalism is the poorest weapon wherewith to fight for lasting righteousness. The men who with stern sobriety and truth assail the many evils of our time, whether in the public press, or in magazines, or in books, are the leaders and allies of all engaged in the work for social and political betterment. But if they give good reason for distrust of what they say, if they chill the ardour of those who demand truth as a primary virtue, they thereby betray the good cause and play into the hands of the very men against whom they are nominally at war. In his Ecclesiastical Polity that fine old Elizabethan divine, Bishop Hooker, wrote:

He that goeth about to persuade a multitude that they are not so well governed as they ought to be shall never want attentive and favourable hearers, because they know the manifold defects where unto every kind of regimen is subject, but the secret lets and difficulties, which in public proceedings are innumerable and inevitable, they have not ordinarily the judgment to consider.

This truth should be kept constantly in mind by every free people desiring to preserve the sanity and poise indispensable to the permanent success of self-government. Yet, on the other hand, it is vital not to permit this spirit of sanity and self-command to degenerate into mere mental stagnation. Bad though a state of hysterical excitement is, and evil though the results are which come from the violent oscillations such excitement invariably produces, yet a sodden acquiescence in evil is even worse.

At this moment we are passing through a period of great unrest—social, political, and industrial unrest. It is of the utmost importance for our future that this should prove to be not the unrest of mere rebelliousness against life, of mere dissatisfaction with the inevitable inequality of conditions, but the unrest of a resolute and eager ambition to secure the betterment of the individual and the nation.

So far as this movement of agitation throughout the country takes the form of a fierce discontent with evil, of a determination to punish the authors of evil, whether in industry or politics, the feeling is to be heartily welcomed as a sign of healthy life.

If, on the other hand, it turns into a mere crusade of appetite against appetite, of a contest between the brutal greed of the 'have nots' and the brutal greed of the 'haves,' then it has no significance for good, but only for evil. If it seeks to establish a line of cleavage, not along the line which divides good men from bad, but along that other line, running at right angles thereto, which divides those who are well off from those who are less well off, then it will be fraught with immeasurable harm to the body politic.

We can no more and no less afford to condone evil in the man of capital than evil in the man of no capital. The wealthy man who exults because there is a failure of justice in the effort to bring some trust magnate to account for his misdeeds is as bad as, and no worse than, the so-called labour leader who clamorously strives to excite a foul class feeling on behalf of some other labour leader who is implicated in murder. One attitude is as bad as the other, and no worse; in each case the accused is entitled to exact justice; and in neither case is there need of action by others which can be construed into an expression of sympathy for crime.

It is a prime necessity that if the present unrest is to result in permanent good the emotion shall be translated into action, and that the action shall be marked by honesty, sanity, and self-restraint. There is mighty little good in a mere spasm of reform. The reform that counts is that which comes through steady, continuous growth; violent emotionalism leads to exhaustion.

It is important to this people to grapple with the problems connected with the amassing of enormous fortunes, and the use of those fortunes, both corporate and individual, in business. We should discriminate in the sharpest way between fortunes well won and fortunes ill won; between those gained as an incident to performing great services to the community as a whole and those gained in evil fashion by keeping just within the limits of mere law honesty. Of course, no amount of charity in spending such fortunes in any way compensates for misconduct in making them. As a matter of personal conviction, and without pretending to discuss the details or formulate the system, I feel that we shall ultimately have to consider the adoption of some such scheme as that of a progressive tax on all fortunes, beyond a certain amount, either given in life or devised or bequeathed upon death to any individual—a tax so framed as to put it out of the power of the owner of one of these enormous fortunes to hand on more than a certain amount to any one individual; the tax of course, to be imposed by the national and not the state government. Such taxation should, of course, be aimed merely at the inheritance or transmission in their entirety of those fortunes swollen beyond all healthy limits. Again, the national government must in some form exercise supervision over corporations engaged in interstate business—and all large corporations engaged in interstate business—whether by licence or otherwise, so as to permit us to deal with the far reaching evils of overcapitalization.

This year we are making a beginning in the direction of serious effort to settle some of these economic problems by the railway rate legislation. Such legislation, if so framed, as I am sure it will be, as to secure definite and tangible results, will amount to something of itself; and it will amount to a great deal more in so far as it is taken as a first step in the direction of a policy of superintendence and control over corporate wealth engaged in interstate commerce; this superintendence and control not to be exercised in a spirit of malevolence toward the men who have created the wealth, but with the firm purpose both to do justice to them and to see that they in their turn do justice to the public at large.

The first requisite in the public servants who are to deal in this shape with corporations, whether as legislators or as executives, is honesty. This honesty can be no respecter of persons. There can be no such thing as unilateral honesty. The danger is not really from corrupt corporations; it springs from the corruption itself, whether exercised for or against corporations.

The eighth commandment reads, 'Thou shalt not steal.' It does not read, 'Thou shalt not steal from the rich man.' It does not read, 'Thou shalt not steal from the poor man.' It reads simply and plainly, 'Thou shalt not steal.'

No good whatever will come from that warped and mock morality which denounces the misdeeds of men of wealth and forgets the misdeeds practiced at their expense; which denounces bribery, but blinds itself to blackmail; which foams with rage if a corporation secures favours by improper methods, and merely leers with hideous mirth if the corporation is itself wronged.

The only public servant who can be trusted honestly to protect the rights of the public against the misdeeds of a corporation is that public man who will just as surely protect the corporation itself from wrongful aggression.

If a public man is willing to yield to popular clamour and do wrong to the men of wealth or to rich corporations, it may be set down as certain that if the opportunity comes he will secretly and furtively do wrong to the public in the interest of a corporation.

But in addition to honesty, we need sanity. No honesty will make a public man useful if that man is timid or foolish, if he is a hot-headed zealot or an impracticable visionary. As we strive for reform we find that it is not at all merely the case of a long uphill pull. On the contrary, there is almost as much of breeching work as of collar work. To depend only on traces means that there will soon be a runaway and an upset.

The men of wealth who today are trying to prevent the regulation and control of their business in the interest of the public by the proper government authorities will not succeed, in my judgment, in checking the progress of the movement. But if they did succeed they would find that they had sown the wind and would surely reap the whirlwind, for they would ultimately provoke the violent excesses which accompany a reform coming by convulsion instead of by steady and natural growth.

On the other hand, the wild preachers of unrest and discontent, the wild agitators against the entire existing order, the men who act crookedly, whether because of sinister design or from mere puzzle headedness, the men who preach destruction without proposing any substitute for what they intend to destroy, or who propose a substitute which would be far worse than the existing evils—all these men are the most dangerous opponents of real reform. If they get their way they will lead the people into a deeper pit than any into which they could fall under the present system. If they fail to get their way they will still do incalculable harm by provoking the kind of reaction which in its revolt against the senseless evil of their teaching would enthrone more securely than ever the evils which their misguided followers believe they are attacking.

More important than aught else is the development of the broadest sympathy of man for man. The welfare of the wage worker, the welfare of the tiller of the soil, upon these depend the welfare of the entire country; their good is not to be sought in pulling down others; but their good must be the prime object of all our statesmanship.

Materially we must strive to secure a broader economic opportunity for all men, so that each shall have a better chance to show the stuff of which he is made. Spiritually and ethically we must strive to bring about clean living and right thinking. We appreciate that the things of the body are important; but we appreciate also that the things of the soul are immeasurably more important.

The foundation stone of national life is, and ever must be, the high individual character of the average citizen.

50

A TRYST WITH DESTINY

Jawaharlal Nehru

The following speech delivered at New Delhi 14 August 1947 by Jawaharlal Nehru was made while introducing the 'pledge' to be taken by the members of the Constituent Assembly in New Delhi, 14 August 1947.

Long years ago we made a tryst with destiny, and now the time comes when we shall redeem our pledge, not wholly or in full measure, but very substantially. At the stroke of the midnight hour, when the world sleeps, India will awake to life and freedom. A moment comes, which comes but rarely in history; when we step out from the old to the new, when an age ends, and when the soul of a nation, long suppressed, finds utterance. It is fitting that at this solemn moment we take the pledge of dedication to the service of India and her people and to the still larger cause of humanity.

At the dawn of history India started on her unending quest, and trackless centuries are filled with her striving and the grandeur of her successes and her failures. Through good and ill fortune alike she has never lost sight of that quest or forgotten the ideals which gave her strength. We end, today, a period of ill fortune and India discovers herself again. The achievement we celebrate today is but a step, an opening of opportunity, to the greater triumphs and achievements that await us. Are we brave enough and wise enough to grasp this opportunity and accept the challenge of the future?

Freedom and power bring responsibility, that responsibility rests upon this Assembly, a sovereign body representing the sovereign people of India.

Before the birth of freedom we have endured all the pains of labour and our hearts are heavy with the memory of this sorrow. Some of those pains continue even now. Nevertheless the past is over and it is the future that beckons to us now.

That future is not one of ease or resting but of incessant striving so that we might fulfill the pledges we have so often taken and the one we shall take today. The service of India means the service of the millions who suffer. It means the ending of poverty, ignorance, disease and inequality of opportunity; The ambition of the greatest man of our generation has been to wipe every tear from every eye. That may be beyond us but as long as there are tears and suffering, so long our work will not be over.

And so we have to labour and work hard to give reality to our dreams. Those dreams are for India, but they are also for the world, for all the nations and peoples are too closely knit together today for any one of them to imagine that it can live apart. Peace has been said to be indivisible, so is freedom, so is prosperity now, and so also is disaster in this one world that can no longer be split into isolated fragments.

To the people of India, whose representatives we are, we appeal to join us with faith and confidence in this great adventure. This is no time for petty and destructive criticism, no time for ill will or blaming others. We have to build the noble mansion of free India where all her children may dwell.

The Pledge

At this solemn moment when the people of India, through suffering and sacrifice, have secured freedom, I...a member of the Constituent Assembly of India, do dedicate myself in all humility to the service of India and her people to the end that this ancient land attain her rightful place in the world and make her full and willing contribution to the promotion of world peace and the welfare of mankind.

51

SIXTH ANNUAL MESSAGE

Thomas Jefferson

2 December 1806: Thomas Jefferson addresses the crisis with Spain at length, outlining the measures he has taken to defend the country. The president also highlights the important contributions that the Lewis and Clark expedition and other expeditions have made to the knowledge of the country.

To the Senate and House of Representatives of The United States in Congress Assembled:

It would have given me, fellow citizens, great satisfaction to announce in the moment of your meeting that the difficulties in our foreign relations, existing at the time of your last separation, had been amicably and justly terminated. I lost no time in taking those measures which were most likely to bring them to such a termination, by special missions charged with such powers and instructions as in the event of failure could leave no imputation on either our moderation or forbearance. The delays which have since taken place in our negotiations with the British government appears to have proceeded from causes which do not forbid the expectation that during the course of the session I may be enabled to lay before you their final issue. What will be that of the negotiations for settling our differences with Spain, nothing which had taken place at the date of the last despatches enables us to pronounce. On the western side of the Mississippi she advanced in considerable force, and took post at the settlement of Bayou Pierre, on the Red river. This village was originally settled by France, was held by her as long as she held Louisiana, and was delivered to Spain only as a part of

Louisiana. Being small, insulated, and distant, it was not observed, at the moment of redelivery to France and the United States, that she continued a guard of half a dozen men which had been stationed there. A proposition, however, having been lately made by our commander-in-chief, to assume the Sabine river as a temporary line of separation between the troops of the two nations until the issue of our negotiations shall be known; this has been referred by the Spanish commandant to his superior, and in the meantime, he has withdrawn his force to the western side of the Sabine river. The correspondence on this subject, now communicated, will exhibit more particularly the present state of things in that quarter.

The nature of that country requires indispensably that an unusual proportion of the force employed there should be cavalry or mounted infantry. In order, therefore, that the commanding officer might be enabled to act with effect, I had authorized him to call on the governors of Orleans and Mississippi for a corps of five hundred volunteer cavalry. The temporary arrangement he has proposed may perhaps render this unnecessary. But I inform you with great pleasure of the promptitude with which the inhabitants of those territories have tendered their services in defence of their country. It has done honour to themselves, entitled them to the confidence of their fellow-citizens in every part of the Union, and must strengthen the general determination to protect them efficaciously under all circumstances which may occur.

Having received information that in another part of the United States a great number of private individuals were combining together, arming and organizing themselves contrary to law, to carry on military expeditions against the territories of Spain, I thought it necessary, by proclamations as well as by special orders, to take measures for preventing and suppressing this enterprise, for seizing the vessels, arms, and other means provided for it, and for arresting and bringing to justice its authors and abettors. It was due to that good faith which ought ever to be the rule of action in public as well as in private transactions; it was due to good order and regular government, that while the public force was acting strictly on the defensive and merely to protect our citizens from aggression, the criminal attempts of private individuals to decide for their country the question of peace or war, by commencing active and unauthorized hostilities, should be promptly and efficaciously suppressed.

Whether it will be necessary to enlarge our regular force will depend on the result of our negotiation with Spain; but as it is uncertain when that result will be known, the provisional measures requisite for that, and to meet any pressure intervening in that quarter, will be a subject for your early consideration.

The possession of both banks of the Mississippi reducing to a single point the defence of that river, its waters, and the country adjacent, it becomes highly necessary to provide for that point a more adequate security. Some position above its mouth, commanding the passage of the river, should be rendered sufficiently strong to cover the armed vessels which may be stationed there for defence, and in conjunction with them to present an insuperable obstacle to any force attempting to pass. The approaches to the city of New Orleans, from the eastern quarter also, will require to be examined, and more effectually guarded. For the internal support of the country, the encouragement of a strong settlement on the western side of the Mississippi, within reach of New Orleans, will be worthy the consideration of the legislature.

The gun-boats authorized by an act of the last session are so advanced that they will be ready for service in the ensuing spring. Circumstances permitted us to allow the time necessary for their more solid construction. As a much larger number will still be wanting to place our seaport towns and waters in that state of defence to which we are competent and they entitled, a similar appropriation for a further provision for them is recommended for the ensuing year.

A further appropriation will also be necessary for repairing fortifications already established, and the erection of such works as may have real effect in obstructing the approach of an enemy to our seaport towns, or their remaining before them.

In a country whose constitution is derived from the will of the people, directly expressed by their free suffrages; where the principal executive functionaries, and those of the legislature, are renewed by them at short periods; where under the characters of jurors, they exercise in person the greatest portion of the judiciary powers; where the laws are consequently so formed and administered as to bear with equal weight and favour on all, restraining no man in the pursuits of honest industry, and securing to every one the property which that acquires, it would not be supposed that any safeguards could be needed against insurrection or enterprise on the public peace or authority. The laws, however, aware that these should not be trusted to moral restraints only, have wisely provided punishments for these crimes when committed. But would it not be salutary to give also the means of preventing their commission? Where an enterprise is meditated by private individuals against a foreign nation in amity with the United States, powers of prevention to a certain extent are given by the laws; would they not be as reasonable and useful were the enterprise preparing against the United States? While adverting to this branch of the law, it is proper to observe, that in enterprises meditated against foreign nations, the ordinary process of binding to the observance of the peace and good behavior, could it be extended to acts to be done out of the jurisdiction of the United States, would be effectual in some cases where the offender is able to keep out of sight every indication of his purpose which could draw on him the exercise of the powers now given by law.

The states on the coast of Barbary seem generally disposed at present to respect our peace and friendship; with Tunis alone some uncertainty remains. Persuaded that it is our interest to maintain our peace with them on equal terms, or not at all, I propose to send in due time a reinforcement into the Mediterranean, unless previous information shall show it to be unnecessary.

We continue to receive proofs of the growing attachment of our Indian neighbours, and of their disposition to place all their interests under the patronage of the United States. These dispositions are inspired by their confidence in our justice, and in the sincere concern we feel for their welfare; and as long as we discharge these high and honourable functions with the integrity and good faith which alone can entitle us to their continuance, we may expect to reap the just reward in their peace and friendship.

The expedition of Messrs. Lewis and Clarke, for exploring the river

Missouri, and the best communication from that to the Pacific ocean, has had all the success which could have been expected. They have traced the Missouri nearly to its source, descended the Columbia to the Pacific ocean, ascertained with accuracy the geography of that interesting communication across our continent, learned the character of the country, of its commerce, and inhabitants; and it is but justice to say that Messrs. Lewis and Clarke, and their brave companions, have by this arduous service deserved well of their country.

The attempt to explore the Red river, under the direction of Mr Freeman, though conducted with a zeal and prudence meriting entire approbation, has not been equally successful. After proceeding up it about six hundred miles, nearly as far as the French settlements had extended while the country was in their possession, our geographers were obliged to return without completing their work.

Very useful additions have also been made to our knowledge of the Mississippi by Lieutenant Pike, who has ascended to its source, and whose journal and map, giving the details of the journey, will shortly be ready for communication to both houses of Congress. Those of Messrs. Lewis and Clarke, and Freeman, will require further time to be digested and prepared. These important surveys, in addition to those before possessed, furnish materials for commencing an accurate map of the Mississippi, and its western waters. Some principal rivers, however, remain still to be explored, toward which the authorization of Congress, by moderate appropriations, will be requisite.

I congratulate you, fellow-citizens, on the approach of the period at which you may interpose your authority constitutionally, to withdraw the citizens of the United States from all further participation in those violations of human rights which have been so long continued on the unoffending inhabitants of Africa, and which the morality, the reputation, and the best interests of our country, have long been eager to proscribe. Although no law you may pass can take prohibitory effect till the first day of the year one thousand eight hundred and eight, yet the intervening period is not too long to prevent, by timely notice, expeditions which cannot be completed before that day.

The receipts at the treasury during the year ending on the 30th of September last, have amounted to near fifteen millions of dollars, which have enabled us, after meeting the current demands, to pay two millions seven hundred thousand dollars of the American claims, in part of the price of Louisiana; to pay of the funded debt upward of three millions of principal, and nearly four of interest; and in addition, to reimburse, in the course of the present month, near two millions of five and a half per cent stock. These payments and reimbursements of the funded debt, with those which have been made in the four years and a half preceding, will, at the close of the present year, have extinguished upwards of twenty-three millions of principal.

The duties composing the Mediterranean fund will cease by law at the end of the present season. Considering, however, that they are levied chiefly on luxuries, and that we have an impost on salt, a necessary of life, the free use of which otherwise is so important, I recommend to your consideration the suppression of the duties on salt, and the continuation of the Mediterranean fund, instead thereof, for a short time, after which that also will become unnecessary for any purpose now within contemplation.

When both of these branches of revenue shall in this way be relinquished, there will still ere long be an accumulation of moneys in the treasury beyond the instalments of public debt which we are permitted by contract to pay. They cannot, then, without a modification assented to by the public creditors, be applied to the extinguishment of this debt, and the complete liberation of our revenues—the most desirable of all objects; nor, if our peace continues, will they be wanting for any other existing purpose. The question, therefore, now comes forward—to what other objects shall these surpluses be appropriated, and the whole surplus of impost, after the entire discharge of the public debt, and during those intervals when the purposes of war shall not call for them? Shall we suppress the impost and give that advantage to foreign over domestic manufactures? On a few articles of more general and necessary use, the suppression in due season will doubtless be right, but the great mass of the articles on which impost is paid is foreign luxuries, purchased by those only who are rich enough to afford themselves the use of them. Their patriotism would certainly prefer its continuance and application to the great purposes of the public education, roads, rivers, canals, and such other objects of public improvement as it may be thought proper to add to the constitutional enumeration of federal powers. By these operations, new channels of communication will be opened between the States; the lines of separation will disappear, their interests will be identified, and their union cemented by new and indissoluble ties. Education is here placed among the articles of public care, not that it would be proposed to take its ordinary branches out of the hands of private enterprise, which manages so much better all the concerns to which it is equal; but a public institution can alone supply those sciences which, though rarely called for, are yet necessary to complete the circle, all the parts of which contribute to the improvement of the country, and some of them to its preservation. The subject is now proposed for the consideration of Congress, because, if approved by the time the State legislatures shall have deliberated on this extension of the federal trusts, and the laws shall be passed, and other arrangements made for their execution, the necessary funds will be on hand and without employment. I suppose an amendment to the constitution, by consent of the States, necessary, because the objects now recommended are not among those enumerated in the constitution, and to which it permits the public moneys to be applied.

The present consideration of a national establishment for education, particularly, is rendered proper by this circumstance also, that if Congress, approving the proposition, shall yet think it more eligible to found it on a donation of lands, they have it now in their power to endow it with those which will be among the earliest to produce the necessary income. This foundation would have the advantage of being independent on war, which may suspend other improvements by requiring for its own purposes the resources destined for them.

This, fellow citizens, is the state of the public interest at the present moment, and according to the information now possessed. But such is the situation of the nations of Europe, and such too the predicament in which we stand with some of them, that we cannot rely with certainty on the present aspect of our affairs that may change from moment to moment, during the course of your session or after you shall have separated. Our duty is, therefore, to act upon things as they are, and to make a reasonable provision for whatever they may be. Were armies to be raised whenever a speck of war is visible in our horizon, we never should have been without them. Our resources would have been exhausted on dangers which have never happened, instead of being reserved for what is really to take place. A steady, perhaps a quickened pace in preparations for the defence of our seaport towns and waters; an early settlement of the most exposed and vulnerable parts of our country; a militia so organized that its effective portions can be called to any point in the Union, or volunteers instead of them to serve a sufficient time, are means which may always be ready yet never preying on our resources until actually called into use. They will maintain the public interests while a more permanent force shall be in course of preparation. But much will depend on the promptitude with which these means can be brought into activity. If war be forced upon us in spite of our long and vain appeals to the justice of nations, rapid and vigorous movements in its outset will go far toward securing us in its course and issue, and toward throwing its burdens on those who render necessary the resort from reason to force.

The result of our negotiations, or such incidents in their course as may enable us to infer their probable issue; such further movements also on our western frontiers as may show whether war is to be pressed there while negotiation is protracted elsewhere, shall be communicated to you from time to time as they become known to me, with whatever other information I possess or may receive, which may aid your deliberations on the great national interests committed to your charge.

52

ACRES OF DIAMONDS

Russell Herman Conwell

Russell Herman Conwell was a Baptist minister, lawyer, writer, and outstanding orator. He is best remembered as the founder and first president of Temple University in Philadelphia, Pennsylvania, and for his lecture and book Acres of Diamonds. He was born in South Worthington, Massachusetts on 15 February 1843. He passed away on 6 December 1925 and was buried in Founder's Garden at Temple University. Russell Conwell delivered his 'Acres of Diamonds' speech over 5,000 times at various times and places from the 1890s to 1925. He delivered it in Camden on 21 March 1893 at the First Baptist Church, 28 North 4th Street.

When going down the Tigris and Euphrates rivers many years ago with a party of English travellers I found myself under the direction of an old Arab guide whom we hired up at Baghdad, and I have often thought how that guide resembled our barbers in certain mental characteristics. He thought that it was not only his duty to guide us down those rivers, and do what he was paid for doing, but to entertain us with stories curious and weird, ancient and modern strange, and familiar. Many of them I have forgotten, and I am glad I have, but there is one I shall never forget.

The old guide was leading my camel by its halter along the banks of those ancient rivers, and he told me story after story until I grew weary of his story-telling and ceased to listen. I have never been irritated with that guide when he lost his temper as I ceased listening. But I remember that he took off his Turkish cap and swung it in a circle to get my attention. I could see it through the corner of my eye, but I determined not to look straight at him for fear he would tell another story. But although I am not a woman, I did finally look, and as soon as I did he went right into another story. Said he, 'I will tell you a story now which I reserve for my particular friends.' When he emphasized the words 'particular friends,' I listened and I have ever been glad I did. I really feel devoutly thankful, that there are 1,674 young men who have been carried through college by this lecture who are also glad that I did listen.

The old guide told me that there once lived not far from the River Indus an ancient Persian by the name of Ali Hafed. He said that Ali Hafed owned a very large farm; that he had orchards, grain-fields, and gardens; that he had money at interest and was a wealthy and contented man. One day, there visited that old Persian farmer one of those ancient Buddhist priests, one of the wise men of the East. He sat down by the fire and told the old farmer how this old world of ours was made.

He said that this world was once a mere bank of fog, and that the Almighty thrust His finger into this bank of fog, and began slowly to move His finger around, increasing the speed until at last He whirled this bank of fog into a solid ball of fire. Then it went rolling through the universe, burning its way through other banks of fog, and condensed the moisture without, until it fell in floods of rain upon its hot surface, and cooled the outward crust. Then the internal fires bursting outward through the crust threw up the mountains and hills, the valleys, the plains and prairies of this wonderful world of ours. If this internal molten mass came bursting out and cooled very quickly, it became granite; less quickly copper, less quickly silver, less quickly gold, and, after gold, diamonds were made. Said the old priest, 'A diamond is a congealed drop of sunlight.' Now that is literally scientifically true, that a diamond is an actual deposit of carbon from the sun.

The old priest told Ali Hafed that if he had one diamond the size of his thumb he could purchase the county, and if the had a mine of diamonds he could place his children upon thrones through the influence of their great wealth. Ali Hafed heard all about diamonds, how much they were worth, and went to his bed that night a poor man. He had not lost anything, but he was poor because he was discontented, and discontented because he feared he was poor. He said, 'I want a mine of diamonds,' and he lay awake all night. Early in the morning he sought out the priest. I know by experience that a priest is very cross when awakened early in the morning, and when he shook that old priest out of his dreams, Ali Hafed said to him:

'Will you tell me where I find diamonds?'

'Diamonds! What do you want with diamonds?'

'Why, I wish to be immensely rich.'

'Well, then, go along and find them. That is all you have to do; go and find them, and then you have them.'

'But I don't know where to go.'

'Well, if you will find a river that runs through white sands, between high mountains, in those white sands you will always find diamonds.'

'I don't believe there is any such river.'

'Oh yes, there are plenty of them. All you have to do is to go and find them, and then you have them.'

Said Ali Hafed, 'I will go.'

So he sold his farm, collected his money, left his family in charge of a neighbour, and away he went in search of diamonds. He began his search, very properly to my mind, at the Mountains of the Moon. Afterward he came around into Palestine, then wandered on into Europe, and at last when his money was all spent and he was in rags, wretchedness, and poverty, he stood on the shore of that bay at Barcelona, in Spain, when a great tidal wave came rolling in between the pillars of Hercules, and the poor, afflicted, suffering, dying man could not resist the awful temptation to cast himself into that incoming tide, and he sank beneath its foaming crest, never to rise in this life again.

Then after that old guide had told me that awfully sad story, he stopped the camel I was riding on and went back to fix the baggage that was coming off another camel, and I had an opportunity to muse over his story while he was gone. I remember saying to myself, 'Why did he reserve that story for his "particular friends"?' There seemed to be no beginning, no middle, no end, nothing to it.

That was the first story I had ever heard told in my life, and would be the first one I ever read, in which the hero was killed in the first chapter. I had but one chapter of that story, and the hero was dead. When the guide came back and took up the halter of my camel, he went right ahead with the story, into the second chapter, just as though there had been no break.

The man who purchased Ali Hafed's farm one day led his camel into the garden to drink, and as that camel put its nose into the shallow water of that garden brook, Ali Hafed's successor noticed a curious flash of light from the white sands of the stream. He pulled out a black stone having an eye of light reflecting all the hues of the rainbow. He took the pebble into the house and put it on the mantel which covers the central fires, and forgot all about it.

A few days later this same old priest came in to visit Ali Hafed's successor, and the moment he opened that drawing room door he saw that flash of light on the mantel, and he rushed up to it, and shouted:

'Here is a diamond! Has Ali Hafed returned?'

'Oh no, Ali Hafed has not returned, and that is not a diamond. That is nothing but a stone we found right out here in our own garden.'

'But,' said the priest, 'I tell you I know a diamond when I see it. I know positively that is a diamond.'

Then together they rushed out into that old garden and stirred up the white sands with their fingers, and lo! There came up other more beautiful and valuable gems then the first. 'Thus,' said the guide to me, 'was discovered the diamond mine of Golconda, the most magnificent diamond mine in all the history of mankind, excelling the Kimberly itself. The Kohinoor, and the Orloff of the crown jewels of England and Russia, the largest on earth, came from that mine.'

When that old Arab guide told me the second chapter of his story, he then took off his Turkish cap and swung it around in the air again to get my attention to the moral. Those Arab guides have morals to their stories, although they are not always moral. As he swung his hat, he said to me, 'Had Ali Hafed remained at home and dug in his own cellar, or underneath his own wheat fields or in his own garden, instead of wretchedness, starvation, and death by suicide in a strange land, he would have had "acres of diamonds." For every acre of that old farm, yes, every shovelful, afterward revealed gems which since have decorated the crowns of monarchs.'

When he had added the moral of his story I saw why he reserved it for 'his particular friends.' But I did not tell him that I could see it. It was that mean old Arab's way of going around a thing like a lawyer, to say indirectly what he did not dare say directly, that 'in his private opinion there was a certain young man then traveling down the Tigris River that might better be at home in America.' I did not tell him I could see that, but I told it to him quick, and I think I will tell it to you.

I told him of a man out in California in 1847, who owned a ranch. He heard they had discovered gold in southern California, and so with a passion for gold he sold his ranch to Colonel Sutter, and away he went, never to come back. Colonel Sutter put a mill upon a stream that ran through that ranch, and one day his little girl brought some wet sand from the raceway into their home and sifted it through her fingers before the fire, and in that falling sand a visitor saw the first shining scales of real gold that were ever discovered in California. The man who had owned that ranch wanted gold, and he could have secured it for the mere taking. Indeed, thirty-eight millions of dollars has been taken out of a very few acres since then.

About eight years ago, I delivered this lecture in a city that stands on that farm, and they told me that a one-third owner for years and years had been getting one hundred and twenty dollars in gold every fifteen minutes, sleeping or waking, without taxation. You and I would enjoy an income like that—if we didn't have to pay an income tax.

But a better illustration really than that occurred here in our town of Pennsylvania. If there is anything I enjoy above another on the platform, it is to get one of these German audiences in Pennsylvania, and fire that at them, and I enjoy it tonight. There was a man living in Pennsylvania, not unlike some Pennsylvanians you have seen, who owned a farm, and he did with that farm just what I should do with a farm if I owned one in Pennsylvania—he sold it. But before he sold it he decided to secure employment collecting coal-oil for his cousin, who was in the business in Canada, where they first discovered oil on this continent. They dipped it from the running streams at that early time. So this Pennsylvania farmer wrote to his cousin asking for employment. You see, friends, this farmer was not altogether a foolish man. No, he was not. He did not leave his farm until he had something else to do. Of all the simpletons the stars shine on I don't know of a worse one than the man who leaves one job before he has gotten another. That has especial reference to my profession, and has no reference whatever to a man seeking a divorce. When he wrote to his cousin for employment, his cousin replied, 'I cannot engage you because you know nothing about the oil business.' Well, then the old farmer said, 'I will know,' and with most commendable zeal (characteristic of the students of Temple University) he sat himself at the study of the whole subject. He began away back at the second day of God's creation when this world was covered thick and deep with that rich vegetation which since has turned to the primitive beds of coal. He studied the subject until he found that the drainings really of those rich beds of coal furnished the coal-oil that was worth pumping, and then he found how it came up with the living springs. He studied until he knew what it looked like, smelled like, tasted like, and how to refine it. Now said he in his letter to his cousin, 'I understand the oil business.' His cousin answered, 'All right, come on.'

So he sold his farm, according to the county record, for $833 (even money, 'no cents'). He had scarcely gone from that place before the man who purchased the spot went out to arrange for the watering of the cattle. He found the previous owner had gone out years before and put a plank across the brook back of the barn, edgewise into the surface of the water just a few inches. The purpose of that plank at that sharp angle across the brook was to throw over to the other bank a dreadful-looking scum through which the cattle would not put their noses. But with that plank there to throw it all over to one side, the cattle would drink below, and thus that man who had gone to Canada had been himself damming back for twenty-three years a flood of coal-oil which the state geologists of Pennsylvania declared to us ten years later was even then worth a hundred millions of dollars to our state, a thousand millions of dollars. The man who owned that territory on which the city to Titusville now stands, and those Pleasantville valleys, had studied the subject from the second day of God's creation clear down to the present time. He studied it until he knew all about it, and yet he is said to have sold the whole of it for $833, and again I say, 'no sense.'

But I need another illustration. I found it in Massachusetts, and I am sorry I did because that is the state I came from. This young man in Massachusetts furnishes just another phase of my thought. He went to Yale College and studied mines and mining, and became such an adept as a mining engineer that he was employed by the authorities of the university to train students who were behind their classes. During his senior years he earned $15 a week for doing that work. When he graduated they raised his pay from $15 to $45 a week, and offered him a professorship, as soon as they did he went right home to his mother. If they had raised that boy's pay from $14 to $15.60 he would have stayed and been proud of the place, but when they put it up to $45 at one leap, he said, 'Mother, I won't work for $45 a week. The idea of a man with a brain like mine working for $45 a week! Let's go out to California and stake out gold-mines and silver-mines, and be immensely rich.' Said his mother, 'Now, Charlie, it is just as well to be happy as it is to be rich.' 'Yes,' said Charlie, 'But it is just as well to be rich and happy too.' And they were both right about it. As he was an only son and she a widow, of course he had his way. They always do.

They sold out in Massachusetts, and instead of going to California they went to Wisconsin, where he went into the employ of the superior Copper Mining Company at $15 a week again, but with the proviso in his contract that he should have an interest in any mines he should discover for the company. I don't believe he ever discovered a mine, and if I am looking in the face of any stockholder of that copper company you wish he had discovered something or other. I have friends who are not here because they could not afford a ticket, who did have stock in that company at the time this young man was employed there. This young man went out there and I have not heard a word from him. I don't know what became of him, and I don't know whether he found any mines or not, but I don't believe he ever did.

But I do know the other end of the line. He had scarcely gotten the other end of the old homestead before the succeeding owner went out to dig potatoes. The potatoes were already growing in the ground when he bought the farm, and as the old farmer was bringing in a basket of potatoes it hugged very tight between the ends of the stone fence. You know in Massachusetts our farms are nearly all stone wall. There you are obliged to be very economical of front gateways in order to have some place to put the stone. When that basket hugged so tight he set it down on the ground, and then dragged on one side, and pulled on the other side, and as he was dragging that basket though this farmer noticed in the upper and outer corner of that stone wall, right next the gate, a block of native silver eight inches square. That professor of mines, mining, and mineralogy who knew so much about the subject that he would not work for $45 a week, when he sold that homestead in Massachusetts sat right on that silver to make the bargain. He was born on that homestead, was brought up there, and had gone back and forth rubbing the stone with his sleeve until it reflected his countenance, and seemed to say, 'Here is a hundred thousand dollars right down here just for the taking.' But he would not take it. It was in a home in Newburyport, Massachusetts, and there was no silver there, all away off—well, I don't know were, and he did not, but somewhere else, and he was a professor of mineralogy.

My friends, that mistake is very universally made, and why should we even smile at him. I often wonder what has become of him. I do not know at all, but I will tell you what I 'guess' as a Yankee. I guess that he sits out there by his fireside tonight with his friends gathered around him, and he is saying to them something like this: 'Do you know that man Conwell who lives in Philadelphia?' 'Oh yes, I have heard of him.' 'Do you know of that man Jones that lives in Philadelphia?' 'Yes, I have heard of him, too.'

Then he begins to laugh, and shakes his sides, and says to his friends, 'Well, they have done just the same thing I did, precisely.'—and that spoils the whole joke, for you and I have done the same thing he did, and while we sit here and laugh at him he has a better right to sit out there and laugh at us. I know I have made the same mistakes, but, of course, that does not make any difference, because we don't expect the same man to preach and practice, too.

As I come here tonight and look around this audience I am seeing again what through these fifty years I have continually seen—men that are making precisely that same mistake. I often wish I could see the younger people, and would that the Academy had been filled tonight with our high school scholars and our grammar-school scholars, that I could have them to talk to. While I would have preferred such an audience as that, because they are most susceptible, as they have not gotten into any custom that they cannot break, they have not met with any failures as we have; and while I could perhaps do such an audience as that more good than I can do grown-up people, yet I will do the best I can with the material I have. I say to you that you have 'acres of diamonds' in Philadelphia right where you now live. 'Oh,' but you will say, 'you cannot know much about your city if you think there are any "acres of diamonds" here.'

I was greatly interested in that account in the newspaper of the young man who found that diamond in North Carolina. It was one of the purest diamonds that has ever been discovered, and it has several predecessors near the same locality. I went to a distinguished professor in mineralogy and asked him where he thought those diamonds came from. The professor secured the map of the geologic formations of our continent, and traced it. He said it went either through the underlying carboniferous strata adapted for such production, westward through Ohio and the Mississippi, or in more probability came eastward through Virginia and up the shore of the Atlantic Ocean. It is a fact that the diamonds were there, for they have been discovered and sold; and that they were carried down there during the drift period, from some northern locality. Now who can say but some person going down with his drill in Philadelphia will find some trace of a diamond mine yet down here? Oh, friends! You cannot say that you are not over one of the greatest diamond mines in the world, for such a diamond as that only comes from the most profitable mines that are found on earth.

But it serves to simply to illustrate my thought, which I emphasize by saying if you do not have the actual diamond mines literally you have all that they would be good for to you. Because now that the Queen of England has given the greatest compliment ever conferred upon American woman for her attire because she did not appear with any jewels at all at the late reception in England, it has almost done away with the use of diamonds anyhow. All you would care for would be the few you would wear if you wish to be modest, and the rest of you would sell for money.

Now then, I say again that the opportunity to get rich, to attain unto great wealth, is here in Philadelphia now, within the reach of almost every man and woman who hears me speak tonight, and I mean just what I say. I have not come to this platform even under these circumstances to recite something to you. I have come to tell you what in God's sight I believe to be the truth, and if the years of life have been of any value to me in the attainment of common sense, I know I am right; that the men and women sitting here, who found it difficult perhaps to buy a ticket to this lecture or gathering tonight, have within their reach 'acres of diamonds,' opportunities to get largely wealthy. There never was a place on earth more adapted than the city of Philadelphia today, and never in the history of the world did a poor man without capital have such an opportunity to get rich quickly and honestly as he has now in our city. I say it is the truth, and I want you to accept it as such; for if you think I have come to simply recite something, then I would better not be here. I have no time to waste in any such talk, but to say the things I believe, and unless some of you get richer for what I am saying to night my time is wasted.

I say that you ought to get rich, and it is our duty to get rich. How many of my pious brethren say to me, 'Do you, a Christian minister, spend your time going up and down the country advising young people to get rich, to get money?' 'Yes, of course I do.' They say, 'Isn't that awful! Why don't you preach the gospel instead of preaching about man's making money?' 'Because to make money honestly is to preach the gospel.' That is the reason. The men who get rich may be the most honest men you find in the community. 'Oh,' but says some young man here tonight, 'I have been told all my life that if a person has money he is very dishonest and dishonourable and mean and contemptible.'

My friend, that is the reason why you have none, because you have that idea of people. The foundation of your faith is altogether false. Let me say here clearly, and say it briefly, though subject to discussion which I have not time for here, ninety-eight out of one hundred of the rich men of America are honest. That is why they are rich. That is why they carry on great enterprises and find plenty of people to work with them. It is because they are honest men.

Says another young man, 'I hear sometimes of men that get millions of dollars dishonestly.' Yes, of course you do, and so do I. But they are so rare a thing in fact that the newspapers talk about them all the time as a matter of news until you get the idea that all the other rich men got rich dishonestly.

My friend, you take and drive me—if you furnish the auto—out into the suburbs of Philadelphia, and introduce me to the people who own their homes around this great city, those beautiful homes with gardens and flowers, those magnificent homes so lovely in their art, and I will introduce you to the very best people in character as well as in enterprise in our city, and you know I will. A man is not really a true man until he owns his own home, and they that own their homes are made more honourable and honest and pure, true and economical and careful, by owning the home.

For a man to have money, even in large sum, is not an inconsistent thing. We preach against covetousness, and you know we do, in the pulpit, and oftentimes preach against it so long and use the terms about filthy lucre: so extremely that Christians get the idea that when we stand in the pulpit we believe it is wicked for any man to have money—until the collection basket goes around, and then we almost swear at the people because they don't give more money. Oh, the inconsistency of such doctrines as that!

Money is power, and you ought to be reasonably ambitious to have it. You ought because you can do more good with it than you could without it. Money printed your Bible, money builds your churches, money sends your missionaries, and money pays your preachers, and you would not have many of them, either, if you did not pay them. I am always willing that my church should raise my salary, because the church that pays the largest salary always raises it the easiest. You never knew an exception to it in your life. The man who gets the largest salary can do the most good with the power that is furnished to him. Of course he can if his spirit be right to use it for what it is given to him.

I say, then, you ought to have money. If you can honestly attain unto riches in Philadelphia, it is our Christian and godly duty to do so. It is an awful mistake of these pious people to think you must be awfully poor in order to be pious.

Some men say, 'Don't you sympathize with the poor people?' Of course I do, or else I would not have been lecturing these years. I won't give in but what I sympathize with the poor, but the number of poor who are to be with is very small. To sympathize with a man whom God has punished for his sins, thus to help him when God would still continue a just punishment, is to do wrong, no doubt about it, and we do that more than we help those who are deserving. While we should sympathize with God's poor—that is, those who cannot help themselves—let us remember that is not a poor person in the United States who was not made poor by his own shortcomings, or by the shortcomings of some one else. It is all wrong to be poor, anyhow. Let us give in to that argument and pass that to one side.

A gentleman gets up back there, and says, 'Don't you think there are some things in this world that are better than money?' Of course I do, but I am talking about money now. Of course there are some things higher than money. Oh yes, I know by the grave that has left me standing alone that there are some things in this world that are higher and sweeter and purer than money. Well do I know there are some things higher and grander than gold. Love is the grandest thing on God's earth, but fortunate the lover who has plenty of money. Money is power, money is force, money will do good as harm. In the hands of good men and women it could accomplish, and it has accomplished, good.

I hate to leave that behind me. I heard a man get up in a prayer-meeting in our city and thank the Lord he was 'one of God's poor.' Well, I wonder what his wife thinks about that? She earns all the money that comes into that house, and he smokes a part of that on the veranda. I don't want to see any more of the Lord's poor of that kind, and I don't believe the Lord does. And yet there are some people who think in order to be pious you must be awfully poor and awfully dirty. That does not follow at all. While we sympathize with the poor, let us not teach a doctrine like that.

Yet the age is prejudiced against advising a Christian man (or, as a Jew would say, a godly man) from attaining unto wealth. The prejudice is so universal and the years are far enough back, I think, for me to safely mention that years ago up at Temple University there was a young man in our theological school who thought he was the only pious student in that department. He came into my office on evening and sat down by my desk, and said to me: 'Mr President, I think it is my duty sir, to come in and labour with you.' 'What has happened now?' Said he, 'I heard you say at the Academy, at the pierce School commencement, that you thought it was an honourable ambition for a young man to desire to have wealth, and that you thought it made him temperate, made him anxious to have a good name, and made him industrious. You spoke to make him a good man. Sir, I have come to tell you the Holy Bible says that "money is the root of all evil".' I told him I had never seen it in the Bible, and advised him to go out into the chapel and get the Bible, and show me the place. So out he went for the Bible, and soon he stalked into my office with the Bible open, with all the bigoted pride of the narrow sectarian, of one who founds his Christianity on some misinterpretation of Scripture. He flung the Bible down on my desk, and fairly squealed into my ear: 'There it is Mr President; you can read it yourself.' I said to him: 'Well young man, you will learn when you get a little older that you cannot trust another denomination to read the Bible for you. You belong to another denomination. You are taught in the theological school, however, that emphasis is the exegesis. Now, will you take that Bible and read it yourself, and give the proper emphasis to it?'

He took the Bible, and proudly read, 'The love of money is the root of all evil.' Then he had it right, and when one does quote aright from that same old Book he quotes the absolute truth. I have lived through fifty years of the mightiest battle that old Book has ever fought, and I have lived to see its banners flying free; for never in the history of this world did the great minds of earth so universally agree that the Bible is true-all true-as they do at this very hour.

So I say that when he quoted right, of course he quoted the absolute truth.

The love of money is the root of all evil.' He who tries to attain unto it too quickly, or dishonestly, will fall into many snares, no doubt about that. The love of money. What is that? It is making an idol of money, and idolatry pure and simple every where is condemned by the Holy Scriptures and by man's common sense. The man that worships the dollar instead of thinking of the purposes for which it ought to be used, the man who idolizes simply money, the miser that hordes his money in the cellar, or hides it in his staking, or refuses to invest it where it will do the world good, that man who hugs the dollar until the eagle squeals has in him the root of all evil.

I think I will leave that behind me now and answer the question of nearly all of you who are asking, 'Is there opportunity to get rich in Philadelphia?' Well, now, how simple a thing it is to see where it is, and the instant you see where it is it is yours. Some old gentleman gets up back there and says, 'Mr Conwell, have you lived in Philadelphia for thirty-one years and don't know that the time has gone by when you can make anything in this city?' 'No, I don't think it is.' 'Yes, it is; I have tried it.'

'What business are you in?' 'I kept a store here for twenty years, and never made a thousand dollars in the whole twenty years.' 'Well, then, you can measure the good you have been to this city by what this city has paid you, because a man can judge very well what he is worth by what he receives that is, in what he is to the world at this time. If you have not made over a thousand dollars in twenty years in Philadelphia, it would have been better for Philadelphia if they had kicked you out of the city nineteen years and nine months ago. A man has no right to keep a store in Philadelphia twenty years and not make at least five hundred thousand dollars, even thought it be a corner grocery-up-town.' You say, 'You cannot make five hundred thousand dollars in a store now.' Oh, my friends, if you will just take only four blocks around you, and find out what the people want and what you ought to supply them, you would very soon see it. There is wealth right within the sound of your voice.

Some one says: 'You don't know anything about business. A preacher never knows a thing about business.' Well, then I will have to prove that I am an expert. I don't like to do this, but I have to do it because my testimony will not be taken if I am not an expert. My father kept a country store, and if there is any place under the stars where a man gets all sorts of experience in every kind of mercantile transactions, it is in the country store. I am not proud of my experience, but sometimes when my father was away he would leave me in charge of the store, thought fortunately for him that was not very often. But this did occur many times, friends: A man would come onto the store, and say to me, 'Do you keep jack-knives?' 'No we don't keep jack-knives,' and I went off whistling a tune. What did I care about that man, anyhow?

Then another farmer would come in and say, 'Do you keep jack-knives?' 'No, we don't keep jack-knives.' Then I went away and whistled another tune. Then a third man came right in the same door and said, 'Do you keep jack-knives?' 'No. Why is every one around here asking for jack-knives? Do you suppose we are keeping this store to supply the whole neighbourhood with jack-knives?' Do you carry on your store like that in Philadelphia? The difficulty was I had not then learned that the foundation of godliness and the foundation principle of success in business are both the same precisely. The man who says, 'I cannot carry my religion into business' advertises himself either as being an imbecile in business, or on the road to bankruptcy, or a thief, one of the three, sure. He will fail within a very few years. He certainly will if he doesn't carry his religion into business. If I had been carrying on my father's store on a Christian plan, godly plan, I would have had a jackknife for the third man when he called for it. Then I would have actually done him a kindness, and I would have received a reward myself, which it would have been my duty to take.

There are some over-pious Christian people who think if you take any profit on anything you sell that you are an unrighteous man. On the contrary, you would be a criminal to sell goods for less than they cost. You have no right to do that. You cannot trust a man with your money who cannot take care of his own. You cannot trust a man in your family that is not true to his wife. You cannot trust a man in the world that does not begin with his own heart, his own character, and his own life. It would have been my duty to have furnished a jack-knife to the third, man or to the second, and to have sold it to him and actually profited myself. I have no more right to sell goods without making a profit on them than I have to overcharge him dishonestly beyond what they are worth. But I should so sell each bill of goods that the person to whom I sell shall make as much as I make.

To live and let live is the principle of the gospel, and the principle of every-day common sense. Oh, young man, hear me; live as you go along. Do not wait until you have reached my years before you begin to enjoy anything of this life. If I had the millions back, of fifty cents of it, which I have tried to earn in these years, it would not do me anything like the good that it does me now in this almost sacred presence tonight. Oh, yes, I am paid over and over a hundredfold tonight for dividing as I have tried to do in some measure as I went along through the years. I ought not to speak that way, it sounds egotistic, but I am old enough now to be excused for that. I should have helped my fellow men, which I have tried to do, and everyone should try to do, and get the happiness of it. The man who goes home with the sense that he has stolen a dollar that day, that he has robbed a man of what was his honest due, is not going home to sweet rest. He arises tired in the morning, and goes with an unclean conscience to his work the next day. He is not a successful man at all, although he may have laid up millions. But the man who has gone through life dividing always with is fellow men, making and demanding his own rights and his own profits, and giving to every other man his rights and profits, lives every day, and not only that, but it is the royal road to great wealth. The history of the thousands of millionaires shows that to be the case.

Then man over there who said he could not make anything in a store in Philadelphia has been carrying on his store on the wrong principle. Suppose I go into your store tomorrow morning and ask, 'Do you know a neighbour A, who lives one square away, at house No. 1240?' 'Oh yes, I have met him. He deals here at the corner store.' 'Where did he come from?' 'I don't know.' 'How many does he have in his family?' 'I don't know.' 'What ticket does he vote?' 'I don't know.' 'What church does he go to?' 'I don't know, and don't care. What are you asking all these questions for?'

If you had a store in Philadelphia, would you answer me like that? If so, then you are conducting your business just as I carried on my father's business in Worthington, Massachusetts. You don't know where your neighbour came from when he moved to Philadelphia, and you don't care. If you had cared you would rich by now. If you had cared enough about him to take an interest in his affairs, to find out what he needed, you would have been rich. But you go through the world saying, 'No opportunity to get rich,' and there is the fault right at your door.

But another young man gets up over there and says, 'I cannot take the mercantile business,' (While I am talking of trade it applies to every occupation.) 'Why can't you go into the mercantile business?' 'Because I haven't any capital.' Oh, the weak and dudish creature that can't see over its collar! It makes a person weak to see these little dudes standing around the corners and saying, 'Oh, if I had plenty of capital, how rich would I get.' 'Young man, do you think you are going to get rich on capital?' 'Certainly.' Well, I say, 'Certainly not.' If your mother has plenty of money, and she will set you up in business, you will 'set her up in business,' supplying you with capital.

The moment a young man or woman gets more money than he or she has grown to by practical experience, that moment he has gotten a curse. It is no help to a young man or woman to inherit money. It is no help to your children to leave them money, but if you leave them education, if you leave them Christian and noble character, if you leave them a wide circle of friends, if you leave them an honourable name, it is far better than that they should have money. It would be worse for them, worse for the nation, that they should have any money at all. Oh, young man, if you have inherited money, don't regard it as a help. It will curse you through your years, and deprive you of the very best things of human life. There is no class of people to be pitied so much as the inexperienced sons and daughters of the rich of our generation. I pity the rich man's son. He can never know the best things in life.

One of the best things in our life is when a young man has earned his own living, and when he becomes engaged to some lovely young woman, and makes up his mind to have a home of his own. Then with that same love comes also that divine inspiration toward better things, and he begins to save his money. He begins to leave off his bad habits and put money in the bank. When he has a few hundred dollars he goes out in the suburbs to look for a home. He goes to the savings bank, perhaps, for half of the value, and then goes for his wife, and when he takes his bride over the threshold of that door for the first time he says in words of eloquence my voice can never touch: 'I have earned this home myself. It is all mine, and I divide with thee.' That is the grandest moment a human heart may ever know.

But a rich man's son can never know that. He takes his bride into a finer mansion, it may be, but he is obliged to go all the way through it and say to his wife, 'My mother gave me that, my mother gave me that, and my mother gave me this,' until his wife wishes she had married his mother. I pity the rich man's son.

The statistics of Massachusetts showed that not one rich man's son out of seventeen ever dies rich. I pity the rich man's sons unless they have the good sense of the elder Vanderbilt, which sometimes happens. He went to his father and said, 'Did you earn all your money?' 'I did, my son. I began to work on a ferry boat for twenty-five cents a day.' 'Then,' said his son, 'I will have none of your money,' and he, too, tried to get employment on a ferry boat that Saturday night. He could not get one there, but he did get a place for three dollars a week. Of course, if a rich man's son will do that, he will get the discipline of a poor boy that is worth more than a university education to any man. He would then be able to take care of the millions of his father. But as a rule, the rich men will not let their sons do the very thing that made them great. As a rule, the rich man will not allow his son to work-and his mother! Why, she would think it was a social disgrace if her poor, weak, little lily-fingered, sissy sort of a boy had to earn his living with honest toil. I have no pity for such rich men's sons.

I remember one at Niagara Falls. I think I remember one a great deal nearer. I think there are gentlemen present who were at a great banquet, and I beg pardon of his friends. At a banquet here in Philadelphia there sat beside me a kind-hearted young man, and he said, 'Mr Conwell, you have been sick for two or three years. When you go out, take my limousine, and it will take you up to your house on Broad Street.' I thanked him very much, and perhaps I ought not to mention the incident in this way, but I follow the facts. I got on to the seat with the driver of that limousine, outside, and when we were going up I asked the driver, 'How much did this limousine cost?' 'Six thousand eight hundred, and he had to pay the duty on it.' 'Well,' I said, 'does the owner of this machine ever drive it himself?' At the chauffeur laughed so heartily that he lost control of his machine. He was so surprised at the question that he ran up on the sidewalk, and around a corner lamp post into the street again.

And when he got into the street he laughed till the whole machine trembled. He said: 'He drive this machine! Oh, he would be lucky if he knew enough to get our when we get there.'

I must tell you about a rich man's son at Niagara Falls. I came in from the lecture to the hotel, and as I approached the desk of the clerk there stood a millionaire's son from New York. He was an indescribable specimen of anthropologic potency. He had a skull-cap on one side of his head, with a gold tassel in the top of it, and a gold-headed cane under his arm with more in it than in his head. It is a very difficult thing to describe that young man. He wore an eye-glass that he could not see through, patent leather boots that he could not walk in, and pants that he could not sit down in—dressed like a grasshopper. This human cricket came up to the clerk's desk just as I entered, adjusted his unseeing eye-glass, and spake in this wise to the clerk. You see, he thought it was 'Hinglish, you know,' to lisp. 'Thir, will you have the kindness to supply me with thome papah and enwelophs!' The hotel clerk measured the man quick, and he pulled the envelopes and paper out of a drawer, threw them across the counter toward the young man, and then turned away to his books. You should have seen that young man when those envelopes came across that counter.

He swelled up like a gobbler turkey, adjusted his unseeing eye-glass, and yelled: 'Come right back here. Now, thir, will you order a thervant to take that papah and enwelophs to yondah dethk.' Oh, the poor, miserable, contemptible American monkey! He could not carry paper and envelopes twenty feet. I suppose he could not get his arms down to do it. I have no pity for such travesties upon human nature. If you have not capital, young man, I am glad of it. What you need is common sense, not copper cents.

The best thing I can do is to illustrate by actual facts well known to you all. A.T. Stewart, a poor boy in New York, had $1.50 to begin life on. He lost 87½ cents of that on the very first venture. How fortunate that young man who loses the first time he gambles. That boy said, 'I will never gamble again in business,' and he never did.

How came he to lose 87½ cents? You probably all know the story how he lost it—because he bought some needles, threads, and buttons to sell which people did not want, and had them left on his hands, a dead loss. Said the boy, 'I will not lose any more money in that way.' Then he went around first to the doors and asked the people what they did want. Then when he had found out what they wanted he invested his 62½ cents to supply a known demand. Study it, wherever you choose—in business, in your profession, in your housekeeping, whatever your life, that one thing is the secret of success. You must first know the demand. You must first know what people need, and then invest yourself where you are most needed. A.T. Stewart went on that principle until he was worth what amounted afterward to forty millions of dollars, owning the very store in which Mr Wanamaker carries on his great work in New York. His fortune was made by his losing something, which taught him the great lesson that he must only invest himself or his money in something that people need. When will you salesmen learn it? When will you manufactures learn that you must know the changing needs of humanity if you would succeed in life? Apply yourselves, all you Christian people, as manufacturers or merchants or workmen to supply that human need. It is a great principle as broad as humanity and as deep as the Scripture itself.

The best illustration I ever heard was of John Jacob Astor. You know that he made the money of the Astor family when he lived in New York. He came across the sea in debt for his fare. But that poor boy with nothing in his pocket made the fortune of the Astor family on one principle. Some young man here tonight will say, 'Well, they could make these over in New York, but they could not do it in Philadelphia!' My friends, did you ever read that wonderful book of Riss (his memory is sweet to us because of his recent death), wherein is given his statistical account of the records taken in 1889 of 107 millionaires of New York. If you read the account you will see that out of the 107 millionaires only seven made their money in New York. Out of the 107 millionaires worth ten million dollars in real estate then, 67 of them made their money in towns of less than 3,500 inhabitants. The richest man in this country today, if you read the real estate values, has never moved away from a town of 3,500 inhabitants.

It makes not so much difference where you are as who you are. But if you cannot get rich in Philadelphia you certainly cannot do it in New York Now John Jacob Astor illustrated what can be done anywhere. He had a mortgage once on a millinery-store, and they could not sell bonnets enough to pay the interest on his money. So he foreclosed that mortgage. took possession of the store, and went in to partnership with the very same people, in the very same store, with the same capital. He did not give them a dollar of capital. They had to sell goods to get any money. Then he left them alone in the store just as they had been before, and he went out and sat down on a bench in the park in the shade. What was John Jacob Astor doing out there, and in partnership with people who had failed on his own hands? Had the most important and, to my mind, the most pleasant part of that partnership on his hands. For as John Jacob Astor sat on that bench he was watching the ladies as they went by; and where is the man who would not get rich at that business? As he sat on the bench if a lady passed him with her shoulders back and head up, and looked straight to the front, as if she did not care if all the world did gaze on her, then he studied her bonnet, and by the time it was out of sight he know the shape of the frame, the colour of the trimmings, and the crinklings in the feather. I sometimes try to describe a bonnet, but not always. I would not try to describe a modern bonnet.

Where is the man that could describe one? This aggregation of all sorts of driftwood stuck on the back of the head, or the side of the neck, like a rooster with only one tail feather left. But in John Jacob Astor's day there was some art about the millinery business, and he went to the millinery-store and said to them: 'Now put into the show-window just such a bonnet as I describe to you, because I have already seen a lady who likes such a bonnet. Don't make up any more until I come back.' Then he went out and sat down again, and another lady passed him of a different form, of a different complexion, with a different shape and colour of bonnet. 'Now,' said he, 'put such a bonnet as that in the show-window.' He did not fill his show-window uptown with a lot of hats and bonnets to drive people away, and then sit on the back stairs and bawl because people went to Wanamaker's to trade. He did not have a hat or a bonnet in that show-window but what some lady liked before it was made up. The tide of custom began immediately to turn in, and that has been the foundation of the greatest store in New York in that line, and still exists as one of three stores. Its fortune was made by John Jacob Astor after they had failed in business, not by giving them any more money, but by finding out what the ladies liked for bonnets before they wasted any material in making them up. I tell you if a man could foresee the millinery business he could foresee anything under heaven!

Suppose I were to go through this audience tonight and ask you in this great manufacturing city if there are not opportunities to get rich in manufacturing. 'Oh yes,' some young man says, 'there are opportunities here still if you build with some trust and if you have two or three millions of dollars to begin with as capital.' Young man, the history of the breaking up of the trusts by that attack upon 'big business' is only illustrating what is now the opportunity of the smaller man. The time never came in the history of the world when you could get rich so quickly manufacturing without capital as you can now.

But you will say, 'You cannot do anything of the kind. You cannot start without capital.' Young man, let me illustrate for a moment. I must do it. It is my duty to every young man, and woman, because we are all going into business very soon on the same plan. Young man, remember if you know what people need you have gotten more knowledge of a fortune than any amount of capital can give you.

There was a poor man out of work living in Hingham, Massachusetts. He lounged around the house until one day his wife told him to get out and work, and, as he lived in Massachusetts, he obeyed his wife. He went out and sat down on the shore of the bay, and whittled a soaked shingle into a wooden chain. His children that evening quarreled over it, and he whittled a second one to keep peace. While he was whittling the second one a neighbour came in and said: 'Why don't you whittle toys and sell them? You could make money doing that.' 'Oh,' he said, 'I would not know what to make.' 'Why don't you ask your own children right here in your own house what to make?' 'What is the use of trying that?' said the carpenter. 'My children are different from other people's children.' (I used to see people like that when I taught school.) But he acted upon the hint, and the next morning when Mary came down the stairway, he asked, 'What do you want for a toy?' She begin to tell him she would like a doll's bed, a doll's washstand, and went on with a list of things that would take him a lifetime to supply. So, consulting his own children, in his own house, he took the firewood, for he had no money to buy lumber, and whittled those strong, unpainted Hingham toys that were that were for so many years known all over the world. Then man began to make those toys for his own children, and then made copies and sold them through the boot-and-shoe store next door. He began to make a little money, and then a little more, and Mr Lawson, in is Frenzied Finance says that man is the richest man in old Massachusetts, and I think it is the truth. And that man is worth a hundred millions of dollars today, and has been only thirty-four years making it on that one principle—that one must judge that what his own children like at home other people's children would like in their homes, too; to judge the human heart by oneself, by one's wife or by one's children. It is the royal road to success in manufacturing.

'Oh,' But you say, 'didn't he have any capital?' Yes, a penknife, but I don't know that he had paid for that.

I spoke thus to an audience in New Britain, Connecticut, and a lady four seats back went home and tried to take off her collar, and the collar-button stuck in the buttonhole. She threw it out and said, 'I am going to get up something better than that to put on collars.' Her husband said: 'After what Conwell said tonight, you see there is a need of an improved collar-fastener that is easier to handle. There is a human need; there is a great fortune. Now, then, get up a collar-button and get rich.' He made fun of her, and consequently made fun of me, and that is one of the saddest things which comes over me like a deep cloud of midnight sometimes—although I have worked so hard for more than half a century, yet how little I have ever really done. Notwithstanding the greatness and the handsomeness of your compliment tonight, I do not believe there is one in ten of you that is going to make a million of dollars because you are here tonight; but it is not my fault, it is yours. I say that sincerely. What is the use of my talking if people never do what I advise them to do? When her husband ridiculed her, she made up her mind she would make a better collar-button, and when a woman makes up her mind 'she will,' and does not say anything about it, she does it. It was that New England woman who invented the snap button which you can find anywhere now. It was a collar-button with a spring cap attached to the outer side. Any of you who wear modern waterproofs know the button that simply pushes together, and when you unbutton it you simply pull it apart. That is the button to which I refer, and which she invented. She afterward invented several other buttons, and then invested in more, and then was taken into partnership with great factories. Now that woman goes over the sea every summer in her private steamship—yes, and takes her husband with her! If her husband were to die, she would have money enough to buy a foreign duke or count or some such title as that at the latest quotations.

Now what is my lesson in that incident? It is this: I told her then, though I did not know her, what I say to you, 'Your wealth is too near to you. You are looking right over it'; and she had to look over it because it was right under her chin.

I have read in the newspaper that a woman never invented anything. Well, that newspaper ought to begin again. Of course, I do not refer to gossip—I refer to machines—and if I did I might better include the men. That newspaper could never appear if women had not invented something. Friends, think. Ye women, think! You say you cannot make a fortune because you are in some laundry, or running a sewing machine it may be, or walking before some loom, and yet you can be a millionaire if you will but follow this almost infallible direction.

When you say a woman doesn't invent anything, I ask—who invented the Jacquard loom that wove every stitch you wear? Mrs Jacquard. The printer's roller, the printing press, were invented by farmers' wives. Who invented the cotton-gin of the South that enriched our country so amazingly? Mrs General Green invented the cotton gin and showed the idea to Mr Whitney, and he like a man, seized it. Who was it that invented the sewing machine? If I would go to school tomorrow and ask your children they would say, 'Elias Howe.'

He was in the Civil War with me, and often in my tent, and I often heard him say that he worked fourteen years to get up that sewing-machine. But his wife made up her mind one day they would starve to death if there wasn't something or other invented pretty soon, and so in two hours she invented the sewing machine. Of course he took out the patent in his name. Men always do that. Who was it that invented the mower and the reaper? According to Mr McCormick's confidential communication, so recently published, it was a West Virginia woman, who, after his father and he had failed altogether in making a reaper and gave it up, took a lot of shears and nailed them together on the edge of a board, with one shaft of each pair loose, and then wired them so that when she pulled the wire the other way it opened them, and there she had the principle of the mowing-machine. If you look at a mowing-machine, you will see it is nothing but a lot of shears. If a woman can invent a mowing-machine, if a woman can invent a Jacquard loom, if a woman can invent a cotton-gin, if a woman can invent a trolley switch—as she did and made the trolleys possible; if a woman can invent, as Mr Carnegie said, the great iron squeezers that laid the foundation of all the steel millions of the United States, 'we men' can invent anything under the stars! I say that for the encouragement of the men.

Who are the great inventors of the world? Again this lesson comes before us. The great inventor sits next to you, or you are the person yourself. 'Oh,' but you will say,' I have never invented anything in my life.' Neither did the great inventors until they discovered one great secret. Do you think that it is a man with a head like a bushel measure or a man like a stroke of lighting? It is neither. The really great man is a plain, straightforward, everyday common sense man. You would not dream that he was a great inventor if you did not see something he had actually done. His neighbours do not regard him so great.

You never see anything great over your back fence. You say there is no greatness among your neighbours. It is all away off somewhere else. Their greatness is ever so simple, so plain, so earnest, so practical, that the neighbours and friends never recognize it.

True greatness is often unrecognized. That is sure. You do not know anything about the greatest men and women. I went out to write the life of General Garfield, and a neighbour, knowing I was in a hurry, and as there was a great crowd around the front door, took me around to General

Garfield's back door and shouted, 'Jim! Jim!' And very soon 'Jim' came to the door and let me in, and I wrote the biography of one of the grandest men of the nation, and yet he was just the same old 'Jim' to his neighbour. If you know a great man in Philadelphia and you should meet him tomorrow, you would say, 'How are you, Sam?' or 'Good morning, Jim.' Of course you would. That is just what you would do.

One of my soldiers in the Civil War had been sentenced to death, and I went up to the White House in Washington—sent there for the first time in my life—to see the President. I went into the waiting room and sat down with a lot of others on the benches, and the secretary asked one after another to tell him what they wanted. After the secretary had been through the line, he went in, and then came back to the door and motioned for me. I went up to that anteroom, and the secretary said: 'That is the President's door right over there. Just rap on it and go right in.' I was never so taken aback, friends, in all my life, never. The secretary himself made it worse for me, because he had told me how to go in and then went out another door to the left and shut that. There I was, in the hallway by myself before the President of the United States of America's door. I had been on fields of battle, where the shells did sometimes shriek and the bullets did sometimes hit me, but I always wanted to run. I have no sympathy with the old man who says, 'I would just as soon march up into the cannon's mouth as eat my dinner.' I have no faith in a man who doesn't know enough to be afraid when he is being shot at. I never was so afraid when the shells came around us at Antietam as I was when I went into that room that day; but I finally mustered the courage—I don't know how I ever did—and at arm's length tapped on the door. The man inside did not help me at all, but yelled out, 'Come in and sit down!'

Well, I went in and sat down on the edge of a chair, and wished I were in Europe, and the man at the table did not look up. He was one of the world's greatest men, and was made great by one single rule. Oh, that all the young people of Philadelphia were before me now and I could say just this one thing, and that they would remember it. I would give a lifetime for the effect it would have on our city and on civilization. Abraham Lincoln's principle for greatness can be adopted by nearly all. This was his rule: whatsoever he had to do at all, he put his whole mind in to it and held it and held it all there until that was all done. That makes men great almost anywhere. He stuck to those papers at that table and did not look up at me, and I sat there trembling. Finally, when he put the string around his papers, he pushed them over to one side and looked over at me, and a smile came over his worn face. He said: 'I am a very busy man and have only a few minutes to spare. Now tell me in the fewest words what it is you want.' I began to tell him, and mentioned the case, and he said: 'I have heard all about it and you do not need to say any more. Mr Stanton was talking to me only a few days ago about that. You can go to the hotel and rest assured that the President never did sign an order to shoot a boy under twenty years of age, and never will. You can say that to his mother anyhow.'

Then he said to me, 'How is it going in the field?' I said, 'We sometimes get discouraged.' And he said: 'It is all right. We are going to win out now. We are getting very near the light. No man ought to wish to be President of the United States, and I will be glad when I get through; the Tad and I are going out to Springfield, Illinois. I have bought a farm out there and I don't care if I again earn only twenty-five cents a day. Tad has a mule team, and we are going to plant onions.'

Then he asked me, 'Were you brought up on a farm?' I said, 'Yes; in the Berkshire Hills of Massachusetts.' He then threw his leg over the corner of the big chair and said, 'I have heard many a time, ever since I was young, that up there in those hills you have to sharpen the noses of the sheep in order to get down to the grass between the rocks.' He was so familiar, so everyday, so farmer-like, that I felt right at home with him at once.

He then took hold of another roll of paper, and looked up at me and said, 'Good morning.' I took the hint then and got up and went out. After I had gotten out I could not realize I had seen the President of the United States at all. But a few days later, when still in the city, I saw the crowd pass through the East Room by the coffin of Abraham Lincoln, and when I looked at the upturned face of the murdered President I felt then that the man I had seen such a short time before, who, so simple a man, so plain a man, was one of the greatest men that God ever raised up to lead a nation on to ultimate liberty. Yet he was only 'Old Abe' to his neighbours. When they had the second funeral, I was invited among others, and went out to see that some coffin put back in the tomb at Springfield. Around the tomb stood Lincoln's old neighbours, to whom he was just 'Old Abe.'

Of course that is all they would say. Did you ever see a man who struts around altogether too large to notice an ordinary working mechanic? Do you think he is great? He is nothing but a puffed-up balloon, held down by his big feet. There is no greatness there. Who are the great men and women? My attention was called the other day to the history of a very little thing that made the fortune of a very poor man. It was an awful thing, and yet because of that experience he—not a great inventor or genius—invented the pin that now is called the safety-pin, and out of that safety-pin made the fortune of one of the great aristocratic families of this nation.

A poor man in Massachusetts who had worked in the nail-works was injured at thirty-eight, and he could earn but little money. He was employed in the office to rub out the marks on the bills made by pencil memorandums, and he used a rubber until his hand grew tired. He then tied a piece of rubber on the end of a stick and worked it like a plane. His little girl came and said, 'Why, you have a patent, haven't you?' The father said afterward, 'My daughter told me when I took the stick and put the rubber on the end that there was a patent, and that was the first thought of that.' He went to Boston and applied for his patent, and every one of you that has a rubber-tipped pencil in your pocket is now paying tribute to the millionaire. All was income, all the way up into the millions.

But let me hasten to one other greater thought. 'Show me the great men and women who live in Philadelphia.' A gentleman over there will get up and say: 'We don't have any great men in Philadelphia. They don't live here. They live away off in Rome or St. Petersburg or London or Manayunk, or anywhere else but here in our town.' I have come now to the apex of my thought. I have come now to the heart of the whole matter and to the center of my struggle: Why isn't Philadelphia a greater city in its greater wealth? Why does New York excel Philadelphia? People say, 'Because of her harbour.' Why do many other cities of the United States get ahead of Philadelphia now? There is only one answer, and that is because our own people talk down their own city. If there ever was a community on earth that has to be forced ahead, it is the city of Philadelphia. If we are to have a boulevard, talk it down; if we are going to have better schools, talk them down; if you wish to have wise legislation, talk it down; talk all the proposed improvements down. That is the only great wrong that I can lay at the feet of the magnificent Philadelphia that has been so universally kind to me. I say it is time we turn around in our city and begin to talk up the things that are in our city, and begin to set them before the world as the people of Chicago, New York, St. Louis, and San Francisco do. Oh, if we only could get that spirit out among our people, that we can do things in Philadelphia and do them well!

Arise, you millions of Philadelphians, trust in God and man, and believe in the great opportunities that are right here—not over in New York or Boston, but here—for business, for everything that is worth living for on earth. There was never an opportunity greater. Let us talk up our won city.

But there are two other young men here tonight, and that is all I will venture to say, because it is too late. One over there gets up and says, 'There is going to be a great man in Philadelphia, but never was one.' 'Oh, is that so? When are you going to be great?' 'When I am elected to some political office.' Young man, won't you learn a lesson in the primer of politics that is a prima facie evidence of littleness to hold office under our form of government? Great men get into office sometimes, but what this country needs is men that will do what we tell them to do. This nation—where the people rule—is governed by the people, for the people, and so long as it is, then the office-holder is but the servant of the people, and the Bible says the servant cannot be greater than the master. The Bible says, 'He that is sent cannot be greater than Him who sent Him.' The people rule, or should rule; and if they do, we do not need the greater men in office. If the great men in America took our offices, we would change to an empire in the next ten years.

I know of a great many young women, now that woman's suffrage is coming, who say, 'I am going to be President of the United States some day.' I believe in woman's suffrage, and there is no doubt but what is coming, and I am getting out of the way, anyhow. I may want an office by and by myself; but if the ambition of an office influences the women in their desire to vote, I want to say right here what I say to the young men, that if you only get the privilege of casting one vote, you don't get anything that is worth while. Unless you can control more than one vote, you will be unknown, and your influence so dissipated as practically not to be felt. This country is not run by votes. Do you think it is? It is governed by influence. It is governed by the ambitions and the enterprises which control votes. The young woman that thinks she is going to vote for the sake of holding an office is making an awful blunder.

That other young man gets up and says, 'There are going to great men in this country and in Philadelphia.' 'Is that so? When?' When there comes a great war, when we get into difficulty through watchful waiting in Mexico; when we get into war with England over, some frivolous deed, or with Japan or China or New Jersey or some distant country. Then I will march up to the cannon's mouth; I will sweep up among the glistening bayonets; I will leap into the arena and tear down the flag and bear it away in triumph. I will come home with stars on my shoulder, and hold every office in the gift of the nation, and I will be great.' No, you won't. You think you are going to be made great by an office, but remember that if you are not great before you get the office, you won't be great when you secure it. It will only be a burlesque in that shape.

We had a Peace Jubilee here after the Spanish War. Out West they don't believe this, because they said, 'Philadelphia would not have heard of any Spanish War until fifty years hence.' Some of you saw the procession go up Broad Street, I was away, but the family wrote to me that the tally-ho coach with Lieutenant Hobson upon it stopped right at the front door and the people shouted, 'Hurrah for Hobson!' and if I had been there I would have yelled too, because he deserves much more of his country than he has ever received. But suppose I go into school and say, 'Who sunk the Merrimac at Santiago?' and if the bys answer me, 'Hobson,' they will tell me seven-eighths of a lie. There were seven other heroes on that steamer, and they, by virtue of their position, were continually exposed to the Spanish fire, while Hobson, as an officer, might reasonably be behind the smoke-stack. You have gathered in this house your most intelligent people, and yet, perhaps, not one here can name the other seven men.

We ought not to so teach history. We ought to teach that, however humble a man's station may be, if he does his full duty in that place he is just as much entitled to the American people's honour as is the king upon his throne. But we do not so teach. We are now teaching everywhere that the generals do all the fighting.

I remember that, after the war, I went down to see General Robert E. Lee, that magnificent Christian gentleman of whom both North and South are now proud as one of our great Americans. The general told me about his servant, 'Rastus,' who was an enlisted coloured soldier. He called him in one day to make fun of him, and said, 'Rastus, I hear that all the rest of your company are killed, and why are you not killed?' Rastus winked at him and said, 'Cause when there is any fightin' goin' on I stay back with the generals.'

I remember another illustration. I would leave it out but for the fact that when you go to the library to read this lecture, you will find this has been printed in it for twenty-five years. I shut my eyes—shut them close—and lo! I see the faces of my youth. Yes, they sometimes say to me, 'You hair is not white; you are working night and day without seeming ever to stop; you can't be old.' But when I shut my eyes, like any other man of my years, oh, then come trooping back the faces of the loved and lost of long ago, and I know, whatever men may say, it is evening-time.

I shut my eyes now and look back to my native town in Massachusetts, and I see the cattle show ground on the mountain top; I can see the horse-sheds there. I can see the Congregational church; see the town hall and mountaineers' cottages; see a great assembly of people turning out, dressed resplendently, and I can see flags flying and handkerchiefs waving and hear bands playing. I can see that company of soldiers that had re-enlisted marching up on that cattle-show ground. I was but a boy, but I was captain of that company and puffed out with pride. A cambric needle would have burst me all to pieces. Then I thought it was the greatest event that ever came to man on earth. If you have ever thought you would like to be king or queen, you go and be received by the mayor.

The bands played, and all the people turned out to receive us. I marched up that Common so proud at the head of my troops, and we turned down into the town hall. Then they seated my soldiers down the center aisle and I sat down on the front seat. A great assembly of people—a hundred or two—came in to fill the town hall, so that they stood up all around. Then the town officers came in and formed a half-circle. The mayor of the town sat in the middle of the platform. He was a man who had never held office before; but he was a good man, and his friends have told me that I might use this without giving them offence. He was a good man, but he thought an office made a man great. He came up and took his seat, adjusted his powerful spectacles, and looked around, when he suddenly spied me sitting there on the front seat.

He came right forward on the platform and invited me up to sit with the town officers. No town officer ever took any notice of me before I went to war, except to advise the teacher to thrash me, and now I was invited up on the stand with the town officers. Oh my! The town mayor was then the emperor, the kind of our day and our time. As I came up on the platform they gave me a chair about this far, I would say, from the front.

When I had got seated, the chairman of the Selectmen arose and came forward to the table, and we all supposed he would introduce the Congregational minister, who was the only orator in town, and that he would give the oration to the returning soldiers. But, friends, you should have seen the surprise which ran over the audience when they discovered that the old fellow was going to deliver that speech himself. He had never made a speech in his life, but he fell into the same error that hundreds of other men have fallen into. It seems so strange that a man won't learn he must speak his piece as a boy if he intends to be an orator when he is grown, but he seems to think all he has to do is to hold an office to be a great orator.

So he came up to the front, and brought with him a speech which he had learned by heart walking up and down the pasture, where he had frightened the cattle. He brought the manuscript with him and spread it out on the table so as to be sure he might see it. He adjusted his spectacles and leaned over it for a moment and marched back on that platform, and then came forward like this—tramp, tramp, tramp. He must have studied the subject a great deal, then you come to think of it, because he assumed an 'elocutionary' attitude. He rested heavily upon his left heel, threw back

The World's 100 Greatest Speeches

his shoulders, slightly advanced the right foot, opened the organs of speech, and advanced his right foot at an angle of forty-five. As he stood in that elocutionary attitude, friends, this is just the way that speech went. Some people say to me, 'Don't you exaggerate?' That would be impossible. But I am here for the lesson and not for the story, and this is the way it went'— 'Fellow-citizens'—As soon as he heard his voice his fingers began to go like that, his knees begin to shake, and then he trembled all over. He choked and swallowed and came around to the table to look at the manuscript. Then he gathered himself up with clenched fists and came back, 'Fellow-citizens, we are very happy to welcome back to their native town these soldiers who have fought and bled—and come back again to their native town. We are especially pleased to see with us today this young hero' (that meant me)—'this young hero who in imagination' (friends remember he said that' if he had not said 'in imagination' I would have not be egotistic enough to refer to it at all)—'this young hero who in imagination we have seen leading his troops on the deadly breach. We have seen his shining sword flashing. Flashing in the sunlight, as he shouted to his troops, "Come on!"'

Oh dear, dear, dear! How little that good man knew about war. If he had known anything about war at all he ought to have now that any of my G. A. R. comrades here tonight will tell you is true, that it is next to a crime for an officer of infantry ever in time of danger to go ahead of his men. 'I, with my shining sword flashing in the sunlight, shouting to my troops, "Come on!"' I never did it. Do you suppose I would get in front of my men to be shot in front by the enemy and in the back by my own men? That is no place for an officer. The place for the officer in actual battle is behind the line. How often, as a staff officer, I rode down the line, when our men were suddenly called to the line of a battle, and the rebel yells were coming out of the woods, and shouted: 'Officers to the rear! Officers to the rear!' Then every officer gets behind the line of private soldiers, and the higher the officer's rank the farther behind he goes. Not because he is any less brave, but because the laws of war require that.

And yet he shouted, 'I, with my shining sword.' In that house there sat the company of my soldiers who had carried that boy across the Carolina rivers that he might not wet his feet. Some of them had gone far out to wet his feet. Some of them had gone far out to get a pig or a chicken. Some of them had gone to death under the shell-swept pines in the mountains of Tennessee, yet in the good man's speech they were scarcely known. He did refer to them, but only incidentally. The hero of the hour was this boy. Did the nation own him anything? No, nothing then and nothing now. Why was he the hero? Simply because that man fell into that same human error—that this boy was great because he was an officer and these were only private soldiers.

Oh, I learned the lesson then that I will never forget so long as the tongue of the bell of time continues to swing for me. Greatness consists not in the holding of some future office, but really consists in doing great deeds with little means and the accomplishment of vast purposes from the private ranks of life. To be great at all one must be great here, now, in Philadelphia. He who can give to this city better streets and better sidewalks, better schools and more colleges, more happiness and more civilization, more of God, he will be great anywhere. Let every man or woman here, if you never hear me again, remember this, that if you wish to be great at all, you must begin where you are and what you are, in Philadelphia, now. He that can give you to his city any blessing, he who can be a good citizen while he lives here, he that can make better homes, he that can be a blessing whether he works in the shop or sits behind the counter or keeps house, whatever be his life, he who would be great anywhere must first be great in his own Philadelphia.

53

WHAT IT MEANS TO BE COLOURED IN THE US

Mary Church Terell

This speech was delivered on 10 October 1906 at United Women's Club, Washington, D.C.

Washington, D.C., has been called 'The Coloured Man's Paradise.' Whether this sobriquet was given to the national capital in bitter irony by a member of the handicapped race, as he reviewed some of his own persecutions and rebuffs, or whether it was given immediately after the war by an ex-slaveholder who for the first time in his life saw coloured people walking about like free men, minus the overseer and his whip, history saith not. It is certain that it would be difficult to find a worse misnomer for Washington than 'The Coloured Man's Paradise' if so prosaic a consideration as veracity is to determine the appropriateness of a name.

For fifteen years I have resided in Washington, and while it was far from being a paradise for coloured people when I first touched these shores it has been doing its level best ever since to make conditions for us intolerable. As a coloured woman I might enter Washington any night, a stranger in a strange land, and walk miles without finding a place to lay my head. Unless I happened to know coloured people who live here or ran across a chance acquaintance who could recommend a coloured boarding-house to me, I should be obliged to spend the entire night wandering about. Indians, Chinamen, Filipinos, Japanese and representatives of any other dark race can find hotel accommodations, if they can pay for them. The coloured man alone is thrust out of the hotels of the national capital like a leper.

As a coloured woman I may walk from the Capitol to the White House, ravenously hungry and abundantly supplied with money with which to purchase a meal, without finding a single restaurant in which I would be permitted to take a morsel of food, if it was patronized by white people, unless I were willing to sit behind a screen. As a coloured woman I cannot visit the tomb of the Father of this country, which owes its very existence to the love of freedom in the human heart and which stands for equal opportunity to all, without being forced to sit in the Jim Crow section of an electric car which starts form the very heart of the city—midway between the Capital and the White House. If I refuse thus to be humiliated, I am cast into jail and forced to pay a fine for violating the Virginia laws…

As a coloured woman I may enter more than one white church in Washington without receiving that welcome which as a human being I have the right to expect in the sanctuary of God…

Unless I am willing to engage in a few menial occupations, in which the pay for my services would be very poor, there is no way for me to earn an honest living, if I am not a trained nurse or a dressmaker or can secure a position as teacher in the public schools, which is exceedingly difficult to do. It matters not what my intellectual attainments may be or how great is the need of the services of a competent person, if I try to enter many of the numerous vocations in which my white sisters are allowed to engage, the door is shut in my face.

From one Washington theater I am excluded altogether. In the remainder certain seats are set aside for coloured people, and it is almost impossible to secure others…

With the exception of the Catholic University, there is not a single white college in the national capitol to which coloured people are admitted… A few years ago the Columbian Law School admitted coloured students, but in deference to the Southern white students the authorities have decided to exclude them altogether.

Some time ago a young woman who had already attracted some attention in the literary world by her volume of short stories answered an advertisement which appeared in a Washington newspaper, which called for the services of a skilled stenographer and expert typewriter... The applicants were requested to send specimens of their work and answer certain questions concerning their experience and their speed before they called in person. In reply to her application the young coloured woman...received a letter from the firm stating that her references and experience were the most satisfactory that had been sent and requesting her to call. When she presented herself there was some doubt in the mind of the man to whom she was directed concerning her racial pedigree, so he asked her point-blank whether she was coloured or white. When she confessed the truth, the merchant expressed...deep regret that he could not avail himself of the services of so competent a person, but frankly admitted that employing a coloured woman in his establishment in any except a menial position was simply out of the question...

Not only can coloured women secure no employment in the Washington stores, department and otherwise, except as menials, and such positions, of course, are few, but even as customers they are not infrequently treated with discourtesy both by the clerks and the proprietor himself...

Although white and coloured teachers are under the same Board of Education and the system for the children of both races is said to be uniform, prejudice against the coloured teachers in the public schools is manifested in a variety of ways. From 1870 to 1900 there was a coloured superintendent at the head of the coloured schools. During all that time the directors of the cooking, sewing, physical culture, manual training, music and art departments were coloured people. Six years ago a change was inaugurated. The coloured superintendent was legislated out of office and the directorships, without a single exception, were taken from coloured teachers and given to the whites...

Now, no matter how competent or superior the coloured teachers in our public schools may be, they know that they can never rise to the height of a directorship, can never hope to be more than an assistant and receive the meager salary therefore, unless the present regime is radically changed...

Strenuous efforts are being made to run Jim Crow cars in the national capital...

Representative Heflin, of Alabama, who introduced a bill providing for Jim Crow street cars in the District of Columbia last winter, has just received a letter from the president of the East Brookland Citizens' Association 'endorsing the movement for separate street cars and sincerely hoping that you will be successful in getting this enacted into a law as soon as possible.' Brookland is a suburb of Washington.

The coloured labourer's path to a decent livelihood is by no means smooth. Into some of the trades unions here he is admitted, while from others he is excluded altogether. By the union men this is denied, although I am personally acquainted with skilled workmen who tell me they are not admitted into the unions because they are coloured. But even when they are allowed to join the unions they frequently derive little benefit, owing to certain tricks of the trade. When the word passes round that help is needed and coloured labourers apply, they are often told by the union officials that they have secured all the men they needed, because the places are reserved for white men, until they have been provided with jobs, and coloured men must remain idle, unless the supply of white men is too small...

And so I might go on citing instance after instance to show the variety of ways in which our people are sacrificed on the altar of prejudice in the Capital of the United States and how almost insurmountable are the obstacles which block his path to success...

It is impossible for any white person in the United States, no matter how sympathetic and broad, to realize what life would mean to him if his incentive to effort were suddenly snatched away. To the lack of incentive to effort, which is the awful shadow under which we live, may be traced the wreck and ruin of score of coloured youth. And surely nowhere in the world do oppression and persecution based solely on the colour of the skin appear more hateful and hideous than in the capital of the United States, because the chasm between the principles upon which this Government was founded, in which it still professes to believe, and those which are daily practiced under the protection of the flag, yawn so wide and deep.

54

SPEECH AT THE ROUND
TABLE CONFERENCE

Mohandas Karamchand Gandhi

This speech was delivered in November 1931.

It will be after all and at best a paper solution. But immediately you withdraw that wedge, the domestic ties, the domestic affection, the knowledge of common birth—do you suppose that all these will count for nothing?

Were Hindus and Mussalmans and Sikhs always at war with one another when there was no British rule, when there was no English face seen there? We have chapter and verse given to us by Hindu historians and by Mussalman historians to say that we were living in comparative peace even then. And Hindus and Mussalmans in the villages are not even today quarrelling. In those days, they were not known to quarrel at all. The late Maulana Muhammad Ali often used to tell me, and he was himself a bit of an historian. He said: 'If God'—'Allah' as he called out—gives me life, I propose to write the history of Mussalman rule in India; and then I will show, through that documents that British people have preserved, that was not so vile as he has been painted by the British historian; that the Mogul rule was not so bad as it has been shown to us in British history; and so on. And so have Hindu historians written. This quarrel is not old; this quarrel is coeval with this acute shame. I dare to say, it is coeval with the British Advent, and immediately this relationship, the unfortunate, artificial, unnatural relationship between Great Britain and India is transformed into a natural relationship, when it becomes, if it dose become, a voluntary partnership to be given up, to be dissolved at the will of either party, when it becomes that you will find that Hindus, Mussalmans, Sikhs, Europeans, Anglo-Indians, Christians, Untouchables, will all live together as one man.

I do not intend to say much tonight about the Princes, but I should be wronging them and should be wronging the Congress if I did not register my claim, not with the Round Table Conference but with the Princes. It is open to the Princes to give their terms on which they will join the Federation. I have appealed to them to make the path easy for those who inhabit the other part of India, and therefore, I can only make these suggestions for their favourable consideration, for their earnest consideration. I think that if they accepted, no matter what they are, but some fundamental rights as the common property of all India, and if they accepted that position and allowed those rights to be tested by the Court, which will be again of their own creation, and if they introduced elements—only elements—of representation on behalf of their subject, I think that they would have gone a long way to conciliate their subjects. They would have gone a long way to show to the world and to show to the whole of India that they are also fired with a democratic spirit, that they do not want to remain undiluted autocrats, but that they want to become constitutional monarch even as King George of Great Britain is. An Autonomous Frontier Province: Let India get what she is entitled to and what she can really take, but whatever she gets, and whenever she gets it, let the Frontier Province get complete autonomy today. That Frontier will then be a standing demonstration to the whole of India, and therefore, the whole vote of the Congress will be given in favour of the Frontier Province getting provincial Autonomy tomorrow. Prime Minister, if you can possibly get your Cabinet to endorse the proposition that from tomorrow the Frontier Province becomes a full-fledged autonomous province, I shall then have a proper footing amongst the Frontier tribes and convince them to my assistance when those over the border cast an evil eye on India.

Thanks; last of all, my last is pleasant task for me. This is perhaps the last time that I shall be sitting with you at negotiations. It is not that I want that. I want to sit at the same table with you in your closets and to negotiate and to plead with you and to go down on bended knees before I take the final lead and final plunge. But whether I have the good fortune to continue to tender my cooperation or not does not depend upon me. It largely depends upon you. It depends upon so many circumstances over which neither you nor we may have any control whatsoever. Then, let me perform this pleasant task of giving my thanks to all form Their Majesties down to the poorest men in the East End where I have taken up my habitation.

In that settlement, which represent the poor people of the East End of London, I have become one of them. They have accepted me as a member, and as a favoured member of their family. It will be one of the richest treasures that I shall carry with me. Here, too, I have found nothing but courtesy and nothing but a genuine affection from all with whom I have come in touch. I have come in touch with so many Englishmen. It has been a priceless privilege to me. They have listened to what must have often appeared to them to be unpleasant, although it was true. Although I have often been obliged to say these things to them they have never shown the slightest impatience or irritation. It is impossible for me to forget these things. No matter what befalls me, no matter what the fortunes may be of this Round Table Conference, one thing I shall certainly carry with me, that is, that from high to low I have found nothing but the utmost courtesy and that utmost affection. I consider that it was well worth my paying this visit to England in order to find this human affection.

It has enhanced, it has deepened my irrepressible faith in human nature that although English men and English women have been fed upon lies that I see so often disfiguring your press, that although in Lancashire, the Lancashire people had perhaps some reason for becoming irritated against me, I found no irritation and no resentment even in the operatives. The operatives, men and women, hugged me. They treated me as one of their own. I shall never forget that. I am carrying with me thousands upon thousands of English friendship. I do not know them but I read that affection in their eyes as early in the morning I walk through your streets. All this hospitality, all this kindness will never be effaced from my memory, no matter what befalls my unhappy land. I thank you for your forbearance.

55

INDIA MUST BE BLED

Dadabhai Naoroji

This speech was made by Dadabhai Naoroji in England, 6 July 1900. Dadabhai Naoroji borrowed the title of this speech from a speech by Lord Salisbury, secretary of state.

I feel exceedingly pleased at having to address so large a meeting of English ladies and gentlemen. I assure you it is a great consolation to me that the English are willing to hear what Indians have to say. I will speak boldly and heartily, in order that you may know the truth. I will take as a text the following true words: 'As India must be bled'. These words were delivered by a secretary of state for India, Lord Salisbury himself. I don't mention them as any complaint against Lord Salisbury. On the contrary, I give him credit for saying the truth. I want to impress upon you what these important words mean. Let us clearly understand what is meant by bleeding a nation. It is perfectly true that when there is a government people must pay taxes, but there is a great difference between taxing people and bleeding people. You, in England, pay something like fifty shillings, or more now, of taxes per head per annum. We, in India, pay only three to four shillings per head per annum. From this you may conclude that we must be the most lightly-taxed people in the world. However, that is not the case. Our burden is nearly twice as heavy as yours. The taxes you pay in this country go from the hands of the taxpayers into the hands of the government, from which they flow back into the country again in various forms, fertilizing trade and returning to the people themselves. There is no diminution of your wealth; your taxes simply change hands. Whatever you give out you must get back.

Any deficit means that much loss of strength. Supposing you pay a hundred million pounds every year, and the government uses that money in—such a way that only a part comes back to you, the other part is going out of the country. In that case, you are being bled, part of your life is going away. Suppose out of the hundred million pounds only eighty million pounds return to you in the shape of salaries, commerce, or manufacturers. You will have lost twenty million pounds. Next year you will be so much the weaker and so on each year; This is the difference between taxing people and bleeding people. Suppose a body of Frenchmen were your rulers, and that out of the hundred million pounds of taxes, they took tell to twenty million pounds each year; you would then be said to be bleeding. The nation would then be losing a portion of its life. How is India bled? I gave an example of your own case with the French as your rulers. We Indians are governed by you. You manage our expenditure and our taxes in such a way that while we pay a hundred million pounds in taxes, this hundred million never returns to us intact. Only about eighty million returns to us. There is a continual bleeding of about twenty million annually from the revenue. Ever since you obtained territorial jurisdiction and power in India in the middle of the last century the English and other Europeans who went to India have treated that country in the most oppressive way. The most oppressive means were adopted in order to bring away enormous quantities of wealth from the country. How was the Indian Empire taken over by you? It has generally been said that you have won it by the sword, and that you will keep it by the sword which is not so. The people who say this do not know what they are talking about. They also forget that you may lose it 'by force'. You have not won the Indian Empire by the sword. During these 150 years you have carried on wars through which this great Empire has been built up, costing hundreds of millions of rupees. Have you paid a single farthing of it? You have made the Indians pay every farthing. You have formed this great British Empire at our expense, and you will hear what reward we have received from you. The European army in India at any time was comparatively insignificant. During the Indian Mutiny, you had only forty thousand troops there. It was the two hundred thousand Indian troops that shed their blood and fought your battles which gave you this magnificent Empire. It is at India's cost and blood that this Empire has been formed and maintained up to the present day. It is in consequence of the tremendous cost of these wars and because of the millions you draw rom us every years that India is so completely exhausted and bled. It is no wonder that the time has come when India is bleeding to death.

You impose upon us an immense European military and civil service, you draw from us a heavy taxation. But in the disbursement and the disposal of that taxation we have not the slightest voice. I ask anyone here to stand up and say the he would be satisfied, if after having to pay a heavy taxation, he was given no voice in governance. I ask any one of you whether there is any great mystery in these dire famines and plagues? No other country exhausted, as India has been exhausted by an evil system of government would have taken it for even half the time. It is extraordinary that the loyalty of the Indians who are bled by you is still so great. The reason is that one of the most cherished and religious duties of the Hindus is that they should be obedient and loyal to the powers that govern them. They have been loyal to that sentiment, and you have derived its benefits. It is a true and genuine loyalty, but do not expect that loyalty not to fail and that it would continue in the same condition in which it is at the present time. It is for the British to rouse themselves and to open their minds, and to think whether they are doing their duty in India. The theory maintained by the statement is that India is governed for the benefit of India. You claim that you do not derive any benefit from the taxation. But this is incorrect. The reality is that India, up to the present day, has been governed so as to bring about the impoverishment of the people. I ask you is this to continue? Is it necessary, that, for your benefit, we must be destroyed? I will conclude with Lord Salisbury's other true words: Injustice will bring down the mightiest to ruin.

56

SPEECH AT BANARAS HINDU UNIVERSITY, INDIA

Mohandas Karamchand Gandhi

This speech was given by Mahatma Gandhi on 4 February 1916 to rouse the upper class of people in the country who were the dominant force in the freedom movement against the British. Citing the submissive nature of the struggle and the slack displayed by the ones responsible, his speech sought to bring the common Indian man into the struggle.

I wish to tender my humble apology for the long delay that took place before I was able to reach this place. And you will readily accept the apology when I tell you that I am not responsible for the delay nor is any human agency responsible for it. The fact is that I am like animal on show, and my keeper in their overkindness always manage to neglect a necessary chapter in this life, and, that is, pure accident. In this case, they did not provide for the series of accidents that happened to us—to me, keepers, and my carriers. Hence this delay.

Friends, under the influence of the matchless eloquence of Mrs Besant who has just sat down, pray, do not believe that our University has become a finished product, and that all the young men who are to come to the University, that has yet to rise and come into existence, have also come and returned from it finished citizens of a great empire. Do not go away with any such impression, and if you, the student world to which my remarks are supposed to be addressed this evening, consider for one moment that the spiritual life, for which this country is noted and for which this country has no rival, can be transmitted through the lip, pray, believe me, you are wrong. You will never be able merely through the lip, to give the message that India, I hope, will one day deliver to the world. I myself have been fed up with speeches and lectures, except the lectures that have been delivered here during the last two days from this category, because they are necessary. But I do venture to suggest to you that we have now reached almost the end of our resources in speech-making; it is not enough that our ears are feasted, that our eyes are feasted, but it is necessary that our hearts have got to be touched and that out hands and feet have got to be moved.

We have been told during the last two days how necessary it is, if we are to retain our hold upon the simplicity of Indian character, that our hands and feet should move in unison with our hearts. But this is only by way of preface. I wanted to say it is a matter of deep humiliation and shame for us that I am compelled this evening under the shadow of this great college, in this sacred city, to address my countrymen in a language that is foreign to me. I know that if I was appointed an examiner, to examine all those who have been attending during these two days this series of lectures, most of those who might be examined upon these lectures would fail. And why? Because they have not been touched.

I was present at the sessions of the great Congress in the month of December. There was a much vaster audience, and will you believe me when I tell you that the only speeches that touched the huge audience in Bombay were the speeches that were delivered in Hindustani? In Bombay, mind you, not in Banaras where everybody speaks Hindi. But between the vernaculars of the Bombay Presidency on the one hand and Hindi on the other, no such great dividing line exists as there does between English and the sister language of India; and the Congress audience was better able to follow the speakers in Hindi. I am hoping that this University will see to it that the youths who come to it will receive their instruction through the medium of their vernaculars. Our languages are the reflection of ourselves, and if you tell me that our languages are too poor to express the best thought, then say that the sooner we are wiped out of existence the better for us. Is there a man who dreams that English can ever become the national language of India? Why this handicap on the nation? Just consider for one moment what an equal race our lads have to run with every English lad.

I had the privilege of a close conversation with some Poona professors. They assured me that every Indian youth, because he reached his knowledge through the English language, lost at least six precious years of life. Multiply that by the numbers of students turned out by our schools and colleges and find out for yourselves how many thousand years have been lost to the nation. The charge against us is that we have no initiative. How can we have any, if we are to devote the precious years of our life to the mastery of a foreign tongue? We fail in this attempt also. Was it possible for any speaker yesterday and today to impress his audience as was possible for Mr Higginbotham? It was not the fault of the previous speakers that they could not engage the audience. They had more than substance enough for us in their addresses. But their addresses could not go home to us. I have heard it said that after all it is English educated India which is leading and doing all the things for the nation. It would be monstrous if it were otherwise. The only education we receive is English education. Surely we must show something for it. But suppose that we had been receiving during the past fifty years education through our vernaculars, what should we have today? We should have today a free India, we should have our educated men not as if they were foreigners in their own land but speaking to the heart of the nation; they would be working amongst the poorest of the poor and whatever they would have gained during these fifty years would be a heritage for the nation. Today even our wives are not the sharers in our best thought. Look at Professor Bose and Professor Ray and their brilliant researches. Is it not a shame that their researches are not the common property of the masses?

Let us now turn to another subject.

The Congress has passed a resolution about self-government, and I have no doubt that the All-India Congress Committee and the Muslim League will do their duty and come forward with some tangible suggestions. But I, for one, must frankly confess that I am not so much interested in what they will be able to produce as I am interested in anything that the student world is going to produce or the masses are going to produce. No paper contribution will ever give us self-government. No amount of speeches will ever make us fit for self-government. It is only our conduct that will fit us for it. And how are we trying to govern ourselves?

want to think audibly this evening. I do not want to make a speech and if you find me this evening speaking without reserve, pray, consider that you are only sharing the thoughts of a man who allows himself to think audibly, and if you think that I seem to transgress the limits that courtesy imposes upon me, pardon me for the liberty I may be taking. I visited the Vishwanath temple last evening, and as I was walking through those lanes, these were the thoughts that touched me. If a stranger dropped from above on to this great temple, and he had to consider what we as Hindus were, would he not be justified in condemning us? Is not this great temple a reflection of our own character? I speak feelingly, as a Hindu. Is it right that the lanes of our sacred temple should be as dirty as they are? The houses round about are built anyhow. The lanes are tortuous and narrow. If even our temples are not models of roominess and cleanliness, what can our self-government be? Shall our temples be abodes of holiness, cleanliness and peace as soon as the English have retired from India, either of their own pleasure or by compulsion, bag and baggage?

I entirely agree with the President of the Congress that before we think of self-government, we shall have to do the necessary plodding. In every city there are two divisions, the cantonment and the city proper. The city mostly is a stinking den. But we are a people unused to city life. But if we want city life, we cannot reproduce the easy-going hamlet life. It is not comforting to think that people walk about the streets of Indian Bombay under the perpetual fear of dwellers in the storeyed building spitting upon them. I do a great deal of railway traveling. I observe the difficulty of third-class passengers. But the railway administration is by no means to blame for all their hard lot. We do not know the elementary laws of cleanliness. We spit anywhere on the carriage floor, irrespective of the thoughts that it is often used as sleeping space. We do not trouble ourselves as to how we use it; the result is indescribable filth in the compartment. The so-called better class passengers over we their less fortunate brethern. Among them I have seen the student world also; sometimes they behave no better. They can speak English and they have worn Norfolk jackets and, therefore, claim the right to force their way in and command seating accommodation.

I have turned the searchlight all over, and as you have given me the privilege of speaking to you, I am laying my heart bare. Surely we must set these

things right in our progress towards self-government. I now introduce you
to another scene. His Highness the Maharaja who presided yesterday over
our deliberations spoke about the poverty of India. Other speakers laid
great stress upon it. But what did we witness in the great pandal in which
the foundation ceremony was performed by the Viceroy? Certainly it was
a most gorgeous show, an exhibition of jewellery, which made a splendid
feast for the eyes of the greatest jeweller who chose to come from Paris.
I compare with the richly bedecked noble men the millions of the poor.
And I feel like saying to these noble men, 'There is no salvation for India
unless you strip yourselves of this jewellery and hold it in trust for your
countrymen in India.' I am sure it is not the desire of the King-Emperor
or Lord Hardinge that in order to show the truest loyalty to our King
Emperor, it is necessary for us to ransack our jewellery boxes and to appear
bedecked from top to toe. I would undertake, at the peril of my life, to
bring to you a message from King George himself that he excepts nothing
of the kind.

Sir, whenever I hear of a great palace rising in any great city of India, be
it in British India or be it in India which is ruled by our great chiefs, I
become jealous at once, and say, 'Oh, it is the money that has come
from the agriculturists.' Over seventy-five per cent of the population are
agriculturists and Mr Higginbotham told us last night in his own felicitous
language, that they are the men who grow two blades of grass in the place
of one. But there cannot be much spirit of self-government about us, if we
take away or allow others to take away from them almost the whole of the
results of their labour. Our salvation can only come through the farmer.
Neither the lawyers, nor the doctors, nor the rich landlords are going to
secure it.

Now, last but not the least, it is my bounden duty to refer to what agitated
our minds during these two or three days. All of us have had many anxious
moments while the Viceroy was going through the streets of Banaras. There
were detectives stationed in many places. We were horrified. We asked
ourselves, 'Why this distrust?' Is it not better that even Lord Hardinge
should die than live a living death? But a representative of a mighty
sovereign may not. He might find it necessary to impose these detectives
on us? We may foam, we may fret, we may resent, but let us not forget that

ndia of today in her impatience has produced an army of anarchists. I
myself am an anarchist, but of another type. But there is a class of anarchists
amongst us, and if I was able to reach this class, I would say to them that
their anarchism has no room in India, if India is to be conquered. It is a
sign of fear. If we trust and fear God, we shall have to fear no one, not the
Maharajas, not the Viceroys, not the detectives, not even King George.

honour the anarchist for his love of the country. I honour him for his
bravery in being willing to die for his country; but I ask him—is killing
honourable? Is the dagger of an assassin a fit precursor of an honourable
death? I deny it. There is no warrant for such methods in any scriptures.
If I found it necessary for the salvation of India that the English should
retire, that they should be driven out, I would not hesitate to declare that
they would have to go, and I hope I would be prepared to die in defence of
that belief. That would, in my opinion, be an honourable death. The bomb-
thrower creates secret plots, is afraid to come out into the open, and when
caught pays the penalty of misdirected zeal.

have been told, 'Had we not done this, had some people not thrown
bombs, we should never have gained what we have got with reference to
the partition movement.' (Mrs Besant: 'Please stop it.') This was what I said
in Bengal when Mr Lyon presided at the meeting. I think what I am saying
is necessary. If I am told to stop I shall obey. (Turning to the Chairman) I
await your orders. If you consider that by my speaking as I am, I am not
serving the country and the empire I shall certainly stop. (Cries of 'Go
on.') (The Chairman: 'Please, explain your object.') I am simply... (another
interruption). My friends, please do not resent this interruption. If Mrs
Besant this evening suggests that I should stop, she does so because she
loves India so well, and she considers that I am erring in thinking audibly
before you young men. But even so, I simply say this, that I want to purge
India of this atmosphere of suspicion on either side, if we are to reach our
goal; we should have an empire which is to be based upon mutual love and
mutual trust. Is it not better that we talk under the shadow of this college
than that we should be talking irresponsibly in our homes? I consider
that it is much better that we talk these things openly. I have done so with
excellent results before now. I know that there is nothing that the students
do not know. I am, therefore, turning the searchlight towards ourselves. I

hold the name of my country so dear to me that I exchange these thought with you, and submit to you that there is no room for anarchism in India Let us frankly and openly say whatever we want to say our rulers, and fac the consequences if what we have to say does not please them. But let u not abuse.

I was talking the other day to a member of the much-abused Civil Service I have not very much in common with the members of that Service, bu I could not help admiring the manner in which he was speaking to me He said: 'Mr Gandhi, do you for one moment suppose that all we, Civi Servants, are a bad lot, that we want to oppress the people whom we hav come to govern?' 'No,' I said. 'Then if you get an opportunity put in a wor for the much-abused Civil Service.' And I am here to put in that word. Yes many members of the Indian Civil Service are most decidedly overbearing they are tyrannical, at times thoughtless. Many other adjectives may b used. I grant all these things and I grant also that after having lived in Indi for a certain number of years some of them become somewhat degraded But what does that signify? They were gentlemen before they came here and if they have lost some of the moral fibre, it is a reflection upon ourselves

Just think out for yourselves, if a man who was good yesterday has becom bad after having come in contact with me, is he responsible that he ha deteriorated or am I? The atmosphere of sycophancy and falsity tha surrounds them on their coming to India demoralizes them, as it woul many of us. It is well to take the blame sometimes. If we are to receiv self-government, we shall have to take it. We shall never be granted self government. Look at the history of the British Empire and the Britis nation; freedom loving as it is, it will not be a party to give freedom to people who will not take it themselves. Learn your lesson if you wish t from the Boer War. Those who were enemies of that empire only a few years ago have now become friends.

57

THE TENETS OF THE NEW PARTY

Bal Gangadhar Tilak

Bal Gangadhar Tilak (1849-1920) was a major political leader of Maharashtra. Shortly after the Calcutta Congress of December 1906 when the split in the Congress was narrowly avoided he spoke in Calcutta on 2 January 1907 outlining the tenets of the 'Extremists'. In 1908 he was sentenced to six years imprisonment for 'sedition'. After his release in 1914, he became a leader of the 'Home Rule League'. His famous slogan 'Swaraj (Home Rule) is my birthright—and I will have it,' was often quoted by Indian nationalists.

Two new words have recently come into existence with regard to our politics, and they are Moderates and Extremists. These words have a specific relation to time, and they, therefore, will change with time. The Extremists of today will be Moderates tomorrow, just as the Moderates of today were Extremists yesterday…

Pax Britannica has been established in this country in order that a foreign government may exploit the country. That this is the effect of Pax Britannica is gradually realized in these days. It was an unhappy circumstance that it was not realized sooner. We believed in the benevolent intentions of the Government, but in politics there is no benevolence. Benevolence is used to sugar-coat the declarations of self-interest, and we were in those days deceived by the apparent benevolent intentions under which rampant self-interest was concealed. It is said there is a revival of Liberalism, but how long will it last? Next year it might be they are out of power and are we to wait till there is another revival of Liberalism…and after all what can a Liberal Government do? I laughed when I read the proceedings of the meeting in Calcutta congratulating people on the appointment of Mr Morley to the Secretaryship of State for India. Passages were read from Mr Morley's books…. They utterly misunderstood the position or ignored the distinction between a philosopher and a statesman….

To convert the whole electorate of England to your opinion and then to get indirect pressure to bear upon the Members of Parliament, they in their turn to return a Cabinet favourable to India and the whole Parliament, the Liberal Party and the Cabinet to bring pressure on the bureaucracy to yield—we say this is hopeless, yet can now understand the difference between the Old and the New Party…. The Old Party believes in appealing to the British nation and we do not. That being our opinion, it logically follows we must have some other method…. We have come forward with a scheme which if you accept, shall better enable you to remedy this state of things than the scheme of the Old school. Your industries are ruined utterly, ruined by foreign rule, your wealth is going out of the country and you are reduced to the lowest level which no human being can occupy. In this state of things is there any other remedy by which you can help yourself? The remedy is not petitioning but boycott. We say prepare your forces, organize your power, and then go to work so that they cannot refuse you what you demand. We have perceived one fact, that the whole of the administration, which is carried on by a handful of Englishmen, is carried on with your assistance. We are all in subordinate service. The whole government is carried on with our assistance and they try to keep us in ignorance of our power of cooperation between ourselves by which that which is in our own hands can be claimed by us and administered by us. The point is to have the entire control in our hands. We shall not give them assistance to collect revenue and keep peace. We shall not assist them in fighting beyond the frontiers or outside India with Indian blood and money. We shall not assist them in carrying on the administration of justice. We shall have our own courts and when time comes we shall not pay taxes. Can you do that by your united efforts? If you can, you are free from tomorrow. We have not raised this cry from a mere impulse… I do not ask you to blindly follow us. Think over the whole problem for yourselves. If you accept our advice, we feel sure, we can achieve our salvation thereby. This is the advice of the New Party.

58

RESIGNATION SPEECH

George Washington

The resignation speech given by George Washington on 23 December 1784 in Annapolis, Maryland at the end of the Revolutionary War supposedly brought tears to the eyes of the members of the Congress and to all the spectators present. As Major General and Commander in Chief, he had the possibility of retaining power but instead chose to do the right thing by tendering his resignation. It was so emotional and Washington trembled so much that he had to hold on to the parchment with both of his hands to keep it steady while delivering the speech.

The great events on which my resignation depended having at length taken place; I have now the honour of offering my sincere Congratulations to Congress and of presenting myself before them to surrender into their hands the trust committed to me, and to claim the indulgence of retiring from the Service of my Country.

Happy in the confirmation of our Independence and Sovereignty, and pleased with the opportunity afforded the United States of becoming a respectable Nation, I resign with satisfaction the Appointment I accepted with diffidence. A diffidence in my abilities to accomplish so arduous a task, which however was superseded by a confidence in the rectitude of our Cause, the support of the Supreme Power of the Union, and the patronage of Heaven.

The Successful termination of the War has verified the most sanguine expectations, and my gratitude for the interposition of Providence, and the assistance I have received from my Countrymen, increases with every review of the momentous Contest.

While I repeat my obligations to the Army in general, I should do injustice to my own feelings not to acknowledge in this place the peculiar services and distinguished merits of the gentlemen who have been attached to my person during the War. It was impossible the choice of confidential officers to compose my family should have been more fortunate. Permit me Sir, to recommend in particular those, who have continued in service to the present moment, as worthy of the favourable notice and patronage of Congress.

I consider it an indispensable duty to close this last solemn act of my official life, by commending the interests of our dearest country to the protection of Almighty God, and those who have the superintendence of them, to his holy keeping.

Having now finished the work assigned to me, I retire from the great theatre of action; and bidding an affectionate farewell to this August body under whose orders I have so long acted, I here offer my Commission, and take my leave of all the employments of public life.

59

DUTIES OF AMERICAN CITIZENSHIP

Theodore Roosevelt

A speech given by Theodore Roosevelt in Buffalo, New York on 26 January 1883, it probed into the theoretical reasons why every citizen must be involved in politics and the practicality of serving in that capacity. People must not excuse themselves from politics just because they are too busy and then blame the government for its ineptitude.

Of course, in one sense, the first essential for a man's being a good citizen is his possession of the home virtues of which we think when we call a man by the emphatic adjective of manly. No man can be a good citizen who is not a good husband and a good father, who is not honest in his dealings with other men and women, faithful to his friends and fearless in the presence of his foes, who has not got a sound heart, a sound mind, and a sound body; exactly as no amount of attention to civil duties will save a nation if the domestic life is undermined, or there is lack of the rude military virtues which alone can assure a country's position in the world. In a free republic, the ideal citizen must be one willing and able to take arms for the defence of the flag, exactly as the ideal citizen must be the father of many healthy children. A race must be strong and vigorous; it must be a race of good fighters and good breeders, else its wisdom will come to naught and its virtue be ineffective; and no sweetness and delicacy, no love for and appreciation of beauty in art or literature, no capacity for building up material prosperity can possibly atone for the lack of the great virile virtues.

But this is aside from my subject, for what I wish to talk of is the attitude of the American citizen in civic life. It ought to be axiomatic in this country that every man must devote a reasonable share of his time to doing his duty in the political life of the community. No man has a right to shirk his political duties under whatever plea of pleasure or business; and while such shirking may be pardoned in those of small means it is entirely unpardonable in those among whom it is most common—in the people whose circumstances give them freedom in the struggle for life. In so far as the community grows to think rightly, it will likewise grow to regard the young man of means who shirks his duty to the State in time of peace as being only one degree worse than the man who thus shirks it in time of war. A great many of our men in business, or of our young men who are bent on enjoying life (as they have a perfect right to do if only they do not sacrifice other things to enjoyment), rather plume themselves upon being good citizens if they even vote; yet voting is the very least of their duties, Nothing worth gaining is ever gained without effort. You can no more have freedom without striving and suffering for it than you can win success as a banker or a lawyer without labour and effort, without self-denial in youth and the display of a ready and alert intelligence in middle age. The people who say that they have not time to attend to politics are simply saying that they are unfit to live in a free community. Their place is under a despotism; or if they are content to do nothing but vote, you can take despotism tempered by an occasional plebiscite, like that of the second Napoleon. In one of Lowell's magnificent stanzas about the Civil War he speaks of the fact which his countrymen were then learning, that freedom is not a gift that tarries long in the hands of cowards: nor yet does it tarry long in the hands of the sluggard and the idler, in the hands of the man so much absorbed in the pursuit of pleasure or in the pursuit of gain, or so much wrapped up in his own easy home life as to be unable to take his part in the rough struggle with his fellow men for political supremacy. If freedom is worth having, if the right of self-government is a valuable right, then the one and the other must be retained exactly as our forefathers acquired them, by labour, and especially by labour in organization, that is in combination with our fellows who have the same interests and the same principles. We should not accept the excuse of the business man who attributed his failure to the fact that his social duties were so pleasant and engrossing that he had no time left for work in his office; nor would we pay much heed to his further statement that he did not like business anyhow because he thought the morals of the business community by no means what they should be, and saw that the great successes were most often won by men of the Jay Gould stamp. It is just the same way with politics. It makes one feel half angry and half amused, and wholly contemptuous, to find men of high business or social standing in the community saying that they really have not got time to go to ward meetings, to organize political clubs, and to take a personal share in all the important details of practical politics; men who further urge against their going the fact that they think the condition of political morality low, and are afraid that they may be required to do what is not right if they go into politics.

The first duty of an American citizen, then, is that he shall work in politics; his second duty is that he shall do that work in a practical manner; and his third is that it shall be done in accord with the highest principles of honour and justice. Of course, it is not possible to define rigidly just the way in which the work shall be made practical. Each man's individual temper and convictions must be taken into account. To a certain extent his work must be done in accordance with his individual beliefs and theories of right and wrong. To a yet greater extent it must be done in combination with others, he yielding or modifying certain of his own theories and beliefs so as to enable him to stand on a common ground with his fellows, who have likewise yielded or modified certain of their theories and beliefs. There is no need of dogmatizing about independence on the one hand or party allegiance on the other. There are occasions when it may be the highest duty of any man to act outside of parties and against the one with which he has himself been hitherto identified; and there may be many more occasions when his highest duty is to sacrifice some of his own cherished opinions for the sake of the success of the party which he on the whole believes to be right. I do not think that the average citizen, at least in one of our great cities, can very well manage to support his own party all the time on every issue, local and otherwise; at any rate if he can do so he has been more fortunately placed than I have been. On the other hand, I am fully convinced that to do the best work people must be organized; and of course an organization is really a party, whether it be a great organization covering the whole nation and numbering its millions of adherents, or an association of citizens in a particular locality, banded together to win a certain specific victory, as, for instance, that of municipal reform. Somebody has said that a racing-yacht, like a good rifle, is a bundle of incompatibilities; that you must get the utmost possible sail power without sacrificing some other quality if you really do get the utmost sail power, that, in short you have got to make more or less of a compromise on each in order to acquire the dozen things needful; but, of course, in making this compromise you must be very careful for the sake of something unimportant not to sacrifice any of the great principles of successful naval architecture. Well, it is about so with a man's political work. He has got to preserve his independence on the one hand; and on the other, unless he wishes to be a wholly ineffective crank, he has got to have some sense of party allegiance and party responsibility, and he has got to realize that in any given exigency it may be a matter of duty to sacrifice one quality, or it may be a matter of duty to sacrifice the other.

If it is difficult to lay down any fixed rules for party action in the abstract; it would, of course, be wholly impossible to lay them down for party action in the concrete, with reference to the organizations of the present day. I think that we ought to be broad-minded enough to recognize the fact that a good citizen, striving with fearlessness, honesty, and common sense to do his best for the nation, can render service to it in many different ways, and by connection with many different organizations. It is well for a man if he is able conscientiously to feel that his views on the great questions of the day, on such questions as the tariff, finance, immigration, the regulation of the liquor traffic, and others like them, are such as to put him in accord with the bulk of those of his fellow citizens who compose one of the greatest parties: but it is perfectly supposable that he may feel so strongly for or against certain principles held by one party, or certain principles held by the other, that he is unable to give his full adherence to either. In such a case, I feel that he has no right to plead this lack of agreement with either party as an excuse for refraining from active political work prior to election. It will, of course, bar him from the primaries of the two leading parties, and preclude him from doing his share in organizing their management; but, unless he is very unfortunate, he can surely find a number of men who are in the same position as himself and who agree with him on some specific piece of political work, and they can turn in practically and effectively long before election to try to do this new piece of work in a practical manner.

One seemingly very necessary caution to utter is, that a man who goes into politics should not expect to reform everything right off, with a jump. I know many excellent young men who, when awakened to the fact that they have neglected their political duties, feel an immediate impulse to form themselves into an organization which shall forthwith purify politics everywhere, national, State, and city alike; and I know of a man who having gone round once to a primary, and having, of course, been unable to accomplish anything in a place where he knew no one and could not combine with anyone, returned saying it was quite useless for a good citizen to try to accomplish anything in such a manner. To these too hopeful or too easily discouraged people I always feel like reading Artemus Ward's article upon the people of his town who came together in a meeting to resolve that the town should support the Union and the Civil War, but were unwilling to take any part in putting down the rebellion unless they could go as brigadier-generals. After the battle of Bull Run there were a good many hundreds of thousands of young men in the North who felt it to be their duty to enter the Northern armies; but no one of them who possessed much intelligence expected to take high place at the outset, or anticipated that individual action would be of decisive importance in any given campaign. He went in as private or sergeant, lieutenant or captain, as the case might be, and did his duty in his company, in his regiment, after a while in his brigade. When Ball's Bluff and Bull Run succeeded the utter failure of the Peninsular campaign, when the terrible defeat of Fredericksburg was followed by the scarcely less disastrous day at Chancellorsville he did not announce (if he had any pluck or manliness about him) that he considered it quite useless for any self-respecting citizen to enter the Army of the Potomac, because he really was not of much weight in its councils, and did not approve of its management; he simply gritted his teeth and went doggedly on with his duty, grieving over, but not disheartened at the innumerable shortcomings and follies committed by those who helped to guide the destinies of the army, recognizing also the bravery, the patience, intelligence, and resolution with which other men in high places offset the follies and shortcomings and persevering with equal mind through triumph and defeat until finally he saw the tide of failure turn at Gettysburg and the full flood of victory come with Appomattox.

I do wish that more of our good citizens would go into politics, and would do it in the same spirit with which their fathers went into the Federal armies. Begin with the little thing, and do not expect to accomplish anything without an effort. Of course, if you go to a primary just once, never having taken the trouble to know any of the other people who go there you will find yourself wholly out of place; but if you keep on attending and try to form associations with other men whom you meet at the political gatherings, or whom you can persuade to attend them, you will very soon find yourself a weight. In the same way, if a man feels that the politics of his city, for instance, are very corrupt and wants to reform them, it would be an excellent idea for him to begin with his district. If he joins with other people, who think as he does, to form a club where abstract political virtue will be discussed he may do a great deal of good. We need such clubs; but he must also get to know his own ward or his own district, put himself in communication with the decent people in that district, of whom we may rest assured there will be many, willing and able to do something practical for the procurance of better government. Let him set to work to procure a better assemblyman or better alderman before he tries his hand at making a mayor, a governor, or a president. If he begins at the top he may make a brilliant temporary success, but the chances are a thousand to one that he will only be defeated eventually; and in no event will the good he does stand on the same broad and permanent foundation as if he had begun at the bottom. Of course, one or two of his efforts may be failures; but if he has the right stuff in him he will go ahead and do his duty irrespective of whether he meets with success or defeat. It is perfectly right to consider the question of failure while shaping one's efforts to succeed in the struggle for the right; but there should be no consideration of it whatsoever when the question is as to whether one should or should not make a struggle for the right. When once a band of one hundred and fifty or two hundred honest, intelligent men, who mean business and know their business, is found in any district, whether in one of the regular organizations or outside, you can guarantee that the local politicians of that district will begin to treat it with a combination of fear, hatred, and respect, and that its influence will be felt; and that while sometimes men will be elected to office in direct defiance of its wishes, more often the successful candidates will feel that they have to pay some regard to its demands for public decency and honesty.

But in advising you to be practical and to work hard, I must not for one moment be understood as advising you to abandon one iota of your self-respect and devotion to principle. It is a bad sign for the country to see one class of our citizens sneer at practical politicians, and another at Sunday-school politics. No man can do both effective and decent work in public life unless he is a practical politician on the one hand, and a sturdy believer in Sunday-school politics on the other. He must always strive manfully for the best, and yet, like Abraham Lincoln, must often resign himself to accept the best possible. Of course when a man verges on to the higher ground of statesmanship, when he becomes a leader, he must very often consult with others and defer to their opinion, and must be continually settling in his mind how far he can go in just deference to the wishes and prejudices of others while yet adhering to his own moral standards: but I speak not so much of men of this stamp as I do of the ordinary citizen, who wants to do his duty as a member of the commonwealth in its civic life; and for this man I feel that the one quality which he ought always to hold most essential is that of disinterestedness. If he once begins to feel that he wants office himself, with a willingness to get it at the cost of his convictions, or to keep it when gotten, at the cost of his convictions, his usefulness is gone. Let him make up his mind to do his duty in politics without regard to holding office at all, and let him know that often the men in this country who have done the best work for our public life have not been the men in office. If, on the other hand, he attains public position, let him not strive to plan out for himself a career. I do not think that any man should let himself regard his political career as a means of livelihood, or as his sole occupation in life; for if he does he immediately becomes most seriously handicapped. The moment that he begins to think how such and such an act will affect the voters in his district, or will affect some great political leader who will have an influence over his destiny, he is hampered and his hands are bound. Not only may it be his duty often to disregard the wishes of politicians, but it may be his clear duty at times to disregard the wishes of the people. The voice of the people is not always the voice of God; and when it happens to be the voice of the devil, then it is a man's clear duty to defy its behests. Different political conditions breed different dangers. The demagogue is as unlovely a creature as the courtier, though one is fostered under republican and the other under monarchical institutions. There is every reason why a man should have an honourable ambition to enter public life, and an honourable ambition to stay there when he is in; but he ought to make up his mind that he cares for it only as long as he can stay in it on his own terms, without sacrifice of his own principles; and if he does thus make up his mind he can really accomplish twice as much for the nation, and can reflect a hundredfold greater honour upon himself, in a short term of service, than can the man who grows gray in the public employment at the cost of sacrificing what he believes to be true and honest. And moreover, when a public servant has definitely made up his mind that he will pay no heed to his own future, but will do what he honestly deems best for the community, without regard to how his actions may affect his prospects, not only does he become infinitely more useful as a public servant, but he has a far better time. He is freed from the harassing care which is inevitably the portion of him who is trying to shape his sails to catch every gust of the wind of political favour.

But let me reiterate, that in being virtuous he must not become ineffective, and that he must not excuse himself for shirking his duties by any false plea that he cannot do his duties and retain his self-respect. This is nonsense, he can; and when he urges such a plea it is a mark of mere laziness and self-indulgence. And again, he should beware how he becomes a critic of the actions of others, rather than a doer of deeds himself; and in so far as he does act as a critic (and of course the critic has a great and necessary function) he must beware of indiscriminate censure even more than of indiscriminate praise. The screaming vulgarity of the foolish spread-eagle orator who is continually yelling defiance at Europe, praising everything American, good and bad, and resenting the introduction of any reform because it has previously been tried successfully abroad, is offensive and contemptible to the last degree; but after all it is scarcely as harmful as the peevish, fretful, sneering, and continual fault-finding of the refined, well-educated man, who is always attacking good and bad alike, who genuinely distrusts America, and in the true spirit of servile colonialism considers us inferior to the people across the water. It may be taken for granted that the man who is always sneering at our public life and our public men is a thoroughly bad citizen, and that what little influence he wields in the community is wielded for evil. The public speaker or the editorial writer who teaches men of education that their proper attitude toward American politics should be one of dislike or indifference is doing all he can to perpetuate and aggravate the very evils of which he is ostensibly complaining. Exactly as it is generally the case that when a man bewails the decadence of our civilization he is himself physically, mentally, and morally a first-class type of the decadent, so it is usually the case that when a man is perpetually sneering at American politicians, whether worthy or unworthy, he himself is a poor citizen and a friend of the very forces of evil against which he professes to contend. Too often these men seem to care less for attacking bad men, than for ruining the characters of good men with whom they disagree on some pubic question; and while their influence against the bad is almost nil, they are sometimes able to weaken the hands of the good by withdrawing from them support to which they are entitled, and they thus count in the sum total of forces that work for evil. They answer to the political prohibitionist, who, in a close contest between a temperance man and a liquor seller diverts enough votes from the former to elect the liquor seller. Occasionally it is necessary to beat a pretty good man, who is not quite good enough, even at the cost of electing a bad one- but it should be thoroughly recognized that this can be necessary only occasionally and indeed, I may say, only in very exceptional cases, and that as a rule where it is done the effect is thoroughly unwholesome in every way, and those taking part in it deserve the severest censure from all honest men.

Moreover, the very need of denouncing evil makes it all the more wicked to weaken the effect of such denunciations by denouncing also the good. It is the duty of all citizens, irrespective of party, to denounce, and, so far as may be, to punish crimes against the public on the part of politicians or officials. But exactly as the public man who commits a crime against the public is one of the worst of criminals, so, close on his heels in the race for iniquitous distinction, comes the man who falsely charges the public servant with outrageous wrongdoing; whether it is done with foul-mouthed and foolish directness in the vulgar and violent party organ, or with sarcasm, innuendo, and the half-truths that are worse than lies, in some professed organ of independence. Not only should criticism be honest, but it should be intelligent, in order to be effective. I recently read in a religious paper an article railing at the corruption of our public life, in which it stated incidentally that the lobby was recognized as all-powerful in Washington. This is untrue. There was a day when the lobby was very important at Washington, but its influence in Congress is now very small indeed; and from a pretty intimate acquaintance with several Congresses I am entirely satisfied that there is among the members a very small proportion indeed who are corruptible, in the sense that they will let their action be influenced by money or its equivalent. Congressmen are very often demagogues; they are very often blind partisans; they are often exceedingly short-sighted, narrow-minded, and bigoted; but they are not usually corrupt; and to accuse a narrow-minded demagogue of corruption when he is perfectly honest, is merely to set him more firmly in his evil course and to help him with his constituents, who recognize that the charge is entirely unjust, and in repelling it lose sight of the man's real shortcomings. I have known more than one State legislature, more than one board of aldermen against which the charge of corruption could perfectly legitimately be brought, but it cannot be brought against Congress. Moreover, these sweeping charges really do very little good. When I was in the New York legislature, one of the things that I used to mind most was the fact that at the close of every session the papers that affect morality invariably said that particular legislature was the worst legislature since the days of Tweed. The statement was not true as a rule; and, in any event, to lump all the members, good and bad, in sweeping condemnation simply hurt the good and helped the bad. Criticism should be fearless, but I again reiterate that it should be honest and should be discriminating. When it is sweeping and unintelligent, and directed against good and bad alike, or against the good and bad qualities of any man alike, it is very harmful. It tends steadily to deteriorate the character of our public men; and it tends to produce a very unwholesome spirit among young men of education, and especially among the young men in our colleges.

Against nothing is fearless and specific criticism more urgently needed than against the 'spoils system,' which is the degradation of American politics. And nothing is more effective in thwarting the purposes of the spoilsmen than the civil service reform. To be sure, practical politicians sneer at it. One of them even went so far as to say that civil service reform is asking a man irrelevant questions. What more irrelevant question could there be than that of the practical politician who asks the aspirant for his political favour—'Whom did you vote for in the last election?' There is certainly nothing more interesting, from a humorous point of view, than the heads of departments urging changes to be made in their underlings, 'on the score of increased efficiency' they say; when as the result of such a change the old incumbent often spends six months teaching the new incumbent how to do the work almost as well as he did himself! Occasionally the civil service reform has been abused, but not often. Certainly the reform is needed when you contemplate the spectacle of a New York City treasurer who acknowledges his annual fees to be eighty-five thousand dollars, and who pays a deputy one thousand five hundred dollars to do his work—when you note the corruptions in the New York legislature, where one man says he has a horror of the Constitution because it prevents active benevolence, and another says that you should never allow the Constitution to come between friends! All these corruptions and vices are what every good American citizen must fight against.

Finally, the man who wishes to do his duty as a citizen in our country must be imbued through and through with the spirit of Americanism. I am not saying this as a matter of spread-eagle rhetoric; I am saying it quite soberly as a piece of matter-of-fact, common-sense advice, derived from my own experience of others. Of course, the question of Americanism has several sides. If a man is an educated man, he must show his Americanism by not getting misled into following out and trying to apply all the theories of the political thinkers of other countries, such as Germany and France, to our own entirely different conditions. He must not get a fad, for instance, about responsible government; and above all things he must not, merely because he is intelligent, or a college professor well read in political literature, try to discuss our institutions when he has had no practical knowledge of how they are worked. Again, if he is a wealthy man, a man of means and standing, he must really feel, not merely affect to feel, that no social differences obtain save such as a man can in some way himself make by his own actions. People sometimes ask me if there is not a prejudice against a man of wealth and education in ward politics. I do not think that there is, unless the man in turn shows that he regards the facts of his having wealth and education as giving him a claim to superiority aside from the merit he is able to prove himself to have in actual service. Of course, if he feels that he ought to have a little better treatment than a carpenter, a plumber, or a butcher, who happens to stand beside him, he is going to be thrown out of the race very quickly, and probably quite roughly; and if he starts in to patronize and elaborately condescend to these men he will find that they resent this attitude even more. Do not let him think about the matter at all. Let him go into the political contest with no more thought of such matters than a college boy gives to the social standing of the members of his own and rival teams in a hotly contested football match. As soon as he begins to take an interest in politics (and he will speedily not only get interested for the sake of politics, but also take a good healthy interest in playing the game itself—an interest which is perfectly normal and praiseworthy, and to which only a prig would object), he will begin to work up the organization in the way that will be most effective, and he won't care a rap about who is put to work with him, save in so far as he is a good fellow and an efficient worker. There was one time that a number of men who think as we do here tonight (one of the number being myself) got hold of one of the assembly districts of New York, and ran it in really an ideal way, better than any other assembly district has ever been run before or since by either party. We did it by hard work and good organization; by working practically, and yet by being honest and square in motive and method: especially did we do it by all turning in as straight-out Americans without any regard to distinctions of race origin. Among the many men who did a great deal in organizing our victories was the son of a Presbyterian clergyman, the nephew of a Hebrew rabbi, and two well-known Catholic gentlemen. We also had a Columbia College professor (the stroke-oar of a university crew), a noted retail butcher, and the editor of a local German paper, various brokers, bankers, lawyers, bricklayers and a stone-mason who was particularly useful to us, although on questions of theoretic rather than applied politics he had a decidedly socialistic turn of mind.

Again, questions of race origin, like questions of creed, must not be considered: we wish to do good work, and we are all Americans, pure and simple. In the New York legislature, when it fell to my lot to choose a committee—which I always esteemed my most important duty at Albany—no less than three out of the four men I chose were of Irish birth or parentage; and three abler and more fearless and disinterested men never sat in a legislative body; while among my especial political and personal friends in that body was a gentleman from the southern tier of counties, who was, I incidentally found out, a German by birth, but who was just as straight United States as if his ancestors had come over here in the Mayflower or in Henry Hudson's yacht. Of course, none of these men of Irish or German birth would have been worth their salt had they continued to act after coming here as Irishmen or Germans, or as anything but plain straight-out Americans. We have not any room here for a divided allegiance. A man has got to be an American and nothing else; and he has no business to be mixing us up with questions of foreign politics, British or Irish, German or French, and no business to try to perpetuate their language and customs in the land of complete religious toleration and equality. If, however, he does become honestly and in good faith an American, then he is entitled to stand precisely as all other Americans stand, and it is the height of un-Americanism to discriminate against him in any way because of creed or birthplace. No spirit can be more thoroughly alien to American institutions, than the spirit of the Know-Nothings.

In facing the future and in striving, each according to the measure of his individual capacity, to work out the salvation of our land, we should be neither timid pessimists nor foolish optimists. We should recognize the dangers that exist and that threaten us: we should neither overestimate them nor shrink from them, but steadily fronting them should set to work to overcome and beat them down. Grave perils are yet to be encountered in the stormy course of the Republic—perils from political corruption, perils from individual laziness, indolence and timidity, perils springing from the greed of the unscrupulous rich, and from the anarchic violence of the thriftless and turbulent poor. There is every reason why we should recognize them, but there is no reason why we should fear them or doubt our capacity to overcome them, if only each will, according to the measure of his ability, do his full duty, and endeavor so to live as to deserve the high praise of being called a good American citizen.

60

SURRENDER SPEECH

Chief Joseph

Chief Joseph of the Nez Perce (1840-1904) was known to his people as 'Thunder Traveling to the Loftier Mountain Heights.' He led his people in an attempt to resist the takeover of their lands in the Oregon Territory by white settlers. In 1877, the Nez Perce were ordered to move to a reservation in Idaho. Chief Joseph agreed at first. But after members of his tribe killed a group of settlers, he tried to flee to Canada with his followers, travelling over 1500 miles through Oregon, Washington, Idaho, and Montana. Along the way they fought several battles with the pursuing U.S. Army. Chief Joseph spoke these words when they finally surrendered on 5 October 1877.

I am tired of fighting. Our chiefs are killed. Looking Glass is dead. Toohulhulsote is dead. The old men are all dead. It is the young men who say yes or no. He who led the young men is dead.

It is cold and we have no blankets. The little children are freezing to death. My people, some of them, have run away to the hills and have no blankets, no food. No one knows where they are—perhaps freezing to death. I want to have time to look for my children and see how many I can find. Maybe I shall find them among the dead.

Hear me, my chiefs. I am tired. My heart is sick and sad. From where the sun now stands, I will fight no more forever.

61

ABOLITION SPEECH

William Wilberforce

William Wilberforce was a member of the British Parliament who converted to Christianity and later became an abolitionist. As a Christian, he sought to reform the evils within himself and the world and since one of the glaring moral issues of his day was slavery, he read up on the subject and met some anti-slavery activists. On 12 May 1789, he delivered his Abolition Speech before the House of Commons where he passionately made his case as to why the slave trade must be abolished. He also introduced a bill to abolish the trade and though it failed, it did not stop him from attempting to pass the bill year after year until finally, the Slave Trade Act was passed in 1807.

When I consider the magnitude of the subject which I am to bring before the House, a subject, in which the interests, not of this country, nor of Europe alone, but of the whole world, and of posterity, are involved: and when I think, at the same time, on the weakness of the advocate who has undertaken this great cause, when these reflections press upon my mind, it is impossible for me not to feel both terrified and concerned at my own inadequacy to such a task. But when I reflect, however, on the encouragement which I have had, through the whole course of a long and laborious examination of this question, and how much candour I have experienced, and how conviction has increased within my own mind, in proportion as I have advanced in my labours; when I reflect, especially, that however averse any gentleman may now be, yet we shall all be of one opinion in the end; When I turn myself to these thoughts, I take courage I determine to forget all my other fears, and I march forward with a firmer step in the full assurance that my cause will bear me out, and that I shall be able to justify upon the clearest principles, every resolution in my hand, the avowed end of which is, the total abolition of the slave trade.

I wish exceedingly, in the outset, to guard both myself and the House from entering into the subject with any sort of passion. It is not their passions I shall appeal to I ask only for their cool and impartial reason; and I wish not to take them by surprise, but to deliberate, point by point, upon every part of this question. I mean not to accuse any one, but to take the shame upon myself, in common, indeed, with the whole parliament of Great Britain, for having suffered this horrid trade to be carried on under their authority.

We are all guilty we ought all to plead guilty, and not to exculpate ourselves by throwing the blame on others; and I therefore deprecate every kind of reflection against the various descriptions of people who are more immediately involved in this wretched business.

Having now disposed of the first part of this subject, I must speak of the transit of the slaves in the West Indies. This I confess, in my own opinion, is the most wretched part of the whole subject. So much misery condensed in so little room, is more than the human imagination had ever before conceived. I will not accuse the Liverpool merchants: I will allow them, nay, I will believe them to be men of humanity; and I will therefore believe, if it were not for the enormous magnitude and extent of the evil which distracts their attention from individual cases, and makes them think generally, and therefore less feelingly on the subject, they would never have persisted in the trade.

I verily believe therefore, if the wretchedness of any one of the many hundred Negroes stowed in each ship could be brought before their view, and remain within the sight of the African Merchant, that there is no one among them whose heart would bear it. Let any one imagine to himself six or 700 of these wretches chained two and two, surrounded with every object that is nauseous and disgusting, diseased, and struggling under every kind of wretchedness! How can we bear to think of such a scene as this? One would think it had been determined to heap upon them all the varieties of bodily pain, for the purpose of blunting the feelings of the mind; and yet, in this very point (to show the power of human prejudice) the situation of the slaves has been described by Mr Norris, one of the Liverpool delegates, in a manner which, I am sure will convince the House how interest can draw a film across the eyes, so thick, that total blindness could do no more; and how it is our duty therefore to trust not to the reasonings of interested men, or to their way of colouring a transaction. Their apartments, says Mr Norris, are fitted up as much for their advantage as circumstances will admit.

The right ankle of one, indeed is connected with the left ankle of another by a small iron fetter, and if they are turbulent, by another on their wrists. They have several meals a day; some of their own country provisions, with the best sauces of African cookery; and by way of variety, another meal of pulse, according to European taste. After breakfast they have water to wash themselves, while their apartments are perfumed with frankincense and lime juice. Before dinner, they are amused after the manner of their country. The song and dance are promoted, and, as if the whole was really a scene of pleasure and dissipation it is added, that games of chance are furnished. The men play and sing, while the women and girls make fanciful ornaments with beads, which they are plentifully supplied with.

Such is the sort of strain in which the Liverpool delegates, and particularly Mr Norris, gave evidence before the privy council. What will the House think when, by the concurring testimony of other witnesses, the true history is laid open.

The slaves who are sometimes described as rejoicing at their captivity, are so wrung with misery at leaving their country, that it is the constant practice to set sail at night, lest they should be sensible of their departure. The pulse which Mr Norris talks of are horse beans; and the scantiness, both of water and provision, was suggested by the very legislature of Jamaica in the report of their committee, to be a subject that called for the interference of parliament.

Mr Norris talks of frankincense and lime juice; when surgeons tell you the slaves are stowed so close, that there is not room to tread among them; and when you have it in evidence from Sir George Yonge, that even in a ship which wanted 200 of her complement, the stench was intolerable.

The song and the dance, says Mr Norris, are promoted. It had been more fair, perhaps, if he had explained that word promoted. The truth is, that for the sake of exercise, these miserable wretches, loaded with chains, oppressed with disease and wretchedness, are forced to dance by the terror of the lash, and sometimes by the actual use of it. I, says one of the other evidences, was employed to dance the men, while another person danced the women. Such, then is the meaning of the word promoted; and it may be observed too, with respect to food, that an instrument is sometimes carried out, in order to force them to eat which is the same sort of proof how much they enjoy themselves in that instance also. As to their singing, what shall we say when we are told that their songs are songs of lamentation upon their departure which, while they sing, are always in tears, insomuch that one captain (more humane as I should conceive him, therefore, than the rest) threatened one of the women with a flogging, because the mournfulness of her song was too painful for his feelings. In order, however, not to trust too much to any sort of description, I will call the attention of the House to one species of evidence which is absolutely infallible.

Death, at least, is a sure ground of evidence, and the proportion of deaths will not only confirm, but if possible will even aggravate our suspicion of their misery in the transit. It will be found, upon an average of all the ships of which evidence has been given at the privy council, that exclusive of those who perish before they sail, not less than 12½ per cent perish in the passage. Besides these, the Jamaica report tells you, that not less than 4½ per cent die on shore before the day of sale, which is only a week or two from the time of landing.

One third more die in the seasoning, and this in a country exactly like their own, where they are healthy and happy as some of the evidences would pretend. The diseases, however, which they contract on shipboard, the astringent washes which are to hide their wounds, and the mischievous tricks used to make them up for sale, are, as the Jamaica report says, (a most precious and valuable report, which I shall often have to advert to) one principle cause of this mortality.

Upon the whole, however, here is a mortality of about 50 per cent and this among negroes who are not bought unless (as the phrase is with cattle) they

e sound in wind and limb. How then can the House refuse its belief to
he multiplied testimonies before the privy council, of the savage treatment
f the negroes in the middle passage? Nay, indeed, what need is there of
ny evidence? The number of deaths speaks for itself, and makes all such
nquiry superfluous.

s soon as ever I had arrived thus far in my investigation of the slave
ade, I confess to you sir, so enormous so dreadful, so irremediable did
s wickedness appear that my own mind was completely made up for the
bolition. A trade founded in iniquity, and carried on as this was, must be
bolished, let the policy be what it might, let the consequences be what
ney would, I from this time determined that I would never rest till I had
fected its abolition.

62

DUTY, HONOUR, COUNTRY

General Douglas MacArthur

General Douglas MacArthur was the then famous commander of Allied Forces in the Pacific Theatre during World War II. His chivalry, his experience in the battlefield, and his selfless sacrifice were all done for the sake of 'Duty, Country, Honour'. This 1962 speech was given while accepting the Sylvanus Thayer Award for outstanding service to the nation. His address was intended for the soldiers who would tread the same course he did, reminding them of their purpose in becoming soldiers.

General Westmoreland, General Grove, distinguished guests, and gentlemen of the Corps!

As I was leaving the hotel this morning, a doorman asked me, 'Where are you bound for, General?' And when I replied, 'West Point,' he remarked, 'Beautiful place. Have you ever been there before?'

No human being could fail to be deeply moved by such a tribute as this [Thayer Award]. Coming from a profession I have served so long, and people I have loved so well, it fills me with an emotion I cannot express. But this award is not intended primarily to honour a personality, but to symbolize a great moral code—the code of conduct and chivalry of those who guard this beloved land of culture and ancient descent. That is the animation of this medallion. For all eyes and for all time, it is an expression of the ethics of the American soldier. That I should be integrated in this way with so noble an ideal, arouses a sense of pride and yet of humility which will be with me always.

Duty, Honour, Country: those three hallowed words reverently dictate what you ought to be, what you can be, what you will be. They are your rallying points: to build courage when courage seems to fail; to regain faith when there seems to be little cause for faith; to create hope when hope becomes forlorn.

Unhappily, I possess neither that eloquence of diction, that poetry of imagination, nor that brilliance of metaphor to tell you all that they mean.

The unbelievers will say they are but words, but a slogan, but a flamboyant phrase. Every pedant, every demagogue, every cynic, every hypocrite, every troublemaker, and I am sorry to say, some others of an entirely different character, will try to downgrade them even to the extent of mockery and ridicule.

But these are some of the things they do; they build your basic character. They mold you for your future roles as the custodians of the nation's defence. They make you strong enough to know when you are weak, and brave enough to face yourself when you are afraid. They teach you to be proud and unbending in honest failure, but humble and gentle in success; not to substitute words for actions, not to seek the path of comfort, but to face the stress and spur of difficulty and challenge; to learn to stand up in the storm but to have compassion on those who fall; to master yourself before you seek to master others; to have a heart that is clean, a goal that is high; to learn to laugh, yet never forget how to weep; to reach into the future yet never neglect the past; to be serious yet never to take yourself too seriously; to be modest so that you will remember the simplicity of true greatness, the open mind of true wisdom, the meekness of true strength. They give you a temper of the will, a quality of the imagination, a vigour of the emotions, a freshness of the deep springs of life, a temperamental predominance of courage over timidity, of an appetite for adventure over love of ease. They create in your heart the sense of wonder, the unfailing hope of what next, and the joy and inspiration of life. They teach you in this way to be an officer and a gentleman.

And what sort of soldiers are those you are to lead? Are they reliable? Are they brave? Are they capable of victory? Their story is known to all of you. It is the story of the American man-at-arms. My estimate of him was formed on the battlefield many, many years ago, and has never changed. I regarded him then as I regard him now—as one of the world's noblest figures, not only as one of the finest military characters, but also as one of the most stainless. His name and fame are the birthright of every American citizen. In his youth and strength, his love and loyalty, he gave all that mortality can give.

He needs no eulogy from me or from any other man. He has written his own history and written it in red on his enemy's breast. But when I think of his patience under adversity, of his courage under fire, and of his modesty in victory, I am filled with an emotion of admiration I cannot put into words. He belongs to history as furnishing one of the greatest examples of successful patriotism. He belongs to posterity as the instructor of future generations in the principles of liberty and freedom. He belongs to the present, to us, by his virtues and by his achievements. In 20 campaigns, on a hundred battlefields, around a thousand campfires, I have witnessed that enduring fortitude, that patriotic self-abnegation, and that invincible determination which have carved his statue in the hearts of his people. From one end of the world to the other he has drained deep the chalice of courage.

As I listened to those songs [of the glee club], in memory's eye I could see those staggering columns of the First World War, bending under soggy packs, on many a weary march from dripping dusk to drizzling dawn, slogging ankle-deep through the mire of shell-shocked roads, to form grimly for the attack, blue-lipped, covered with sludge and mud, chilled by the wind and rain, driving home to their objective, and for many, to the judgment seat of God.

I do not know the dignity of their birth, but I do know the glory of their death. They died unquestioning, uncomplaining, with faith in their hearts, and on their lips the hope that we would go on to victory. Always, for them: Duty, Honour, Country; always their blood and sweat and tears, as we sought the way and the light and the truth.

And 20 years after, on the other side of the globe, again the filth of murky oxholes, the stench of ghostly trenches, the slime of dripping dugouts; hose boiling suns of relentless heat, those torrential rains of devastating storms; the loneliness and utter desolation of jungle trails; the bitterness of ong separation from those they loved and cherished; the deadly pestilence of tropical disease; the horror of stricken areas of war; their resolute and determined defence, their swift and sure attack, their indomitable purpose, their complete and decisive victory—always victory. Always through the bloody haze of their last reverberating shot, the vision of gaunt, ghastly men reverently following your password of: Duty, Honour, Country.

The code which those words perpetuate embraces the highest moral laws and will stand the test of any ethics or philosophies ever promulgated for the uplift of mankind. Its requirements are for the things that are right, and its restraints are from the things that are wrong.

The soldier, above all other men, is required to practice the greatest act of religious training—sacrifice.

In battle and in the face of danger and death, he discloses those divine attributes which his Maker gave when he created man in his own image. No physical courage and no brute instinct can take the place of the divine help which alone can sustain him. However horrible the incidents of war may be, the soldier who is called upon to offer and to give his life for his country is the noblest development of mankind.

You now face a new world—a world of change. The thrust into outer space of the satellite, spheres, and missiles mark the beginning of another epoch in the long story of mankind. In the five or more billions of years the scientists tell us it has taken to form the earth, in the three or more billion years of development of the human race, there has never been a more abrupt or staggering evolution. We deal now not with things of this world alone, but with the illimitable distances and as yet unfathomed mysteries of the universe. We are reaching out for a new and boundless frontier.

We speak in strange terms: of harnessing the cosmic energy; of making winds and tides work for us; of creating unheard synthetic materials to supplement or even replace our old standard basics; to purify sea water for our drink; of mining ocean floors for new fields of wealth and food of disease preventatives to expand life into the hundreds of years; or controlling the weather for a more equitable distribution of heat and cold of rain and shine; of space ships to the moon; of the primary target in war no longer limited to the armed forces of an enemy, but instead to include his civil populations; of ultimate conflict between a united human race and the sinister forces of some other planetary galaxy; of such dreams and fantasies as to make life the most exciting of all time.

And through all this welter of change and development, your mission remains fixed, determined, inviolable: it is to win our wars. Everything else in your professional career is but corollary to this vital dedication. All other public purposes, all other public projects, all other public needs, great or small, will find others for their accomplishment. But you are the ones who are trained to fight. Yours is the profession of arms, the will to win, the sure knowledge that in war there is no substitute for victory; that if you lose the nation will be destroyed; that the very obsession of your public service must be: Duty, Honour, Country.

Others will debate the controversial issues, national and international, which divide men's minds; but serene, calm, aloof, you stand as the Nation's war-guardian, as its lifeguard from the raging tides of international conflict, as its gladiator in the arena of battle. For a century and a half you have defended, guarded, and protected its hallowed traditions of liberty and freedom, of right and justice.

Let civilian voices argue the merits or demerits of our processes of government; whether our strength is being sapped by deficit financing, indulged in too long, by federal paternalism grown too mighty, by power groups grown too arrogant, by politics grown too corrupt, by crime grown too rampant, by morals grown too low, by taxes grown too high, by extremists grown too violent; whether our personal liberties are as thorough and complete as they should be. These great national problems are not for your professional participation or military solution. Your guidepost stands out like a ten-fold beacon in the night: Duty, Honour, Country.

You are the leaven which binds together the entire fabric of our national system of defence. From your ranks come the great captains who hold the nation's destiny in their hands the moment the war tocsin sounds. The Long Gray Line has never failed us. Were you to do so, a million ghosts in olive drab, in brown khaki, in blue and gray, would rise from their white crosses thundering those magic words: Duty, Honour, Country. This does not mean that you are war mongers.

On the contrary, the soldier, above all other people, prays for peace, for he must suffer and bear the deepest wounds and scars of war. But always in our ears ring the ominous words of Plato, that wisest of all philosophers: Only the dead have seen the end of war.

The shadows are lengthening for me. The twilight is here. My days of old have vanished, tone and tint. They have gone glimmering through the dreams of things that were. Their memory is one of wondrous beauty, watered by tears, and coaxed and caressed by the smiles of yesterday. I listen vainly, but with thirsty ears, for the witching melody of faint bugles blowing reveille, of far drums beating the long roll. In my dreams, I hear again the crash of guns, the rattle of musketry, the strange, mournful mutter of the battlefield.

But in the evening of my memory, always I come back to West Point. Always there echoes and re-echoes: Duty, Honour, Country.

Today marks my final roll call with you, but I want you to know that when I cross the river my last conscious thoughts will be of The Corps, and The Corps, and The Corps.

I bid you farewell.

63

FUNERAL ORATION

Pericles

Pericles, who was dubbed by Thuciydies as 'the first citizen of Athens,' delivered this oratory piece in Athens in 431 BC. A statesman, general and an orator, he was a product of Sophistas, tutored personally by the great philosopher Anaxagoras. He was a highly persuasive orator who influenced Athenians to build hundreds of temples, including the famous Pantheon. His speeches also inspired Athenians to become the most powerful in Greece. However, his skills in rhetoric were put to the test on February 431 BC during the annual public funeral for those who were slain in the war. He stood to the occasion to laud the glory of Athens and in inspiring the Athenians that their fallen heroes have not died in vain, like what Abraham Lincoln did during the Gettysburg Address, two thousand years later.

Most of those who have spoken here before me have commended the lawgiver who added this oration to our other funeral customs. It seemed to them a worthy thing that such an honour should be given at their burial to the dead who have fallen on the field of battle. But I should have preferred that, when men's deeds have been made, they should be honoured in deed only, and with such an honour as this public funeral, which you are now witnessing. Then the reputation of many would not have been imperiled on the eloquence or want of eloquence of one, and their virtues believed or not as he spoke well or ill. For it is difficult to say neither too little nor too much; and even moderation is apt not to give the impression of truthfulness.

The friend of the dead who knows the facts is likely to think that the words of the speaker fall short of his knowledge and of his wishes; another who is not so well informed, when he hears of anything which surpasses his own powers, will be envious and will suspect exaggeration. Mankind are tolerant of the praises of others so long as each hearer thinks that he can do as well or nearly as well himself, but, when the speaker rises above him, jealousy is aroused and he begins to be incredulous. However, since our ancestors have set the seal of their approval upon the practice, I must obey, and to the utmost of my power shall endeavor to satisfy the wishes and beliefs of all who hear me.

I will speak first of our ancestors, for it is right and seemly that now, when we are lamenting the dead, a tribute should be paid to their memory. There has never been a time when they did not inhabit this land, which by their valour they will have handed down from generation to generation, and we have received from them a free state. But if they were worthy of praise, still more were our fathers, who added to their inheritance, and after many a struggle transmitted to us their sons this great empire. And we ourselves assembled here today, who are still most of us in the vigour of life, have carried the work of improvement further, and have richly endowed our city with all things, so that she is sufficient for herself both in peace and war. Of the military exploits by which our various possessions were acquired, or of the energy with which we or our fathers drove back the tide of war, Hellenic or Barbarian, I will not speak; for the tale would be long and is familiar to you. But before I praise the dead, I should like to point out by what principles of action we rose to power, and under what institutions and through what manner of life our empire became great. For I conceive that such thoughts are not unsuited to the occasion, and that this numerous assembly of citizens and strangers may profitably listen to them.

Our form of government does not enter into rivalry with the institutions of others. Our government does not copy our neighbours', but is an example to them. It is true that we are called a democracy, for the administration is in the hands of the many and not of the few. But while there exists equal justice to all and alike in their private disputes, the claim of excellence is also recognized; and when a citizen is in any way distinguished, he is preferred to the public service, not as a matter of privilege, but as the reward of merit. Neither is poverty an obstacle, but a man may benefit his country whatever the obscurity of his condition. There is no exclusiveness in our public life, and in our private business we are not suspicious of one another, nor angry with our neighbour if he does what he likes; we do not put on sour looks at him which, though harmless, are not pleasant. While we are thus unconstrained in our private business, a spirit of reverence pervades our public acts; we are prevented from doing wrong by respect for the authorities and for the laws, having a particular regard to those which are ordained for the protection of the injured as well as those unwritten laws which ping upon the transgressor of them the reprobation of the general sentiment.

And we have not forgotten to provide for our weary spirits many relaxations from toil; we have regular games and sacrifices throughout the year; our homes are beautiful and elegant; and the delight which we daily feel in all these things helps to banish sorrow. Because of the greatness of our city the fruits of the whole earth flow in upon us; so that we enjoy the goods of other countries as freely as our own.

Then, again, our military training is in many respects superior to that of our adversaries. Our city is thrown open to the world, though and we never expel a foreigner and prevent him from seeing or learning anything of which the secret if revealed to an enemy might profit him. We rely not upon management or trickery, but upon our own hearts and hands. And in the matter of education, whereas they from early youth are always undergoing laborious exercises which are to make them pave, we live at ease, and yet are equally ready to face the perils which they face. And here is the proof: The Lacedaemonians come into Athenian territory not by themselves, but with their whole confederacy following; we go alone into a neighbour's country; and although our opponents are fighting for their homes and we on a foreign soil, we have seldom any difficulty in overcoming them. Our enemies have never yet felt our united strength, the care of a navy divides our attention, and on land we are obliged to send our own citizens everywhere. But they, if they meet and defeat a part of our army, are as proud as if they had routed us all, and when defeated they pretend to have been vanquished by us all.

If then we prefer to meet danger with a light heart but without laborious training, and with a courage which is gained by habit and not enforced by law, are we not greatly the better for it? Since we do not anticipate the pain, although, when the hour comes, we can be as pave as those who never allow themselves to rest; thus our city is equally admirable in peace and in war. For we are lovers of the beautiful in our tastes and our strength lies, in our opinion, not in deliberation and discussion, but that knowledge which is gained by discussion preparatory to action. For we have a peculiar power of thinking before we act, and of acting, too, whereas other men are courageous from ignorance but hesitate upon reflection. And they are surely to be esteemed the pavest spirits who, having the clearest sense both of the pains and pleasures of life, do not on that account shrink from danger. In doing good, again, we are unlike others; we make our friends by conferring, not by receiving favours. Now he who confers a favour is the firmer friend, because he would rather by kindness keep alive the memory of an obligation; but the recipient is colder in his feelings, because he knows that in requiting another's generosity he will not be winning gratitude but only paying a debt. We alone do good to our neighbours not upon a calculation of interest, but in the confidence of freedom and in a frank and fearless spirit.

To sum up: I say that Athens is the school of Hellas, and that the individual Athenian in his own person seems to have the power of adapting himself to the most varied forms of action with the utmost versatility and grace. This is no passing and idle word, but truth and fact; and the assertion is verified by the position to which these qualities have raised the state. For in the hour of trial Athens alone among her contemporaries is superior to the report of her. No enemy who comes against her is indignant at the reverses which he sustains at the hands of such a city; no subject complains that his masters are unworthy of him. And we shall assuredly not be without witnesses; there are mighty monuments of our power which will make us the wonder of this and of succeeding ages; we shall not need the praises of Homer or of any other panegyrist whose poetry may please for the moment, although his representation of the facts will not bear the light of day. For we have compelled every land and every sea to open a path for our valour, and have everywhere planted eternal memorials of our friendship and of our enmity. Such is the city for whose sake these men nobly fought and died; they could not bear the thought that she might be taken from them; and every one of us who survive should gladly toil on her behalf.

I have dwelt upon the greatness of Athens because I want to show you that we are contending for a higher prize than those who enjoy none of these privileges, and to establish by manifest proof the merit of these men whom I am now commemorating. Their loftiest praise has been already spoken. For in magnifying the city I have magnified them, and men like them whose virtues made her glorious. And of how few Hellenes can it be said as of them, that their deeds when weighed in the balance have been found equal to their fame! Methinks that a death such as theirs has been the true measure of a man's worth; it may be the first revelation of his virtues, but is at any rate their final seal. For even those who come short in other ways may justly plead the valour with which they have fought for their country; they have blotted out the evil with the good, and have benefited the state more by their public services than they have injured her by their private actions. None of these men were enervated by wealth or hesitated to resign the pleasures of life; none of them put off the evil day in the hope, natural to poverty, that a man, though poor, may one day become rich.

But, deeming that the punishment of their enemies was sweeter than any of these things, and that they could fall in no nobler cause, they determined at the hazard of their lives to be honourably avenged, and to leave the rest. They resigned to hope their unknown chance of happiness; but in the face of death they resolved to rely upon themselves alone. And when the moment came they were minded to resist and suffer, rather than to fly and save their lives; they ran away from the word of dishonour, but on the battlefield their feet stood fast, and in an instant, at the height of their fortune, they passed away from the scene, not of their fear, but of their glory.

Such was the end of these men; they were worthy of Athens, and the living need not desire to have a more heroic spirit, although they may pray for a less fatal issue. The value of such a spirit is not to be expressed in words. Any one can discourse to you for ever about the advantages of a Pave defence, which you know already. But instead of listening to him I would have you day by day fix your eyes upon the greatness of Athens, until you become filled with the love of her; and when you are impressed by the spectacle of her glory, reflect that this empire has been acquired by men who knew their duty and had the courage to do it, who in the hour of conflict had the fear of dishonour always present to them, and who, if ever they failed in an enterprise, would not allow their virtues to be lost to their country, but freely gave their lives to her as the fairest offering which they could present at her feast.

The sacrifice which they collectively made was individually repaid to them; for they received again each one for himself a praise which grows not old, and the noblest of all tombs—I speak not of that in which their remains are laid, but of that in which their glory survives, and is proclaimed always and on every fitting occasion both in word and deed. For the whole earth is the tomb of famous men; not only are they commemorated by columns and inscriptions in their own country, but in foreign lands there dwells also an unwritten memorial of them, graven not on stone but in the hearts of men. Make them your examples, and, esteeming courage to be freedom and freedom to be happiness, do not weigh too nicely the perils of war. The unfortunate who has no hope of a change for the better has less reason to throw away his life than the prosperous who, if he survive, is always liable to a change for the worse, and to whom any accidental fall makes the most serious difference. To a man of spirit, cowardice and disaster coming together are far more bitter than death striking him unperceived at a time when he is full of courage and animated by the general hope.

Wherefore I do not now pity the parents of the dead who stand here; I would rather comfort them. You know that your dead have passed away amid manifold vicissitudes; and that they may be deemed fortunate who have gained their utmost honour, whether an honourable death like theirs, or an honourable sorrow like yours, and whose share of happiness has been so ordered that the term of their happiness is likewise the term of their life. I know how hard it is to make you feel this, when the good fortune of others will too often remind you of the gladness which once lightened your hearts. And sorrow is felt at the want of those blessings, not which a man never knew, but which were a part of his life before they were taken from him.

Some of you are of an age at which they may hope to have other children, and they ought to bear their sorrow better; not only will the children who may hereafter be born make them forget their own lost ones, but the city will be doubly a gainer. She will not be left desolate, and she will be safer.

For a man's counsel cannot have equal weight or worth, when he alone has no children to risk in the general danger. To those of you who have passed their prime, I say: Congratulate yourselves that you have been happy during the greater part of your days; remember that your life of sorrow will not last long, and be comforted by the glory of those who are gone. For the love of honour alone is ever young, and not riches, as some say, but honour is the delight of men when they are old and useless.

To you who are the sons and fathers of the departed, I see that the struggle to emulate them will be an arduous one. For all men praise the dead, and, however pre-eminent your virtue may be, I do not say even to approach them, and avoid living their rivals and detractors, but when a man is out of the way, the honour and goodwill which he receives is unalloyed. And, if I am to speak of womanly virtues to those of you who will henceforth be widows, let me sum them up in one short admonition: To a woman not to show more weakness than is natural to her sex is a great glory, and not to be talked about for good or for evil among men.

I have paid the required tribute, in obedience to the law, making use of such fitting words as I had. The tribute of deeds has been paid in part; for the dead have them in deeds, and it remains only that their children should be maintained at the public charge until they are grown up: this is the solid prize with which, as with a garland, Athens crowns her sons living and dead, after a struggle like theirs. For where the rewards of virtue are greatest, there the noblest citizens are enlisted in the service of the state. And now, when you have duly lamented everyone his own dead, you may depart.

64

ON THE DEATH OF MARIE ANTOINETTE

Edmund Burke

In October 1793, Marie Antoinette, the downfallen Queen of France, was beheaded amid the violent aftermath of the French Revolution. By that time, Irish statesman and orator Edmund Burke (1729-1797) had become an outspoken critic of the Revolutionaries' ongoing reign of terror. Persons of Royal ancestry in France were subject to arbitrary imprisonment and execution, along with anyone accused of aiding or sympathizing with them. In this speech, Burke laments the death of the Queen and the passing of an era.

It is now sixteen or seventeen years since I saw the Queen of France, then the Dauphiness, at Versailles; and surely never lighted on this orb, which she hardly seemed to touch, a more delightful vision. I saw her just above the horizon, decorating and cheering the elevated sphere she had just begun to move in, glittering like the morning star full of life and splendour and joy.

Oh, what a revolution! And what a heart must I have, to contemplate without emotion that elevation and that fall! Little did I dream, when she added titles of veneration to those of enthusiastic, distant, respectful love, that she should ever be obliged to carry the sharp antidote against disgrace concealed in that bosom; little did I dream that I should have lived to see such disasters fallen upon her, in a nation of gallant men, in a nation of men of honour, and of cavaliers! I thought ten thousand swords must have leaped from their scabbards, to avenge even a look that threatened her with insult.

But the age of chivalry is gone; that of sophisters, economists, and calculators has succeeded, and the glory of Europe is extinguished forever. Never, never more, shall we behold that generous loyalty to rank and sex, that proud submission, that dignified obedience, that subordination of the heart, which kept alive, even in servitude itself, the spirit of an exalted freedom! The unbought grace of life, the cheap defence of nations, the nurse of manly sentiment and heroic enterprise is gone. It is gone, that sensibility of principle, that chastity of honour, which felt a stain like a wound, which inspired courage whilst it mitigated ferocity, which ennobled whatever it touched, and under which vice itself lost half its evil, by losing all its grossness.

65

ON THE NAZI INVASION OF POLAND

Neville Chamberlaine

British Prime Minister Neville Chamberlain gave this speech to the House of Commons on 1 September 1939, just hours after Hitler's troops had invaded Poland. Chamberlain and others had spent years negotiating with Hitler in order to prevent another war in Europe, two decades after the Great War in which an entire generation of young men had been wiped out. Negotiations with Hitler had included ceding the German-speaking portions of Czechoslovakia, amid promises by Hitler he would have no further territorial demands. Unknown to Chamberlain, Hitler yearned for war all along and was simply biding his time until his armies were prepared.

I do not propose to say many words tonight. The time has come when action rather than speech is required. Eighteen months ago in this House I prayed that the responsibility might not fall upon me to ask this country to accept the awful arbitrament of war. I fear that I may not be able to avoid that responsibility.

But, at any rate, I cannot wish for conditions in which such a burden should fall upon me in which I should feel clearer than I do today as to where my duty lies.

No man can say that the government could have done more to try to keep open the way for an honourable and equitable settlement of the dispute between Germany and Poland. Nor have we neglected any means of making it crystal clear to the German government that if they insisted on using force again in the manner in which they had used it in the past we were resolved to oppose them by force.

Now that all the relevant documents are being made public we shall stand at the bar of history knowing that the responsibility for this terrible catastrophe lies on the shoulders of one man, the German Chancellor, who has not hesitated to plunge the world into misery in order to serve his own senseless ambitions...

Only last night the Polish Ambassador did see the German Foreign Secretary, Herr von Ribbentrop. Once again he expressed to him what, indeed, the Polish government had already said publicly, that they were willing to negotiate with Germany about their disputes on an equal basis.

What was the reply of the German government? The reply was that without another word the German troops crossed the Polish frontier this morning at dawn and are since reported to be bombing open towns. In these circumstances there is only one course open to us.

His Majesty's Ambassador in Berlin and the French Ambassador have been instructed to hand to the German government the following document:

'Early this morning the German Chancellor issued a proclamation to the German army which indicated that he was about to attack Poland. Information which has reached His Majesty's government in the United Kingdom and the French government indicates that attacks upon Polish towns are proceeding. In these circumstances, it appears to the Governments of the United Kingdom and France that by their action the German government have created conditions, namely, an aggressive act of force against Poland threatening the independence of Poland, which call for the implementation by the Government of the United Kingdom and France of the undertaking to Poland to come to her assistance. I am accordingly to inform your Excellency that unless the German government are prepared to give His Majesty's government satisfactory assurances that the German government have suspended all aggressive action against Poland and are prepared promptly to withdraw their forces from Polish territory, His Majesty's government in the United Kingdom will without hesitation fulfill their obligations to Poland.'

If a reply to this last warning is unfavourable, and I do not suggest that it is likely to be otherwise, His Majesty's Ambassador is instructed to ask for his passports. In that case we are ready.

Yesterday, we took further steps towards the completion of our defensive preparation. This morning we ordered complete mobilization of the whole of the Royal Navy, Army and Royal Air Force. We have also taken a number of other measures, both at home and abroad, which the House will not perhaps expect me to specify in detail. Briefly, they represent the final steps in accordance with pre-arranged plans. These last can be put into force rapidly, and are of such a nature that they can be deferred until war seems inevitable. Steps have also been taken under the powers conferred by the House last week to safeguard the position in regard to stocks of commodities of various kinds.

The thoughts of many of us must at this moment inevitably be turning back to 1914, and to a comparison of our position now with that which existed then. How do we stand this time? The answer is that all three Services are ready, and that the situation in all directions is far more favourable and reassuring than in 1914, while behind the fighting Services we have built up a vast organization of Civil Defence under our scheme of Air Raid Precautions.

As regards the immediate manpower requirements, the Royal Navy, the Army and the Air Force are in the fortunate position of having almost as many men as they can conveniently handle at this moment. There are, however, certain categories of service in which men are immediately required, both for Military and Civil Defence. These will be announced in detail through the press and the BBC.

The main and most satisfactory point to observe is that there is today no need to make an appeal in a general way for recruits such as was issued by Lord Kitchener 25 years ago. That appeal has been anticipated by many months, and the men are already available. So much for the immediate present. Now we must look to the future. It is essential in the face of the tremendous task which confronts us, more especially in view of our past experiences in this matter, to organize our manpower this time upon as methodical, equitable and economical a basis as possible.

We, therefore, propose immediately to introduce legislation directed to that end. A Bill will be laid before you which for all practical purposes will amount to an expansion of the Military Training Act. Under its operation all fit men between the ages of 18 and 41 will be rendered liable to military service if and when called upon. It is not intended at the outset that any considerable number of men other than those already liable shall be called up, and steps will be taken to ensure that the manpower essentially required by industry shall not be taken away.

There is one other allusion which I should like to make before I end my speech, and that is to record my satisfaction of His Majesty's government, that throughout these last days of crisis Signor Mussolini also has been doing his best to reach a solution. It now only remains for us to set our teeth and to enter upon this struggle, which we ourselves earnestly endeavoured to avoid, with determination to see it through to the end.

We shall enter it with a clear conscience, with the support of the Dominions and the British Empire, and the moral approval of the greater part of the world.

We have no quarrel with the German people, except that they allow themselves to be governed by a Nazi government. As long as that government exists and pursues the methods it has so persistently followed during the last two years, there will be no peace in Europe. We shall merely pass from one crisis to another, and see one country after another attacked by methods which have now become familiar to us in their sickening technique.

We are resolved that these methods must come to an end. If out of the struggle we again re-establish in the world the rules of good faith and the renunciation of force, why, then even the sacrifices that will be entailed upon us will find their fullest justification.

66

SERMON TO THE BIRDS

Saint Francis of Assisi

Saint Francis of Assisi (1182-1226) was born into a wealthy family at Assisi, Italy, the son of a cloth merchant. After much contemplation, including vivid dreams and mystic visions, he turned away from the pursuit of all worldly pleasures, sold all of his property and donated the money to the Church. He then began a lifelong passion of caring for society's castoffs, the sick and poor, including lepers. His wealthy father reacted to his son's odd new lifestyle by disinheriting him. Thus, Francis lived in utter poverty and even went without shoes. But his humbleness, extraordinary kindness and love for humanity attracted the attention of other young men and they also chose to give up worldly pleasures and follow him to spread the gospel and serve the poor. Eventually, as the brotherhood grew, its members travelled to other parts of Europe to preach, including France, Germany, Spain and England. A separate order for women was formed, now known as the Franciscan Nuns or Poor Clares. Francis had much love for animals with special fondness for the birds. He liked to refer to animals as his brothers and sisters. Legend has it that wild animals had no fear of Francis and even came to him seeking refuge from harm. In 1224, Francis went up onto a mountain and began a 40-day fast. During that time he is said to have had a miraculous vision and received the marks of the nails and spear exactly as they appeared on the body of Jesus during his crucifixion. After his death in 1226, Francis was declared a saint by Pope Gregory IX.

My little sisters, the birds, much bounden are ye unto God, your Creator, and always in every place ought ye to praise Him, for that He hath given you liberty to fly about everywhere, and hath also given you double and triple rainment; moreover, He preserved your seed in the ark of Noah, that your race might not perish out of the world; still more are ye beholden to Him for the element of the air which He hath appointed for you; beyond all this, ye sow not, neither do you reap; and God feedeth you, and giveth you the streams and fountains for your drink; the mountains and valleys for your refuge and the high trees whereon to make your nests; and because ye know not how to spin or sow, God clotheth you, you and your children; wherefore your Creator loveth you much, seeing that He hath bestowed on you so many benefits; and therefore, my little sisters, beware of the sin of ingratitude, and study always to give praises unto God.

67

ENCOURAGES HIS SOLDIERS

Guiseppe Garibaldi

Giuseppe Garibaldi (1807-1882) was an Italian patriot and military leader who helped free the Italians from foreign rule and unify the country. He was a master of guerrilla warfare and raised volunteers beginning in 1848 to conduct daring military campaigns to overcome the rule of Imperial Austria. In 1860, Garibaldi's thousand 'red shirts' took Sicily in the name of Victor Emmanuel II of Italy. Thousands of volunteers then rushed to join Garibaldi's army. In August, he crossed to the mainland to march on Naples, where he was greeted by jubilant crowds singing the national anthem, now known as 'Garibaldi's Hymn.' After turning over the city to Victor Emmanuel II, Garibaldi resumed a humble life on the island of Caprera. The speech is an eloquent appeal he made to his soldiers in 1860. A year later, as a result of his daring military leadership and the political leadership of fellow patriots, Giuseppe Mazzini and Camillo Cavour, the independent Kingdom of Italy was finally proclaimed.

We must now consider the period which is just drawing to a close as almost the last stage of our national resurrection, and prepare ourselves to finish worthily the marvelous design of the elect of twenty generations, the completion of which Providence has reserved for this fortunate age.

Yes, young men, Italy owes to you an undertaking which has merited the applause of the universe. You have conquered and you will conquer still, because you are prepared for the tactics that decide the fate of battles. You are not unworthy of the men who entered the ranks of a Macedonian phalanx, and who contended not in vain with the proud conquerors of Asia. To this wonderful page in our country's history another more glorious still will be added, and the slave shall show at last to his free brothers a sharpened sword forged from the links of his fetters.

To arms, then, all of you! All of you! And the oppressors and the mighty shall disappear like dust. You, too, women, cast away all the cowards from your embraces; they will give you only cowards for children, and you who are the daughters of the land of beauty must bear children who are noble and brave. Let timid doctrinaires depart from among us to carry their servility and their miserable fears elsewhere. This people is its own master. It wishes to be the brother of other peoples, but to look on the insolent with a proud glance, not to grovel before them imploring its own freedom. It will no longer follow in the trail of men whose hearts are foul. No! No! No!

Providence has presented Italy with Victor Emmanuel. Every Italian should rally round him. By the side of Victor Emmanuel every quarrel should be forgotten, all rancor depart. Once more I repeat my battle-cry: 'To arms, all of you!' If March, 1861, does not find one million of Italians in arms, then alas for liberty, alas for the life of Italy. Ah, no, far be from me a thought which I loathe like poison. March of 1861, or if need be February, will find us all at our post-Italians of Calatafimi, Palermo, Ancona, the Volturno, Castelfidardo, and Isernia, and with us every man of this land who is not a coward or a slave. Let all of us rally round the glorious hero of Palestro and give the last blow to the crumbling edifice of tyranny. Receive, then, my gallant young volunteers, at the honoured conclusion of ten battles, one word of farewell from me.

I utter this word with deepest affection and from the very bottom of my heart. Today I am obliged to retire, but for a few days only. The hour of battle will find me with you again, by the side of the champions of Italian liberty. Let those only return to their homes who are called by the imperative duties which they owe to their families, and those who by their glorious wounds have deserved the credit of their country. These, indeed, will serve Italy in their homes by their counsel, by the very aspect of the scars which adorn their youthful brows. Apart from these, let all others remain to guard our glorious banners. We shall meet again before long to march together to the redemption of our brothers who are still slaves of the stranger. We shall meet again before long to march to new triumphs.

68

WHAT IS AN AMERICAN?

Harold Ickes

This remarkable speech was delivered on 18 May 1941 during an I am an American Day gathering in New York's Central Park by Harold Ickes, President Franklin Roosevelt's Secretary of the Interior. It came at a perilous moment in history, May of 1941, when Adolf Hitler and the Nazis seemed headed toward possible world domination. By this time, countries that had fallen to the Nazis included Austria, Czechoslovakia, Poland, Norway, Denmark, France, Belgium, Luxembourg, the Netherlands, and areas in North Africa. Airfields and cities in England were now under ferocious air attack from the German Luftwaffe while wolf-packs of Nazi U-boats attempted to blockade the British Isles. Many Americans, however, still questioned the wisdom and necessity of direct U.S. involvement in the European war. Pacifist sentiment was steadily growing, while at the same time Fascism was sometimes referred to as the 'wave of the future' by respected Americans, buoyed in part by the ceaseless barrage of highly effective anti-democratic propaganda emanating from the Fascist countries of Europe including Germany. In this speech, Harold Ickes counters that propaganda, defines what it means to be a free American, and offers a blunt assessment of the perilous future the United States would face standing alone against a victorious Hitler.

I want to ask a few simple questions. And then I shall answer them.

What has happened to our vaunted idealism? Why have some of us been behaving like scared chickens? Where is the million-throated, democratic voice of America?

For years it has been dinned into us that we are a weak nation; that we are an inefficient people; that we are simple-minded. For years we have been told that we are beaten, decayed, and that no part of the world belongs to us any longer.

Some amongst us have fallen for this carefully pickled tripe. Some amongst us have fallen for this calculated poison. Some amongst us have begun to preach that the 'wave of the future' has passed over us and left us a wet, dead fish.

They shout—from public platforms in printed pages, through the microphones—that it is futile to oppose the 'wave of the future.' They cry that we Americans, we free Americans nourished on Magna Carta and the Declaration of Independence, hold moth-eaten ideas. They exclaim that there is no room for free men in the world any more and that only the slaves will inherit the earth. America—the America of Washington and Jefferson and Lincoln and Walt Whitman—they say, is waiting for the undertaker and all the hopes and aspirations that have gone into the making of America are dead too.

However, my fellow citizens, this is not the real point of the story. The real point—the shameful point—is that many of us are listening to them and some of us almost believe them.

I say that it is time for the great American people to raise its voice and cry out in mighty triumph what it is to be an American. And why it is that only Americans, with the aid of our brave allies—yes, let's call them 'allies'—the British, can and will build the only future worth having. I mean a future, not of concentration camps, not of physical torture and mental straitjackets, not of sawdust bread or of sawdust Caesars—I mean a future when free men will live free lives in dignity and in security.

This tide of the future, the democratic future, is ours. It is ours if we show ourselves worthy of our culture and of our heritage.

But make no mistake about it; the tide of the democratic future is not like the ocean tide—regular, relentless, and inevitable. Nothing in human affairs is mechanical or inevitable. Nor are Americans mechanical. They are very human indeed.

What constitutes an American? Not colour nor race nor religion. Not the pedigree of his family nor the place of his birth. Not the coincidence of his citizenship. Not his social status nor his bank account. Not his trade nor his profession. An American is one who loves justice and believes in the dignity of man. An American is one who will fight for his freedom and that of his neighbour. An American is one who will sacrifice property, ease and security in order that he and his children may retain the rights of free men. An American is one in whose heart is engraved the immortal second sentence of the Declaration of Independence.

Americans have always known how to fight for their rights and their way of life. Americans are not afraid to fight. They fight joyously in a just cause.

We Americans know that freedom, like peace, is indivisible. We cannot retain our liberty if three-fourths of the world is enslaved. Brutality, injustice and slavery, if practiced as dictators would have them, universally and systematically, in the long run would destroy us as surely as a fire raging in our nearby neighbour's house would burn ours if we didn't help to put out his.

If we are to retain our own freedom, we must do everything within our power to aid Britain. We must also do everything to restore to the conquered peoples their freedom. This means the Germans too.

Such a program, if you stop to think, is selfishness on our part. It is the sort of enlightened selfishness that makes the wheels of history go around. It is the sort of enlightened selfishness that wins victories.

Do you know why? Because we cannot live in the world alone, without friends and without allies. If Britain should be defeated, then the totalitarian undertaker will prepare to hang crepe on the door of our own independence.

Perhaps you wonder how this could come about? Perhaps you have heard 'them'—the wavers of the future—cry, with calculated malice, that even if Britain were defeated we could live alone and defend ourselves single handed, even against the whole world.

I tell you that this is a cold blooded lie.

The World's 100 Greatest Speeches

We would be alone in the world, facing an unscrupulous military-economic bloc that would dominate all of Europe, all of Africa, most of Asia, and perhaps even Russia and South America. Even to do that, we would have to spend most of our national income on tanks and guns and planes and ships. Nor would this be all. We would have to live perpetually as an armed camp, maintaining a huge standing army, a gigantic air force, two vast navies. And we could not do this without endangering our freedom, our democracy, our way of life.

Perhaps such is the America 'they'—the wavers of the future—foresee. Perhaps such is the America that a certain aviator, with his contempt for democracy, would prefer. Perhaps such is the America that a certain Senator desires. Perhaps such is the America that a certain mail order executive longs for.

But a perpetually militarized, isolated and impoverished America is not the America that our fathers came here to build.

It is not the America that has been the dream and the hope of countless generations in all parts of the world.

It is not the America that one hundred and thirty million of us would care to live in.

The continued security of our country demands that we aid the enslaved millions of Europe—yes, even of Germany—to win back their liberty and independence. I am convinced that if we do not embark upon such a program we will lose our own freedom.

We should be clear on this point. What is convulsing the world today is not merely another old-fashioned war. It is a counter revolution against our ideas and ideals, against our sense of justice and our human values.

Three systems today compete for world domination. Communism, fascism, and democracy are struggling for social-economic-political world control. As the conflict sharpens, it becomes clear that the other two, fascism and communism, are merging into one. They have one common enemy, democracy. They have one common goal, the destruction of democracy.

This is why this war is not an ordinary war. It is not a conflict for markets or territories. It is a desperate struggle for the possession of the souls of men.

This is why the British are not fighting for themselves alone. They are fighting to preserve freedom for mankind. For the moment, the battleground is the British Isles. But they are fighting our war; they are the first soldiers in trenches that are also our front-line trenches.

In this world war of ideas and of loyalties we believers in democracy must do two things. We must unite our forces to form one great democratic international. We must offer a clear program to freedom-loving peoples throughout the world.

Freedom-loving men and women in every land must organize and tighten their ranks. The masses everywhere must be helped to fight their oppressors and conquerors. We, free, democratic Americans are in a position to help. We know that the spirit of freedom never dies. We know that men have fought and bled for freedom since time immemorial. We realize that the liberty-loving German people are only temporarily enslaved. We do not doubt that the Italian people are looking forward to the appearance of another Garibaldi. We know how the Poles have for centuries maintained a heroic resistance against tyranny. We remember the brave struggle of the Hungarians under Kossuth and other leaders. We recall the heroic figure of Masaryk and the gallant fight for freedom of the Czech people. The story of the Yugoslavs', especially the Serbs' blows for liberty and independence is a saga of extraordinary heroism. The Greeks will stand again at Thermopylae, as they have in the past. The annals of our American sister-republics, too, are glorious with freedom-inspiring exploits. The noble figure of Simon Bolivar, the great South American liberator, has naturally been compared with that of George Washington.

No, liberty never dies. The Genghis Khans come and go. The Attilas come and go. The Hitlers flash and sputter out. But freedom endures.

Destroy a whole generation of those who have known how to walk with heads erect in God's free air, and the next generation will rise against the oppressors and restore freedom. Today in Europe, the Nazi Attila may gloat that he has destroyed democracy. He is wrong. In small farmhouses all over Central Europe, in the shops of Germany and Italy, on the docks of Holland and Belgium, freedom still lives in the hearts of men. It will endure like a hardy tree gone into the wintertime, awaiting the spring.

And, like spring, spreading from the South into Scandinavia, the democratic revolution will come. And men with democratic hearts will experience comradeship across artificial boundaries.

These men and women, hundreds of millions of them, now in bondage or threatened with slavery, are our comrades and our allies. They are only waiting for our leadership and our encouragement, for the spark that we can supply.

These hundreds of millions, of liberty-loving people, now oppressed, constitute the greatest sixth column in history. They have the will to destroy the Nazi gangsters.

We have always helped in struggles for human freedom. And we will help again. But our hundreds of millions of liberty-loving allies would despair if we did not provide aid and encouragement. The quicker we help them the sooner this dreadful revolution will be over. We cannot, we must not, we dare not delay much longer.

The fight for Britain is in its crucial stages. We must give the British everything we have. And by everything, I mean everything needed to beat the life out of our common enemy.

The second step must be to aid and encourage our friends and allies everywhere. And by everywhere I mean Europe and Asia and Africa and America.

And finally, the most important of all, we Americans must gird spiritually for the battle. We must dispel the fog of uncertainty and vacillation. We must greet with raucous laughter the corroding arguments of our appeasers and fascists. They doubt democracy. We affirm it triumphantly so that all the world may hear:

Here in America we have something so worth living for that it is worth dying for! The so-called 'wave of the future' is but the slimy backwash of the past. We have not heaved from our necks the tyrant's crushing heel, only to stretch our necks out again for its weight. Not only will we fight for democracy, we will make it more worth fighting for. Under our free institutions, we will work for the good of mankind, including Hitler's victims in Germany, so that all may have plenty and security.

We American democrats know that when good will prevails among men there will be a world of plenty and a world of security.

In the words of Winston Churchill, 'Are we downhearted?' No, we are not! But someone is downhearted! Witness the terrified flight of Hess, Hitler's Number Three Man. And listen to this—listen carefully:

'The British nation can be counted upon to carry through to victory any struggle that it once enters upon no matter how long such a struggle may last or however great the sacrifices that may be necessary or whatever the means that have to be employed; and all this even though the actual military equipment at hand may be utterly inadequate when compared with that of other nations.'

Do you know who wrote that? Adolf Hitler in Mein Kampf. And do you know who took down that dictation? Rudolf Hess.

We will help to make Hitler's prophecy come true. We will help brave England drive back the hordes from Hell who besiege her and then we will join for the destruction of savage and blood-thirsty dictators everywhere. But we must be firm and decisive. We must know our will and make it felt. And we must hurry.

69

HOPES BELIED

Gopal Krishna Gokhale

This speech was delivered at London, 30 November 1908. G.K. Gokhale had several meetings with John Morley, secretary of state, during his stay in England and had developed a good rapport with him and from whom he had great hopes. In the speech, Gokhale expected that the proposed reforms would be generous and meet the aspirations of the people. His claim that 'those who want reforms are still in vast majority—quite nine-tenth of the number', however, contradicts his earlier statements. In a letter Lord Minto wrote to Morley in March 1907 it is mentioned that: 'He (Gokhale) says that the whole younger generation of India is going over to the Extremists' side; that they are quite unreasonable and attracted by the idea of getting rid of British rule.' The latter statement described the situation prevailing in the country at that time more truthfully. Gokhale, though a confirmed Moderate, who did not like to offend the British, was bold enough to recommend that the best solution to tackle the situation could be to annul the partition of Bengal and to offer 'amnesty' to those who have been punished for their opinions. That is what the British government did in 1911. When the reforms under Indian Councils Act (Morley—Minto Act, 1909) were announced, Gokhale was very much disappointed, especially by that part of the Act by which the Muslims were given separate electorates and several other undemocratic privileges. This was expressed in the resolutions passed in the Lahore Session of the Congress in December, 1909. The following speech was delivered by Gokhale at the New Reform Club, and was chaired by J.E. Ellis, member of Parliament, former under secretary for India.

I came to this country more than six months ago, deputed by the Presidency Association of Bombay, to present before the authorities here, the views of the association on the subject of the forthcoming reforms. I am now about to return to India, and before leaving I am glad to have had this opportunity to address a la word to friends of Indian reform in this country.

The situation in India at the present moment is undoubtedly serious and even anxious but I think it is necessary that considerable caution should be exercised in accepting or interpreting the somewhat alarmist telegrams that have of late been coming from that country. India is a large country, and news collected over so vast an area and poured into another country thousands of miles away in a single stream, is apt at times, to prove misleading in its effect on the public mind. A section of the Anglo-Indian community; especially in upper India, has undoubtedly grown apprehensive about the scope and character of the proposed reforms. It is not difficult to discover traces of this nervousness through the telegrams which appear here from day to day. Lastly, the advocates of disorder and their instruments, I fear, are not pleased at the prospect of important reforms. This may account to some extent for what appears to be a spurt of renewed activity on their part. But when all these things are said, and allowances made for them, the fact remains—and I hope all who are in a position to influence the course of events in India will adequately realize this—that the Indian situation today is most serious. We are in the midst of a grave crisis in that country, and that the next two or three years will really determine what is to be the future of India's connection with England.

And now, what is the position today? That, after all, is the all important question. In dealing with it, let me say at once that we have to keep in view principally, what are known as the educated classes of the country. It is true that these classes were numerically a small minority in the country, though they were not quite so small in numbers as was sometimes imagined. But they were the brain of the country, and what they thought today the rest of India thought tomorrow. They formed the public opinion for the land. There are about a million people in India today who have received some sort of English education; and between fifteen to twenty millions have received an education in the vernaculars. However, the number of those who take an interest in public issues is larger than this. All who come directly or indirectly under the influence of the vernacular press take such interest, and it is not an extravagant estimate to put this number between forty to fifty millions—equal practically to the entire population of these islands.

Taking the educated class, you may first divide it into those who want reforms arid those who want separation from England or independence. It is quite safe to say that those who want reforms are still the vast majority—nearly about a nineteenth of the number. The bulk of these men, though they want reforms, have now practically lost all hope of receiving any substantial reforms.

If the reforms, which are to be shortly announced, turn out to be substantial, the effective conciliation of the nineteenth who want reforms is not impossible. If such conciliation is achieved, the air will be cleared of that anti-English feeling with which it is so heavily charged today, and which is really the gravest danger in the present situation. There will then be very little sympathy in the country with the advocates of disorder or their instruments and the task of dealing with disorder will be comparatively simple.

The administration at present is carried, on by a fleeting body of foreign officials, who stay in the country just long enough to complete their period of service and then retire with a pension. There is no one among them who is permanently interested in the country; the way the children of the country can be. 'When they retire, they take with them all the knowledge and experience and training which they have acquired at our expense, and which can no longer be available to us. New officials take their place to acquire, in their turn, similar knowledge, experience and training, and then similarly, to carry it out of the country. The administration, thus, is largely in the hands of men who are either leaving or rare preparing to leave the country. Larger issues concerning the permanent well-being of the people, such as mass education, relief of agricultural indebtedness, and so on, which require continuous examination, discussion and persevering effort made every year naturally cannot receive much attention—at their hands. The present efficiency can at best be only a mechanical kind of efficiency—the result of the capacity, sense of discipline and duty. It can never attain the level of that higher efficiency which can spring only from self-government.

In less than a fortnight from today we shall know, what the reforms are. We shall then be in a position to say how far they would really conciliate the people. It will be unfortunate, and even disastrous, if they fail to satisfy. I think if these reforms are granted, they will give us a real interest in provincial, district, and local administration. Moreover, if they are accompanied by conciliatory action in two important matters—the partition of Bengal and amnesty to political prisoners—there is every probability of the present crisis being successfully overcome. I am absolutely convinced that unless the partition of Bengal is modified in some way, there will be no peace there, and as a result, no peace in India, Much of the effects of the coming reforms will be lost, unless the bitter exasperation that has been caused in the public mind by recent prosecutions for sedition is removed by an amnesty to those who have been punished for their views. This, in my humble opinion, is the only true path of conciliation. If Lord Morley and Lord Minto would take this path, and take it without delay, I think it would prove effective. Their names would go down to a grateful posterity with those of Lord Canning and Lord Ripon. But if they miss this opportunity; if the reforms turn out to be less substantial than they should be, or if they are not accompanied by either of the two conciliatory measures I have mentioned, I really fear we shall not be far from martial law in parts of India. If martial law is proclaimed, it will at once mean an end all over the country of the moral influence which still lies behind British rule and the mind reels to think of the consequences which will ensue.

70

WHY HOME RULE?

This speech was delivered at Calcutta, 26 December 1917. Annie Besant belonged to that small group of Britishers who devoted their lives for the emancipation of India and was even interned for her activities, which included the demand for home rule. In the presidential address at the thirty-second Session of the Indian National Congress at Calcutta, she elaborated the effects of war on the Indian economy and Indians in general. The facts and figures quoted by her are very revealing. She also elaborated why India wanted home rule. Before she was elected president of the Indian National Congress she, along with B.G. Tilak, had electrified the country through their Home Rule Movement. The Congress now passed in the hands of extremists and the moderates who had been controlling the Congress since 1907, were marginalized. This was made easy by the death of G.K. Gokhale and Pherozeshah Mehta in 1915. Besant gave a great fillip to the Congress and the freedom movement. Hers was one of the most eloquent speeches made at a Congress session. Never before had Indians witnessed such sentiments.

The Great War, into the whirlpool of which nation after nation has been drawn, has entered its fourth year. The rigid censorship which has been established makes it impossible for any outside government to forecast its duration. To me, speaking for a moment not as a politician but as a student of spiritual laws, its end is sure. For the true object of this War is to prove the evil of, and to destroy, autocracy; the enslavement of one nation by another, and to place on sure foundations the God-given right to self-rule and self-development of every nation Also, the right of the individual, of the smaller self, so far as is consisted with the welfare of the larger self of the nation.

When Great Britain sprang to arms, it was in defence of the freedom of a small nation, guaranteed by treaties, and the great principles she proclaimed electrified India and the dominions. The all sprang to her side without question, without delay; they heard th voice of old England, the soldier of liberty, and it thrilled their hearts All were unprepared, save the small territorial army of Great Britain due to the genius and foresight of Lord Haldane. The readily mobilized army of India, hurled into the fray by the swift decision of Lord Hardinge.

Since 1885, the Congress constantly protested against the ever-increasing military expenditure, but the voice of the Congress supposedly the voice of sedition and of class ambition, became the voice of the educated Indian, the most truly patriotic and loyal class of the population.

Year after year the Congress continued to remonstrate against the costs of the army, until in 1902 after the futile protests of the intervening years, it condemned an increase of pay to British soldiers in India which put an additional burden on Indian revenues by £786,000 a year. It pointed out that the British garrison was unnecessarily large, as was shown by the withdrawal of large bodies of British soldiers for services in South Africa and China, between 1859 and 1904, for forty-five years—Indian troops were engaged in thirty-seven wars and expeditions. In 1863, the Indian army consisted of 140,000 men, with 65,300 white officers.

The Great War began on 4 August, and in that very month and in the early part of September, India sent an expeditionary force of three divisions consisting of two infantry and one cavalry. Another cavalry division joined them in France in November. 'The first arrived,' said Lord Hardinge, 'in time to fill a gap that could not otherwise have been filled.' He added pathetically: 'There are very few survivors of those two splendid divisions of infantry.' Truly, their homes are empty, but their sons shall enjoy in India the liberty for which their fathers died in France. The army in India has thus proved a great imperial asset, and in weighing India's contribution to the War, it should be remembered that India's forces were no hasty improvisation, but were a fully equipped and well-supplied army which had previously cost India annually a large sum to maintain. Great Britain needs India as much as India needs England, both for prosperity in peace as well as for safety in war. Mr Montagu has wisely said that 'for equipment in war a nation needs freedom in peace.' Therefore, I say that for both countries alike, the lesson of the war is home rule for India.

Let me close this part of the subject by laying at the feet of His Imperial Majesty the loving homage of the thousands assembled here, with the hope and belief that, before long we shall lay there the willing and grateful homage of a free nation.

Apart from the natural exchange of thought between the east and the west, the influence of English education, literature and ideals, the effect of travel in Europe, Japan and the United States of America, and other recognized causes for the changed outlook in India, there have been special forces at work during the last few years to arouse a new spirit in India, and to alter her attitudes of mind.

Englishmen in India must give up the idea that English dominance is necessary for protection of their interests, amounting in 1915 to £3,653,999,000 sterling. They do not claim to dominate the United States of America, because they have invested £688, 078,000 there. They do not claim to dominate the Argentine Republic, because they have invested about £269,808,000 there. Why then should they claim to dominate India on grounds of their investment?

India, for all these reasons, was forced to see before her a future of perpetual subordination: the Briton rules in Great Britain, the Frenchman in France, the American in America, each dominion in its own area but the Indian was to rule nowhere; alone among the peoples of the world, he was not to feel his own country as his own. 'Britain for the British' was right and natural; 'India for the Indians' was wrong, even seditious. It must be 'India for the Empire', or not even for the Empire, but 'for the rest of the Empire'. India's attitude has changed to meet the changed attitude of the Government of India and Great Britain. But let no one imagine that the consequential change of attitude connotes any change in her determination to win home rule, i.e. is ready to consider terms of peace, but it must be 'peace with honour', and honour in this context implies freedom. If this not be granted, a more vigorous agitation will commence.

The undermining of this belief dates from the spreading of the Arya Samaj and the Theosophical Society. Both bodies sought to lead the Indian people to value their own civilization, to take pride in their past, create self-respect in the present and self-confidence in the future. They destroyed the unhealthy inclination to imitate the West in all aspects, and taught discrimination, assimilating only what was valuable in Western thought and culture. Another great force was that of Swami Vivekananda, alike in his passionate love and admiration for India, and his exposure of the evils resulting from materialism in the West.

I know for certain that millions, I say deliberately, millions, in every civilized land are waiting for the message that will save them from the hideous abysmal of materialism, into which modern-money-worship is driving them headlong. Several leaders of the new social movements have already discovered that vedanta in its highest form can alone spiritualize their social aspirations.

India demands Home Rule for the following reasons: one essential and vital, the other less important but weighty. First because freedom is the birthright of every nation. Secondly, because her most important interests are now made subservient to the interests of the British Empire without her consent, and her resources are not utilized for her greatest needs. It is enough only to mention the money spent on her army, not for local defence, but for imperial purposes, as compared with that spent on primary education.

It is not a question whether the rule is good or bad, German efficiency in Germany is far greater than English efficiency in England. The Germans were better fed, had more amusements and leisure, less crushing poverty than the English. But would any Englishman, therefore, desire to see Germans occupying all the highest positions in England? And why not? Because the self-respect and dignity of a free man would revolt against foreign domination, however superior.

All we say in the matter is: you have not succeeded in bringing education, health and prosperity to the masses of the people. Is it not time to give the Indians a chance of doing for their own country, similar to what Japan and other nations have done for theirs? Surely the claim is not unreasonable.

We have been assured time after time that India is totally unfit for democratic institutions, having always lived under absolute rule of sorts But that is not the opinion of historians, based on facts, though it may be the opinion of the Indian Civil Service, based on prejudices. The people of India are quite capable of administering their own affairs. They have deeply rooted in them the workings of the local government. The village communities, each of which is a little republic, are the most abiding of Indian institutions. Holding the position we do in India, every little duty and policy should induce us to leave as much governance as possible to the people.

I do not propose to dwell on the isolated reforms which the Congress has asked during the period of its existence. The majority of Congressmen are tired of asking for the same thing over and over again and feel that it is better to concentrate on Home Rule, since, once the people have power, they can get rid of bad laws and make good ones for themselves. Think of the joy of being a free man in a free country equal to other civilized men; of breathing in an India purged of the poisonous atmosphere of coercion.

To see India free, to see her hold her head high among other nations, to see her sons and daughters respected everywhere, to see her worthy of her mighty past, engaged in building a yet mightier future—is not this worth working for, worth suffering for, worth living and worth dying for? Is there any other land which evokes such love for her spirituality, such admiration for her literature, such homage for her valour, as this glorious mother of nations, from whose womb went forth the races that now, in Europe and America, are leading the world? Has any land suffered as our India has suffered, since her sword was broken on Kurukshetra, and the peoples of Europe and Asia swept across her borders, laid waste her cities, and discrowned her kings? They came to conquer, but they got absorbed. At last, out of those mingled people, the divine artificer has welded the nation, assimilating not only her own virtues, but also those her foes Liad brought in, and gradually eliminating the vices.

After a history of millennia, stretching far back out of the ken of mortal yes; having lived with, but not died with, the mighty civilizations of the past; having seen them rise and flourish and decay, until only their sepulchres remained, deep buried in the earth's crust; having wrought, and triumphant, and having suffered, and having survived all changes, unbroken India, who has been verily the crucified among nations, now stands on this her resurrection morning, the immortal, the glorious, the ever-young, and India shall soon be seen proud and self-reliant, strong and free, the radiant splendour of Asia, is the light and the blessing of the world.

71

IN NON-COOPERATION LIES SUCCESS

Chittaranjan Das

This speech was delivered at Ahmedabad, 27 December 1921. Chittaranjan Das was arrested on 10 December 1921 for organizing boycott and a 'hartal' on the eve of the Prince of Wales's visit to Calcutta. In prison, he was in the company of leaders like Subhas Chandra Bose and Maulana Abul Kalam Azad among several others who were also arrested on the same charge. Das had been elected president of the Congress for that year and he had to deliver the presidential address at Ahmedabad. But before he could complete writing his address he was arrested. Nonetheless, he sent it to the Congress office from jail. The speech was brushed up by Gandhi and was published in Young India on 12 January 1922 with Gandhi's introductory remarks. 'In appreciating the address the reader will be helped to know that it was prepared just before his arrest,' Gandhi wrote. The address was read by Sarojini Naidu and Hakim Ajmal Khan presided. In the speech, Das explains the meaning of freedom and the methods of both the Non-cooperation and Civil Disobedience Movements to achieve it. He wholeheartedly supported the movements under Gandhi's leadership. But while Das was still in jail, Gandhi suspended the Non-cooperation Movement on 12 February 1922—only forty-five days after Das's speech and stunned the nation. Das was released in August 1922, by which time the movement was dead. As a result, Gandhi's leadership came under a cloud. While Gandhi was still in jail, the Swaraj Party was formed under the leadership of Das, Motilal Nehru, Lala Lajpat Rai, Subhas Bose and others. They decided to participate in the councils but remained in the Congress. Das's transformation from an enthusiastic non-cooperator to a swarajist was an event of great significance for the freedom movement. Unfortunately, Das died quite suddenly in 1925 and the void created was not easy to fill, though he had groomed Subhas Chandra Bose for the purpose.

At the very outset we ought to define our attitude in relation to the resent struggle. 'What is our aim?' 'Where are we going?' I think that most people would agree that we are out to secure freedom, freedom from foreign subjection, freedom from foreign interference. It is as well, however, that we should have a clear grasp of what is meant by the word 'freedom': In the first place, it does not imply an absence of all restraint. Secondly, freedom does not necessarily imply the absence of the idea of dependence. Dependence there must be so long as we live in a society, and need its protection. There is no necessary opposition between freedom and such dependence that is willingly suffered by the people.

'What then is freedom?' It is impossible to define the term, but one may describe it as that state, that condition, which makes it possible for a nation to realize its own individuality and to evolve its own destiny. The history of mankind is full of stirring stories as to how nations have fought for freedom in order to retain their nationalism and their individuality inviolate and untarnished. We stand then for freedom, because we claim the right to develop our own selves, evolve our own destiny based on our rules, and not be ashamed of what Western civilization has to teach us, and be unhampered by the institutions which have been imposed on us. But here a voice interrupts me, the voice of Rabindranath Tagore, one of India's greatest poets. He says, 'Western culture is standing at our door; must we be so inhospitable as to turn it away, or ought we not acknowledge that in the union of the cultures of the east and the west lies the salvation of the world?' I admit that if Indian nationalism has to live, it cannot afford to isolate itself from other nations. But I have two criticisms on what Rabindranath Tagore has to say: first, we must have a house of our own before we can receive a guest; and second, Indian culture must discover itself before it can be ready to assimilate Western culture. In my opinion, there can be no true assimilation before freedom comes, although there may be as there has been, a slavish imitation. India's cultural conquest is all but complete; it was the inevitable result of her political conquest. India must resist it. She must come alive, and then we may talk of the union of the two civilizations. I object to the perpetuation of British domination as, in my opinion it is impossible to find fulfilment of our nationality, individuality, and personality, so long as that domination continues. In arriving at this conclusion, I have entirely ignored the character of the British rule in India. That rule may be good or bad, or it may be conceded that it is partly good and partly bad, but my conclusion is based on the view that there is something inherent in subjection which injures national life and hampers its growth and self-fulfilment. Whether within the Empire or outside it, India must have freedom so that she may realize her individuality and evolve her destiny without any help or hindrance from the British people.

I now come to the question—what are the methods which we ought to adopt in our fight against the bureaucracy? There are three, and only three methods that I know of: the first is, armed resistance, second, cooperation with the bureaucracy in the councils that have been established under the Government of India Act, and third, non-violent non-cooperation. The first I must dismiss as beyond the range of practical politics. Even if it were not so, on principle, I am opposed to violence. We must then choose between cooperation and non-cooperation. I confess, that in considering the question of cooperation, I am not a bit troubled by the fact that some of our leaders who assisted at the birth of India's political life, are against us on this issue. I, therefore, propose to consider some of the arguments that are advanced against us by these supporters of the Government of India Act. In doing so, I shall first consider whether the freedom of the Indian nation, that is to say, its right to develop its own individuality and evolve its own destiny, has been recognized in the Act; secondly, whether the act, either expressly or by necessary implication, gives even the beginnings of responsible government to the Indian people; and lastly, whether the legislature has any control, effective or otherwise, over the purse. Ladies and gentlemen, I have very great respect for the opinion of my political opponents but I cannot accept the fundamental principle on which the Reform Act is based. I think that we should preserve our self-esteem, whatever the stage of our progress may be. I think that we should solemnly declare in an open Congress, that freedom is inherent in every nation. India has and possesses the right to develop her own individuality and to evolve her own destiny unhampered by what the British Parliament has decided or may decide for us. I think we should recognize that any power which in any way hampers or embarrasses the self-realization and self-fulfilment of the Indian nation is an enemy of India and must be resisted. I am willing to cooperate with England, but on one condition only, that she recognizes this inherent right of India. You will not find that recognition anywhere in the Government of India Act. I, for one, will not be party to the perpetuation of British domination in India. Freedom is my birthright, and I demand a recognition of that right, not in instalments or compartments, but whole and entire. I do not doubt that victory will be ours; but supposing we fail, we would at least have preserved, inviolate, our national self-respect and dignity. At any rate we would have repudiated the insult on which the Government of India Act is based.

Therefore, the only method of warfare open to us is non-cooperation and that is the programme which we adopted at two successive Congress sessions. We are devoted to the doctrine of non-cooperation. Do not expect me to discuss its ethics, but there are friendly critics whose doubts we ought to dispel, if it is within our power to do so. They say that the doctrine of non-cooperation is a doctrine of negation, a doctrine of despair; they stand aghast at the narrowness, the exclusiveness such a doctrine implies. They draw our attention to the trend of political events in the world, and they ask us whether there is any hope for a nation that is determined to live a life of isolation. I feel bound to answer the question which has been raised by these critics, and in doing so, I must ask myself the question, 'What is non-cooperation? I find it easier to answer it by considering for a moment what is not non-cooperation. Non-cooperation is not a refusal to cooperate with the English people because they are English. Non-cooperation does not advocate a policy of separation or isolation. What then is non-cooperation? I cannot do better than quote the eloquent words of Mr Stokes: 'It is the refusal to be a party to preventable evil; it is the refusal to accept or have any part in injustice; it is the refusal to acquiesce in wrongs that can be righted, or to submit to a state of affairs which is manifestly inconsistent with the dictates of righteousness.' But it is, however, argued that the whole doctrine is a doctrine of negation, a doctrine of despair. I agree, that in form the doctrine is one of negation, but I maintain that in substance it is one of affirmation. We break in order to build; we destroy in order to construct; we reject in order to accept. This is the history of human endeavour. If subjection be an evil, then we are bound not to cooperate with every agency that seeks to perpetuate our subjection. That is a negation; but it affirms our determination to be free, to win our liberty at any cost. Nor do I agree that the doctrine is one of despair. It is a doctrine of hope, confidence and unbounded faith in its efficacy.

72

NEED FOR A NATIVE SYSTEM

Motilal Nehru

This speech was delivered at New Delhi, 17 March 1924. After the suspension of the Non-cooperation Movement by Gandhi in 1922, several leaders of the Congress Party decided to enter the legislative bodies forsaking the boycott of the councils. This resulted in the formation of the Swaraj Party. The aim of the Swaraj Party was to fight elections for the assembly and the councils under the Act of 1919. After being elected, their aim was to wreck the working of these bodies and consequently of the government from within. The leading lights of the Swaraj Party were Motilal Nehru and C.R. Das. Their party fought the elections in 1923 and were successful beyond expectations. They were able to acquire a working majority in the Central Legislative Assembly under the leadership of Motilal Nehru, and were able to influence the decision-making process to a considerable degree. The following speech by Motilal Nehru in the Legislative Assembly in New Delhi on the Indian Finance Bill, is a fine example of the obstructionist method adopted by the Swaraj Party. After the forceful speech of Motilal Nehru, the Finance Bill was overruled by sixty votes against fifty-seven. However, the grants and the Bill were certified by the governor general.

The hon'ble home member has on more occasion than one during my brief experience of this House, with his special polemics shows himself to be a master in the art which is usually practised by the Government of India. That art is the art of 'divide and rule'. We have seen on many occasions that the great argument which he has against any proposition which is advanced by this section of the House, is to point out to those, who he fears, will follow us into the lobby and vote in favour of that proposition, the grave danger in which they stand if they do so. He never fails to point out to the non-swarajists the dangers of their associating themselves with the swarajists, and to those who are not in the Nationalist Party, the very grave and serious dangers of their joining or voting with the Nationalist Party. Today we have witnessed an exhibition of that art almost to perfection. My hon'ble friend has told all those who are not for a policy which destroys all, to beware how they cast in their lot with those who openly and professedly, before they came into this Assembly, were wreckers, and whose object was to make the government impossible.

I have made the effort to point out on previous occasions as to how it was that I, a sworn swarajist, a confirmed swarajist, was using the instruments and the means that lay at my disposal in this assembly to push forward the national demand and to see what response that demand elicited from the authorities before whom it was pressed. I said in clear terms and with no room for any doubt that we had come into this assembly, non-cooperators as we were, to offer you our cooperation, but on our own terms. Those terms were not dictated by a spirit of hostility to the government but were considered in consultation with other friends who were not swarajists. Those terms were put before the whole country and opinions were invited. All schools of thought concurred that we could not, in the interests of our country, place national demand any lower. Having satisfied overselves as to the nature of the demand and the acceptance it had found in the entire country, we put it forward not on behalf of the swarajists or any particular section but, as I submitted when I was moving my amendment to the motion of my hon'ble friend Mr Rangachariar, we put it forward on behalf of the country.

Now, sir, after the discussion of the demands, we have the Finance Bill confronting us. What is our position regarding that? I should like to know what the hon'ble home member expected it would be? I am sure he did not expect us to readily agree the motion. He might have heard 'Ayes', as he did in the case of my hon'ble friend, Pandit Madan Mohan Malaviya, who informs us that he never voted on any of the demands. It is obvious that the Finance Bill, as it stands, could not possibly have our approval. Well, if it did not have our entire approval, was it merely the amendments of the various clauses proposing reductions of the various taxes that would have satisfied us? Was that all we wanted? What reason did my hon'ble friend have to make that guess? After my statement that these demands would now be discussed in the ordinary course, no division was called for during the entire debate on the remaining grants with the exception of two. All the demands were discussed and done with. The whole idea was to put forward all the objections that could be raised on the merits.

Our position in regard to the Government of India Act, is that it is a false beginning. You assume much when you tell us that we the people of India would have to train ourselves in parliamentary institutions before we can aspire to have parliamentary rights. Your conception of parliamentary duties, parliamentary rights and parliamentary procedures may be quite different to what the genius of the people might dictate to its representatives. Now, sir, it is stated in the report of the speech of Lord Olivier which I have before me:

We claim to know by centuries of experience in Europe and America the laws and conditions indispensable for the stable working of that system, which is not native to India.

That claim admits the whole of my case. I do not want a system which is not native to India. What I want the Round Table Conference to determine is a system which is native to India and of which you have no experience in Europe or America. Your experience of centuries of Europe and America will not assist you in the least to find out what system is native to India.

What we are doing, I say again, merely amounts to the strongest protest we can make. We are using the strongest weapon available to us. We can do no more. I expect that in the step proposed to be taken, the House is with me. I beg the House to vote with one voice in support of my hon'ble friend Pandit Malaviya, and to reject the motion to take the Bill into consideration. It will then, not be necessary for us to go into the amendments proposed which were put in as a matter of ordinary precaution.

73

BENGAL LEADING THE FREEDOM MOVEMENT

Tulsi Chandra Goswami

This speech was delivered at New Delhi, 19 February 1926. Several leaders, who devoted their lives working for the cause of freedom, have been relegated to the background. One such leader was Tulsi Chandra Goswami. He played an important role in the national movement during the 20s and 30s. Like Subhas Chandra Bose, he too was a protégé of C.R. Das. He had joined the Swaraj Party and was a deputy to Motilal Nehru in the Central Legislative Assembly, of which he was a member from 1923 to 1928. He was only twenty five when he entered the assembly as the youngest member. His speeches in the Central Legislative Assembly have been rarely surpassed by their eloquence and style.

I think we have to put up with a lot in connection with this constitution. One of the things we have to put up with in this assembly is the importation of mofussil officials as nominated members who came to assist in our labours probably for a month or so and then disappear into thin air. I submit again that the serious business of legislature is not compatible with the visits, the holiday visits, of these mofussil officials. Well, as I said, I have only one thing to say and that is bring your suspected people of justice by all means. It may be that we have no faith in the system of justice in this country. It may be that from the moralistic point of view an offence against the laws of the country is not necessarily to be regarded as a sinful act; but I will allow—as I think most of my friends this side will allow—that the government has the right to bring to trial all their suspects. I say to the government, 'You have your ordinary laws; you have your judiciary; play the game.' A government becomes despicable, becomes an object of contempt, when in spite of all these weapons in its armoury to which such a confident reference was made this morning by the foreign secretary, it has recourse to the underhand method of imprisoning people without even framing charges against them. I do not mind you calling even some of our patriots, who have been convicted of technical offence 'criminals', because in the history of criminals you find some of the most illustrious men of history. You have Christ, who was convicted and crucified; you have Socrates; you have Galileo. Mahatma Gandhi was convicted as a criminal, and a hired hangman of Bengal had the privilege of calling the great C.R. Das a criminal. So, I do not mind your applying the law against those who seek to subvert your government, provided you can prove a technical offence. I repeat again, it is not necessarily morally wrong to try to subvert a government which one does not like and cannot be otherwise mended. This, however, is an offence, and that as such is punishable; and no true patriot would resent being punished under the ordinary law of the land. This is his martyrdom.

It was said in this House that Bengal, of all provinces was tainted with revolutionary spirit. I feel proud of the fact that in Bengal national consciousness and love of freedom are so powerful. Why it was asked, I think by Mr Donovan it was necessary only in Bengal to apply drastic measure? I will tell him why. It is because Bengal has to wipe off the traitors' guilt. It has to wipe out the guilt of Omi Chand and Mir Jaffar, who sold their country to foreigners; because Bengal remembers the glorious regime of your Warren Hastings; because Bengal remembers the treatment that was meted out by government officials to indigo planters; because Bengal remembers the Risley circular which made singing of 'Bande Mataram' an offence. Would any civilized government dare to defend an action like that? Is singing your national song a crime? This is why Bengal leads the national movement. I may add, Bengal has a literature, she has a great literature, and the motive power of that literature is nationalism. May Bengal forever lead the Nationalist Movement, that is my prayer. I do not care whether Bengal is accused of revolutionary crime, I do not care what is said of Bengal patriots who are either convicted or detained in jail without any charges being framed against them. It shall always be a matter of pride for me to feel that Bengal always leads the onward movement to freedom, which I have not the slightest doubt, shall be realized.

74

BOYCOTT THE SIMON COMMISSION

Lala Lajpat Rai

This speech was delivered at New Delhi, 16 February 1928. The Tory Government in Britain had created the Royal Statutory Commission on 8 November 1927 with John Simon as chairman (hence the name Simon Commission) and six other members. All seven were members of the British Parliament; all equally uninformed about India. The genesis of the commission lay in a provision contained in the Government of India Act of 1919 that at the end of ten years the working of the reforms introduced by the act will be inquired into by a commission with a view to determine what further action, if any, should be taken. Indian reaction to the appointment of the commission was one of shock and resentment because not a single Indian was included as a member. The exclusion of Indians from a body which was to prepare the future Constitution of India was unreasonable on the face of it. The nations' decision to boycott the commission met with great success. On 3 February 1928, the day when the commission members arrived in Bombay, a complete 'hartal' was observed in all important towns of India and huge demonstrations were witnessed, people waving black flags and shouting 'Simon, go back.' While people demonstrated in the street, Lala Lajpat Rai echoed their sentiments in the legislative council with forceful arguments in a memorable speech while introducing a resolution for boycotting the commission.

I rise to move the resolution that stands in my name and I do so with the profoundest sense of responsibility that I have ever felt in the discharge of any public duty I shall at the beginning, give very briefly and categorically my reasons for the action that I am taking. My first reason is that I have no faith in the bona fides of the government or of the people who have appointed this commission. Why I have no faith in them I shall state later on. My second reason is that I have no faith in the competency of the commission that has been appointed. I acknowledge, sir, that Sir John Simon is one of the ablest members of the British nation and I give the member of the commission the fullest possible credit for their good intentions and good motives. But the very fact which has been made a ground of their appointment, namely, their ignorance of India, Indian history and Indian politics, is, in my judgement, their greatest disqualification to take on the task which has been entrusted to them. The problems of India are so vast and so complicated that even if the gods were to descend from the heavens they cannot master it in such a short time as is at the disposal of this commission. The members of the commission cannot in this short space time make any intelligent recommendations which may be acceptable both to England and to India. My impression is that all the commission will do is to practically record in a gramophone what they will be told by the bureaucracy here.

Eventually they will record, their recommendations in another gramophone in consultation with other people in England. The very secretive niethàds, which they are employing even now at the present moment in going about their business justifies my making this statement. They are very much afraid of going out to public and informing the people of their movements. They move from place to place in secrecy and an air of mystery surrounds them. That in itself shows that the people who guide them will practically choose what they want to present before them. My third ground for the action which I am taking is that I have no faith in my commission's ability to settle the Indian problem. I can understand commissions being appointed for inquiry into facts which are disputed or which are not clear but I question the competency of any commission to decide the ability of nations to rule themselves and to settle constitutions for them which have to be worked by them in their own interests. In my judgement the problem of India is not for commissions. In must be tackled by representative men both from England and India in a spirit of conciliation and negotiations. It is only then that it may be possible to solve this problem by an agreement, which may eventually be ratified by Parliament.

Now, having given these grounds briefly, I will come to the arguments that have been given by the Secretary of State for the appointment of such a commission. The Secretary of State has told us many things. One of the things he has told us is that it is the duty of Parliament, and Parliament alone, to, consider and decide this question. He says that the Parliament took the government of the country from the East India Company, saved India from a welter of anarchy, and if today the British were to go out of India, India would again be thrown into a welter of anarchy. Unfortunately the Secretary of State's and our notions of anarchy differ very much. He has spoken of the glorious and the great association of England with India. Yes, great and glorious from the British point of view, but inglorious and infamous from the Indian point of view. I do not admit that the association of England with India has done us any substantial good. This is the chief point of difference between us and the Secretary of State for India.

He talks of anarchy. What anarchy can be greater than the anarchy of the law imposed at the point of the bayonet by a foreigner or body of foreigners? That is the greatest anarchy which can be inflicted on any self-respecting nation. What anarchy can be greater than the anarchy involved in the position that the people for whom governments are made, for whom governments are constituted, should have no voice in the determination of their fate? There can be no anarchy greater than that. All anarchies are followed at some time or the other by established and sound systems of government. No progress is made by threats. We are not scared by these threats of anarchy. I wish to say from my position in this House that I am not at all afraid of any anarchy that might follow the withdrawal of the British from this country. I am prepared for the worst. What can be worse than the conditions in which we are now living? There can be nothing worse. We have reached the lowest depths of misery and degradation imaginable. There can be nothing lower than that and if the British government thinks that by their withdrawal we shall be warring with each other, I shall welcome even that condition, because quite naturally after a few years of warring and quarrelling, and even bloodshed, we shall settle down and form some kind of government, which will be our own handiwork, and which we can improve later on. The members of the European group are laughing at me. My reply is: 'You can have a hearty laugh, because you are like the painter who paints his own picture. If you were in our position you would not be laughing but weeping. Let us have a trial of ruling England for even two years and then we shall see who laughs and who weeps.'

75

ON THE CUBAN CRISIS

John F. Kennedy

At 7 p.m. on Monday, 22 October 1962, President Kennedy appeared on television to inform the American people of the recently discovered installation of Russian nuclear missiles in Cuba. The President had first learned of the missiles on 16 October, when he was shown aerial photos taken by an American U-2 spy plane over Cuba, located some ninety miles off the coast of Florida. Two days later, the President conferred with the Soviet Minister of Foreign Affairs, Andrei Gromyko, who claimed the weapons were for defensive purposes only. The President then met with top military aides and his brother Robert to discuss possible military options. On Sunday, 21 October, the President spent the entire day conferring with his top advisors considering two principal military options—a surgical air strike against the bases in Cuba, or a Naval blockade of Cuba. The President chose the blockade option, which he labelled in this speech as a 'strict quarantine.' Additionally, in this speech, the President warned the Russians that any missile attack from Cuba would be considered an attack from Soviet Russia and bring 'a full retaliatory response' from the United States against Russia itself.

Good evening, my fellow citizens:

This government, as promised, has maintained the closest surveillance of the Soviet military build-up on the island of Cuba. Within the past week, unmistakable evidence has established the fact that a series of offensive missile sites is now in preparation on that imprisoned island. The purpose of these bases can be none other than to provide a nuclear strike capability against the Western Hemisphere.

Upon receiving the first preliminary hard information of this nature last

384

Tuesday morning at 9 a.m., I directed that our surveillance be stepped up. And having now confirmed and completed our evaluation of the evidence and our decision on a course of action, this government feels obliged to report this new crisis to you in fullest detail.

The characteristics of these new missile sites indicate two distinct types of installations. Several of them include medium-range ballistic missiles capable of carrying a nuclear warhead for a distance of more than 1,000 nautical miles. Each of these missiles, in short, is capable of striking Washington, D.C., the Panama Canal, Cape Canaveral, Mexico City, or any other city in the southeastern part of the United States, in Central America, or in the Caribbean area.

Additional sites not yet completed appear to be designed for intermediate range ballistic missiles—capable of traveling more than twice as far—and thus capable of striking most of the major cities in the Western Hemisphere, ranging as far north as Hudson Bay, Canada, and as far south as Lima, Peru. In addition, jet bombers, capable of carrying nuclear weapons, are now being uncrated and assembled in Cuba, while the necessary airbases are being prepared.

This urgent transformation of Cuba into an important strategic base—by the presence of these large, long-range, and clearly offensive weapons of sudden mass destruction—constitutes an explicit threat to the peace and security of all the Americas, in flagrant and deliberate defiance of the Rio Pact of 1947, the traditions of this nation and hemisphere, the joint resolution of the 87th Congress, the Charter of the United Nations, and my own public warnings to the Soviets on 4 and 13 September. This action also contradicts the repeated assurances of Soviet spokesmen, both publicly and privately delivered, that the arms build-up in Cuba would retain its original defensive character, and that the Soviet Union had no need or desire to station strategic missiles on the territory of any other nation.

The size of this undertaking makes clear that it has been planned for some months. Yet only last month, after I had made clear the distinction between any introduction of ground-to-ground missiles and the existence of defensive anti-aircraft missiles, the Soviet government publicly stated on

11 September, and I quote, 'the armaments and military equipment sent to Cuba are designed exclusively for defensive purposes,' that, and I quote the Soviet government, 'there is no need for the Soviet government to shift its weapons…for a retaliatory blow to any other country, for instance Cuba,' and that, and I quote their government, 'the Soviet Union has so powerful rockets to carry these nuclear warheads that there is no need to search for sites for them beyond the boundaries of the Soviet Union.' That statement was false.

Only last Thursday, as evidence of this rapid offensive build-up was already in my hand, Soviet Foreign Minister Gromyko told me in my office that he was instructed to make it clear once again, as he said his government had already done, that Soviet assistance to Cuba, and I quote, 'pursued solely the purpose of contributing to the the defence capabilities of Cuba,' that, and I quote him, 'training by Soviet specialists of Cuban nationals in handling defensive armaments was by no means offensive, and if it were otherwise,' Mr Gromyko went on, 'the Soviet Government would never become involved in rendering such assistance.' That statement also was false.

Neither the United States of America nor the world community of nations can tolerate deliberate deception and offensive threats on the part of any nation, large or small. We no longer live in a world where only the actual firing of weapons represents a sufficient challenge to a nation's security to constitute maximum peril. Nuclear weapons are so destructive and ballistic missiles are so swift, that any substantially increased possibility of their use or any sudden change in their deployment may well be regarded as a definite threat to peace.

For many years both the Soviet Union and the United States, recognizing this fact, have deployed strategic nuclear weapons with great care, never upsetting the precarious status quo which insured that these weapons would not be used in the absence of some vital challenge. Our own strategic missiles have never been transferred to the territory of any other nation under a cloak of secrecy and deception; and our history—unlike that of the Soviets since the end of World War II—demonstrates that we have no desire to dominate or conquer any other nation or impose our system upon its people. Nevertheless, American citizens have become adjusted to living daily on the bullseye of Soviet missiles located inside the USSR or in submarines.

In that sense, missiles in Cuba add to an already clear and present danger—although it should be noted the nations of Latin America have never previously been subjected to a potential nuclear threat.

But this secret, swift, and extraordinary build-up of Communist missiles—in an area well known to have a special and historical relationship to the United States and the nations of the Western Hemisphere, in violation of Soviet assurances, and in defiance of American and hemispheric policy—this sudden, clandestine decision to station strategic weapons for the first time outside of Soviet soil—is a deliberately provocative and unjustified change in the status quo which cannot be accepted by this country, if our courage and our commitments are ever to be trusted again by either friend or foe.

The 1930s taught us a clear lesson: aggressive conduct, if allowed to go unchecked and unchallenged, ultimately leads to war. This nation is opposed to war. We are also true to our word. Our unswerving objective, therefore, must be to prevent the use of these missiles against this or any other country, and to secure their withdrawal or elimination from the Western Hemisphere.

Our policy has been one of patience and restraint, as befits a peaceful and powerful nation, which leads a worldwide alliance. We have been determined not to be diverted from our central concerns by mere irritants and fanatics. But now further action is required—and it is underway; and these actions may only be the beginning. We will not prematurely or unnecessarily risk the costs of worldwide nuclear war in which even the fruits of victory would be ashes in our mouth—but neither will we shrink from that risk at any time it must be faced.

Acting, therefore, in the defence of our own security and of the entire Western Hemisphere, and under the authority entrusted to me by the Constitution as endorsed by the resolution of the Congress, I have directed that the following initial steps be taken immediately:

First: To halt this offensive build-up, a strict quarantine on all offensive military equipment under shipment to Cuba is being initiated. All ships of any kind bound for Cuba from whatever nation or port will, if found to contain cargoes of offensive weapons, be turned back. This quarantine will be extended, if needed, to other types of cargo and carriers. We are not at this time, however, denying the necessities of life as the Soviets attempted to do in their Berlin blockade of 1948.

Second: I have directed the continued and increased close surveillance of Cuba and its military build-up. The foreign ministers of the OAS, in their communique of 6 October, rejected secrecy in such matters in this hemisphere. Should these offensive military preparations continue, thus increasing the threat to the hemisphere, further action will be justified. I have directed the Armed Forces to prepare for any eventualities; and I trust that in the interest of both the Cuban people and the Soviet technicians at the sites, the hazards to all concerned in continuing this threat will be recognized.

Third: It shall be the policy of this nation to regard any nuclear missile launched from Cuba against any nation in the Western Hemisphere as an attack by the Soviet Union on the United States, requiring a full retaliatory response upon the Soviet Union.

Fourth: As a necessary military precaution, I have reinforced our base at Guantanamo, evacuated today the dependents of our personnel there, and ordered additional military units to be on a standby alert basis.

Fifth: We are calling tonight for an immediate meeting of the Organ of Consultation under the Organization of American States, to consider this threat to hemispheric security and to invoke articles 6 and 8 of the Rio Treaty in support of all necessary action. The United Nations Charter allows for regional security arrangements—and the nations of this hemisphere decided long ago against the military presence of outside powers. Our other allies around the world have also been alerted.

Sixth: Under the Charter of the United Nations, we are asking tonight hat an emergency meeting of the Security Council be convoked without elay to take action against this latest Soviet threat to world peace. Our esolution will call for the prompt dismantling and withdrawal of all ffensive weapons in Cuba, under the supervision of UN observers, before ne quarantine can be lifted.

eventh and finally: I call upon Chairman Khrushchev to halt and liminate this clandestine, reckless and provocative threat to world peace nd to stable relations between our two nations. I call upon him further o abandon this course of world domination, and to join in an historic ffort to end the perilous arms race and to transform the history of man. He has an opportunity now to move the world back from the abyss of lestruction—by returning to his government's own words that it had no need to station missiles outside its own territory, and withdrawing these weapons from Cuba—by refraining from any action which will widen or deepen the present crisis—and then by participating in a search for peaceful and permanent solutions.

This nation is prepared to present its case against the Soviet threat to peace, and our own proposals for a peaceful world, at any time and in any forum—in the OAS, in the United Nations, or in any other meeting that could be useful—without limiting our freedom of action. We have in the past made strenuous efforts to limit the spread of nuclear weapons. We have proposed the elimination of all arms and military bases in a fair and effective disarmament treaty. We are prepared to discuss new proposals for the removal of tensions on both sides—including the possibility of a genuinely independent Cuba, free to determine its own destiny. We have no wish to war with the Soviet Union—for we are a peaceful people who desire to live in peace with all other peoples.

But it is difficult to settle or even discuss these problems in an atmosphere of intimidation. That is why this latest Soviet threat—or any other threat which is made independently or in response to our actions this week—must and will be met with determination. Any hostile move anywhere in the world against the safety and freedom of peoples to whom we are committed—including in particular the brave people of West Berlin—will be met by whatever action is needed.

Finally, I want to say a few words to the captive people of Cuba, to whom this speech is being directly carried by special radio facilities. I speak to you as a friend, as one who knows of your deep attachment to your fatherland, as one who shares your aspirations for liberty and justice for all. And I have watched and the American people have watched with deep sorrow how your nationalist revolution was betrayed—and how your fatherland fell under foreign domination. Now your leaders are no longer Cuban leaders inspired by Cuban ideals. They are puppets and agents of an international conspiracy which has turned Cuba against your friends and neighbours in the Americas—and turned it into the first Latin American country to become a target for nuclear war—the first Latin American country to have these weapons on its soil.

These new weapons are not in your interest. They contribute nothing to your peace and well-being. They can only undermine it. But this country has no wish to cause you to suffer or to impose any system upon you. We know that your lives and land are being used as pawns by those who deny your freedom.

Many times in the past, the Cuban people have risen to throw out tyrants who destroyed their liberty. And I have no doubt that most Cubans today look forward to the time when they will be truly free—free from foreign domination, free to choose their own leaders, free to select their own system, free to own their own land, free to speak and write and worship without fear or degradation. And then shall Cuba be welcomed back to the society of free nations and to the associations of this hemisphere.

My fellow citizens: let no one doubt that this is a difficult and dangerous effort on which we have set out. No one can see precisely what course it will take or what costs or casualties will be incurred. Many months of sacrifice and self-discipline lie ahead—months in which our patience and our will will be tested—months in which many threats and denunciations will keep us aware of our dangers. But the greatest danger of all would be to do nothing.

The path we have chosen for the present is full of hazards, as all paths are—but it is the one most consistent with our character and courage as a nation

The World's 100 Greatest Speeches   390

and our commitments around the world. The cost of freedom is always high—and Americans have always paid it. And one path we shall never choose, and that is the path of surrender or submission.

Our goal is not the victory of might, but the vindication of right—not peace at the expense of freedom, but both peace and freedom, here in this hemisphere, and, we hope, around the world. God willing, that goal will be achieved.

Thank you and goodnight.

76

JUSTICE FOR IRELAND

Daniel O'Connell

Daniel O'Connell (1775–1847) was a great Irish statesman, called the Liberator of Ireland. He led a movement that successfully forced the British to pass the Catholic Emancipation Act of 1829, allowing Roman Catholics to become members of the British House of Commons. Until 1800, Ireland had its own separate Parliament which included many Catholic members. However, the British Act of Union abolished local political control by establishing the United Kingdom of England and Ireland. King George III permitted only Church of England Irish to participate in the British Parliament, which had a centuries-old history of discrimination against Catholics. This left the majority of Irish Catholics without proper representation. O'Connell worked to pressure the British to end this discrimination. In 1828, he even ran for Parliament and received a huge margin of Irish votes. Although he could not be seated, his victory favourably impressed the British prime minister and reform finally occurred in 1829 with the passage of the Catholic Emancipation Act. O'Connell thus became a full-fledged member of the House of Commons and an eloquent spokesman for the Irish cause. He succeeded in getting more reforms enacted improving the treatment of the Irish. On 4 February 1836, he gave this speech in the House of Commons calling for equal justice.

It appears to me impossible to suppose that the House will consider me presumptuous in wishing to be heard for a short time on this question, especially after the distinct manner in which I have been alluded to in the course of the debate. If I had no other excuse, that would be sufficient; but I do not want it; I have another and a better—the question is one in the highest degree interesting to the people of Ireland. It is, whether we mean to do justice to that country—whether we mean to continue the injustice which has been already done to it, or to hold out the hope that it will be reated in the same manner as England and Scotland. That is the question. We know what 'lip service' is; we do not want that. There are some men who will even declare that they are willing to refuse justice to Ireland; while there are others who, though they are ashamed to say so, are ready to consummate the iniquity, and they do so.

England never did do justice to Ireland—she never did. What we have got of it we have extorted from men opposed to us on principle—against which principle they have made us such concessions as we have obtained from them. The right honourable baronet opposite [Sir Robert Peel] says he does not distinctly understand what is meant by a principle. I believe him. He advocated religious exclusion on religious motives; he yielded that point at length, when we were strong enough to make it prudent for him to do so.

Here am I calling for justice to Ireland; but there is a coalition tonight— not a base unprincipled one—God forbid!—it is an extremely natural one; I mean that between the right honourable baronet and the noble lord the member for North Lancashire [Lord Stanley]. It is a natural coalition, and it is impromptu; for the noble lord informs us he had not even a notion of taking the part he has until the moment at which he seated himself where he now is. I know his candour; he told us it was a sudden inspiration which induced him to take part against Ireland. I believe it with the most potent faith, because I know that he requires no preparation for voting against the interests of the Irish people. [*Groans.*] I thank you for that groan—it is just of a piece with the rest. I regret much that I have been thrown upon arguing this particular question, because I should have liked to have dwelt upon the speech which has been so graciously delivered from the throne today—to have gone into its details, and to have pointed out the many great and beneficial alterations and amendments in our existing institutions which it hints at and recommends to the House. The speech of last year was full of reforms in words, and in words only; but this speech contains the great leading features of all the salutary reforms the country wants; and if they are worked out fairly and honestly in detail, I am convinced the country will require no further amelioration of its institutions, and that it will become the envy and admiration of the world. I, therefore, hail the speech with great satisfaction.

It has been observed that the object of a king's speech is to say as little in as many words as possible; but this speech contains more things than words—it contains those great principles which, adopted in practice, will be most salutary not only to the British Empire, but to the world. When speaking of our foreign policy, it rejoices in the cooperation between France and this country; but it abstains from conveying any ministerial approbation of alterations in the domestic laws of that country which aim at the suppression of public liberty, and the checking of public discussion, such as call for individual reprobation, and which I reprobate as much as any one. I should like to know whether there is a statesman in the country who will get up in this House and avow his approval of such proceedings on the part of the French government. I know it may be done out of the House amid the cheers of an assembly of friends; but the government have, in my opinion, wisely abstained from reprobating such measures in the speech, while they have properly exulted in such a union of the two countries as will contribute to the national independence and the public liberty of Europe.

Years are coming over me, but my heart is as young and as ready as ever in the service of my country, of which I glory in being the pensionary and the hired advocate. I stand in a situation in which no man ever stood yet—the faithful friend of my country—its servant—its stave, if you will—I speak its sentiments by turns to you and to itself. I require no £20,000,000 on behalf of Ireland—I ask you only for justice: will you—can you—I will not say dare you refuse, because that would make you turn the other way. I implore you, as English gentlemen, to take this matter into consideration now, because you never had such an opportunity of conciliating. Experience makes fools wise; you are not fools, but you have yet to be convinced. I cannot forget the year 1825. We begged then as we would for a beggar's boon; we asked for emancipation by all that is sacred amongst us, and I remember how my speech and person were treated on the Treasury Bench, when I had no opportunity of reply. The other place turned us out and sent us back again, but we showed that justice was with us. The noble lord says the other place has declared the same sentiments with himself; but he could not use a worse argument. It is the very reason why we should acquiesce in the measure of reform, for we have no hope from that House—all our hopes are centred in this; and I am the living representative of those hopes. I have o other reason for adhering to the ministry than because they, the chosen epresentatives of the people of England, are anxiously determined to give the same measure of reform to Ireland as that which England has received. have not fatigued myself, but the House, in coming forward upon this ccasion. I may be laughed and sneered at by those who talk of my power; ut what has created it but the injustice that has been done in Ireland? hat is the end and the means of the magic, if you please—the groundwork f my influence in Ireland. If you refuse justice to that country, it is a nelancholy consideration to me to think that you are adding substantially o that power and influence, while you are wounding my country to its very eart's core; weakening that throne, the monarch who sits upon which, ou say you respect; severing that union which, you say, is bound together y the tightest links, and withholding that justice from Ireland which she ·ill not cease to seek till it is obtained; every man must admit that the ourse I am taking is the legitimate and proper course—I defy any man to ay it is not. Condemn me elsewhere as much as you please, but this you nust admit. You may taunt the ministry with having coalesced me, you nay raise the vulgar cry of 'Irishman and Papist' against me, you may send ·ut men called ministers of God to slander and calumniate me; they may ssume whatever garb they please, but the question comes into this narrow ompass. I demand, I respectfully insist: on equal justice for Ireland, on the ame principle by which it has been administered to Scotland and England. will not take less. Refuse me that if you can.

77

D-DAY PRAYER

Franklin D. Roosevelt

This is the prayer originally entitled 'Let Our Hearts Be Stout' written by President Franklin D. Roosevelt as Allied troops were invading German-occupied Europe during World War II. The prayer was read to the nation on radio on the evening of D-Day, 6 June 1944, while American, British and Canadian troops were fighting to establish five beachheads on the coast of Normandy in northern France. The previous night, 5 June the President had also been on the radio to announce that Allied troops had entered Rome. The spectacular news that Rome had been liberated was quickly superceded by news of the gigantic D-Day invasion which began at 6.30 a.m. on 6 June. By midnight, about 57,000 American and 75,000 British and Canadian soldiers had made it ashore, amid losses that included 2,500 killed and 8,500 wounded.

My fellow Americans:

Last night, when I spoke with you about the fall of Rome, I knew at tha moment that troops of the United States and our Allies were crossing th Channel in another and greater operation. It has come to pass with succes thus far.

And so, in this poignant hour, I ask you to join with me in prayer.

Almighty God: Our sons, pride of our nation, this day have set upon mighty endeavour, a struggle to preserve our republic, our religion, an our civilization, and to set free a suffering humanity.

Lead them straight and true; give strength to their arms, stoutness to thei hearts, steadfastness in their faith.

They will need Thy blessings. Their road will be long and hard. For the enemy is strong. He may hurl back our forces. Success may not come with rushing speed, but we shall return again and again; and we know that by Thy grace, and by the righteousness of our cause, our sons will triumph.

They will be sore tried, by night and by day, without rest—until the victory is won. The darkness will be rent by noise and flame. Men's souls will be shaken with the violences of war.

For these men are lately drawn from the ways of peace. They fight not for the lust of conquest. They fight to end conquest. They fight to liberate. They fight to let justice arise, and tolerance and goodwill among all Thy people. They yearn but for the end of battle, for their return to the haven of home.

Some will never return. Embrace these, Father, and receive them, Thy heroic servants, into Thy kingdom.

And for us at home—fathers, mothers, children, wives, sisters, and brothers of brave men overseas, whose thoughts and prayers are ever with them—help us, Almighty God, to rededicate ourselves in renewed faith in Thee in this hour of great sacrifice.

Many people have urged that I call the nation into a single day of special prayer. But because the road is long and the desire is great, I ask that our people devote themselves in a continuance of prayer. As we rise to each new day, and again when each day is spent, let words of prayer be on our lips, invoking Thy help to our efforts.

Give us strength, too—strength in our daily tasks, to redouble the contributions we make in the physical and the material support of our armed forces. And let our hearts be stout, to wait out the long travail, to bear sorrows that may come, to impart our courage unto our sons wheresoever they may be.

And, O Lord, give us faith. Give us faith in Thee; faith in our sons; faith in each other; faith in our united crusade. Let not the keeness of our spirit ever be dulled. Let not the impacts of temporary events, of temporal matters of but fleeting moment—let not these deter us in our unconquerable purpose.

With Thy blessing, we shall prevail over the unholy forces of our enemy. Help us to conquer the apostles of greed and racial arrogances. Lead us to the saving of our country, and with our sister nations into a world unity that will spell a sure peace—a peace invulnerable to the schemings of unworthy men. And a peace that will let all of men live in freedom, reaping the just rewards of their honest toil.

Thy will be done, Almighty God.

Amen.

78

THE DESTRUCTIVE MALE

Elizabeth Cady Stanton

Women's rights pioneer Elizabeth Cady Stanton (1815–1902) gave this powerful speech in 1868 at the Women's Suffrage Convention in Washington, D.C. Twenty years earlier, at Seneca Falls, New York, she had helped launch the women's rights movement in America. Stanton worked tirelessly for more than a half-century to obtain voting rights for American women and also questioned the social and political norms of her day, which excluded women.

urge a sixteenth amendment, because 'manhood suffrage,' or a man's government, is civil, religious, and social disorganization. The male element is a destructive force, stern, selfish, aggrandizing, loving war, violence, conquest, acquisition, breeding in the material and moral world like discord, disorder, disease, and death. See what a record of blood and cruelty the pages of history reveal! Through what slavery, slaughter, and sacrifice, through what inquisitions and imprisonments, pains and persecutions, black codes and gloomy creeds, the soul of humanity has struggled for the centuries, while mercy has veiled her face and all hearts have been dead alike to love and hope!

The male element has held high carnival thus far; it has fairly run riot from the beginning, overpowering the feminine element everywhere, crushing out all the diviner qualities in human nature, until we know but little of true manhood and womanhood, of the latter comparatively nothing, for it has scarce been recognized as a power until within the last century. Society is but the reflection of man himself, untempered by woman's thought; the hard iron rule we feel alike in the church, the state, and the home.

No one need wonder at the disorganization, at the fragmentary condition of everything, when we remember that man, who represents but half complete being, with but half an idea on every subject, has undertaken the absolute control of all sublunary matters.

People object to the demands of those whom they choose to call the strong-minded, because they say 'the right of suffrage will make the women masculine'. That is just the difficulty in which we are involved today. Though disfranchised, we have few women in the best sense; we have simply so many reflections, varieties, and dilutions of the masculine gender. The strong, natural characteristics of womanhood are repressed and ignored in dependence, for so long as man feeds woman she will try to please the giver and adapt herself to his condition. To keep a foothold in society, woman must be as near like man as possible, reflect his ideas, opinions, virtues, motives, prejudices, and vices. She must respect his statutes, though they strip her of every inalienable right, and conflict with that higher law written by the finger of God on her own soul.

She must look at everything from its dollar-and-cent point of view, or she is a mere romancer. She must accept things as they are and make the best of them. To mourn over the miseries of others, the poverty of the poor, their hardships in jails, prisons, asylums, the horrors of war, cruelty, and brutality in every form, all this would be mere sentimentalizing. To protest against the intrigue, bribery, and corruption of public life, to desire that her sons might follow some business that did not involve lying, cheating, and a hard, grinding selfishness, would be arrant nonsense.

In this way man has been moulding woman to his ideas by direct and positive influences, while she, if not a negation, has used indirect means to control him, and in most cases developed the very characteristics both in him and herself that needed repression. And now man himself stands appalled at the results of his own excesses, and mourns in bitterness that falsehood, selfishness, and violence are the law of life. The need of this hour is not territory, gold mines, railroads, or special payments but a new evangel of womanhood, to exalt purity, virtue, morality, true religion, to lift man up into the higher realms of thought and action.

We ask woman's enfranchisement, as the first step toward the recognition of that essential element in government that can only secure the health, strength, and prosperity of the nation. Whatever is done to lift woman to her true position will help to usher in a new day of peace and perfection for the race.

In speaking of the masculine element, I do not wish to be understood to say that all men are hard, selfish, and brutal, for many of the most beautiful spirits the world has known have been clothed with manhood; but I refer to those characteristics, though often marked in woman, that distinguish what is called the stronger sex. For example, the love of acquisition and conquest, the very pioneers of civilization, when expended on the earth, the sea, the elements, the riches and forces of nature, are powers of destruction when used to subjugate one man to another or to sacrifice nations to ambition.

Here that great conservator of woman's love, if permitted to assert itself, as it naturally would in freedom against oppression, violence, and war, would hold all these destructive forces in check, for woman knows the cost of life better than man does, and not with her consent would one drop of blood ever be shed, one life sacrificed in vain.

With violence and disturbance in the natural world, we see a constant effort to maintain an equilibrium of forces. Nature, like a loving mother, is ever trying to keep land and sea, mountain and valley, each in its place, to hush the angry winds and waves, balance the extremes of heat and cold, of rain and drought, that peace, harmony, and beauty may reign supreme. There is a striking analogy between matter and mind, and the present disorganization of society warns us that in the dethronement of woman we have let loose the elements of violence and ruin that she only has the power to curb. If the civilization of the age calls for an extension of the suffrage, surely a government of the most virtuous educated men and women would better represent the whole and protect the interests of all than could the representation of either sex alone.

79

PREVENT THE REVOLT OF HIS OFFICERS

George Washington

At the close of the Revolutionary War in America, a perilous moment in the life of the fledgling American republic occurred as officers of the Continental Army met in Newburgh, New York, to discuss grievances and consider a possible insurrection against the rule of Congress. They were angry over the failure of Congress to honour its promises to the army regarding salary, bounties and life pensions. The officers had heard from Philadelphia that the American government was going broke and that they might not be compensated at all. On 10 March 1783, an anonymous letter was circulated among the officers of General Washington's main camp at Newburgh. It addressed those complaints and called for an unauthorized meeting of officers to be held the next day to consider possible military solutions to the problems of the civilian government and its financial woes. General Washington stopped that meeting from happening by forbidding the officers to meet at the unauthorized meeting. Instead, he suggested they meet a few days later, on 15 March, at the regular meeting of his officers. Meanwhile, another anonymous letter was circulated, this time suggesting Washington himself was sympathetic to the claims of the malcontent officers. And so, on 15 March 1783, Washington's officers gathered in a church building in Newburgh, effectively holding the fate of America in their hands. Unexpectedly, General Washington himself showed up. He was not entirely welcomed by his men, but nevertheless, personally addressed them.

Gentlemen:

By an anonymous summons, an attempt has been made to convene you together; how inconsistent with the rules of propriety, how unmilitary, and how subversive of all order and discipline, let the good sense of the army decide...

hus much, gentlemen, I have thought it incumbent on me to observe o you, to show upon what principles I opposed the irregular and hasty neeting which was proposed to have been held on Tuesday last—and not •ecause I wanted a disposition to give you every opportunity consistent vith your own honour, and the dignity of the army, to make known your ¸rievances. If my conduct heretofore has not evinced to you that I have •een a faithful friend to the army, my declaration of it at this time would •e equally unavailing and improper. But as I was among the first who ∙mbarked in the cause of our common country. As I have never left your ˏide one moment, but when called from you on public duty. As I have been he constant companion and witness of your distresses, and not among he last to feel and acknowledge your merits. As I have ever considered my ɔwn military reputation as inseparably connected with that of the army. ⅄s my heart has ever expanded with joy, when I have heard its praises, and ʍny indignation has arisen, when the mouth of detraction has been opened ɑgainst it, it can scarcely be supposed, at this late stage of the war, that I am ˏndifferent to its interests.

But how are they to be promoted? The way is plain, says the anonymous ɑddresser. If war continues, remove into the unsettled country, there ᵊstablish yourselves, and leave an ungrateful country to defend itself. But who are they to defend? Our wives, our children, our farms, and other property which we leave behind us. Or, in this state of hostile separation, ɑre we to take the two first (the latter cannot be removed) to perish in a wilderness, with hunger, cold, and nakedness? If peace takes place, never sheathe your swords, says he, until you have obtained full and ample justice; this dreadful alternative, of either deserting our country in the extremest hour of her distress or turning our arms against it (which is the apparent object, unless Congress can be compelled into instant compliance), has something so shocking in it that humanity revolts at the idea. My God! What can this writer have in view, by recommending such measures? Can he be a friend to the army? Can he be a friend to this country? Rather, is he not an insidious foe? Some emissary, perhaps, from New York, plotting the ruin of both, by sowing the seeds of discord and separation between the civil and military powers of the continent? And what a compliment does he pay to our understandings when he recommends measures in either alternative, impracticable in their nature?

I cannot, in justice to my own belief, and what I have great reason to conceive is the intention of Congress, conclude this address, without giving it as my decided opinion, that that honourable body entertain exalted sentiments of the services of the army; and, from a full conviction of its merits and sufferings, will do it complete justice. That their endeavours to discover and establish funds for this purpose have been unwearied, and will not cease till they have succeeded, I have not a doubt. But, like all other large bodies, where there is a variety of different interests to reconcile, their deliberations are slow. Why, then, should we distrust them? And, in consequence of that distrust, adopt measures which may cast a shade over that glory which has been so justly acquired; and tarnish the reputation of an army which is celebrated through all Europe, for its fortitude and patriotism? And for what is this done? To bring the object we seek nearer? No! most certainly, in my opinion, it will cast it at a greater distance.

For myself (and I take no merit in giving the assurance, being induced to it from principles of gratitude, veracity, and justice), a grateful sense of the confidence you have ever placed in me, a recollection of the cheerful assistance and prompt obedience I have experienced from you, under every vicissitude of fortune, and the sincere affection I feel for an army I have so long had the honour to command will oblige me to declare, in this public and solemn manner, that, in the attainment of complete justice for all your toils and dangers, and in the gratification of every wish, so far as may be done consistently with the great duty I owe my country and those powers we are bound to respect, you may freely command my services to the utmost of my abilities.

While I give you these assurances, and pledge myself in the most unequivocal manner to exert whatever ability I am possessed of in your favour, let me entreat you, gentlemen, on your part, not to take any measures which, viewed in the calm light of reason, will lessen the dignity and sully the glory you have hitherto maintained; let me request you to rely on the plighted faith of your country, and place a full confidence in the purity of the intentions of Congress; that, previous to your dissolution as an army, they will cause all your accounts to be fairly liquidated, as directed in their resolutions, which were published to you two days ago, and that they will adopt the most effectual measures in their power to render ample ustice to you, for your faithful and meritorious services. And let me conjure you, in the name of our common country, as you value your own sacred honour, as you respect the rights of humanity, and as you regard the military and national character of America, to express your utmost horror and detestation of the man who wishes, under any specious pretenses, to overturn the liberties of our country, and who wickedly attempts to open the floodgates of civil discord and deluge our rising empire in blood.

By thus determining and thus acting, you will pursue the plain and direct road to the attainment of your wishes. You will defeat the insidious designs of our enemies, who are compelled to resort from open force to secret artifice. You will give one more distinguished proof of unexampled patriotism and patient virtue, rising superior to the pressure of the most complicated sufferings. And you will, by the dignity of your conduct, afford occasion for posterity to say, when speaking of the glorious example you have exhibited to mankind, 'Had this day been wanting, the world had never seen the last stage of perfection to which human nature is capable of attaining.'

80

TRIBUTE TO THE DOG

George Graham Vest

George Graham Vest (1830–1904) served as US Senator from Missouri from 1879 to 1903 and became one of the leading orators and debaters of his time. This delightful speech is from an earlier period in his life when he practiced law in a small Missouri town. It was given in court while representing a man who sued another for the killing of his dog. During the trial, Vest ignored the testimony, and when his turn came to present a summation to the jury, he made the following speech and won the case.

Gentlemen of the Jury: The best friend a man has in the world may turn against him and become his enemy. His son or daughter that he has reared with loving care may prove ungrateful. Those who are nearest and dearest to us, those whom we trust with our happiness and our good name may become traitors to their faith. The money that a man has, he may lose. It flies away from him, perhaps when he needs it most. A man's reputation may be sacrificed in a moment of ill-considered action. The people who are prone to fall on their knees to do us honour when success is with us, may be the first to throw the stone of malice when failure settles its cloud upon our heads.

The one absolutely unselfish friend that man can have in this selfish world, the one that never deserts him, the one that never proves ungrateful or treacherous is his dog. A man's dog stands by him in prosperity and in poverty, in health and in sickness. He will sleep on the cold ground, where the wintry winds blow and the snow drives fiercely, if only he may be near his master's side. He will kiss the hand that has no food to offer. He will lick the wounds and sores that come in encounters with the roughness of he world. He guards the sleep of his pauper master as if he were a prince. When all other friends desert, he remains. When riches take wings, and eputation falls to pieces, he is as constant in his love as the sun in its ourney through the heavens.

f fortune drives the master forth, an outcast in the world, friendless nd homeless, the faithful dog asks no higher privilege than that of ccompanying him, to guard him against danger, to fight against his nemies. And when the last scene of all comes, and death takes his master n its embrace and his body is laid away in the cold ground, no matter if ll other friends pursue their way, there by the graveside will the noble dog be found, his head between his paws, his eyes sad, but open in alert watchfulness, faithful and true even in death.

81

'MUSLIM INDIA' WITHIN INDIA

Muhammad Iqbal

This speech was delivered at Allahabad, 29 December 1930. Iqbal is famous in India for his poem 'Saare Jahan se Achcha, Hindustan Hamara' (India is the best in the entire world) which he wrote in 1905. The same year he went to England for higher studies. He stayed in England for three years (1905–1908), but was a changed man on his return—a fundamentalist who had begun to believe in Pan-Islamism and started writing against nationalism. In 1908, he wrote a poem Tarane-i-Milli the first line of which reads, 'Chino-Arab hamara, Hindustan hamara, Muslim ham hum, watah hai saara jahan hamara' (China and Arabia are ours, Hindustan is ours; we are Muslims and the whole world is ours). In the late 20s Iqbal became an active member of the Muslim League and was close to Jinnah. In 1929, he was one of the leaders of the anti-Nehru Committee Report movement of the Muslim League. In the following speech which was his presidential address at the All India Muslim League Session at Allahabad, in which Iqbal demanded 'Muslim India' within India should not have come as a surprise to many. He asserts in the speech that the formation of a consolidated northwest Indian Muslim state appears to me to be the final destiny of the Muslims. As a consequence of Iqbal's speech the demand for a separate homeland for the Muslims in India grew. Rahmat Au, who was a student at Cambridge University (where Iqbal also had studied,) gave this idea a name—Pakistan. He distributed a pamphlet explaining the concept of Pakistan to the delegates of the Round Table Conference in London (1931–1932,). Ten years later Jinnah had to add the eastern wing and some other areas and the picture of Pakistan was complete. It took only seven more years to become a reality. Communalism, in its higher aspect, is indispensable to the formation of a harmonious whole in a country like India. The units of Indian society are not territorial as in European countries. India is a continent of human groups belonging to different races, speaking different languages, and professing different religions. Their behaviour is not determined by a common race-consciousness. Even the Hindus do not form a homogeneous group. The principle of European democracy cannot be applied to India without recognizing the presence of communal groups. The Muslim demand for the creation of a Muslim India within India is, therefore, perfectly justified. The resolution of the All-Parties Muslim Conference at Delhi is to my mind wholly inspired by this noble ideal of a harmonious whole which, instead of stiffening the respective individualities, of its component wholes, affords them chances of fully working out the possibilities that may be latent in them. I have no doubt that this House will emphatically endorse the Muslim demand embodied in this resolution.

Personally, I would go further than the demands which are embodied in the resolution. I would like to see Punjab, the North West Frontier Province, Sind and Baluchistan amalgamated into a single state. Self-government within the British Empire, or without the British Empire, the formation of a consolidated North-West Indian Muslim state appears to me to be the final destiny of the Muslims, at least of Northwest India. The proposal was put forward before the Nehru Committee but it was rejected on the ground that, if carried into effect, it would give a very unwieldy state. This is true in so far as the area is concerned; but the population of the state contemplated by the proposal would be much smaller than some of the present Indian provinces. The exclusion of Ambala division, and perhaps of some of the districts where non-Muslims predominate, will make it less extensive and more Muslim in population—so that the exclusion suggested will enable this consolidated state to give a more effective protection to non-Muslim minorities within its area. The idea need not alarm the Hindus or the British. India is the greatest Muslim country in the world. The life of Islam as a cultural force in this living country depends very largely on its centralization in a specified territory. This centralization of the most active portion of the Muslims in India, whose military and police service has, not withstanding unfair treatment from the British made British rule possible in this country, will eventually solve the problems of India as well as of Asia. It will intensify their sense of responsibility and deepen their patriotic feeling. Thus, possessing full opportunity of development within the body politic of India, the North-West Indian Muslims will prove the best defenders of India against a foreign invasion, be that one of ideas or of bayonets. Punjab with a fifty-six per cent Muslim population supplies fifty-four per cent of total combatant troops in the Indian army and if the nineteen thousand gurkhas recruited from the independent state of Nepal are excluded, the Punjab contingent amounts to sixty-two per cent of the entire Indian Army. This percentage does not take into account nearly si thousand combatants supplied to the Indian Army by the North-Wes Frontier Province and Baluchistan. From this, you can easily calculat the possibilities of North-West Indian Muslims in regard India's defenc against foreign aggression. The hon'ble Srinivasa Sastri thinks that th Muslim demand for the creation of autonomous Muslim states along th northwest border is actuated by a desire 'to acquire means of exertin pressure in emergencies on the Government of India'. I may frankly tel him that the Muslim demand is not actuated by the kind of motive h imputes to us. It is actuated by a genuine desire for free development, whicl is practically impossible under the unitary government contemplatec by the nationalist Hindu politicians with a view to securing permanen communal dominance in India.

Nor should the Hindus fear that the creation of autonomous Muslim states will mean the introduction of a kind of religious rule in such states. I have already indicated to you the meaning of the word religion, as applied to Islam. The truth is that Islam is not a church. It is a state, conceived as a contractual organism long, long before Rousseau ever thought of such a thing, and animated by an ethical ideal which regards man not as an earth-rooted creature, defined by a portion of the earth, but as a spiritual being understood in terms of a social mechanism, and possessing rights and duties as a living factor in that mechanism. I, therefore, demand the formation of a consolidated Muslim state in the best interests of India and Islam. For India, it means security and peace resulting from an internal balance of power. For Islam it would mean an opportunity to rid itself of the stamp that Arabian imperialism was forced to give, to mobilize its laws, education, culture, and to bring them into close contact with its own original spirit and with the spirit of modern times.

82

PLEADING FOR THE DEPRESSED CLASSES

B.R. Ambedkar

This speech was delivered at London, 31 December 1930. Three sessions of the Round Table Conference were held in London to prepare an outline of the future Constitution of India. Ambedkar was nominated as the representative of the depressed classes (later rechristened as scheduled castes in the Act of 1935) in all the three sessions, along with Rao Bahadur Srinivasan. The speech below was delivered by Ambedkar during the First Round Table Conference (Minorities Sub-Committee). Ambedkar in the speech, argues that the depressed classes were a minority like the Muslims, Sikhs, Christians, etc., and should get the same privileges and safeguards as did the other minorities. This session, which had been boycotted by the Congress, ended without any agreement. A second session was held during September—December, 1931 in which Gandhi also participated as the sole representative of the Congress. In this session, Ambedkar crossed swords with Gandhi on the question of the depressed classes being recognized as a minority (see Gandhi's speech of 8 October 1931), which also ended in failure. As agreed, the chairman, Ramsay Macdonald, announced the famous Communal Award (17 August 1932) in which the depressed classes were declared as a minority. Gandhi went on a fast unto death, which resulted in the Poona Pact. Instead of separate electorates for the depressed classes, reservation of seats in various legislatures was agreed upon. Ambedkar signed the Pact on behalf of the depressed classes and Madan Mohan Malaviya on behalf of the upper castes. Some writers feel that it was a defeat for Gandhi as unwittingly he acknowledged that Ambedkar represented the depressed classes and not him.

I am sure you will readily agree that the task which has fallen upon me to represent the case of the depressed classes is a heavy one. It is for the first time that the case of the depressed classes from the political point of view has come to be considered. The disabilities of the depressed classes were mentioned in almost every despatch that was recorded by the Government of India in connection with the political advancement of the country; bu the despatches only mentioned the difficulties and never attempted to give any solutions of those difficulties. The problem was just allowed to rest.

The first observation that I will make is, that although there are various minority communities in India which require political recognition, it has to be understood that the minorities are not on the same plane and that they differ from each other. They differ in the social standing which each minority occupies vis-à-vis the majority community. We have, for instance, the Parsi community, which is the smallest community in India, and yet, vis-à-vis its social standing with the majority community, it is probably the highest in order of precedence. On the other hand, if you take the depressed classes, they are a minority which comes next to the great Muslim minority in India, and yet their social standard is lower than the social standard of ordinary human beings. Again, if you take the minorities and classify them on the basis of social and political rights, you will find that there are certain minorities which enjoy social and political rights. The fact that they are in a minority does not necessarily stand in the way of their full and free enjoyment of those civic rights. But if you take the case of the depressed classes, the position is totally different. They have no rights in certain matters, and, where they have any, the majority community will not permit them to enjoy them.

My first submission to this committee, then, is that it should realize that although the minorities are all in the same boat, the most important fact to remember is that they are not all in the same class in the same boat. Some are travelling in 'A' class, some in 'B' class and some in 'C' and so on. I have not the slightest doubt in my mind that the depressed classes, though they are a minority and are to that extent in the same boat as other minorities, are not even in 'C' or 'D' class but are actually in the hold.

Starting from that point of view, I agree, that in some respects, the position of the depressed classes is similar to that of the other minorities in India. They, along with the other minorities, fear that under any future Constitution of India by which a majority rule will be established—there can be no doubt that majority rule will be the rule of the orthodox Hindus—there is a great danger of that majority with its orthodox Hindu beliefs and prejudices ontravening the dictates of justice, equality and good conscience. There is a great danger that the minorities may be discriminated against either in legislation or administration or in other public rights of citizenship, and therefore it is necessary to safeguard the position of the minorities in such a manner that the discrimination which is feared, shall not take place.

From that point of view, however, what is asked is that the minorities shall have a fair representation in the legislature and the executive, that they shall have representation in the public services of the country. The constitution shall provide that there shall be imposed certain limitations on the future legislatures of India, both central and provincial on their legislative power which will prevent the majorities from abusing their legislative power in such a manner as to enact laws which would create discrimination between one citizen and another. This circumstance—this danger of discrimination—is common to all minorities, and I, as a representative of the depressed classes, join with the demand which the other minorities have made in this regard.

I now come to those circumstances which mark off the depressed classes and the other minority communities in India. I will at once say that the way in which the position of the depressed classes differs from the positions of the other minority communities in India is this, that in the first place, the depressed classes are not entitled, under present circumstances, to certain civic rights which the other minorities enjoy by law. In other words, in the existing situation the depressed classes suffer from what are called civic disabilities. I will give you just one or two illustrations, because I know I have not much time at my disposal.

Take the case of employment in the police or in the army. In the Government of India Act it is provided that no subject of His Majesty shall be deprived of the right of being employed in any public service by reason of his caste, creed or colour. It is obvious that every member of the depressed class who is capable, who is in a position to satisfy the test laid down for employment in any public department, should have the right to enter that public department. But what do we find? If a depressed class man applied for service in the police department today, he is told point blank by the executive officers of the government that no member of the depressed class can be employed in the police service, because he is an untouchable. In the case of the military the same situation obtains. Up to 1892, practically the whole of the Madras and Bombay armies consisted of members drawn from the depressed classes. All the great wars in the history of India have been fought with the help of sepoys drawn from the depressed classes, both in the Bombay presidency and in Madras. Yet in 1892, a rule or regulation was made which debarred the depressed class from entry into the military service, and even today, if you ask a question in the Legislative Council as to why this was done, the answer is that the bar of untouchability does create insuperable difficulties in the recruitment of these classes. Secondly, and in my opinion, the most hideous distinction which marks the depressed classes, is that they are subject to social persecution unknown in any other part of the world.

As against these special circumstances which affect the depressed classes, we propose the following safeguards. Firstly, we want a fundamental right enacted in the Constitution which will declare 'untouchability' to be illegal for all public purposes. We must be emancipated, so to say from this social curse, before we can at all consent to the Constitution. Secondly, this fundamental right must also invalidate and nullify all such disabilities and discriminations as may have been made hitherto. Lastly, and most importantly, we want legislation against the social persecution to which I have drawn your attention just now.

83

THE UNKINDEST CUT OF ALL

Mohandas Karamchand Gandhi

This speech was delivered in London, 8 October 1931. During the Second Round Table Conference Dr B.R. Ambedkar crossed swords with Gandhi over the question of representation of the depressed classes. Both put their claim, to the amusement of the other members of the conference. Ambedkar wanted separate electorates for the depressed classes on the lines of the Muslims and Sikhs. Gandhi opposed it with uncharacteristic vehemence. He believed that this would divide Hindu society and called it the 'unkindest cut of all' and a 'perpetual bar-sinister'. Under the Communal Award announced by British Prime Minister Ramsay MacDonald, who was the chairman of the conference, depressed classes were given separate electorates in spite of Gandhi's opposition to it in the conference. Gandhi undertook a fast-unto-death on the issue resulting in the famous Poona Pact. Separate electorate for depressed classes were withdrawn and were replaced by reserved seats for them in the legislatures. This was a great success for Gandhi and many believe that he saved Hindu society from disintegration. Following is Gandhi's speech at the Second Round Table Conference in London.

Prime Minister and friends, it is with deep sorrow and deeper humiliation that I have to announce utter failure on my part to secure an agreed solution of the communal question through informal conversations among and with the representatives of different groups. I apologize to you. But to say that the conversations have, failed is not to say the entire truth. The causes of failure were inherent in the composition of the Indian delegation. We are almost all not elected representatives of the parties or groups whom we are presumed to represent, but are here by the nomination of the government. Nor are those whose presence was absolutely necessary for an agreed solution, here. Further, you will allow me to say that this was hardly the time to summon the Minorities Committee. It lacks the sense of reality in that we do not know what it is that we are going to get. The solution can be just the tip of the swaraj constitution, not its foundation—and only because our differences have hardened, and not arisen, by reason of foreign domination. I have not a shadow of doubt that the iceberg of communal differences will melt under the warmth of the sun of freedom. I, therefore venture to suggest that the minorities committee be adjourned sine die and that the fundamentals of the Constitution be hammered into shape as quickly as may be. Meanwhile, the informal work of discovering a real solution of the communal problem will and must continue; only it must not block or be allowed to block the progress of constitution-building. Attention must be diverted from it and concentrated on the main part of the structure. Lastly, the only reason for my appearance at these deliberations is that I represent the Indian National Congress, and so I must clearly set forth its position. In spite of appearances to the contrary; especially in England, the Congress claims to represent the entire nation, and most decidedly the dumb millions, among who are included the numberless untouchables, who are more suppressed than depressed, as also in a way the more unfortunate and neglected classes known as backward races.

It seems to have been represented that I am opposed to any representation of the untouchables on the legislature. This is a travesty of the truth. What I have said, and what I must repeat, is that I am opposed to their special representation. I am convinced that it can do them no good, and may do much harm; but the Congress is wedded to adult franchise. Therefore, millions of them can be placed on the voters' roll. It is impossible to conceive that, with untouchability fast disappearing, nominees of these voters can be boycotted by the others; but what these people need more than election to the legislatures is protection from social and religious persecution. I can well understand the claims advanced by other minorities but the claims advanced on behalf of the untouchables, is to me the 'unkindest cut of all'. It means the perpetual bar-sinister. I would not seal the vital interests of the untouchables even for the sake of winning the freedom of India. I claim myself in my own person to represent the vast mass of the untouchables. Here I speak not merely on behalf of the Congress, but on my own behalf, and I claim that I would get their vote, if there was a referendum of the untouchables, and that I would top the poll. I would work from one end of India to the other to convince them that separate electorates and separate reservation is not the way to remove this bar-sinister, which is not to their shame, but that of orthodox Hinduism. The Sikhs may remain as such in perpetuity; so may Mohammedans, so may Europeans. Will the untouchables remain untouchables in perpetuity? I would rather that Hinduism died than untouchability lived. Therefore, with all my regard for Dr Ambedkar, and for his desire to witness the upliftment of the untouchables, with all regard for his ability; I must say in all humility that here the great wrong under which he has laboured and perhaps the bitter experiences that he has undergone have, for the moment, warped his judgement. It hurts me to have to say this, but I would be untrue to the cause of the untouchables, which is as dear to me as life itself, if I did not say it. I will not bargain away their rights for the kingdom of the whole world. I am speaking with a due sense of responsibility, and I say that it is not a proper claim which is registered by Dr Ambedkar when he seeks to speak for all the untouchables of India. It will create a division in Hinduism which I cannot possibly look forward to with any satisfaction whatsoever. I do not mind untouchables, if they so desire, being converted to Islam or Christianity. I would tolerate that, but I cannot possibly tolerate what is in store for Hinduism if there are two divisions set forth in the villages. Those who speak of the political rights of untouchables do not know their India, do not know how Indian society is today constructed, and, therefore, I want to say with all the emphasis that I can command that if I was the only person to resist this thing I would resist it with my life.

84

DOMINION STATUS: FALSE CARD IN A PACK

Vithalbhai J. Patel

This speech was delivered in London, April 1932. During the freedom movement various terms were used for independence like swaraj, dominion status, independence, self-rule, home-rule, puma swaraj. The connotation of each term was not always clear. From 1885 to 1905, the Congress Party did not use any of these terms in their resolutions and were satisfied with prayers and petitions. The word swaraj was first used by Dadabhai Naoroji in his presidential address in 1906 without defining it. From 1908 to 1915, the moderates who controlled the Congress, again lapsed into prayers and petitions. The Home Rule Leaguers, B.G. Tilak and Annie Besant (1915 onwards) wanted home rule within the British Empire. In 1926, Gandhi in an answer to a question said, 'I shall be quite satisfied with dominion status within the British Empire, if it is a reality and not a sham.' He delivered the following speech at the Foreign Policy Association, London.

The analogy of self-governing colonies such as Canada, Australia and New Zealand does not and cannot apply to India. The colonies were founded by Britain, while India was a conquered territory. The original inhabitants of Canada and Australia were mercilessly exterminated, and the Anglo-Saxon elements—though largely made up of poor white trash—have become the predominant settlers in these unpopulated regions. No ties of blood or race exist between India and Britain; as they do between Britain and its self-governing colonies. The British army and navy, but for the name, belong as much to the colonists as they do to the British. In India, it is different. The prosperity of the colonies implies prosperity for Britain and vice-versa. It is, therefore, easy to understand a close inter alliance and economic community of interests and a mutual defence guarantee society among

Britain and her colonies without a clash of religion, race, culture, or the destruction of cherished historical ambitions. Indians are an alien nation with nothing in common with the British people. Their culture, language, religion, and tradition are quite different from those of the British. The economic interests of the two countries too are very diverse. England's astounding prosperity over the last two centuries has rested and can only continue to rest on our hunger, on our premature death, on our physical weakening, on our illiteracy and darkness. India's economic rise bringing prosperity and happiness to her own children must reduce the British Isles to a second rate overpopulated country of coal-diggers, fishermen and poultry farmers.

The dominion status card of England is a cardsharper's false card in a pack. It is played to deceive the entire world and to continue England's domination over India. While the world permits itself to be fooled, it also permits itself to be crushed by imperialism and militarism. There can be no normal industrial development in the world without total and universal disarmament. And such a disarmament is impossible so long as England insists on retaining control over India. The liberation of India is necessary as much for the world's sake as for her own.

All this is no mere accident. Britain wants to mislead the outside world into believing that there is an alternative to real independence, namely, dominion status within the Empire. Let the world realize once and for all that there is no middle way between the imperialist rule of one country over another, and unconditional independence of the latter country.

85

THE FICKLE LEADER

Subhas Chandra Bose

This speech was delivered in London, 10 June 1933. This was Bose's presidential address at the Third Indian Political Conference; it is considered to be his most controversial speech. In this speech, Bose criticizes Gandhi, without mincing any words, for his capricious behavior. Bose had never accepted Gandhi as his political guru, but had been close to C.R. Das while he was alive. After the failure of the Round Table Conference, Gandhi had restarted the Civil Disobedience Movement with full vigour and publicity. The entire nation was bestirred at Gandhi's call. Nearly 1,20,000 persons, including women and children, had courted arrest; were imprisoned and had boldly faced the inhuman repression by the government. Gandhi, all of a sudden, suspended the movement on 8 May 1933 without consulting anybody. The bravery and sacrifices of millions of people thus came to naught. Bose could not digest this strange behavior of Gandhi. C.R. Das had expressed similar views about Gandhi's fickle mindedness: 'The Mahatma opens a campaign in a brilliant fashion; he works it up with unerring skill; he moves from success to success till he reaches the zenith of his campaign—but after that he loses his nerve and begins to falter.' Bose's assertion that 'the party of the future will have to part company with the erstwhile leaders of the Indian people', reveals his mind. During the remaining years of his life Subhas Bose tried to put into practice this belief and offered the nation an alternative leadership.

Today our condition is analogous to that of an army that has suddenly surrendered unconditionally to the enemy in the midst of a protracted and strenuous campaign. (Here Bose is referring to the sudden suspension of the Civil Disobedience Movement by Mahatma Gandhi). And the surrender has taken place, not because the nation demanded it, not because the national army rose in revolt against its leaders and refused to fight— not because the supply of the sinews of war was cut off—but either because the commander in chief was exhausted as a result of repeated fasting or because both his mind and judgement were clouded owing to subjective causes which it is impossible for an outsider to understand. The surrender of 1933 reminds one of the Bardoli Retreat of 1922. But for 1922, some explanation, however unsatisfactory, could be offered to justify the retreat. The outbreak of violence at Chauri Chaura was suggested as a pretext for suspending the Civil Disobedience Movement in 1922. What explanation or pretext can one suggest to account for the surrender of 1933? Standing today at the crossroads of Indian history it is must and proper that we should try to discover the mistakes of the past so that our future activity may be directed along the right lines and all possible pitfalls may be avoided. In 1922, when the entire nation had been roused to passionate activity and greater daring and sacrifice could be expected of the people, the commander in chief suddenly hoists the white flag. It was, therefore, a mistake to suspend operations on the basis of what is known as the Delhi Pact (the Gandhi-Irwin Pact) of March 1931. Even if the leaders wanted a compromise, they should have waited for a more opportune moment. As matters stood, the Delhi Pact was an advantage to the government and a disaster to the people. If the Delhi pact of March 1931 was a blunder, the surrender of May 1933 is a calamity of the highest magnitude.

The party of the future will have to part company with the erstwhile leaders of the Indian people because there is no possibility that the latter will be able to adopt the principles, programs, policies and tactics that will be required for the next phase of the grim fight with Great Britain. Rarely in history—if ever at all—do we find the leaders of one epoch figuring as the leaders of the next. Times always produce the required men, and this will happen in India also.

86

THE PLEASURE OF BOOKS

William Lyon Phelps

William Lyon Phelps (1865–1943) was an American educator, literary critic and author. He served as a professor of English at Yale University from 1901 to 1933. His works include Advance of the English Novel and Essays on Modern Dramatists. On 6 April 1933, he delivered this speech during a radio broadcast. His reverence for books was not shared by everyone, especially those in Nazi Germany. On 10 May 1933, the Nazis had staged an event unseen since the Middle Ages as young German students from universities, formerly regarded as among the finest in the world, had gathered in Berlin and other German cities to burn books with 'un-German' ideas.

The habit of reading is one of the greatest resources of mankind; and we enjoy reading books that belong to us much more than if they are borrowed. A borrowed book is like a guest in the house; it must be treated with punctiliousness, with a certain considerate formality. You must see that it sustains no damage; it must not suffer while under your roof. You cannot leave it carelessly, you cannot mark it, you cannot turn down the pages, you cannot use it familiarly. And then, some day, although this is seldom done, you really ought to return it.

But your own books belong to you; you treat them with that affectionate intimacy that annihilates formality. Books are for use, not for show; you should own no book that you are afraid to mark up, or afraid to place on the table, wide open and face down. A good reason for marking favourite passages in books is that this practice enables you to remember more easily the significant sayings, to refer to them quickly, and then in later years, it is like visiting a forest where you once blazed a trail. You have the pleasure of going over the old ground, and recalling both the intellectual scenery and your own earlier self.

Everyone should begin collecting a private library in youth; the instinct of private property, which is fundamental in human beings, can here be cultivated with every advantage and no evils. One should have one's own bookshelves, which should not have doors, glass windows, or keys; they should be free and accessible to the hand as well as to the eye. The best of mural decorations is books; they are more varied in colour and appearance than any wallpaper, they are more attractive in design, and they have the prime advantage of being separate personalities, so that if you sit alone in the room in the firelight, you are surrounded with intimate friends. The knowledge that they are there in plain view is both stimulating and refreshing. You do not have to read them all. Most of my indoor life is spent in a room containing six thousand books; and I have a stock answer to the invariable question that comes from strangers. 'Have you read all of these books?'

'Some of them twice.' This reply is both true and unexpected.

There are of course no friends like living, breathing, corporeal men and women; my devotion to reading has never made me a recluse. How could it? Books are of the people, by the people, for the people. Literature is the immortal part of history; it is the best and most enduring part of personality. But book-friends have this advantage over living friends; you can enjoy the most truly aristocratic society in the world whenever you want it. The great dead are beyond our physical reach, and the great living are usually almost as inaccessible; as for our personal friends and acquaintances, we cannot always see them. Perchance they are asleep, or away on a journey. But in a private library, you can at any moment converse with Socrates or Shakespeare or Carlyle or Dumas or Dickens or Shaw or Barrie or Galsworthy. And there is no doubt that in these books you see these men at their best. They wrote for you. They 'laid themselves out,' they did their ultimate best to entertain you, to make a favourable impression. You are necessary to them as an audience is to an actor; only instead of seeing them masked, you look into their innermost heart of heart.

87

ON THE FESTIVAL OF THE SUPREME BEING

Maximilien Robespierre

Maximilien Robespierre (1758-1794) was one of the leaders and orators of the French Revolution of 1789, best known for his involvement in the Reign of Terror that followed. As the revolution approached, Robespierre became head of the powerful Jacobin Club, a radical group advocating exile or death for France's nobility. In 1792, after Paris mobs stormed the palace of the Tuileries and dethroned King Louis XVI and Queen Marie Antoinette, Robespierre helped organize the new revolutionary governing body, the Commune of Paris. Robespierre now developed great love for power along with a reputation for intolerance, self-righteousness and cruelty. He used his considerable oratory skills to successfully demand the execution of the king and queen, saying Louis XVI 'must die that the country may live.' In January 1793, the king was executed, followed ten months later by the queen. Not long after this speech, Robespierre himself was arrested by his political enemies. A rescue attempt followed, during which part of his jaw was shot off. On 28 July 1794, Robespierre and 19 of his comrades were guillotined. After his death, the Reign of Terror subsided, with Robespierre subsequently blamed for much of its horrors.

The day forever fortunate has arrived, which the French people have consecrated to the Supreme Being. Never has the world which He created offered to Him a spectacle so worthy of His notice. He has seen reigning on the earth tyranny, crime, and imposture. He sees at this moment a whole nation, grappling with all the oppressions of the human race, suspend the course of its heroic labours to elevate its thoughts and vows toward the great Being who has given it the mission it has undertaken and the strength to accomplish it.

Is it not He whose immortal hand, engraving on the heart of man the code of justice and equality, has written there the death sentence of tyrants? Is it not He who, from the beginning of time, decreed for all the ages and for all peoples liberty, good faith, and justice?

He did not create kings to devour the human race. He did not create priests to harness us, like vile animals, to the chariots of kings and to give to the world examples of baseness, pride, perfidy, avarice, debauchery, and falsehood. He created the universe to proclaim His power. He created men to help each other, to love each other mutually, and to attain to happiness by the way of virtue.

It is He who implanted in the breast of the triumphant oppressor remorse and terror, and in the heart of the oppressed and innocent calmness and fortitude. It is He who impels the just man to hate the evil one, and the evil man to respect the just one. It is He who adorns with modesty the brow of beauty, to make it yet more beautiful. It is He who makes the mother's heart beat with tenderness and joy. It is He who bathes with delicious tears the eyes of the son pressed to the bosom of his mother. It is He who silences the most imperious and tender passions before the sublime love of the fatherland. It is He who has covered nature with charms, riches, and majesty. All that is good is His work, or is Himself. Evil belongs to the depraved man who oppresses his fellow man or suffers him to be oppressed.

The Author of Nature has bound all mortals by a boundless chain of love and happiness. Perish the tyrants who have dared to break it!

Republican Frenchmen, it is yours to purify the earth which they have soiled, and to recall to it the justice that they have banished! Liberty and virtue together came from the breast of Divinity. Neither can abide with mankind without the other.

O generous People, would you triumph over all your enemies? Practice justice, and render the Divinity the only worship worthy of Him. O People, let us deliver ourselves today, under His auspices, to the just transports of a pure festivity. Tomorrow we shall return to the combat with vice and tyrants. We shall give to the world the example of republican virtues. And that will be to honour Him still.

The monster which the genius of kings had vomited over France has gone back into nothingness. May all the crimes and all the misfortunes of the world disappear with it! Armed in turn with the daggers of fanaticism and the poisons of atheism, kings have always conspired to assassinate humanity. If they are able no longer to disfigure divinity by superstition, to associate it with their crimes, they try to banish it from the earth, so that they may reign there alone with crime.

O People, fear no more their sacrilegious plots! They can no more snatch the world from the breast of its Author than remorse from their own hearts. Unfortunate ones, uplift your eyes toward heaven! Heroes of the fatherland, your generous devotion is not a brilliant madness. If the satellites of tyranny can assassinate you, it is not in their power entirely to destroy you. Man, whoever thou mayest be, thou canst still conceive high thoughts for thyself. Thou canst bind thy fleeting life to God, and to immortality. Let nature seize again all her splendour, and wisdom all her empire! The Supreme Being has not been annihilated.

It is wisdom above all that our guilty enemies would drive from the republic. To wisdom alone it is given to strengthen the prosperity of empires. It is for her to guarantee to us the rewards of our courage. Let us associate wisdom, then, with all our enterprises. Let us be grave and discreet in all our deliberations, as men who are providing for the interests of the world. Let us be ardent and obstinate in our anger against conspiring tyrants, imperturbable in dangers, patient in labours, terrible in striking back, modest and vigilant in successes. Let us be generous toward the good, compassionate with the unfortunate, inexorable with the evil, just toward every one. Let us not count on an unmixed prosperity, and on triumphs without attacks, nor on all that depends on fortune or the perversity of others. Sole, but infallible guarantors of our independence, let us crush the impious league of kings by the grandeur of our character, even more than by the strength of our arms.

Frenchmen, you war against kings; you are therefore worthy to honour divinity. Being of Beings, Author of Nature, the brutalized slave, the vile instrument of despotism, the perfidious and cruel aristocrat, outrages Thee by his very invocation of Thy name. But the defenders of liberty can give themselves up to Thee, and rest with confidence upon Thy paternal bosom. Being of Beings, we need not offer to Thee unjust prayers. Thou knowest Thy creatures, proceeding from Thy hands. Their needs do not escape Thy notice, more than their secret thoughts. Hatred of bad faith and tyranny burns in our hearts, with love of justice and the fatherland. Our blood flows for the cause of humanity. Behold our prayer. Behold our sacrifices. Behold the worship we offer Thee.

88

NAZIS' AIM IS SLAVERY

Edouard Daladier

Edouard Daladier, Premier of France, delivered this radio address to the people of France on 29 January 1940, after the Nazis had conquered Poland and just a few months before Hitler's armies attacked France.

At the end of five months of war one thing has become more and more clear. It is that Germany seeks to establish a domination over the world completely different from any known in history.

The domination at which the Nazis aim is not limited to the displacement of the balance of power and the imposition of supremacy of one nation. It seeks the systematic and total destruction of those conquered by Hitler, and it does not treaty with the nations which he has subdued. He destroys them. He takes from them their whole political and economic existence and seeks even to deprive them of their history and their culture. He wishes to consider them only as vital space and a vacant territory over which he has every right.

The human beings who constitute these nations are for him only cattle. He orders their massacre or their migration. He compels them to make room for their conquerors. He does not even take the trouble to impose any war tribute on them. He just takes all their wealth, and, to prevent any revolt, he wipes out their leaders and scientifically seeks the physical and moral degradation of those whose independence he has taken away.

Under this domination, in thousands of towns and villages in Europe there are millions of human beings now living in misery which, some months ago, they could never have imagined. Austria, Bohemia, Slovakia and Poland are only lands of despair. Their whole peoples have been deprived of the means of moral and material happiness. Subdued by treachery or brutal violence, they have no other recourse than to work for their executioners who grant them scarcely enough to assure the most miserable existence.

There is being created a world of masters and slaves in the image of Germany herself. For, while Germany is crushing beneath her tyranny the men of every race and language, she is herself being crushed beneath her own servitude and her domination mania. The German worker and peasant are the slaves of their Nazi masters while the worker and peasant of Bohemia and Poland have become in turn slaves of these slaves. Before this first realization of a mad dream, the whole world might shudder.

Nazi propaganda is entirely founded on the exploitation of the weakness of the human heart. It does not address itself to the strong or the heroic. It tells the rich they are going to lose their money. It tells the worker this is a rich man's war. It tells the intellectual and the artist that all he cherished is being destroyed by war. It tells the lover of good things that soon he would have none of them. It says to the Christian believer: 'How can you accept this massacre?' It tells the adventurer—'a man like you should profit by the misfortunes of your country.'

It is those who speak this way who have destroyed or confiscated all the wealth they could lay their hands on, who have reduced their workers to slavery, who have ruined all intellectual liberty, who have imposed terrible privations on millions of men and women and who have made murder their law. What do contradictions matter to them if they can lower the resistance of those who wish to bar the path of their ambitions to be masters of the world?

For us there is more to do than merely win the war. We shall win it, but we must also win a victory far greater than that of arms. In this world of masters and slaves, which those madmen who rule at Berlin are seeking to forge, we must also save liberty and human dignity.

The World's 100 Greatest Speeches

89

THE MARSHALL PLAN

George C. Marshall

This was delivered by Secretary of State, George C. Marshall on 5 June 1947. Two years after the defeat of Nazi Germany, U.S. Secretary of State George C. Marshall returned home from a visit to Europe and reported, 'The recovery of Europe is far slower than had been expected. Disintegrating forces are becoming evident. The patient is sinking while the doctors deliberate...' Much of Europe now lay in ruins. People faced shortage of housing, food, raw materials such as coal, and also lacked the money to pay for imports. The survival of Europe was at stake. When asked to deliver the 1947 commencement address at Harvard University, Marshall accepted the invitation and used the opportunity to suggest an economic recovery plan to revitalize Europe.

Mr President, Dr Conant, members of the Board of Overseers, Ladies and Gentlemen:

I'm profoundly grateful and touched by the great distinction and honour and great compliment accorded to me by the authorities of Harvard this morning. I'm overwhelmed, as a matter of fact, and I'm rather fearful of my inability to maintain such a high rating as you've been generous enough to accord to me. In these historic and lovely surroundings, this perfect day, and this very wonderful assembly, it is a tremendously impressive thing to an individual in my position.

But to speak more seriously, I need not tell you that the world situation is very serious. That must be apparent to all intelligent people. I think one difficulty is that the problem is one of such enormous complexity that the very mass of facts presented to the public by press and radio make it exceedingly difficult for the man in the street to reach a clear appraisement of the situation. Furthermore, the people of this country are distant from the troubled areas of the earth and it is hard for them to comprehend the plight and consequent reactions of the long-suffering peoples, and the effect of those reactions on their governments in connection with our efforts to promote peace in the world.

In considering the requirements for the rehabilitation of Europe, the physical loss of life, the visible destruction of cities, factories, mines, and railroads was correctly estimated, but it has become obvious during recent months that this visible destruction was probably less serious than the dislocation of the entire fabric of European economy. For the past ten years conditions have been abnormal. The feverish preparation for war and the more feverish maintenance of the war effort engulfed all aspects of national economies. Machinery has fallen into disrepair or is entirely obsolete. Under the arbitrary and destructive Nazi rule, virtually every possible enterprise was geared into the German war machine.

Long-standing commercial ties, private institutions, banks, insurance companies, and shipping companies disappeared through loss of capital, absorption through nationalization, or by simple destruction. In many countries, confidence in the local currency has been severely shaken. The breakdown of the business structure of Europe during the war was complete. Recovery has been seriously retarded by the fact that two years after the close of hostilities a peace settlement with Germany and Austria has not been agreed upon. But even given a more prompt solution of these difficult problems, the rehabilitation of the economic structure of Europe quite evidently will require a much longer time and greater effort than has been foreseen.

There is a phase of this matter which is both interesting and serious. The farmer has always produced the foodstuffs to exchange with the city dweller for the other necessities of life. This division of labour is the basis of modern civilization. At the present time it is threatened with breakdown. The town and city industries are not producing adequate goods to exchange with the food-producing farmer. Raw materials and fuel are in short supply. Machinery is lacking or worn out. The farmer or the peasant cannot find the goods for sale which he desires to purchase. So the sale of his farm produce for money which he cannot use seems to him an unprofitable transaction. He, therefore, has withdrawn many fields from crop cultivation and is using them for grazing. He feeds more grain to stock and finds for himself and his family an ample supply of food, however short he may be on clothing and the other ordinary gadgets of civilization. Meanwhile, people in the cities are short of food and fuel, and in some places approaching the starvation levels. So the governments are forced to use their foreign money and credits to procure these necessities abroad. This process exhausts funds which are urgently needed for reconstruction. Thus a very serious situation is rapidly developing which bodes no good for the world. The modern system of the division of labour upon which the exchange of products is based is in danger of breaking down.

The truth of the matter is that Europe's requirements for the next three or four years of foreign food and other essential products—principally from America—are so much greater than her present ability to pay that she must have substantial additional help or face economic, social, and political deterioration of a very grave character.

The remedy lies in breaking the vicious circle and restoring the confidence of the European people in the economic future of their own countries and of Europe as a whole. The manufacturer and the farmer throughout wide areas must be able and willing to exchange their product for currencies, the continuing value of which is not open to question.

Aside from the demoralizing effect on the world at large and the possibilities of disturbances arising as a result of the desperation of the people concerned, the consequences to the economy of the United States should be apparent to all. It is logical that the United States should do whatever it is able to do to assist in the return of normal economic health in the world, without which there can be no political stability and no assured peace.

Our policy is directed not against any country or doctrine but against hunger, poverty, desperation, and chaos. Its purpose should be the revival of a working economy in the world so as to permit the emergence of olitical and social conditions in which free institutions can exist. Such ssistance, I am convinced, must not be on a piecemeal basis as various rises develop. Any assistance that this government may render in the uture should provide a cure rather than a mere palliative. Any government hat is willing to assist in the task of recovery will find full cooperation, I m sure, on the part of the United States Government. Any government vhich maneuvers to block the recovery of other countries cannot expect elp from us. Furthermore, governments, political parties, or groups which eek to perpetuate human misery in order to profit therefrom politically or therwise will encounter the opposition of the United States.

t is already evident that, before the United States Government can proceed nuch further in its efforts to alleviate the situation and help start the Euuropean world on its way to recovery, there must be some agreement mong the countries of Europe as to the requirements of the situation and he part those countries themselves will take in order to give proper effect o whatever action might be undertaken by this Government. It would be leither fitting nor efficacious for this Government to undertake to draw up inilaterally a program designed to place Europe on its feet economically. his is the business of the Europeans. The initiative, I think, must come rom Europe. The role of this country should consist of friendly aid in the rafting of a European program and of later support of such a program so ar as it may be practical for us to do so. The program should be a joint one, greed to by a number, if not all, European nations.

An essential part of any successful action on the part of the United States is n understanding on the part of the people of America of the character of he problem and the remedies to be applied. Political passion and prejudice hould have no part. With foresight, and a willingness on the part of our eople to face up to the vast responsibility which history has clearly placed ipon our country the difficulties I have outlined can and will be overcome.

am sorry that on each occasion I have said something publicly in regard o our international situation, I've been forced by the necessities of the ase to enter into rather technical discussions. But to my mind, it is of vast mportance that our people reach some general understanding of what the omplications really are, rather than react from a passion or a prejudice or an emotion of the moment. As I said more formally a moment ago, we are remote from the scene of these troubles. It is virtually impossible at this distance merely by reading, or listening, or even seeing photograph or motion pictures, to grasp at all the real significance of the situation. And yet the whole world of the future hangs on a proper judgement. I hangs, I think, to a large extent on the realization of the American people of just what are the various dominant factors. What are the reactions o the people? What are the justifications of those reactions? What are the sufferings? What is needed? What can best be done? What must be done?

Thank you very much.

90

SEEKING BRITISH WAR AIMS (EDITED)

Maulana Abul Kalam Azad

This speech was delivered at Ramgarh, 19 March 1940. World War II (September 1939) had serious repercussions in India. The British government declared India a belligerent country without consulting the Congress Party which had ministries in eight out of eleven provinces. Congress leaders, led by Gandhi, had been enquiring about the war aims of the British ever since the war had started. The replies given by the government were vague and did not satisfy the Congress leaders. The Congress Working Committee met on 17 October 1939 and advised the Congress ministries to resign because the Congress party did not want to support the government in their war effort. Consequently, all Congress ministries resigned between 27 October and 15 November 1939. The resignation of the ministries proved to be a mistake. The government and the viceroy felt relieved because the Congress with their control of eight provincial governments had the power to hasten the war effort. Now they themselves had relinquished that power. The Muslim League celebrated this in the form of 'Day of Deliverance'. In the presidential address at the Ramgarh Session of the Congress, Maulana Azad, reiterates and justifies the decision of the Congress Working Committee in clearer and stronger terms. However, only three days later (on 22 March 1940) the emboldened Jinnah demanded a separate territory for the Muslims in his presidential address at Lahore.

The first and the most important question before us is where are the steps taken by us in consequence of the declaration of war on 3 September 1939, leading us? Where do we stand now?

Probably in the entire history of the Congress, the 1936 session at Lucknow marked a new ideological phase, when the Congress passed a long resolution on the international situation and placed its viewpoint clearly and categorically before the public. These resolutions embodied at one and the same time, two declarations to the world: firstly, we stated, what I have described as a new ideology in Indian politics, that we could not remain in isolation from the political events of the outside world, even in our present state of helplessness. It is, therefore, impossible for India today to consider her problems while confining herself within her four walls. It is inevitable that events in the outside world should have their repercussions in India. It is equally inevitable that our decisions and the conditions prevailing in India should affect the rest of the world. It was this consciousness and belief which brought about our decisions. We declared these resolutions against reactionary movements like Fascism and Nazism which were directed against democracy and individual and national freedom. India cannot endure the prospect of Nazism and Fascism, but she is even more tired of British imperialism. If India remains deprived of her natural right to freedom, this would clearly mean that British imperialism continued to flourish with all its traditional characteristics. Under such conditions, India would on no account be prepared to lend a helping hand for the triumph of British imperialism. This was the second declaration which was constantly emphasized through these resolutions. These resolutions were repeatedly passed from the Lucknow session onwards till August 1939 and are known by the name of War Resolutions.

War was declared on 3 September, and on 7 September the All India Congress Working Committee met at Wardha to deliberate upon the situation. What did the Working Committee do on this occasion? All the declarations of the Congress made since 1936 were prior to this. It had also to face the action taken by the British government in declaring India as a belligerent country. The Congress postponed its final decisions and asked the British government to state its war aims, for, on this depended not only peace and justice for India, but for the entire world. If India was being invited to participate in this war, she had a right to know why this war was being fought. What was its object? If the result of this grim tragedy was not to be the same as that of the last war, and if it was really being fought to safeguard freedom, democracy and peace and to bring a new order to the world, then, in all fairness, India had a right to know, what effect these aims would have on her own destiny. The Working Committee formulated this demand in a long statement on 14 September 1939. If I

xpress the…occupy an outstanding place in recent…not claiming too
much…of the future irrefutable document, based on truth set aside by
the arrogant pride…the statement which was published… This is a simple
ut and reason, and it can only be armed forces. On 17 October 1939, the
tatement of the Viceroy was published and the Working Committee met
to deliberate upon it on 22 October at Wardha. Without any discussion
came to the conclusion that this reply could, under any circumstances,
be considered satisfactory, and that it should now unhesitatingly give the
ecision, which it had postponed till then. The decision of the Working
Committee was as follows:

n the circumstances, the Committee cannot possibly give any support to
Great Britain, for it would amount to an endorsement of the imperialistic
olicy which the Congress has always sought to end. As a first step in this
irection, the Committee calls upon the Congress Ministries to tender their
esignations. 'When, after the declaration of war, we raised the question of
war aims and their effect on India's destiny, we did not forget the British
olicy of 1917 and 1919. We wanted to know how in the year 1939, when
he world was covering centuries in the course of days, England looked
t India. Had that look changed? We were given a clear reply that it had
ot. Even now there is no change in that imperialist outlook. We are told
to believe that the British government is very desirous that India should
ttain the status of a dominion, in the shortest possible period. We knew
ven earlier that the British government had expressed this desire. We now
now that they are very anxious indeed. But it is not a question of the desire
r of the measure of the desire of the British government. The straight and
imple question is of India's rights—whether she is entitled to determine her
wn fate or not. On this answer depends the answers to all other questions.
his question forms the foundation stone of India's problem; India will not
llow it to be removed, for if it is displaced, the entire structure of Indian
ationalism will collapse. So far as the question of war is concerned our
osition is quite clear. We see the face of British imperialism as clearly now
s we did in the last war, and we are not prepared to assist in its triumph
y participating in the war. Our case is crystal clear. We do not wish to see
British imperialism triumphant and stronger and thus lengthen the period
f our own subjection to it. We absolutely refuse to do so. Our path lies in
he opposite direction.

91

CRIPPS PROPOSALS

Sir Stafford Cripps

This speech was delivered at Delhi, 30 March 1942. The year 1942 was a very critical year for the British. The Empire was crumbling. Singapore had fallen on 15 February, and a garrison of some sixty thousand Indian troops surrendered to the Japanese without firing a shot. The fall of Rangoon on 8 March had brought the war dangerously close to India. The Congress ministries had resigned in October-November 1939 and since then had not been cooperating in the war-effort. There was a desperate need to win the confidence of the Indian leaders and through them of the Indian masses. Towards that end Winston Churchill sent Sir Stafford Cripps, a member of the British War Cabinet, (and supposedly a friend of Nehru) to negotiate with the Indian leaders. Cripps arrived in Delhi on 23 March 1942 armed with the Draft Declaration approved by the British War Cabinet. Actually, Churchill the diehard imperialist, had sent Cripps reluctantly due to the pressure exerted by American President Roosevelt and to a lesser extent by Chiang Kai-shek. And, of course, the worsening situation in Southeast Asia was another compelling reason. In the broadcast from All India Radio, Delhi, Cripps summarizes the offer contained in the Draft Declaration. The proposals may be divided into two parts: one, pertaining to the war period and the other concerning the postwar period. Though Indians were offered a substantial role in the viceroy's Council, the real power was still vested in the viceroy during the war period. The postwar offer entitled the provinces and the Indian rulers to secede from the union. Pakistan, thus, had advanced one step further and Mohammed Ali Jinnah was happy. But when the Congress rejected the proposals, the Muslim League followed suit.

First of all you will want to know what object we had in view. We wanted to make it quite clear and beyond any possibility of doubt or question that the British government and the British people desire the Indians to have full self-government, with a constitution as free in every respect as our own n Great Britain or as of any of the great dominion members of the British Commonwealth of nations. In the words of the Draft Declaration, India would be 'associated with the United Kingdom and other dominions by a common allegiance to the Crown but equal to them in every respect, in no way subordinate in any aspect of its domestic or external affairs.' There is, however, an existing constitution which regulates the central and provincial governments of India and everyone agrees that in these turbulent times we cannot here and now set about forging a new constitution. It is far too important a matter for the future of India to be improvised in a hurried way.

The principle on which these proposals are based is that the new constitution should be framed by the elected representatives of the Indian people themselves. So we propose that immediately hostilities are ended, a constitution-making body should be set up consisting of elected representatives from British India, and if the Indian states wish, as we hope they will, to become part of the new Indian union, they too will be invited to send their representatives to this constitution-making body. Nonetheless if they do, that will not bind them to become members of the union. This is the broad outline of the future. So much for the general framework of the proposals. But, as we all know, the most vital and difficult question is that which concerns the interests of the various communities amongst the Indian peoples. I will not attempt to go into any of the historical origins of these difficulties; let us look at them as a present fact. In the great Indian subcontinent there are many peoples and races like that in the great subcontinent of Russia. Our object is to give to the Indian people full self-government with complete freedom as to how they will devise and organize their own constitution. There are those who claim that India should form a single united country; there are others who say it should be divided up into two, three or more separate countries; there are those who claim that provincial autonomy should be very wide but with few centrally controlled federal services; while others stress the need for centralization in view of the growing complexity of economic development. These and many other various ideas which are worthy enough to be explored and debated upon, but it is for the Indian people, and not for any outside authority, to decide under which of these forms India will govern in the future. If the Indian people ask for our help, it will of course, be gladly given, but it is for you, the Indian people to discuss and decide upon your future constitution. We shall look on with deep interest and hope that your wisdom will guide you truly in this great adventure. We ask you, therefore, to come together—all religions and races—in a constitution-making body as soon as hostilities are over to frame your own constitution. We have specified the form which that body will take, unless, and this is an important joint, the leaders of the principal sections of Indian opinion agree between themselves before the end of hostilities, upon some other and better form. The constitution-making body will have as its object the framing of a single constitution for the whole of India—that is, of British India, together with such of the Indian states as may decide to join in. But we realize this very simple fact: If you want to persuade a number of people who are inclined to be antagonistic to enter the same room, it is unwise to tell them that once they go in there is no way out—they are to be locked in together forever. It is much wiser to tell them they can go in and if they find that they can't come to a common decision, then there is nothing to prevent those who wish from leaving again by another door. They are much more likely to go in if they have the knowledge that they can, by their free will, go out again if they cannot agree.

This is what we say to the provinces of India. Come together to frame a common constitution; if you find even after your discussions and all the give and take of a constitution-making assembly, that you cannot overcome your differences and that some provinces are still not satisfied with the constitution, then such provinces can withdraw and remain out if they wish. Nonetheless, the same degree of self-government and freedom will be available for them as for the union itself, that is to say complete self-government. We provide the means and the road by which you can attain that form of the absolute and united self-government that you desire at the earliest possible moment. In the past, we have waited for the various Indian communities to come to a common decision as to how a new constitution for a self-governing India should be framed and, because there has been no agreement amongst the Indian leaders, the British government has been accused by some of using this as a tactic to delay the granting of freedom to India. We are now giving the lead that has been asked for and it is in the hands of the Indians and the Indians alone whether they will accept that lead and so attain their own freedom. If they fail to accept this opportunity the responsibility for the failure must rest with them.

As regards the position of the minority communities within the new Indian union, I am confident that the constitution-making body will make a just provision for their protection. But in view of the undertakings given to these minorities by His Majesty's government the past, we propose that in the treaty; which, under the Draft Declaration, will be concluded between His Majesty's government and the constitution-making body, the new Indian union should undertake to protect the rights of these minorities. If there should be any non-acceding provinces a similar treaty provision would be made in respect of minority communities within their borders.

I have already indicated to you the position as to the immediate future. I know that His Excellency; the Viceroy, has the greatest hope that the acceptance of this document by the leaders of Indian opinion 'principle will make it possible for him to start forthwith upon the consultations which will enable him, to implement the principle laid down in the last paragraph of the document. It contains one essential reservation—that in respect of the responsibility for defence. This reservation does not mean that the governor general and his executive council will or indeed could be excluded from taking an effective share in the counsels for India's defence. In this wide-flung war, defence cannot be localized in a single country and its preparation must permeate the activities of every department of the government and must demand from every department the fullest cooperation. If His Majesty's government is to take full responsibility for the conduct of naval, military and air defence of India, as is their duty, then India's defence must be dealt with by them as part of the world war effort in which they are now engaged, and the direction of that defence must rest in the hands of the commander-in-chief under the War Cabinet and their highest staff officers. But, as I have already pointed out, the Government of India must also have an effective share in the defence councils and so we have decided that the commander-in-chief must retain his position as a member of the executive council. In order that India may have a full voice in this central control of strategy; defensive and offensive, not only in India itself but in all the interrelated theatres of war, we have invited the appointment of a representative Indian to the War Cabinet and to the Pacific Council of the United Nations. This is one of the ways in which

India will have her full say in the counsels of the Commonwealth and of the United Nations as an equal partner. When it comes to making peace, India will appoint her own representatives to the Peace Conference side by side those of the other free nations and 'so make her contribution to the building of a new world order.

I am confident that nothing further or more complete could be done towards the immediate realization of the just claims and demands of the Indian peoples. Our proposals are definite and precise. If they were to be rejected by the leaders of Indian opinion, there would be neither the time nor the opportunity to reconsider this matter till after the war which would be a bitter blow to the friends of India all over the world.

92

LOOKING TO JAPAN FOR EMANCIPATION

Rashbehari Bose

This speech was delivered at Bangkok, 15 June 1942. The role of Rashbehari Bose in the revolutionary movement of the country is somewhat unique. During the early days of World War I, he along with other revolutionaries of Bengal and Punjab, had motivated the Indian soldiers in various cantonments of the country to revolt against the British. However, the plan leaked out. Hundreds of revolutionaries, including some soldiers, were either executed or imprisoned, but Rashbehari somehow evaded arrest. He was also an accused in the Lahore Conspiracy Case. When he came to know that the police was on his trail he escaped to Japan in June 1915, where he married a Japanese girl. He wrote a book in Japanese and contributed articles educating the Japanese about conditions in India. He became quite a family man. However, he became active when Japan joined the war in December 1941 on the side of Germany and Italy. The speech reproduced below was made by Rashbehari as chairman of the Indian Independence Conference held in Bangkok from 15 to 23 June 1942 and was attended by about a hundred delegates from different parts of East Asia. He unfurled India's tricolour. The Indian Independence League (IIL) was resurrected (which he had formed in the 1920s in Japan). Several resolutions were passed including the one inviting Subhas Bose to East Asia. With the help of army officers like Captain Mohan Singh and others they motivated the Indian prisoners-of-war to join the Indian National Army. More than twenty thousand joined them. When Subhas reached Japan in June 1943 and then Singapore, Rashbehari voluntarily handed over the charge of IIL as well as of the Indian National Army to Subhas, while he served only as adviser. It is only fair to remember that Rashbehari Bose had laid the foundations of the organization on which Subhas Bose built up a huge structure.

I do not want to take your time by going into the details regarding India's struggle for freedom since 1857. It would be enough to say that although the failure of our revolt of 1857 was a great blow to the nation and depression had set in the country, our efforts to overthrow British rule never ceased. Under the circumstances prevailing in those days, the activities had to be carried on underground, and within a limited scope. Whenever an opportunity arose, a revolt was attempted. After minor preparatory stages our first effort on a large scale was made when the war of 1914–18 started. Our workers were active everywhere. The Indian army was prepared to join the revolt, although a part of it had actually revolted rather prematurely. We thought we are going to succeed. Unfortunately, we did not meet with success on that occasion. Thousands were sent to Andamans and Mandalay and hundreds of them still remain rotting in prisons and concentration camps.

During that war of 1914–18 the British had been partially successful in receiving India's cooperation by telling lies and making false promises. Our people were misled by the fine phraseologies of the shrewd British diplomats. They promised us freedom after the war, as they are doing during the present war. But soon after the conclusion of that war, it was realized that the British not only did not mean to keep their promises but definitely wanted to take away even that shadow of civil liberty that the Indians had in the pre-war days. When they protested, the British responded with bombs, bullets and machine-guns. Needless to mention that the tragedy of the Jallianwala Bagh of Amritsar in April 1919 is still fresh in our memory. The wounds have not yet healed and cannot be healed unless and until we have completely destroyed the power that was responsible for that great humiliation of our people.

Every tragedy, however, has a lesson to teach like the tragedy of Jallianwalla Bagh. The blood of more than a thousand of those innocent martyrs, that included even our women and children, could not go without significant results. The great upheavel that swept India from one corner to the other, and the great movements of Non-cooperation and Civil Disobedience that has been carried on by the Indian National Congress since 1919, which wonderfully organized the masses of India for political struggle, were undoubtedly the direct result of the massacres at Jallianwala Bagh.

When the war in Europe started in 1939, Britain once again began to indulge in jugglery of words in order to secure Indian 'cooperation' and help. But to our great delight, to this very day the nationalist leaders in

India have refused to be misled and have continued to resist all British efforts to drag India into war. Our respect goes to Mahatma Gandhi for the most admirable way in which he has led the nation clear of all dangers of being entangled in this war.

With this background in India, the Greater East Asia War was declared on 8 December 1941. No matter in which part of the world he or she might be living, whatever be his or her attitude towards Japan, I refuse to believe that there was a true Indian patriot who was not extremely delighted and gratified in his heart of hearts when the great news of the declaration of war by Japan against the Anglo-Saxon races reached his or her ears. I refuse to believe there is any true Indian patriot, whatever his career or conviction may be, who might not have rejoiced, as from day to day, the mighty imperial forces of Japan on land and sea and in the air went on administering crushing blows against their imperialism in Asia. The British Imperialist based in these parts began falling one after the other like houses of cards. Those of us who were destined to live and work in Japan had particular reasons to be overjoyed at this most welcome happening. We have been working in Japan for decades and can see that Japan is in a position to stand by the oppressed Asiatics and to liberate Asia. We were anxiously awaiting the day when Japan would fully realize the great significance of creating a free and united Asia and would feel convinced that it was in the interests of Japan herself, as also for the rest of Asia, if not for the world as whole, that the octopus grip of the Anglo-Saxon Imperialism in the East must be completely destroyed. We were fully convinced that Japan alone was in the position to do the honour. Thus when on the morning of that most auspicious day, the day of the enlightenment of Lord Buddha, we heard the most auspicious news of Japan's declaration of war against our common enemy, we felt convinced that our mission in Japan was fulfilled. We felt convinced that India's freedom was assured. Now that Japan and Thailand have taken up arms against our common foe the joint efforts of our worthy allies ensure the doom of the British Empire and our complete victory is assured.

These effective efforts on different fronts to destroy our common enemy are a reminder in regards to our own duties and responsibilities in this common effort for our common cause. We must ask ourselves what we have done and what we are going to do to contribute to this great cause. Only praising Japan, Germany and Italy will not elevate us to the position which we are craving. We must contribute our mite and must make the greatest sacrifice we can do and sacrifice all we can. Then alone can we command the respect and consideration of our worthy allies and then alone can we claim a place worthy of a great nation like ours in future international assemblies.

93

QUITTING INDIA

Clement Richard Attlee

This speech was delivered in London, 15 March 1946. The following speech made by Clement Attlee left no doubt in the minds of Indians that swaraj was now a reality. Attlee said that, 'a nation of four hundred million people that twice sent her sons to die for freedom should herself have freedom to decide her own destiny,' the entire House reverberated with cheers for him. To give freedom to India was part of the election manifesto of the Labour Party. Attlee was living up to that promise. Attlee made some important declarations in the speech like sending a Cabinet Mission to India which would pave the way for the interim government. The speech also reveals that there was still hope in British circles that India would remain a united entity and strengthen the British Commonwealth by joining it. This hope was reiterated by him the next year while moving the Indian Independence Bill in the Parliament (see Attlee's speech of 10 July 1947). Gandhi's reaction to the speech was that of bewilderment. When a correspondent asked him on 17 March what he thought of Attlee's speech, Gandhi replied, 'This time I believe that the British mean business. But the offer has come suddenly. Will India be jerked into independence? I feel today like a passenger who has been hoisted in a basket chair on to a ship's deck in a stormy sea and has not yet found his feet. There should have been some psychological preparation but even now it is not too late.' Evidently, Gandhi did not expect that independence would come so soon. The British were in a hurry to leave. It was not possible for them to hold on to India any longer.

I find from our friends in this House who had earlier been out to India and have subsequently returned, from letters received from Indians and from the English in India, to be in complete agreement on the fact that India is today in a state of great tension and that this is indeed a critical moment. Presently, the idea of nationalism is spreading fast in India and indeed all over Asia. It does not seem appropriate to apply the formula of the past to the present position. The mood of 1946 is not what it was in 1920, 1930 or even 1942. The slogans of the earlier days are discarded. Sometimes words that seemed at that time to the Indians to express the height of their aspirations are set on one side and other words and ideas thrust forward. I would like today, therefore, not to stress so much on the differences between the Indians, but let us all realize that there is an underlying demand among the Indians. It is worth remembering that a nation of four hundred million people which twice sent her sons to die for freedom should herself have freedom to decide her own destiny. My colleagues are going to India with the intention of making all their efforts to help her to attain that freedom as speedily and fully as possible. What form of government is to replace the present regime is for India to decide, but our desire is to help her to set up a machinery for making that decision. There, you have met with the initial difficulty of setting up that machinery but we are resolved that a machinery shall be set up, and we seek the utmost cooperation of all the Indian leaders to do so.

India herself must choose as to what will be her future situation and her position in the world. Unity may come through the United Nations or through the Commonwealth but no great nation can stand alone by herself without sharing what is happening in the world. I hope that India may elect to remain within the British Commonwealth. I am certain that she will find great advantage in doing so, but if she does, she must do it of her own free will, for the British Commonwealth and Empire is not bound together by chains of external compulsion. It is a free association of free people. If, on the other hand, she elects for independence—and, in our view, she has a right to do so—it will be for us to help to make the transition as smooth and easy as possible. We want, to set up an interim government—one of the purposes of the Bill which has been discussed today—to give the viceroy greater freedom in order that in the period which would elapse while a constitution is being worked out, you may have a government enjoying the greatest possible support in India. I would not like to fetter the viceroy's decision in any way in regard to the choice of portfolios. I am hoping that the statesmen of Britain and those of princely India will be able to work out a solution of the problem of bringing together the various constituent parts. I do not believe for a moment that the Indian princes would lag behind in India's march towards progress.

I am very well aware of the minority problem in India. I think all Indian leaders are now realizing the need for getting a settlement and I believe that due provision will be made for them in the constitution.

With regard to the treaty, we would not do anything to our own advantage which would be detrimental to India.

In an Asia ravaged by war, we have here the one country that has been seeking to apply the principles of democracy. I myself have always felt that political India might be the light of Asia. We have a very grave anxiety over India's food supply.

Whatever we can do to assist, we shall do. My colleagues are going out to India, resolved to succeed, and I am sure everyone will wish them Godspeed.

94

INDIA FREE AND DIVIDED

Jawaharlal Nehru

This speech was delivered at New Delhi, 3 June 1947. The interim government headed by Nehru was not working smoothly as the Muslim League members were not cooperating. The League also refused to participate in the Constituent Assembly. At the same time, the Muslim League resorted again to Direct Action—this time in Punjab and North-West Frontier Province. There were serious riots in Rawalpindi, Lahore, Amritsar, Peshwar, Multan which later spread to Bombay (now Mumbai), Ranchi and Kanpur. According to official accounts 2049 persons were killed and over 10,000 seriously injured in a matter of just two weeks. On 20 February 1947, Prime Minister Atlee made a statement in the House of Commons which decided the fate of India. He announced that it was the intention of His Majesty's government to take 'necessary steps to effect the transference of power to responsible Indian hands by a date not later than June 1948' and replace Lord Wavell with Lord Mountbatten as viceroy. After this announcement the Muslim league put more fire in their Direct Action. Jenkins (governor of Punjab) reported that 'communal tension was acute in almost all districts—and was spreading to villages.' The number of casualties were rising by the day, and the 'mayhem counted approximately six Hindus and Sikhs for every Muslim murdered.' Ultimately, the Congress took a realistic view of the deteriorating situation and in an emergency meeting of the Working Committee on 8 March 1947 demanded the partition of Punjab. Later, Bengal was added. This was virtually conceding to the partition of the country. Mountbatten replaced Wavell on 24 March 1947. He soon realized that in the circumstances the Cabinet Mission Plan was unworkable and that partition was inevitable. The Congress had already committed itself to partition in their Resolution of 8 March Jawaharlal Nehru's broadcast on 3 June did not come as a surprise. On 14 June, the All-India Congress Committee accepted the Mountbatten Plan of the partition of the country reasoning that 'it was better to accept the statement of June 3 rather than to fritter away their energies in trying to keep unwilling people in the union.'

Nearly nine months ago, soon after my assumption of office, I spoke to you from this place. I told you then that we were on the march and the goal had still to be reached. There were many difficulties and obstacles on the way and our journey's end may not be near, for that end was not the assumption of office in the Government of India but the achievement of full independence for India and the establishment of a cooperative commonwealth in which all would have equal shares in opportunity and in all things that give meaning and value to life.

Nine months have passed, months of sore trial and difficulty of anxiety and sometimes even of heartbreak. Yet looking back at this period with its suffering and sorrow for our people there is much which has been achieved—India has advanced nationally and internationally, and is respected today in the councils of the world. In the domestic sphere something substantial has been achieved, though the burden on the common man still continues to be terribly heavy and millions lack food and cloth and other necessities of life. Several development schemes are nearly ready and yet it is true that most of our dreams about the brave things we are going to accomplish have still to be realized. You know well difficulties which the country had to face, economic, political and communal. These months have been full of tragedy for millions and the burden on those who have the governance of the country in their hands has been great indeed.

My mind is heavy with the thought of the sufferings of our people in the areas of disturbance—the thousands who are dead and those, especially our womenfolk, who have suffered agony worse than death. To their families and to the innumerable people who have been uprooted from their homes and rendered destitute, I offer my deepest sympathy and assurance that we shall do all in our power to bring relief. We must ensure that such tragedies do not recur.

Today, I am speaking to you on another historic occasion when a vital change affecting the future of India is proposed. You have just heard an announcement on behalf of the British government. This announcement lays down a procedure for self-determination in certain areas of India. It envisages, on the one hand, the possibility of these areas seceding from India. On the other, it promises a big advance towards complete independence.

Such a big change must have the full concurrence of the people, for it must always be remembered that the future of India can only be decided by the people of India, and not by any outside authority; however friendly. These proposals will be placed soon before the representative assemblies of the people or consideration. But meanwhile, the sands of time run out and decisions cannot await the normal course of events. So while we must necessarily abide by what the people finally decide, we had to come to certain decisions ourselves and to recommend them to the people for acceptance. We have, therefore, decided to accept these proposals and to recommend to our larger committees that they do likewise. It is with no joy in my heart that I commend these proposals to you, though I have no doubt in my mind that this is the right course. For generations we have dreamt and struggled for a free, independent and united India. The proposal to allow certain parts to secede if they so wish is painful for any of us to contemplate. Nevertheless, I am convinced that our present decision is the right one even from the larger viewpoint. The united India that we have laboured for was not one of compulsion and of coercion but a free and willing association of a free people. In this way, we shall reach that united India sooner than otherwise, and then she will have a stronger and more secure foundation.

We are little men serving a great cause, but because the cause is great, something of that greatness falls upon us also. Mighty forces are at work in the world today and I have no doubt that we are ushering in a period of greatness for India. The India of yesteryears, its history and tradition, the India in our minds and hearts, cannot change.

With a firm faith in our future I appeal to you to cooperate in the great task ahead and to march together to haven of freedom for all in India. Jai Hind.

95

INDIA INTEGRATED

Sardar Vallabhbhai Patel

This speech was delivered at New Delhi, 5 July 1947 after taking charge of the Department of States set up exclusively for dealing with the rulers of Indian states, on 3 July 1947 by Sardar Patel. There were about 565 Indian states at that time varying in size from a few acres to thousands of square miles. Only about half a dozen of these states were within the territory of proposed Pakistan. The rest were within Indian territory. A few had a common border with India and Pakistan like Kashmir, Jaisalmer, Jodhpur, Bikaner. A vast majority of the rulers were Hindus or Sikhs. The integration of all these states with India was a formidable task because some of these states aspired to be independent and a couple of them were even toying with the idea of joining Pakistan after the departure of the British. The British had already made the work of integration of Indian states somewhat easy. As early as 2 April 1946, Pethwick-Lawrence, on behalf of the Cabinet Mission, had told the nawab of Bhopal (who was the chancellor of the Chamber of Princes at that time), 'that if British India became independent, paramountcy would end. The Crown would not be in a position to carry out its treaty obligations and hence the Indian states would be released from their obligations under their treaties'. This was confirmed by Prime Minister Attlee, while making a statement on Indian Independence Bill in the British Parliament. The role played by the British to facilitate Indians to integrate their country (what was left of it) in one administrative whole has not been appreciated by the Indian historians. Sardar Patel's speech is a fine example of precision and clear thinking. Its friendly tone showing concern for the princes, and the privileges offered to them, convinced many of them, who were still in a dilemma, to accept what was offered by him.

It was announced some days back that the Government of India had decided to set up a department to conduct their relations with the states in matters of common concern. This department has come into being today and the states have been informed to this effect. On this important occasion, I have a few words to say to the rulers of Indian states among whom I am happy to count many as my personal friends. It is a lesson from history that it was owing to her politically-fragmented condition and our inability to make a united stand, that India succumbed to successive waves of invaders. Our mutual conflicts and internecine quarrels and jealousies have in the past been the cause of our downfall and us falling victims to foreign domination number of times. We cannot afford to fall into those traps again. We are on the threshold of independence. It is true that we have not been able to preserve the unity of the country entirely unimpaired in the final stage. To the bitter disappointment and sorrow of many of us, some parts have chosen to go out of India and to set up their own government. But there can be no question that despite this separation a fundamental homogeneity of culture and sentiment reinforced by the compulsive logic of mutual interests would continue to govern us. This would be the case with that vast majority of states which, owing to their geographical contiguity and indissoluble ties, economic, cultural and political, must continue to maintain relations of mutual friendship and cooperation with the rest of India. The safety and preservation of these states as well as of India demand unity and mutual cooperation between its different parts.

'When the British established their rule in India, they evolved the doctrine of paramountcy which established the supremacy of British interests. That doctrine has remained undefined to this day, but in its exercise there has, undoubtedly, been more subordination than cooperation. Outside the field of paramountcy there has been a very wide scope in which relations between British India and the states have been regulated by enlightened mutual interests. Now that British rule is ending, the demand has been made that the states should regain their independence. In so far as paramountcy embodies the submission of states to foreign will, I have every sympathy with this demand, but I do not think it can be their desire to utilize this freedom from domination in a manner which is injurious to the common interests of India or which militates against the ultimate paramountcy of popular interests and welfare or which might result in the abandonment of that mutually useful relationship that has developed between British India and the Indian states during the last century. This has been amply demonstrated by the fact that a great majority of Indian states have already come into the Constituent Assembly. To those who have not done so, I appeal that they should join now

This country, with its institutions, is the proud heritage of the people who inhabit it. It is purely by accident that some live in the states and some in British India, but all partake of its culture and character. We are all knit together by bonds of blood and feelings no less than of self-interest. None can segregate us into segments, no impassable barriers can be set up between us. I suggest that it is, therefore, better for us to make laws sitting together as friends than to make treaties as aliens. I invite my friends, the rulers of states and their people, to the councils of the Constituent Assembly in this spirit of friendliness, and cooperation in a joint endeavour, inspired by common allegiance to our motherland for the common good of us all.

There appears to be a great deal of misunderstanding about the attitude of the Congress towards the states. I should like to make it clear that it is not the desire of the Congress to interfere in any manner whatsoever with the domestic affairs of the states. They are no enemies of the princely order, but, on the other hand, they wish them and their people under this aegis all prosperity, contentment and happiness. Nor would it be my policy to conduct the relations of the new department with the states in any manner which savours the domination of one over the other. If there would be any domination, it would be that of our mutual interests and welfare. We have no ulterior motive or selfish interests to serve. Our common objective should be to understand each other's point of view and make decisions acceptable to all and in the best interests of the country. With this object, I propose to explore the possibility of associating with the administration of the new department—a Standing Committee representative—of both the states and British India.

We are at a momentous stage in the history of India. By common endeavour we can raise the country to a new greatness while lack of unity will expose us to fresh calamities. I hope the Indian states will bear in mind that the alternative to cooperation in the general interest is anarchy and chaos which will overwhelm all if we are unable to act together in the minimum of common tasks. Let not the future generations curse us for having had the opportunity but then failing to turn it to our mutual advantage. Instead, let it be our proud privilege to leave a legacy of mutually beneficial relationships which would raise this sacred land to its proper place amongst the nations of the world and turn it into an abode of peace and prosperity.

96

THE CURTAIN FALLS

Clement Richard Attlee

This speech was delivered in London, 10 July 1947. The year 1947 saw the Labour government of Clement Attlee in a hurry to leave India. The parliamentary delegation, the Cabinet Mission, the formation of the interim government and the Constituent Assembly were steps in that direction. Lord Mountbatten, who replaced Lord Wavell as viceroy, had changed the date of quitting India from 3 June 1948 to 15 August 1947 bringing independence about ten months closer. Lord Mountbatten had acted his part well and made both the Congress and the Muslim League accept his plan of the partition of the country. Only some formalities had to be undertaken. The speech was delivered by Prime Minister Attlee in the House of Commons, while introducing the Indian Independence Bill. The Bill was drafted in a hurry. So was the speech. But the Bill and the speech decided the fate of a hundred million Indians in a distant land. The members in the House of Commons listened to their prime minister in ominous silence and dignity as though it was the funeral oration for the British Empire. Winston Churchill, sitting on the opposition bench, grunted but did not say a word. He saw his beloved Empire being consigned to history and with great effort he held back his tears.

This will brings to an end one chapter in the long connection between Britain and India, but it opens another. British rule which has endured so long is now, at the instance of this country, coming to an end.

There have been many times in history when states, at the point of the sword, have been forced to surrender a government over to another people. It is very rare for a people that have long enjoyed power over another nation to surrender it voluntarily. May I recall here a thing that is not always remembered, that just as India owes her unity and freedom from external aggression to the British, so the Indian National Congress itself was founded and inspired by men of our own race. Further, that any judgement passed on British rule in India by the Indians is passed on the basis of the principles which we have ourselves instilled into them.

Many years ago, when we began to encourage Indian participation in the responsibility of government and set ourselves to train them in the methods of democracy, it was obvious that the time would come, sooner or later, when the Indians would seek to secure the entire management of their own affairs. Some twenty years age, I was first brought into contact with it by being placed on the Simon Commission and I think they would agree with me that the major difficulty that has faced all of us in considering the best way of achieving Indian self-government has been the absence of mutual trust and toleration between the communities. Everyone who has touched upon the Indian problem has been brought up against this stumbling block. They have all wanted to maintain the unity of India, to give India complete self-governance and to preserve the rights of minorities. Every one of them has hoped that a solution might be found without resorting to partition. I know that many Indians of all communities passionately desire this, but it has not been found to be practicable.

We and the Indian statesmen have had to accept the only alternative— partition. For myself, I earnestly hope that this severance may not endure, and that the two new dominions which we now propose to set up may in course of time, come together again to form one great member state of the British Commonwealth of Nations.

In Clause one, a provision is made for the setting up, from 15 August next, of two dominions to be known as India and Pakistan. A decision has already come that Bengal and Punjab should be divided. In the North-West Frontier Province (N\XTFP) and in Sylhet voting is taking place to decide the future of those areas.

The House will remember that the Cabinet Mission, in their memorandum of 12 May 1946, informed the states that His Majesty's government could not, and will not, under any circumstances, transfer paramountcy to an Indian government. With the transfer of power to two Indian dominions, it is necessary to terminate the paramountcy and suzerainty of the Crown over the Indian states, and with them, the political engagements concluded under paramountcy and the mutual rights and obligations of the Crown and the States which derive the therefrom.

With the ending of the treaties and agreements, the states regain their independence. But they are part of geographical India, and their rulers and peoples are imbued with a patriotism no less great than that of their fellow Indians in British India. It would, I think, be unfortunate if, owing to the formal severance of their paramountcy relations with the Crown, they were to become units cut off from the rest of India.

The House will recall that the original plan of the Cabinet Mission was for the setting up of a Constituent Assembly for the purpose of framing a constitution for the whole of India, which would then be brought before Parliament as expressing the desires of the people of India. However, that Cabinet plan was not carried out in full, but the Constituent Assembly, which the Muslim League decided not to attend, has been at work for some time for framing a constitution. It is proposed that a Constituent Assembly for Pakistan should be formed as soon as the procedure indicated in Clauses two to four has been carried out.

I have endeavoured to explain to the House the general purposes and provisions of this measure. There will, no doubt be many points of detail which the hon'ble members will raise in the course of this debate and at committee stage. It will be the object of my right hon'ble friends and myself to give the House full information and explanation within our power, but there will inevitably be some matters on which it will not be possible to answer with precision, for this Bill unlike other bills deals with India. It does not lay down, as in the Act of 1935, a new constitution for India, providing every detail. It is far more in the nature of an enabling Bill—a Bill to enable the representatives of India and Pakistan to frame their own constitutions, and to provide for the exceedingly difficult period of transition. Ever since the Cripps's Mission, it has been the desire of successive governments that the future constitution of India should be framed by the Indians and not by the British. Had the Cripps offer been accepted, a Constituent Assembly might have come into being immediately after the end of the War. What has had to be done hurriedly, might have been done at greater leisure. We might have been spared some anxious years. But it is no good crying over lost opportunities.

We must all regret the division of India, but despite this grave drawback, we should, I think, welcome this new chapter in the history of the Commonwealth and Empire. That Indian dominions are to be set up and this House is relinquishing its control and responsibility for the Government of India is not, as a few would have us believe, a sign of weakness. It is, on the contrary; a sign of the strength and vitality of the British Commonwealth. There have been great empires in the past in which many nations have been brought together in one polity, but they perished because their rigidity of structure did not allow growth, and because the peoples which composed it were subjected to the will of one dominant ruler or one dominant race.

The British Commonwealth of Nations survives today, and has survived through the strain of two great wars, precisely because it is not static, is constantly developing, and because it has, throughout the years, steadily changed from an Empire, in which the power of control rested with Britain, to a partnership of free peoples inspired by common ideals and united in a common interest. We are now proposing to welcome two new dominions into that full partnership. We all wish that they will long remain with us, and that the friendship which united so many British and Indians, despite all the strains of recent years, may continue. My hope is that we may forget past differences and remember only how often and in how many fields of human endeavour the British and the Indians have worked together in harmony.

97

OUR NATIONAL FLAG

Jawaharlal Nehru

This speech was delivered at New Delhi, 22 July 1947. The national flag was adopted by the Constituent Assembly on 22 July 1947 and was presented to the nation, on behalf of the women of India, at the midnight session of the Assembly on 14 August 1947. The resolution which Nehru moved in the Constituent Assembly was: It is hereby resolved that the national flag of India shall be a horizontal tricolour of deep saffron (kesari), white and dark green in equal proportion. In the centre of the white band, there shall be a wheel in navy blue to represent the charkha. The design of the wheel shall be that which appears on the abacus of the Sarnath, the capital of Ashoka. The diameter of the wheel shall be approximate to the width of the white band. The ratio of the width to the length of the flag shall ordinarily be 2:3. Gandhi did not like the idea of the charkha being replaced by the Ashoka chakra in the flag. He wrote in Harijan Bandhu 'In my opinion nothing would have been lost if no changes had been made in the original flag. I will refuse to salute the flag that is modified on the above lines, however artistic it may be.' But it was too late. The nation had accepted the new flag.

Behind this resolution and the flag which I have the honour to present to this House for adoption lies history, the concentrated history of a short span in a nation's existence. Nevertheless, sometimes in a brief period we pass through the track of centuries. It is not so much the mere act of living that counts but what one does in this brief life that is ours; it is not so much the mere existence of a nation that counts but what that nation does during the various periods of its existence. I do venture to claim that in the past quarter of a century or so India has lived and acted in a concentrated way and the emotions which have filled the people of India, represent not merely some years but something infinitely more valuable.

I realize fully, as this House does, that this triumph of ours has been marred in many ways. There have been, especially in the past few months, many events which have caused us sorrow. We have seen parts of this dear motherland of ours cut off from the rest. We have seen a large number of people suffering tremendously, large numbers wandering about like waifs and strays without a home. We have seen many other things which I need not repeat to this House, but which we cannot forget. All this sorrow has dogged our footsteps. Even when we have achieved victory and triumph, it still dogs us. We have tremendous problems which we face in the present and which will arise in the future. Nevertheless, I hold it to be true, that this moment does represent a triumph and a victorious conclusion of all our struggles, for the moment.

I present this flag to you. This resolution defines the flag which I trust you will adopt. In a sense this flag was adopted, not by a formal resolution, but by popular acclaim and usage, adopted much more by the sacrifice that surrounded it in the past few decades. We are in a sense only ratifying that popular adoption. It is a flag which has been variously described. Some people, having misunderstood its significance, have thought, of it in communal terms and believe that some part of it represents one community or the other. I would like to add that when this flag was devised there was no communal significance attached to it.

Now, may I say a few words about this particular flag? There is a slight variation in this flag from the one many of us have used during these past years. The colours are the same, a deep saffron, white and dark green. Previously, in the white band there was the charkha which symbolized the common man in India, which symbolized the masses of the people, which symbolized their industry and which came to us from the message which Mahatma Gandhi delivered. Now, this particular charkha has been slightly varied. This is so because normally, the symbol on one side of the flag should be exactly the same as on the other side. Otherwise, there is a difficulty which goes against the rules. The charkha, as it appeared previously on this flag, had the wheel on one side and the spindle on the other. If you see the other side it is reversed. The wheel must be towards the pole, not towards the end of the flag. Therefore, after considerable thought, we were of course convinced that this great symbol which had enthused people should continue but that it should continue in a slightly different form, that the wheel should be there, not the rest of the charkha, that is the spindle and the string which created this confusion, that the essential part of the charkha should be there, that is the wheel. So, the old tradition continues in regard to the charkha and the wheel. But what type of wheel should we have? Our minds went back to many wheels but notably one famous wheel, which had appeared in many places and which all of us have seen, the one at the top of the capital of the Ashoka column and in many other places. That wheel is a symbol of India's ancient culture, it is a symbol of the many things that India had stood for through the ages. So we thought that this chakra emblem should be there, and that wheel appears.

This flag that I have the honour of presenting before you is not, I hope and trust, a flag of the Empire, a flag of imperialism, a flag of domination over anybody, but a flag of freedom not only for ourselves, but a symbol of freedom to all people who may see it.

98

BRITAIN SALUTES FREE INDIA

Lord Mountbatten

This speech was delivered at New Delhi, 14 August 1947. This is Mountbatten's last speech as viceroy in India. A few hours later he would become as the first Governor General of the dominion of India. The congratulatory message from His Majesty, the British monarch, lays emphasis on the fact that India was an independent dominion of the British Commonwealth of Nations. However, to the utter surprise of the British, India declared herself a republic on 26 January 1950 and ceased to be a dominion. The designation of the Governor General was changed to that of president. The constitution of the Commonwealth was modified to accommodate republics and the name British Commonwealth was changed to the Commonwealth of Nations. India is now its important member and has retained the British connection. The rest of the speech describes the role Mountbatten played during his term as viceroy.

Mr President and members of the Constituent Assembly, I have message from His Majesty to deliver to you today:

On this historic day when India takes her place as a free and independent dominion in the British Commonwealth of Nations, I send you all my greetings and heartfelt wishes.

Freedom-loving people everywhere will wish to share in your celebrations, for, with this transfer of power by consent, comes the fulfilment of a great democratic ideal to which the British and Indian peoples alike are firmly dedicated. It is inspiring to think that all this has been achieved by means of peaceful change.

It was barely six months ago that Mr Clement Attlee invited me to accept the appointment of last viceroy. He made it clear that this would be no easy task—since His Majesty's government in the United Kingdom had decided to transfer power to Indian hands by June 1948. At that time it seemed to many that His Majesty's government had set a date far too early. How could this tremendous operation be completed in fifteen months?

However, I had not been more than a week in India before I realized that this date of June 1948 for the transfer of power was too late rather than too early; communal tension and rioting had assumed proportions of which I had had no conception when I left England. It seemed to me that a decision had to be taken at the earliest possible moment unless there was to be risk of a general conflagration throughout the subcontinent.

I entered into discussions with the leaders of all the parties at once—and the result was the Plan of 3 June. Its acceptance has been hailed as an example of fine statesmanship throughout the world. The plan was evolved at every stage by a process of open diplomacy with the leaders. Its success is chiefly attributable to them.

I know well that the rejoicing which the advent of freedom brings is tempered in your hearts by the sadness that it could not come to a united India. That the pain of division, has shorn today's events of some of its joy. In supporting your leaders in the difficult decision which they had to take, you have displayed as much magnanimity and realism as have those patriotic statesmen themselves.

Let me now pass to the Indian states. The Plan of 3 June dealt almost exclusively with the problem of the transfer of power in British India; and the only reference to the states was a paragraph which recognized that on the transfer of power; all the Indian states–565 of them—would become independent. Here then was another gigantic problem and there was apprehension on all sides. But after th formation of the States Department it was possible for me, as a Crown representative, to tackle this great question. Thanks to that far-sighted statesman, Sardar Vallabhbhai Patel, member-in-charge of States Department, a scheme was produced which appeared to me to be equally in the interests of the states as of the dominion of India. The overwhelming majority of the states are geographically linked with India, and therefore, this dominion had by far the bigger stake in the solution of this problem. It is a great triumph for the realism and sense of responsibility of the rulers and governments of the states, as well as of the Government Of India, that it was possible to produce an Instrument of Accession which was equally, acceptable to both sides; and one moreover, so simple and so straightforward that within less than three weeks, practically all the states concerned had signed the Instrument of Accession along with the Standstill Agreement. Thus, a unified political structure covering over three hundred million people and the major part of this great subcontinent has been established.

The only state of importance that has not yet acceded is the premier state, Hyderabad. Hyderabad occupies a unique position in view of its size, population and resources, and it has its special problems. The Nizam, while he does not propose to accede to the dominion of Pakistan, has not up to the present felt able to accede to the dominion of India. His Exalted Highness has, however, assured me of his wish to cooperate in the three essential, subjects of external affairs, defence and communications with that dominion whose territories surround his state. With the assent of the government, negotiations will be continued with the Nizam and I am hopeful that we shall reach a solution satisfactory to all.

From today, I am your constitutional governor general and I would ask you to regard me as one of yourselves, devoted wholly to the furtherance of India's interests.

99

ON THE MILITARY-INDUSTRIAL COMPLEX

Dwight D. Eisenhower

This speech was delivered on 17 January 1961. This is the Farewell Address delivered by President Eisenhower in January 1961, at the conclusion of a successful two-term presidency. Prior to becoming President, Eisenhower had a long and distinguished military career. During World War II in Europe, he was Supreme Commander of the Allied Expeditionary Forces and commanded the forces involved in the D-Day invasion of northern Europe. As the new President in 1953, he forged an armistice to end the Korean War, which had begun three years earlier during the presidency of Harry Truman. As Commander-in-Chief throughout the 1950s, amid the ongoing Cold War between the U.S. and Soviet Russia, Eisenhower oversaw a permanent and ever-expanding military establishment designed to forestall any aggression by Soviet Russia and keep America a step ahead of the Russians in war technology. Remarkably, in this speech, Eisenhower (the old soldier) argues that it is this new military-industrial complex that has the potential to undermine the very freedoms in America it was meant to protect.

Three days from now, after half a century in the service of our country, I shall lay down the responsibilities of office as, in traditional and solemn ceremony, the authority of the Presidency is vested in my successor.

This evening I come to you with a message of leave-taking and farewell, and to share a few final thoughts with you, my countrymen. Like every other citizen, I wish the new President, and all who will labour with him, Godspeed. I pray that the coming years will be blessed with peace and prosperity for all. Our people expect their President and the Congress to find essential agreement on issues of great moment, the wise resolution of which will better shape the future of the nation. My own relations with the Congress, which began on a remote and tenuous basis when, long ago, a member of the Senate appointed me to West Point, have since ranged to the intimate during the war and immediate post-war period, and, finally, to the mutually interdependent during these past eight years.

In this final relationship, the Congress and the Administration have, on most vital issues, cooperated well, to serve the national good rather than mere partisanship, and so have assured that the business of the nation should go forward. So, my official relationship with the Congress ends in a feeling, on my part, of gratitude that we have been able to do so much together.

We now stand ten years past the mid-point of a century that has witnessed four major wars among great nations. Three of these involved our own country. Despite these holocausts America is today the strongest, the most influential and most productive nation in the world. Understandably proud of this pre-eminence, we yet realize that America's leadership and prestige depend, not merely upon our unmatched material progress, riches and military strength, but on how we use our power in the interests of world peace and human betterment.

Throughout America's adventure in free government, our basic purposes have been to keep the peace; to foster progress in human achievement, and to enhance liberty, dignity and integrity among people and among nations. To strive for less would be unworthy of a free and religious people. Any failure traceable to arrogance, or our lack of comprehension or readiness to sacrifice would inflict upon us grievous hurt both at home and abroad.

Progress toward these noble goals is persistently threatened by the conflict now engulfing the world. It commands our whole attention, absorbs our very beings. We face a hostile ideology—global in scope, atheistic in character, ruthless in purpose, and insidious in method. Unhappily the danger it poses promises to be of indefinite duration. To meet it successfully, there is called for, not so much the emotional and transitory sacrifices of crisis, but rather those which enable us to carry forward steadily, surely, and without complaint the burdens of a prolonged and complex struggle—with liberty the stake. Only thus shall we remain, despite every provocation, on our charted course toward permanent peace and human betterment.

Crises there will continue to be. In meeting them, whether foreign or domestic, great or small, there is a recurring temptation to feel that some spectacular and costly action could become the miraculous solution to all current difficulties. A huge increase in newer elements of our defence; development of unrealistic programs to cure every ill in agriculture; a dramatic expansion in basic and applied research—these and many other possibilities, each possibly promising in itself, may be suggested as the only way to the road we wish to travel. But each proposal must be weighed in the light of a broader consideration: the need to maintain balance in and among national programs-balance between the private and the public economy, balance between cost and hoped for advantage—balance between the clearly necessary and the comfortably desirable; balance between our essential requirements as a nation and the duties imposed by the nation upon the individual; balance between actions of the moment and the national welfare of the future. Good judgment seeks balance and progress; lack of it eventually finds imbalance and frustration.

The record of many decades stands as proof that our people and their government have, in the main, understood these truths and have responded to them well, in the face of threats and stress. But threats, new in kind or degree, constantly arise. I mention two only.

A vital element in keeping the peace is our military establishment. Our arms must be mighty, ready for instant action, so that no potential aggressor may be tempted to risk his own destruction. Our military organization today bears little relation to that known by any of my predecessors in peacetime, or indeed by the fighting men of World War II or Korea. Until the latest of our world conflicts, the United States had no armaments industry. American makers of plowshares could, with time and as required, make swords as well. But now we can no longer risk emergency improvisation of national defence; we have been compelled to create a permanent armaments industry of vast proportions. Added to this, three and a half million men and women are directly engaged in the defence establishment. We annually spend on military security alone more than the net income of all United States corporations. This conjunction of an immense military establishment and a large arms industry is new in the American experience. The total influence—economic, political, even spiritual—is felt in every city, every State house, every office of the Federal government. We recognize the imperative need for this development. Yet we must not fail to comprehend its grave implications. Our toil, resources and livelihood are all involved; so is the very structure of our society. In the councils of government, we must guard against the acquisition of unwarranted influence, whether sought or unsought, by the military-industrial complex. The potential for the disastrous rise of misplaced power exists and will persist. We must never let the weight of this combination endanger our liberties or democratic processes. We should take nothing for granted. Only an alert and knowledgeable citizenry can compel the proper meshing of the huge industrial and military machinery of defence with our peaceful methods and goals, so that security and liberty may prosper together.

Akin to, and largely responsible for the sweeping changes in our industrial-military posture, has been the technological revolution during recent decades. In this revolution, research has become central; it also becomes more formalized, complex, and costly. A steadily increasing share is conducted for, by, or at the direction of, the Federal government. Today, the solitary inventor, tinkering in his shop, has been overshadowed by task forces of scientists in laboratories and testing fields. In the same fashion, the free university, historically the fountainhead of free ideas and scientific discovery, has experienced a revolution in the conduct of research. Partly because of the huge costs involved, a government contract becomes virtually a substitute for intellectual curiosity. For every old blackboard there are now hundreds of new electronic computers.

The prospect of domination of the nation's scholars by Federal employment, project allocations, and the power of money is ever present—and is gravely to be regarded. Yet, in holding scientific research and discovery in respect, as we should, we must also be alert to the equal and opposite danger that public policy could itself become the captive of a scientific technological elite. It is the task of statesmanship to mold, to balance, and to integrate these and other forces, new and old, within the principles of our democratic system—ever aiming toward the supreme goals of our free society.

Another factor in maintaining balance involves the element of time. As we peer into society's future, we—you and I, and our government—must avoid the impulse to live only for today, plundering, for our own ease and convenience, the precious resources of tomorrow. We cannot mortgage the material assets of our grandchildren without risking the loss also of their political and spiritual heritage. We want democracy to survive for all generations to come, not to become the insolvent phantom of tomorrow.

Down the long lane of the history yet to be written, America knows that this world of ours, ever growing smaller, must avoid becoming a community of dreadful fear and hate, and be instead, a proud confederation of mutual trust and respect. Such a confederation must be one of equals. The weakest must come to the conference table with the same confidence as do we, protected as we are by our moral, economic, and military strength. That table, though scarred by many past frustrations, cannot be abandoned for the certain agony of the battlefield. Disarmament, with mutual honour and confidence, is a continuing imperative. Together we must learn how to compose differences, not with arms, but with intellect and decent purpose. Because this need is so sharp and apparent I confess that I lay down my official responsibilities in this field with a definite sense of disappointment. As one who has witnessed the horror and the lingering sadness of war— as one who knows that another war could utterly destroy this civilization which has been so slowly and painfully built over thousands of years—I wish I could say tonight that a lasting peace is in sight. Happily, I can say that war has been avoided. Steady progress toward our ultimate goal has been made. But, so much remains to be done. As a private citizen, I shall never cease to do what little I can to help the world advance along that road.

So—in this my last good night to you as your President—I thank you for the many opportunities you have given me for public service in war and in peace. I trust that in that service you find some things worthy; as for the rest of it, I know you will find ways to improve performance in the future.

You and I—my fellow citizens—need to be strong in our faith that all nations, under God, will reach the goal of peace with justice. May we be ever unswerving in devotion to principle, confident but humble with power, diligent in pursuit of the nation's great goals.

To all the peoples of the world, I once more give expression to America's prayerful and continuing aspiration: We pray that peoples of all faiths, all races, all nations, may have their great human needs satisfied; that those now denied opportunity shall come to enjoy it to the full; that all who yearn for freedom may experience its spiritual blessings; that those who have freedom will understand, also, its heavy responsibilities; that all who are insensitive to the needs of others will learn charity; that the scourges of poverty, disease and ignorance will be made to disappear from the earth, and that, in the goodness of time, all peoples will come to live together in a peace guaranteed by the binding force of mutual respect and love.

100

BLOOD AND IRON

Otto Van Bismarck

This speech was delivered on September 1862. 'Not by speeches and decisions of the majorities will the greatest problems of the time be decided.'

The conflict is viewed too tragically, and presented too tragically in the press; the regime does not seek war. If the crisis can be ended with honour, the regime will gladly do so. The great independence of the individual makes it difficult in Prussia to rule under the Constitution. In France, it is otherwise; there, individual independence is lacking. The constitutional crisis, however, is no shame, but rather an honour. We are perhaps too educated to put up with a constitution—we are too critical. Public opinion wavers; the press is not public opinion; we know how that arises. There are too many Catilines, who have revolution at heart. The members [of the House], however, have the task of standing over public sentiment, and of guiding it. Our blood is too hot, we prefer armour too great for our small body to carry, but we should put it to service. Germany does not look to Prussia's liberalism, but to its power. Bavaria, Wurttemberg, and Baden would like to turn to liberalism, but they shall not assume Prussia's role. Prussia must collect its forces for the favourable occasion, which has several times been neglected; Prussia's borders are not favourable to a healthy national life. Not by speeches and decisions of majorities will the greatest problems of the time be decided—that was the mistake of 1848–49—but by iron and blood. This olive branch (he drew it from his memorandum book) I picked up in Avignon, to offer, as a symbol of peace, to the popular party; I see, however, that it is still not the time for it.